PART 7 Effective Style and Language

PART 8 Understanding Grammar

PART 9 Understanding Punctuation and Mechanics

PART 10 If English Is Not Your First Language

How to find what you need in *The Brief Penguin Handbook:*

If you know what Part you want to look at in *The Brief Penguin Handbook*, then use the **colour-coded tabbed dividers** to open to that section.

If you want to know more about what's in a particular chapter or Part, then open the back cover of the handbook and consult the **Detailed Contents**.

If you want to look up a very specific word or problem, then use the **Index** on p. 589.

There are more resources at the back of *The Brief Penguin Handbook* that can help you find answers to your questions:

- A handy list of **Common Errors** on the inside back cover flap, which tells you where to find answers to the most common grammar, punctuation, and mechanics questions
- A **Glossary** with basic grammatical and usage terms, on p. 575
- A list of all the **Staying on Track** boxes that help you avoid pitfalls during writing, on p. 608
- A **Revision Guide** for editing and proofreading symbols, on p. 609

You can find additional help and resources for writing and research in the eText version of *The Brief Penguin Handbook*, available at **www.mywritinglab.com**.

THE BRIEF PENGUIN HANDBOOK

THIRD CANADIAN EDITION

LESTER FAIGLEY
University of Texas at Austin

ROGER GRAVES
University of Alberta

HEATHER GRAVES
University of Alberta

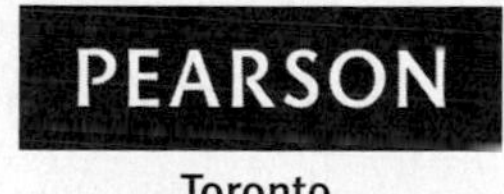

Toronto

Vice-President, Editorial Director: Gary Bennett
Editor-in-Chief: Michelle Sartor
Acquisitions Editor: David S. Le Gallais
Marketing Manager: Jennifer Sutton
Senior Developmental Editor: Patti Altridge
Project Manager: Richard di Santo
Production Editor: Cindy Miller for Cenveo Publisher Services
Copy Editor: Claudia Forgas
Proofreaders: Karen Alliston, Cy Strom
Photo and Permissions Researcher: Christina Beamish
Compositor: Cenveo Publisher Services
Art Director: Julia Hall
Interior and Cover Designer: Julia Hall
Cover Image: Shutterstock

Credits and acknowledgments for materials borrowed from other sources and reproduced, with permission, in this textbook appear on the appropriate page within the text, and on page 587.

10 9 8 7 6 5 4 3 2 1 RRD-C

Library and Archives Canada Cataloguing in Publication

Faigley, Lester, 1947–
The brief Penguin handbook / Lester Faigley, Roger Graves, Heather Graves. — 3rd Canadian ed.

Includes index.
ISBN 978-0-13-397865-0

1. English language—Rhetoric. I. Graves, Roger, 1957– II. Graves, Heather, 1958– III. Title.

PE1408.F33 2012 808′.042 C2013-906646-7

ISBN 978-0-13-397865-0

Preface

The third Canadian edition of *The Brief Penguin Handbook* grows out of our experiences as writing teachers at a time when the tools for writing, the uses of writing, and the nature of writing itself are undergoing astounding and rapid transformation in an era of multimedia. Yet the traditional qualities of good writing—clarity, brevity, readability, consistency, effective design, accurate documentation, freedom from errors, and a human voice—are prized more than ever.

A handbook can be a guide for students throughout the composing process, helping them build on what they already know about writing and demonstrate these qualities of good writing in their work. Many thousands of students have become better writers with the help of *The Brief Penguin Handbook.*

What's new in this edition?

The Brief Penguin Handbook has been revised extensively in order to give students the best, most up-to-date writing instruction available, and to make it easier for them to navigate their handbook.

Specific changes to the Canadian edition

The third Canadian edition of *The Brief Penguin Handbook* incorporates multimedia techniques for writing and researching with the latest knowledge we have about the demands students face when writing in a variety of disciplines. Parts 1 and 2 get students started with the basics of writing in an academic context, and Part 3 moves them to the next level of sophistication by showing how the genres of writing and purposes for writing change from one discipline to the next. This section of the book also provides a guide to the kinds of evidence valued in each academic discipline. With this information, students have a much better chance of writing the kinds of assignments that instructors want to read.

In addition to the many outstanding revisions to the U.S. edition, the Canadian edition includes new chapters in Part 4, "Designing and Presenting," that help students understand the differences between highly structured documents (such as MLA and APA essay formats), template structured documents (such as Facebook pages and WordPress blogs), and more loosely structured documents (such as brochures and flyers). In research we have done in Canadian post-secondary educational institutions, we have found that students must write assignments in a variety of media, both print and online, and integrate visual information into these assignments. Part 4 guides students through the process of understanding how to organize these documents and how to integrate visuals of all kinds into them. Our research also shows that presentations are one genre that occurs widely throughout the disciples. For that reason, we have created a chapter specifically on how to prepare an outstanding presentation.

Parts 5 and 6 provide an outstanding guide to both the process of researching and how to integrate sources into written assignments. The new Research Maps in these sections provide a concise, visual map to guide students through the research and writing process. Part 6 has chapters specifically devoted to plagiarism and strategies for avoiding plagiarism. These chapters are followed by excellent guides to documentation for all of the major documentation styles: MLA, APA, CMS, CSE, and IEEE. Style, grammar, and a special section for non-native speakers of English ensure that *The Brief Penguin Handbook* will also help students with the final stages of the writing process—editing and polishing their written work.

Process-oriented instruction on documentation styles

- The MLA and APA chapters (26 and 27) have been reorganized to emphasize the process of creating the correct citation for any source. These chapters now open with new documentation-process maps that not only remind students of the key steps in citing sources but also help them find their way into each chapter. New "Writer at Work" student examples show a student figuring out how to cite a source. And newly designed source samples, grouped together in one place in each chapter, are easier for students to find and use.

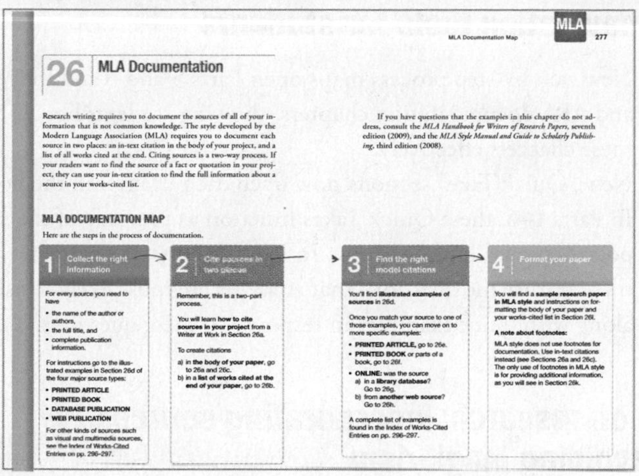

MLA

MLA Documentation Map 277

26 MLA Documentation

Research writing requires you to document the sources of all of your information that is not common knowledge. The style developed by the Modern Language Association (MLA) requires you to document each source in two places: an in-text citation in the body of your project, and a list of all works cited at the end. Citing sources is a two-way process. If your readers want to find the source of a fact or quotation in your project, they can use your in-text citation to find the full information about a source in your works-cited list.

If you have questions that the examples in this chapter do not address, consult the *MLA Handbook for Writers of Research Papers*, seventh edition (2009), and the *MLA Style Manual and Guide to Scholarly Publishing*, third edition (2008).

MLA DOCUMENTATION MAP

Here are the steps in the process of documentation.

1 Collect the right information

For every source you need to have
- the name of the author or authors,
- the full title, and
- complete publication information.

For instructions go to the illustrated examples in Section 26d of the four major source types:
- PRINTED ARTICLE
- PRINTED BOOK
- DATABASE PUBLICATION
- WEB PUBLICATION

For other kinds of sources such as visual and multimedia sources, see the Index of Works-Cited Entries on pp. 296–297.

2 Cite sources in two places

Remember, this is a two-part process.

You will learn **how to cite sources in your project** from a Writer at Work in Section 26a.

To create citations
a) in **the body of your paper**, go to 26a and 26c.
b) in a **list of works cited at the end of your paper**, go to 26b.

3 Find the right model citations

You'll find **illustrated examples of sources** in 26d.

Once you match your source to one of those examples, you can move on to more specific examples:
- **PRINTED ARTICLE,** go to 26e.
- **PRINTED BOOK** or parts of a book, go to 26f.
- **ONLINE:** was the source
  a) in a **library database**? Go to 26g.
  b) from **another web source**? Go to 26h.

A complete list of examples is found in the Index of Works-Cited Entries on pp. 296–297.

4 Format your paper

You will find a **sample research paper in MLA style** and instructions on formatting the body of your paper and your works-cited list in Section 26l.

A note about footnotes:

MLA style does not use footnotes for documentation. Use in-text citations instead (see Sections 26a and 26c). The only use of footnotes in MLA style is for providing additional information, as you will see in Section 26k.

More student models

- New "Writer at Work" sections in the writing, research, and documentation chapters (Parts 5 and 6) highlight the work of one student as he moves through the research process—selecting a topic for a research project, finding and evaluating sources, and drafting a researched argument paper.

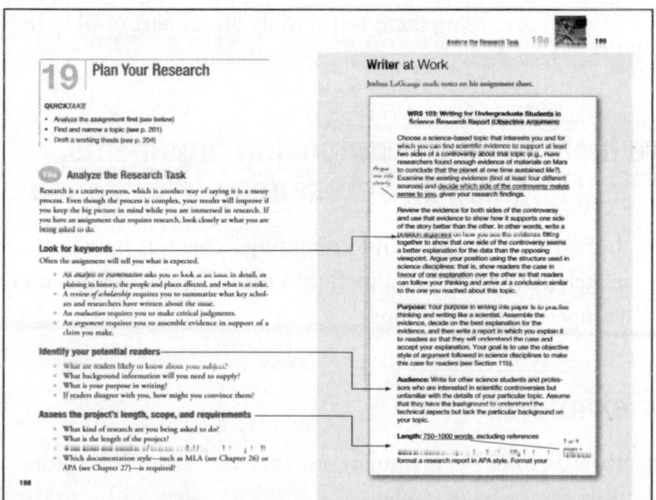

19 Plan Your Research

QUICK*TAKE*
- Analyze the assignment first (see below)
- Find and narrow a topic (see p. 201)
- Draft a working thesis (see p. 204)

19a Analyze the Research Task

Research is a creative process, which is another way of saying it is a messy process. Even though the process is complex, your results will improve if you keep the big picture in mind while you are immersed in research. If you have an assignment that requires research, look closely at what you are being asked to do.

Look for keywords

Often the assignment will tell you what is expected.
- An *analysis* or *examination* asks you to look at an issue in detail, explaining its history, the people and places affected, and what is at stake.
- A *review of scholarship* requires you to summarize what key scholars and researchers have written about the issue.
- An *evaluation* requires you to make critical judgments.
- An *argument* requires you to assemble evidence in support of a claim you make.

Identify your potential readers
- What are readers likely to know about your subject?
- What background information will you need to supply?
- What is your purpose in writing?
- If readers disagree with you, how might you convince them?

Assess the project's length, scope, and requirements
- What kind of research are you being asked to do?
- What is the length of the project?
- Which documentation style—such as MLA (see Chapter 26) or APA (see Chapter 27)—is required?

198

Analyze the Research Task 19a 199

Writer at Work

Joshua LaGrange made notes on his assignment sheet.

WRS 103: Writing for Undergraduate Students in Science Research Report (Objective Argument)

Choose a science-based topic that interests you and for which you can find scientific evidence to support at least two sides of a controversy about that topic (e.g., Have researchers found enough evidence of materials on Mars to conclude that the planet at one time sustained life?). Examine the existing evidence (find at least four different sources) and decide which side of the controversy makes sense to you, given your research findings.

Argue one side clearly

Review the evidence for both sides of the controversy and use that evidence to show how it supports one side of the story better than the other. In other words, write a position argument on how you see the evidence fitting together to show that one side of the controversy seems a better explanation for the data than the opposing viewpoint. Argue your position using the structure used in science disciplines: that is, show readers the case in favour of one explanation over the other so that readers can follow your thinking and arrive at a conclusion similar to the one you reached about this topic.

Purpose: Your purpose in writing this paper is to practise thinking and writing like a scientist. Assemble the evidence, decide on the best explanation for the evidence, and then write a report in which you explain it to readers so that they will understand the case and accept your explanation. Your goal is to use the objective style of argument followed in science disciplines to make this case for readers (see Section 11b).

Audience: Write for other science students and professors who are interested in scientific controversies but unfamiliar with the details of your particular topic. Assume that they have the background to understand the technical aspects but lack the particular background on your topic.

Length: 750–1000 words, excluding references

format a research report in APA style. Format your

- A new informative paper and a new MLA model research paper are included in this edition, as well as added models for business writing.

New navigation tools for students

- New step-by-step process maps open Parts 5 and 6 and the MLA and APA documentation chapters, showing students how to use these chapters effectively.
- New "Quick Take" sections now open each chapter in the book. In Parts 1–6, these Quick Takes function as previews of the major points covered in the chapter. In Parts 7–10 (style, grammar, ESL), these feature the questions that students are most likely to ask, along with quick examples in response to these questions.

More on research, incorporating sources, and avoiding plagiarism

- Part 6 includes a new chapter devoted to plagiarism and strategies for avoiding it.
- MLA, APA, CMS, CSE, and IEEE chapters have been updated to comply with the latest style guidelines.
- The research coverage has been reorganized so that finding sources and evaluating sources are now dealt with in separate chapters.
- The chapters on incorporating sources and avoiding plagiarism are now in Part 6, emphasizing to students that documenting sources properly and using them responsibly are all part of what responsible researchers do.

More instruction on composing arguments, and on designing and presenting information

- In Part 4, "Designing and Presenting," chapters have been completely restructured and include a new chapter on how to prepare compelling presentations.

New examples

- Parts 7–10 (style, grammar, punctuation, and ESL) feature numerous new examples.

Supplements

Accompanying *The Brief Penguin Handbook* is an array of supplements for both instructors and students, including book-specific resources.

MyWritingLab (www.mywritinglab.com)
The moment you know.

Educators know it. Students know it. It's that inspired moment when something that was difficult to understand suddenly makes perfect sense. Our MyLab products have been designed and refined with a single purpose in mind—to help educators create that moment of understanding with their students.

MyWritingLab delivers **proven results** in helping individual students succeed. It provides **engaging experiences** that personalize, stimulate, and measure learning for each student. And, it comes from a **trusted partner** with educational expertise and an eye on the future.

MyWritingLab can be used by itself or linked to any learning management system. To learn more about how MyWritingLab combines proven learning applications with powerful assessment, visit www.mywritinglab.com.

MyWritingLab—the moment you know.

Pearson eText

Pearson eText gives students access to the text whenever and wherever they have access to the internet. eText pages look exactly like the printed text, offering powerful new functionality for students and instructors. Users can create notes, highlight text in different colours, create bookmarks, zoom, click hyperlinked words and phrases to view definitions, and view in single-page or two-page view.

Study on the Go

Featured at the beginning of each part you will find a unique barcode providing access to Study on the Go, an unprecedented mobile integration between text and online content. Students link to Pearson's unique Study on the Go content directly from their smartphones, allowing them to study whenever and wherever they wish! Go to one of the sites below to see how you can download an app to your smartphone for free. Once the app is installed, your phone will scan the code and link to a website containing Pearson's Study on the Go content, including such popular study tools as Videos, Glossary Flashcards, and Quizzes, which can be accessed anytime.

ScanLife

http://getscanlife.com

NeoReader

http://get.neoreader.com

QuickMark

www.quickmark.com.tw

CourseSmart for Students

CourseSmart goes beyond traditional expectations—providing instant, online access to the textbooks and course materials you need at an average savings of 60%. With instant access from any computer and the ability to search your text, you'll find the content you need quickly, no matter where you are. And with online tools like highlighting and note-taking, you can save time and study efficiently. See all the benefits at www.coursesmart.com/students.

CourseSmart for Instructors

CourseSmart goes beyond traditional expectations—providing instant, online access to the textbooks and course materials you need at a lower cost for students. And even as students save money, you can save time and hassle with a digital eTextbook that allows you to search for the most relevant content at the very moment you need it. Whether it's evaluating textbooks or creating lecture notes to help students with difficult concepts, CourseSmart can make life a little easier. See how when you visit www.coursesmart.com/instructors.

Instructor's Resource Manual

An *Instructor's Resource Manual* offers guidance to both new and experienced teachers on using the handbook and its ancillary package to the best advantage.

To see a complete listing of student supplements and instructor support materials available upon adoption of *The Brief Penguin Handbook*, Third Canadian Edition, please visit the book's online catalogue page, which can be accessed at www.pearsoncanada.ca/highered.

Technology Specialists

Pearson's Technology Specialists work with faculty and campus course designers to ensure that Pearson technology products, assessment tools, and online course materials are tailored to meet your specific needs. This highly qualified team is dedicated to helping schools take full advantage of a wide range of educational resources by assisting in the integration of a variety of instructional materials and media formats. Your local Pearson Canada sales representative can provide you with more details on this service program.

Pearson Custom Library

For enrollments of at least 25 students, you can create your own textbook by choosing the chapters that best suit your own course needs. To begin building your custom text, visit www.pearsoncustomlibrary.com. You may also work with a dedicated Pearson Custom editor to create your ideal text—publishing your own original content or mixing and matching Pearson content. Contact your local Pearson representative to get started.

Acknowledgments

The scope and complexity of a handbook require a talented, experienced team, and I have been blessed to have the same team as the previous edition. Executive Editor Lynn Huddon and I have worked together on over twenty books and editions—none of which would have achieved success without Lynn's creative mind and hard work.

Victoria Davis created new exercises for the fourth edition and contributed many good ideas. Susan "George" Schorn contributed to the chapters on writing in the disciplines and writing in specific genres.

As always, my greatest debt of gratitude is to my wife, Linda, who makes it all possible.

LESTER FAIGLEY

This third edition of *The Brief Penguin Handbook* is the product of a wonderful group of people at Pearson Canada. David Le Gallais continues to champion this book and ensure that it meets the needs of instructors throughout higher education. Patti Altridge, our Developmental Editor, did an amazing job of keeping order in the chaos of rapidly multiplying files. We would also like to thank Richard di Santo,

Project Manager; Katie Monrea'L and Cindy Miller, production editors; Claudia Forgas, copyeditor; and Karen Alliston and Cy Strom, proofreaders, for their great work on this project.

We would like to thank the students who have generously provided examples of their work for this edition: Justin Kamal, Lisa Locascio, Joshua LaGrange, Trent Grey, Katie Lee, Kris Sifeldeen, Jennifer LaBranche, Eric Graves, Erin Graves, Danielle Mitchell, and Chelsea Chambers.

ROGER GRAVES

HEATHER GRAVES

THE BRIEF PENGUIN HANDBOOK

THIRD CANADIAN EDITION

PART 1

Planning, Drafting, and Revising

You **can learn more and do more** with MyWritingLab and with the eText version of *The Brief Penguin Handbook*. Find resources in MyWritingLab to help you successfully plan and complete your assignment.

1 Think as a Writer 1

2 Plan and Draft 8

3 Shape Your Paragraphs 20

4 Rewrite, Edit, and Proofread 30

1 Think as a Writer

QUICK*TAKE*

- Think about what post-secondary readers expect (see below)
- Think about the process of communication (see p. 3)
- Think about your credibility (see p. 6)

1a Think About What Post-secondary Readers Expect

Writing in post-secondary education varies considerably from course to course. A lab report for a biology course looks quite different from a paper in your English class, just as a classroom observation in an education course differs from a case study report in an accounting class.

Some common expectations about arguments in post-secondary writing extend across disciplines. For example, you could be assigned to write a proposal for a downtown light-rail system in a number of different classes—civil engineering, urban planning, or management. The emphasis of such a proposal would change depending on the course. In all cases, however, the proposal would require a complex argument in which you describe the problem that the light-rail system would improve, make a specific proposal that addresses the problem, explain the benefits of the system, estimate the cost, identify funding sources, assess alternatives to your plan, and anticipate possible opposition.

Setting out a specific proposal or claim supported by reasons and evidence is at the heart of most post-secondary writing, no matter what the course. Some expectations of arguments (such as including a thesis statement) may be familiar to you, but others (such as the emphasis on finding alternative ways of thinking about a subject and finding facts that might run counter to your conclusions) may be unfamiliar.

Expectations of writers in college and university

WRITING IN POST-SECONDARY EDUCATION . . .	WRITERS ARE EXPECTED TO . . .
States explicit claims	Know that the main claim is often called a *thesis*. (see pages 13–15)
Supports claims with reasons	Express reasons after making a claim (We should do something *because* ________). (see pages 79–80)
Bases reasons on evidence	Provide evidence for reasons in the form of facts, statistics, testimony from reliable sources, and direct observations. (see pages 42–43)
Considers opposing positions	Help readers understand why there are disagreements about issues by accurately representing differing views. (see pages 77–78)
Analyzes with insight	Provide in-depth analysis. (see pages 48–52)
Investigates complexity	Explore the complexity of a subject by asking "Have you thought about this?" or "What if you discard the usual way of thinking about a subject and take the opposite point of view?" (see pages 81–82)
Organizes information clearly	Make the main ideas evident to readers and indicate which parts are subordinate to others. (see page 17)
Signals relationships of parts	Indicate logical relationships clearly so that readers can follow an argument without getting lost. (see pages 23–25)
Documents sources carefully	Provide the sources of information so that readers can consult the same sources the writer used. (see page 255 [23c]; pages 277–398)

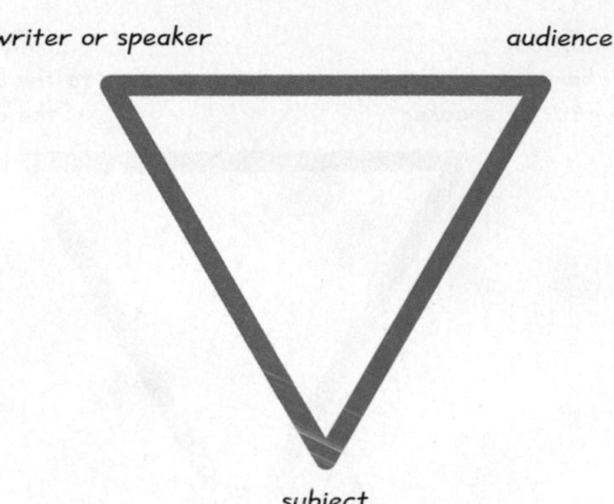

Figure 1.1 The rhetorical triangle

1b Think About the Process of Communication

Whether you are writing a research paper for a political science course, designing a website for a small business, or preparing slides for a sales presentation, you are participating in a complex process. That process—communication—involves the interaction of three essential elements: the writer or speaker, the audience, and the subject. These three elements are often represented visually as a triangle (Figure 1.1).

Speaker, subject, and audience are each necessary for communication to occur. These three elements interact with one another. Speakers make adjustments to their presentations of a subject depending on the audience (think of how you talk to small children). Just as speakers adjust to audiences, audiences continually adjust to speakers (think of how your attitude toward speakers changes when they are able to laugh at themselves).

1c Think About How to Persuade Others

The ancient Greeks recognized that the dynamic nature of the *rhetorical triangle* is the key to understanding how an audience is persuaded. The most important teacher of rhetoric in ancient Greece, Aristotle (384–323 BCE), defined rhetoric as the art of finding the best available means of persuasion in any situation. He set out three primary tactics of persuasion: appeals based on the trustworthiness of the speaker (*ethos*); appeals to the emotions and deepest-held values of the audience (*pathos*); and appeals to logic, reasoning, and evidence (*logos*). These appeals likewise can be represented using the rhetorical triangle (Figure 1.2).

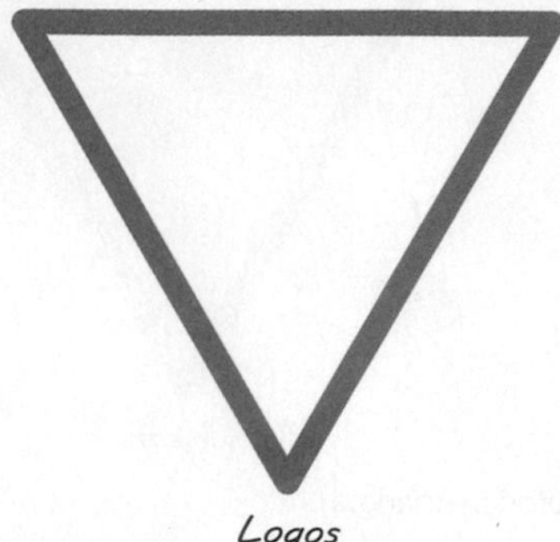

Figure 1.2 Persuasive appeals

Can you tell which is better?
Neither could we…
until we tested them.
ConsumerReports.org®
Get Ratings and Reports on every product and service you use, from cars to computers, treadmills to toasters, banks to bikes. Watch our video clips to see how we put the products to the test. Find out which brands are best and worst. Connect with other consumers through our Discussion Forums. Plus, receive expert advice on the latest product trends and developments with our Cars, Electronics, Shopping, and Money Blogs.
Special discount for CONSUMER REPORTS magazine subscribers
www.Canada.ConsumerReports.org
0707C

Figure 1.3 *Ethos.*

Figure 1.4 *Pathos.* Greenpeace: "Oil-Soaked Bird."

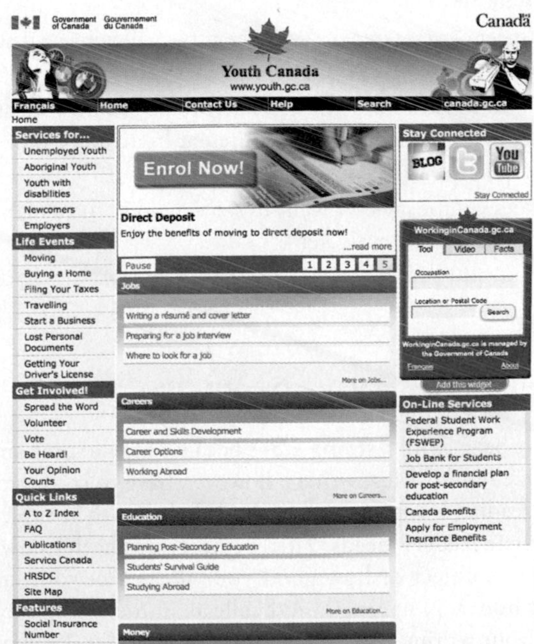

Figure 1.5 *Logos*. The Youth Canada page explains logically how to get a job, a career, or an education.

1d Think About Your Instructor as Your Audience

Readers of post-secondary writing expect more than what they can find out from a Google search or an online encyclopedia. Facts are easy to obtain from databases and print sources. Readers want to know how these facts are connected. Good post-secondary writing also involves an element of surprise. If readers can predict exactly where a writer is going, even if they fully agree, they will either skim to the end or stop reading. Readers expect you to tell them something that they don't know already.

WRITING SMART

Understand your audience

- Who is most likely to read what you write?
- How much does your instructor know about your subject? Does your instructor want you to define key terms or concepts to show that you know them?
- What aspect of your treatment of the topic will your instructor find interesting?
- What is your instructor's attitude likely to be toward your subject? If your instructor holds an attitude different from yours, how can you get him or her to consider your views?
- What does your instructor want to see you do in this assignment: compare, synthesize, evaluate?

1e Think About Your Credibility

Some writers begin with a strong ethos because of who they are; they have immediate credibility. Most writers, however, have to convince their readers to keep reading by demonstrating knowledge of their subject and concern with their readers' needs. Furthermore, no matter how much you know about a subject or how good your ideas are, your credibility is destroyed if readers in university and college, in the workplace, or in public life find your writing poor in quality, especially if it is full of errors and difficult-to-read sentences.

WRITING SMART

Build your credibility

- How can you convince your instructor that you are knowledgeable about your subject? Do you need to do research?
- How can you convince your instructor that you have thought carefully about your subject?
- What strategies can you use that will enhance your credibility? Should you cite experts on your subject? Can you acknowledge opposing positions, indicating that you've taken a balanced view on your subject?
- Does the appearance, accuracy, and clarity of your writing give you credibility?

1f Think About Your Purpose

The starting point for effective writing is determining in advance what you want to accomplish. Knowing your purpose shapes everything else you do as a writer—your choice of the kind of writing, your subject matter, your organization, and your style.

WRITING SMART

Identify your purposes for writing

- Are you analyzing a verbal or visual text to understand how it persuades readers, how it makes us think and feel in certain ways? (See Chapter 6.)
- Are you describing and reflecting on people, places, experiences, and ideas? Are you writing a personal essay, blog, or travel narrative? (See Chapter 7.)
- Are you writing to report information, to explain a process, to explore questions and problems, or to analyze patterns, connections, and causes? (See Chapter 8.)
- Are you arguing for a position on a controversial issue or arguing to convince people to take a particular course of action? (See Chapter 9.)

2 Plan and Draft

QUICK*TAKE*

- Establish your goals (see below)
- Explore your topic (see p. 10)
- Write a working thesis (see p. 13)
- Plan a strategy (see p. 16)

 Establish Your Goals

Your instructor will give you specific suggestions about how to think about your audience and your topic. Two ways to make your task simpler are as follows:

- Be sure you are responding to the assignment appropriately.
- Select a topic that both fits the assignment and appeals to you strongly enough to make you want to write about it.

Look carefully at your assignment

When your instructor gives you a writing assignment, look closely at what you are asked to do. Often the assignment will contain keywords such as *analyze, compare and contrast, critically reflect, define, describe, explore and critique, evaluate,* or *propose* that will assist you in determining what direction to take.

- **Analyze:** Find connections among a set of facts, events, or readings, and make them meaningful.
- **Compare and contrast:** Examine how two or more things are alike and how they differ.
- **Critically reflect:** Apply ideas from the course to the topic you've been given.
- **Define:** Make a claim about how something should be defined, according to features that you set out.
- **Describe:** Observe carefully and select details that create a dominant impression.
- **Explore and critique:** Survey the research on a particular topic and identify the perspectives that inform this research.
- **Evaluate:** Argue that something is good, bad, best, or worst in its class, according to criteria that you set out.
- **Propose:** Identify a particular problem and explain why your solution is the best one.

If you are unclear about what the assignment calls for, talk with your instructor.

Find a topic you care about

If you do not have an assigned topic, a good way to find one is to look first at the materials for your course. You may find something that interests you in the readings for the course or in a topic that came up in class discussion. It's hard to write about something that doesn't engage you, so start by writing down things that do. If your assignment gives you a wide range of options, you might write more than one list, starting with your personal interests. Think also about campus topics, community topics, and national topics that intrigue you. Your lists might resemble these:

Personal

1. Benefits of weight training
2. Wit and humour in Judd Apatow movies
3. How should I decide to commit to a relationship?

Campus

1. Pros and cons of charging computer fees for on-campus labs
2. Should food services provide more alternatives for students with food allergies?
3. Should my school require a program-related internship?

Community

1. Fundraising for community food banks
2. ESL education and literacy programs
3. More bike lanes to encourage more people to ride bicycles
4. The implications of inter-professional collaboration in the medical professions

Nation/World

1. Funding and training of Canadian athletes
2. Separatism in Quebec and the West
3. Private vs. public healthcare clinics
4. Pollution caused by fish farms

Often you will find that, before you can begin writing, you need to analyze exactly what you mean by a phrase such as "private vs. public healthcare clinics." For example, what distinguishes a public clinic from a private one? Is it the services each renders, or is it the cost or freedom to use the clinic at all?

After you make a list (or lists), you should review it:

- Put a checkmark beside the topics that look most interesting or that mean the most to you.
- Put a question mark beside the topics that you don't know very much about. If you choose one of these issues, you will have to do research.
- Select the two or three topics that look the most promising.

2b Explore Your Topic

Once you have identified a potential topic, the next step is to determine what you already know about that topic and what you need to find out. Experienced writers use many strategies for exploring their knowledge of a topic and how interesting it really is to them. Here are a few.

Ask questions

These classic reporter's questions will assist you in thinking through a topic:

1. *Who* is doing it?
2. *What* is happening or at issue?
3. *When* is it happening?
4. *Where* is it happening?
5. *How* is it happening?
6. *Why* is it happening?

Freewrite

Another way to find out how much you know about a topic is to *freewrite:* Write as quickly as you can without stopping for a set time, usually five or ten minutes. The goal of freewriting is to get as much down as possible. Don't stop to correct mistakes. Let your ideas flow wherever they take you, even if they take you well outside the boundaries of your topic. The constant flow of words should generate ideas—some useful, some not.

If you get stuck, write the same sentence over again, or write about how hungry you are, or how difficult freewriting is, until thoughts on your selected topic reappear. After you've finished, read what you have written and single out any key ideas.

You may want to use a keyword or idea as a starting point for a second freewrite. After two or three rounds you will discover how much you already know about your topic and possible directions for developing it.

Brainstorm

An alternative method of discovery is to *brainstorm*. The end result of brainstorming is usually a list—sometimes of questions, sometimes of statements. You might come up with a list of observations and questions, such as these for the topic of images of nursing:

- *Less than 6% of nurses are male—what contributes to this?*
- *Why are images of nurses on television so far from reality?*
- *Why don't television shows include older nurses and women doctors?*

- *Professional nursing brochures portray nurses in offices and with paperwork.*
- *What are the implications for nursing as a profession when television shows offer such a demeaning image of the profession?*

Make an idea map

Still another strategy for exploring how much you know about a potential topic is to make an *idea map*. Idea maps are useful because they let you see everything at once, and you can begin to make connections among the different aspects of an issue—definitions, causes, effects, proposed solutions, and your personal experience. A good way to get started is to write down ideas on sticky notes. Then you can move the sticky notes around until you figure out which ideas fit together. Figure 2.1 shows what an idea map on images of nursing might look like.

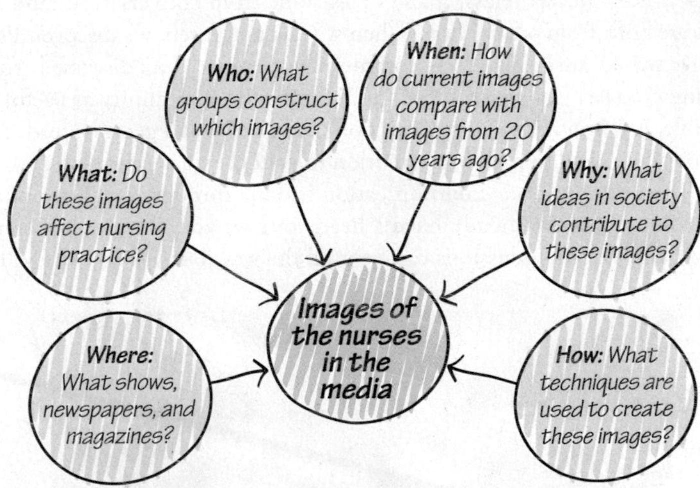

Figure 2.1 Idea map on images of nursing

Respond to something you've read

Most of the writing you do in post-secondary institutions will be linked to texts you are reading. Find time to read about your topic before writing about it. Select a book or an article that you find to be a powerful statement about your topic. You don't have to agree with the author completely; in fact, it's more productive if you can "talk back" to the author.

Imagine you are sitting down face to face with the author. Find places where you can write things like the following:

- *"I agree with your general point, but did you think of this other example? What would you do with it?"*
- *"Here you seem to be arguing for one side, but later you seem to contradict yourself and give credit to the other side."*
- *"Your point about one group might be applied to a different group."*
- *"I don't agree with this claim because your evidence doesn't support your assertion."*

Talking back to a text can help you find your own position: "While X sees it this way, I look at it a different way."

Talk and listen

Writing requires concentration, which for many people depends on quiet and solitude. Nevertheless, many ideas come from conversation, and all ideas are born from other ideas. When we talk and listen, we discover. Productive writers are engaged in a community where ideas are discussed. Your writing class is a writing community. To make the community as useful as possible, it is important to ask your peers for specific and genuine feedback on your drafts and to pay close attention to your classmates' writing as well.

If any of your class communication is done through email or online discussion, you will already have a head start on your assigned writing. Emails and online discussions can be used the way journals and freewrites

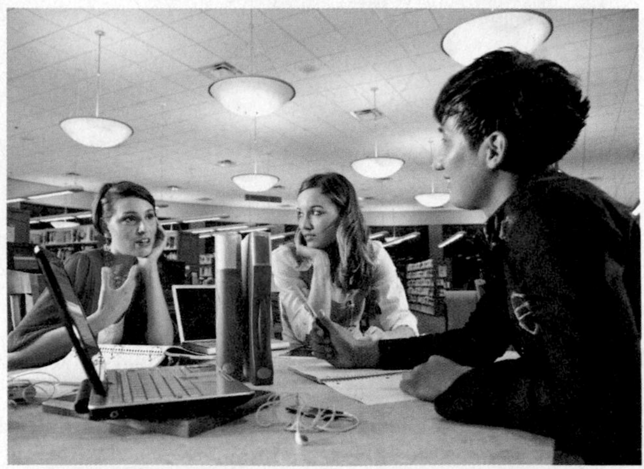

■ You can get one-on-one help in developing your ideas, focusing your topic, and revising your paper at your writing centre.

are—as material for essays. When you are planning your essay, you may find that you already have a wealth of written material to draw from.

WRITING SMART

Explore your topic using a blog

One way of keeping track of your exploratory notes is to keep a blog. *Blogs* are a good way to organize multimedia information, including text, images, links, and audio files. For example, after completing a freewriting or brainstorming session, you could quickly edit your notes and post them to your blog. You could also post your idea maps (export your files in PDF format for posting), links to and short descriptions of online articles you want to keep track of, or summaries of texts you have read as part of your research.

In addition, most blogs have a commenting feature, which allows others to leave responses to your posts. Invite your classmates or friends to read your exploratory blog and give you feedback. By turning your blog into a conversation about your topic, you will be able to take advantage of their questions and responses about your work as you craft your paper.

2c Write a Working Thesis

The initial stage of the planning process involves finding ideas, expanding and broadening your thoughts, and recording ideas from written sources and conversations. The next stage of thinking, after you have decided on a general topic, is *narrowing* your focus to a specific topic. Having a specific focus is the key to writing a strong essay.

Use questions to focus a broad topic

- *Why are nurses depicted working on hospital wards?*
- *How has the role of nurses in healthcare changed over the past 30 years?*
- *Do professions other than nursing suffer from similar distortions of their working lives?*
- *How do publications of nursing organizations depict nurses visually?*
- *What strategies do professional nursing organizations use to present images of nursing that are professional?*

Consider other angles to expand a narrow topic

Too-narrow topics are rarer than topics that are too broad. Although nursing research into the causes of snowmobile accidents is important, very few peer-reviewed articles exist. Consider broadening the topic: Define the topic as "high-risk adolescent behaviour," a more general category, and you will find many articles that examine the causes of a range of behaviours similar to snowmobile accidents.

Turn your topic into a thesis statement

Your *thesis* states your main idea. Much of the writing that you will do both in university and college and in your working career will have an explicit thesis, usually stated near the beginning. The thesis announces your topic and indicates what points you want to make about that topic.

Your thesis should be closely tied to your purpose—to reflect on your own experience, to explain some aspect of your topic, or to argue for a position or a course of action.

A reflective thesis	My experience watching television shows over a long time confirms the large gap in reality between the images on television and real life generally, and nursing is just one example of many.
An informative thesis	While images of nurses on television exaggerate to the point of making the daily life of working nurses unrecognizable, they sometimes present issues that help raise the profile of the nursing profession.
A persuasive thesis	While television often fails to depict any aspect of real life accurately, it does a particular disservice to the nursing profession because the negative stereotypes it portrays limit nursing's potential to grow as a profession.

STAYING ON TRACK

Evaluate your working thesis

Ask yourself these questions about your working thesis:

1. Is it specific?
2. Is it manageable in the length and time I have?
3. Is it interesting to my intended readers?

STAYING ON TRACK *(Continued)*

Consider the following examples:

Example 1

The Canadian cod fishing industry collapsed in 1990 because of overfishing.

Specific? The thesis is too narrow. It states a commonly acknowledged fact.

Manageable? A known fact is stated in the thesis, so there is nothing to research. The general topic of overfishing is too complicated for essay-length treatment.

Interesting? The decline of cod stocks on the Grand Banks is interesting to Atlantic fishermen, but Canadians living inland would need an angle that is appealing.

Revised thesis

The Department of Fisheries and Oceans must ban dragger nets as soon as possible before all Canadian fishing stocks are depleted.

Example 2

Popular media portrayals of the nursing profession damage the nursing profession because they reinforce negative images of nursing as part of the for-profit healthcare industry.

Specific? The thesis is too broad. How are we defining "popular media"? Are we referring to all media images here?

Manageable? Because the thesis is not limited to a specific kind of media or specific example, the topic is too large to research adequately.

Interesting? The topic is potentially interesting, but it is too vague to engage an instructor. What does it tell an instructor that he or she doesn't already know?

Persuasive? This thesis does take a stand by asserting that popular media portrayals damage the nursing profession.

Revised thesis

Media portrayals of the nursing profession that juxtapose images of nurses on strike with stories of the death of a patient damage the nursing profession because they polarize complex issues and create negative images of nursing as part of the for-profit healthcare industry.

These examples suggest that the key to writing an effective thesis is finding a topic that is neither too vast nor too narrow—and not obvious. You may have to adjust your working thesis more than once as you plan and begin drafting.

 Plan a Strategy

People who write frequently on the job or who make their living by writing have many different ways of producing a successful piece of writing. Some may plan extensively in advance, either individually or as a team, specifying exactly what will go in each section. Other writers find that putting ideas into words often changes the ideas and generates new ones. These writers know that writing drafts is a way of discovering their subject, and they count on one or two or more rewrites to get their document into shape.

Consider making an outline

At some point in school you may have been required to produce a formal outline to submit along with a paper. A *formal outline* typically begins with the thesis statement, which anchors the entire outline. Each numbered or lettered item clearly supports the thesis, and the relationship among the items is clear from the outline hierarchy.

Thesis statement: For nursing to be able to establish a professional position in today's culture, the static misrepresented image of nursing in the media must be drastically rebranded.

I. Negative stereotypes of nurses in the popular media
   A. Nurses as sexual objects in *Private Practice* episode involving Dell
   B. Nurses as simple-minded in *Grey's Anatomy*
   C. Nurses as guardian angels in *Nurse Jackie*

II. Implications for nursing practice
   A. The diminished view of nursing in the media risks eroding patient trust and confidence.
   B. Even good television shows contain inaccuracies about nursing.

Consider using a working outline

A working outline is more like an initial sketch of how you will arrange the major sections. Jotting down main points and a few subpoints before you begin can be a great help while you are writing. You can read the complete essay that developed from these outlines in Section 9f.

Media depictions of nursing

Section 1: Begin with setting the context for how the media control understandings of nursing and why that is a problem.

Section 2: Describe the negative stereotypes of nurses (e.g., sexual objects) that exist in popular media such as television shows.
Section 3: Explain that beyond the sexual overtones, the media also depict nurses as simple-minded.
Section 4: Describe more recent shows such as Nurse Jackie, which have started to depict nurses as guardian angels. Although this image is better, it still diminishes the image of nurses in the public eye.
Section 5: Discuss what these depictions imply about nursing and how they risk eroding patient trust and confidence in nursing care.
Section 6: Indicate how the image of nursing in the media could be rehabilitated.

2e Compose a Draft

Skilled writers aim at producing a good draft—not a perfect draft. They know that they can go back and revise later.

Essays typically contain an introduction, body, and conclusion. You do not have to write these parts in that order, though. In your *introduction*, you can offer a short example that illustrates the problem being discussed. You can state a surprising fact. You can begin with a fascinating quotation. Your aim is to interest the reader and to let the reader know the topic of the paper, if not necessarily the thesis.

The *body* of the essay consists of the primary discussion. Remember to guide readers through the discussion by letting them know where you are going. Your readers need road signs to tell them where the discussion is taking them. Road signs are transition words and phrases such as *consequently*, *the third reason is . . .* , and *on the other hand*.

The last section, the *conclusion*, often repeats what has already been said. If the essay has been long and complex, sometimes this repetition is necessary, but usually the repetition is just that—annoying redundancy. The final paragraph does not have to repeat the main point. It can give a compelling last example or propose a course of action. It can ponder the larger significance of the subject under discussion. It can pose an important question for the reader to think about.

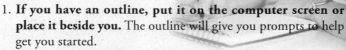

WRITING SMART

Overcome writer's block

1. **If you have an outline, put it on the computer screen or place it beside you.** The outline will give you prompts to help get you started.
2. **Begin writing what you know best.** If you don't know exactly where you are headed, the introduction can be the hardest section to write. The introduction can wait until last.
3. **Resist the urge to revise too soon.** It's more important to keep moving forward. If you stop to polish a section, you will lose momentum, and in the end you may discard that section anyway.
4. **If you get stuck, try working on another section.** Look again at your notes or your outline.
5. **If you are still stuck, talk to someone about what you are trying to write.** If your campus has a writing centre, talk to a consultant. Reading more about your subject can also help you get moving again.

 2f Write as a Member of a Team

Almost without exception people in occupations that require higher education write frequently on the job, and much of that writing is done in collaboration rather than alone. The better you understand how to write effectively with other people, the more enjoyable and more productive the process will be for you.

Determine the goals and identify tasks and roles

- Write down the goals as specifically as you can and discuss them as a team.
- Determine what tasks are required to meet those goals. Be as specific as you can. Write down the tasks and arrange them in the order in which they need to be completed.
- Decide whether the team has the skills and resources to perform those tasks. If you do not possess the necessary skills and resources, adjust the goals to what you can realistically expect to accomplish.

Make a work plan

- Make a timeline that lists the dates when specific tasks need to be completed and distribute it to all team members. Charts are useful tools for keeping track of progress.

- Assign tasks to team members. Find out if anyone possesses additional skills that could be helpful to the team.
- Revisit the team's goals often. To succeed, each team member must keep in mind what the team aims to accomplish.
- Decide on a process for monitoring progress. Set up specific dates for review and assign team members to be responsible for reviewing work that has been done.

Understand the dynamics of a successful team

- Teamwork requires some flexibility. Different people have different styles and contribute in different ways. Keep talking to one another along the way.
- It may be desirable to rotate roles during the project.

Deal with problems when they come up

- If a team member is not participating, find out why.
- If team members have different ideas about what needs to be done, find time to meet so that the team can reach an agreement.
- Get the team together if you are not meeting the deadlines you established in the work plan and devise a new plan, if necessary.

WRITING SMART

Compose wikis

Wikis are communal websites where, in the purest form, each contributor has an equal ability to create and revise a wiki page. Wiki software records each change as it is made, prompting others to make more changes. The most successful wikis have specific goals and methods of communication to discuss problems as they arise.

The best-known wiki is *Wikipedia*, the online encyclopedia founded in 2001 with entries that have been collaboratively written by thousands of users.

On your next collaborative project, try using a wiki to organize your group's work. Create a wiki for the text so that everyone will be able to see changes to the document in real time. You can even use the wiki to list your group's goals, the project's timeline, and the tasks and roles of individual members. Be careful to state explicitly the goals of your wiki and the conditions under which group members can alter important organizational documents.

3 Shape Your Paragraphs

Quick*Take*

- Focus your paragraphs (see below)
- Organize your paragraphs (see p. 23)
- Make your paragraphs coherent (see p. 23)
- Write effective beginning and ending paragraphs (see p. 26)

3a Focus Your Paragraphs

Readers expect sentences in a paragraph to be closely related to one another. Often writers will begin a paragraph with one idea, but other ideas will occur to them while they are writing. Paragraphs confuse readers when they go in different directions. When you revise your paragraphs, check for focus.

In the following example, notice how Kris Sifeldeen keeps the focus on Al Gore's use of data throughout the paragraph.

> The final aspect of convincing his audience of his argument was Al Gore's use of *logos*, or convincing the audience through logic and reasoning that an argument is valid. He does this through his presentations of visuals that seem to be very conclusive evidence that there truly is a problem on earth. A more analytical viewing of *An Inconvenient Truth* shows that Gore provides no references to the data and minimally explains the origins of most of the charts and graphs he uses in his presentation. This can be seen by many as a lack of confidence in his data because not only does he fail to provide sources, he also fails to provide simple additions such as error bars or uncertainties which demonstrate how accurate the information given really is. As well, many scientists argue with the information itself, stating that he may have accidentally misread the data, as described above, or he may have even purposefully altered the information so that the problem of global warming changes appears much worse than it is in actuality. For example, Al Gore warns that in around 25 years, global deaths from global warming will increase to about 300,000 people per year. However, according to Eric Steig, an earth scientist at the University of Washington in Seattle, Gore's data was simply an extrapolation from a heat wave in Europe in 2003.[2] This in reality provides no grounds for Al Gore to make that

type of assumption, even if global warming really is occurring. The main overall points in his movie may in fact be true; however, he misrepresents as well as misinterprets scientific data and therefore provides conclusions that are far more negative than they may be in reality, which some may consider to be a scare tactic. Although some information in his movie may be correct, his failure to provide references, accurate figures, and interpretations of data proves that ethos is also not his strongest argumentative method employed.

When to use explicit topic sentences

You were probably taught to begin a paragraph with a topic sentence. Topic sentences alert readers to the focus of a paragraph and help writers stay on topic. Topic sentences should explain the focus of the paragraph and situate it in the larger argument. However, topic sentences do not have to begin paragraphs, and they need not be just one sentence. You will decide what placement and length will best suit your subject.

Topic sentences at the beginning of a paragraph will quickly orient readers, preparing them for the sentences to come. Each sentence that follows elucidates the topic sentence.

Topic sentence at the beginning

There are many ways that Al Gore attempts to demonstrate his credibility as someone who is qualified to address the public about this particular subject area, also known as *ethos*. The first way in which he does this is by referring back to his presidential campaign race against George W. Bush in 2000, where he unfairly lost the election. This could also be considered an attempt at pathos, but it also serves to show audience members that he has many years of professional experience in politics, which is at its core a service to humanity. He also emphasizes his years in university where he had taken an interest in the topic of global warming since his undergraduate year. This serves both to explain his interest in the subject of global warming as well as provide more evidence that he is a hard-working, educated, and a professional human being. However, the problem with his attempts at ethos is that Gore truly has no real scientific background. It is completely possible for Gore, through no fault of his own, to have misread the data presented to him from real scientists and thus have provided inaccurate results and conclusions which he then gave to his audience. After a closer analysis of the movie, it would not be unreasonable to state that Al Gore's ethos is rightfully accepted around the world. In this particular movie his ethos may have been stronger than it should have been due to the heavy scientific content which he has minimal experience or training in. For these reasons, ethos is not the strongest argumentative method.

When a paragraph builds to make a particular point, the topic sentence is more effective at the end of the paragraph.

Topic sentence at the end

To gain support from the public, scientists will often use rhetoric in their writings or presentations. Most people believe that science writing should be completely factual and not contain any separate attempts to persuade the general public. In the film *An Inconvenient Truth*, Al Gore uses logic, emotion, and credibility to help demonstrate and raise awareness of global warming. Many believe that his use of *ethos* (the method of demonstrating his credibility) is the strongest method of argument to ensure his audience is convinced and aware of global warming. However, through a proper analysis of the film, it is very clear that through the use of irrelevant life accounts, sad stories of casualties in America, etc., Gore utilizes the argumentative appeal of *pathos* (triggering emotional responses in the audience) as the most effective way of convincing his audience. As well, there are many scientific articles and web pages that suggest his data used in the movie are mistaken, or purposely altered to create a stronger response in his audience. If this were true, Gore's *logos* and *ethos* would both be rendered ineffective and false. **Gore uses all the methods of argument in this scientific film, but *pathos* is without a doubt the most effective on his audience because it causes emotional and thus physical responses in individuals.**

When to use implicit topic sentences

In some cases, particularly in narrative prose, writers omit explicit topic sentences because they would clash with the tone or style of the paragraph. Instead, these paragraphs use tightly connected, focused sentences to make the topic implicitly clear.

Implicit topic sentence

Going back into the past could cause many paradoxes. One such paradox is the grandfather paradox. This paradox asks what would happen if a person were to travel to a time before the birth of his or her parents and killed his or her grandfather. If a person's grandfather died before fathering one of his or her parents, that person could never have been created to travel into the past and kill his or her grandfather. Simple paradoxes like this suggest time travel is not possible because nature does not allow paradoxes. Novikov's self-consistency principle states that general relativity could be used to create closed timelike curves (CTC).[2] These curves would prevent anyone who is travelling into the past from doing anything that could alter the future and create a paradox.

The implicit topic sentence is something like "Using today's knowledge and logic, travelling into the past appears unlikely, mainly due to the many paradoxes that could occur."

3b Organize Your Paragraphs

Well-organized paragraphs in essays usually follow a pattern similar to that of a well-organized paper, but in miniature. Chances are you'll use a combination of these strategies in order to get your point across.

- **Description.** Descriptive paragraphs are frequent in informative writing. The key is providing concrete details, including sights, sounds, smells, textures, and tastes.
- **Narration.** Narrative paragraphs are organized by time. They are essential for histories and any how to writing.
- **Comparison and contrast.** Paragraphs of comparison assess one subject in terms of its relation to others, usually highlighting what they have in common. Contrasting paragraphs analyze differences between things.
- **Definition.** Paragraphs organized by definition usually begin with a term and then go on to list its defining characteristics, sometimes using examples.
- **Examples and illustrations.** Examples and illustrations make key points and ideas vivid and memorable.
- **Cause and effect.** Cause and effect paragraphs are structured in two basic ways: They can begin with causes and then state the effect or they can begin with the effect and then analyze the causes.
- **Classification and division.** Classifying places items into categories according to their similarities. Dividing takes a single item or concept and breaks it down into its component parts.

3c Make Your Paragraphs Coherent

Your teachers may have told you that your paragraphs should flow. Writing that flows is coherent, which means readers understand how sentences fit together. Repeating key phrases and signalling relationships with transitional terms help in building coherence.

Reiterate key terms and phrases

When you repeat key terms and phrases within paragraphs, your reader will be able to trace major ideas and stay situated in your argument. In the following paragraph, notice that the writer refers back to two central terms, *grassroots activism* and *battleground*. Notice too that the paragraph isn't repeating itself. Repetition without forward momentum is self-defeating.

> The web has become the primary medium for **grassroots activism**. Among thousands of websites created by individuals are many pages devoted to media criticism and parodies of advertising. **This activism** has come at a time when the internet has become the **battleground** for the deregulated corporate giants. On **this battleground**, control of the coaxial cable and fibre-optic conduits represents only a small part of the potential fortunes to be made from an array of services carried through the pipe.

Signal relationships with transitional terms

Transitional terms act like warning signs for readers, preparing them for whatever is around the bend. Notice how transitions in the following paragraph make it easier to read by preparing you for what is coming.

> **In spite of** all the talk about the internet as cyberspace and a virtual world, the materiality of the internet as a medium is unavoidable. You sit in front of a machine that has to be turned on and connected to the net. **And if** you want to access the resources of the World Wide Web, you need an internet service provider, a modem, and a computer with enough memory to support the current versions of Firefox or Internet Explorer. **In Canada** the lines do not go to every neighbourhood, and **in the rest of the world** almost the entire continent of Africa outside South Africa is not online. **At present** the internet continues the one-way flow of information from the First to the Third World. Can the internet be a factor in promoting a two-way flow between the margins and the centre?

STAYING ON TRACK

Use transitional terms

Be sure to use transitional terms accurately in order to signal the relationships among your sentences.

- **To enumerate:** again, also, and, as well, finally, furthermore, first, second, third, in addition, last, moreover, next, too
- **To generalize:** commonly, in general, for the most part, on the whole, usually, typically

STAYING ON TRACK *(Continued)*

- **To offer an example:** for example, for instance, indeed, in fact, of course, specifically, such as, the following
- **To situate in time:** after a month, afterwards, as long as, as soon as, at the moment, at present, at that time, before, earlier, followed by, in the meantime, in the past, lately, later, meanwhile, now, preceded by, presently, since then, so far, soon, subsequently, suddenly, then, this year, today, until, when, while
- **To situate in space:** above, below, beyond, close to, elsewhere, far from, following, here, near, next to, there
- **To conclude:** as a result, hence, in conclusion, in short, on the whole, therefore, thus
- **To contrast:** although, but, even though, however, in contrast, conversely, in spite of, instead, nevertheless, nonetheless, on the one hand, on the contrary, on the other hand, still, though, yet
- **To compare:** again, also, in the same way, likewise, similarly
- **To signal cause or effect:** as a result, because, consequently, for this reason, hence, if, so, then, therefore, thus
- **To sum up:** as I said, as we have seen, as mentioned earlier, in conclusion, in other words, in short, in sum, therefore, thus
- **To concede a point:** certainly, even though, granted, in fairness, in truth, naturally, of course, to be fair, while it's true

3d Consider Paragraph Length

Paragraph breaks can signal various kinds of shifts:

- A new concept
- The next step in an argument
- The end of the introduction
- The beginning of the conclusion
- A new speaker in dialogue
- A shift in time or place
- A logical pause that gives the reader a breather

What is the ideal length for a paragraph? It depends on what sort of paragraphs you are writing. Business letter writers strive for short paragraphs so their readers can see the essential information at a glance. Paragraphs in academic essays tend to be about 150 to 200 words long. Academic writers need space to make and support arguments in depth. As a general rule, readers' eyes glaze over when they see paragraphs in an essay that stretch beyond one page. Nevertheless, too many short paragraphs in post-secondary writing are a sign that the piece lacks either weighty ideas or sufficient development.

3e Link Across Paragraphs

Transitions at the beginnings and endings of paragraphs guide readers. They explain why a paragraph follows from the previous one. They offer writers the opportunity to highlight the turns in their thinking.

Be aware of transitions in your writing. Ask yourself why one main idea leads into the next. What step or shift takes place between paragraphs? How does this step or shift fit into the overall development of the piece? The answers to these questions can become your transition.

3f Write Effective Beginning and Ending Paragraphs

Beginning paragraphs, like the first scene of a movie, set the story in motion. They identify what topic the essay will examine, and they set the tone—will this be a comedy or a drama? Good ending paragraphs, like the final scenes in a movie, do more than summarize: They comment on key points or leave readers with something to ponder. Because readers are more likely to remember beginning and ending paragraphs, they are your best opportunity to make a good impression.

Understand what beginning paragraphs do

Effective beginning paragraphs convince the reader to read on. They capture the reader's interest and set the tone for the piece. In essays they often state the thesis and briefly map out the way the writing will progress from paragraph to paragraph. Sometimes the work of the beginning paragraph might be carried through three or four paragraphs. A writer might start with a memorable example, then use the example to launch the rest of the essay.

Start beginning paragraphs with a bang

Getting the first few sentences of an essay down on paper can be daunting. Begin with one of the following strategies to get your reader's attention.

A question

What programs and policies are effective in preventing homelessness?

A hard-hitting fact

Over 33 000 people in Canada are homeless, and one-third of them are 25 years old or younger.

A pithy quotation

"'This is my house. I'm not proud of it, but it's the God's honest truth,' he [Smurf, a homeless ex-con] said Tuesday. 'I sleep like a baby. Wind doesn't get me. Rain doesn't get me. Snow doesn't get me. I just curl up there, have a bottle, and a little cat nap.'" Brent Wittmeier of the *Edmonton Journal*, quoted above, has unearthed a piece of our city's underworld that is both shocking and moving.*

Images

"The 52-year-old ex-convict—his street name derived from blue tattoos that mark him 'head to toe'—angles past giant wire spools each night to reach his bed," writes the *Edmonton Journal*'s Brent Wittmeier. The man's bed, as Wittmeier describes it, is "a heap of cardboard and blankets encased by an outer wall, a transformer box, plywood, more cardboard and blankets."

An anecdote

"Edmonton reached a daytime high of -22 C Wednesday, though it felt 10 degrees colder with wind chill. On days like these and the freezing nights that follow," writes the *Edmonton Journal*'s Brent Wittmeier, "the survival of men like Smurf is what motivates 24-year-old Aidan Inglis, one of six Boyle Street outreach workers who build relationships with the homeless to get them closer to housing."

A problem

"Outreach workers said Smurf's shelter wasn't bad compared with the dozens of nooks and crannies where people sleep. Some nights, like Monday, they might even return late at night just to make sure a troubled client is OK," according to Brent Wittmeier of the *Edmonton Journal*, who interviewed outreach worker Aidan Inglis. "'It's really scary for us because we're worried about them,' Inglis said."

A concisely stated thesis

Solutions to homelessness must include affordable housing, money to cover basic living expenses, and access to social services.

---

* Throughout this book, MLA citation style (see Chapter 26) is used for topics in the humanities and social sciences, and APA or CSE citation style (see Chapters 27 and 29) is used for topics in medicine and other sciences.

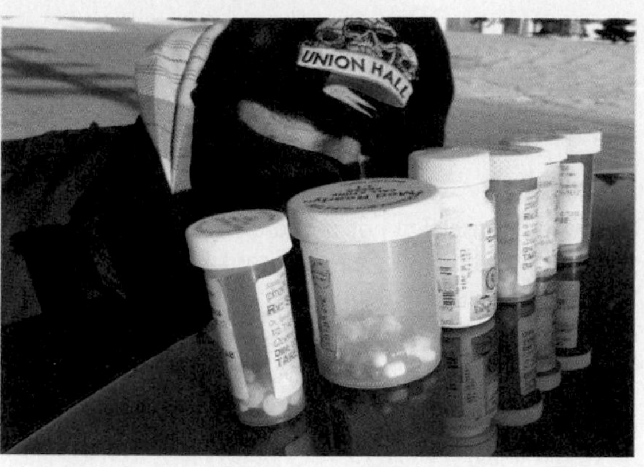

A contradiction or paradox

Homeless youth often stubbornly resist coming into shelters, but once they do come in they often stay.

An odd, ridiculous, or unbelievable fact

"'The homeless are all around us,' Inglis said, 'often just out of sight, a few metres from Jasper Avenue or Saskatchewan Drive apartments.'" The *Edmonton Journal*'s reporter Brent Wittmeier was speaking to Aidan Inglis, a 24-year-old outreach worker.

Essays that begin with obvious, overly general, or exaggerated sentences dampen readers' interest immediately. Use the first sentence to tell readers something they don't know. Begin with a fresh idea, fact, or image.

Understand what ending paragraphs do

Ending paragraphs remind readers where they've been and invite them to carry your ideas forward. Use the ending paragraph to touch on your key points, but do not merely summarize. Leave your readers with something that will inspire them to continue to think about what you have written.

Conclude with strength

The challenge in ending paragraphs is to leave the reader with something provocative, something beyond pure summary of the previous paragraphs. The following are strategies for ending an essay:

Issue a call to action

Because the number of homeless people in Edmonton has dropped by 21 percent since 2008, we should work harder to implement the strategies that are successful there in other urban areas.

Discuss the implications of your argument

The manner in which nerve cells, neurons, and synapses within the brain are organized may be the largest determinant of intelligence. Just as with bottlenose dolphins, brain size is relevant to intelligence only if the nerve cells, neurons, and synapses are organized appropriately.

Explain the applications of your argument

Dilation suggests that travelling into the future is possible and is the only part of time travel that we are able to test. This has convinced many scientists that forward time travel is possible.

Make recommendations

Nurses, along with their associations, must become more involved in rebuilding the media's image of nursing.

Speculate about the future

If sustainable wormholes could be created, then travelling to the past would appear to be more probable, but not certain.

Tell an anecdote that illustrates a key point

The principal character on the show *Nurse Jackie* does not help the image of nursing when she is the epitome of a completely dysfunctional and irrational person (Cabaniss, 2011). Her behaviours and actions thoroughly belittle and misrepresent the nursing profession.

Describe a key image

These fictional and derogatory images of nurses are in stark contrast to what the Canadian Nurses Association (2007) describes a nurse to be. Their definition of a Registered Nurse includes the terms *self-regulated*, *professional*, *autonomous*, *education*, *collaboration*, and *research* (CNA, 2007, p. 6).

Offer a quotation that expresses the essence of your argument

As one youth in a homeless shelter put it, "What is the point of going to a shelter if most of the time they don't have room?"

Ask a rhetorical question

What will be the fate of the nursing profession if the media continue to misrepresent nurses and their diverse roles?

Resist the urge to end on a bright note if what comes before doesn't warrant it; you want your ending to match the body of your essay.

4 Rewrite, Edit, and Proofread

QUICK*TAKE*

- Switch from writer to reader (see below)
- Learn strategies for rewriting (see p. 32)
- Respond to other writers' drafts (see p. 34)
- Proofread carefully (see p. 37)

4a Switch from Writer to Reader

Even the best writers often have to revise several times to get the result they want. To be able to revise effectively, you have to plan your time. You cannot revise an essay effectively if you wait until the last minute to begin working. Allow at least a day to let what you write cool off. With a little time you will gain enough distance to "re-see" it, which, after all, is what *revision* means.

You must also have effective strategies for revising if you're going to be successful. The biggest trap you can fall into is starting off with the little stuff first. *Don't sweat the small stuff at the beginning*. When you see a word that's wrong or a misplaced comma, the great temptation is to fix it. But if you start searching for errors, it's hard to get back to the larger concerns.

Begin your revision by pretending you are someone who either is uninformed about your subject or holds an opposing view. If possible, think of an actual person and pretend to be that person. Read your draft aloud, all the way through. When you read aloud, you will probably hear clunky phrases and outright errors, but do no more at this stage than put checks in the margins so that you can find these things later. Once again, you don't want to get bogged down with the little stuff. What you are after in this stage is an overall sense of how well you have accomplished what you set out to do.

Use the following questions to evaluate your draft. Note any places where you might make improvements.

Does your paper or project meet the assignment?

- Look again at your assignment, especially at the keywords, such as *analyze*, *define*, *evaluate*, and *propose*. Does your paper or project do what the assignment asks?
- Look again at the assignment for specific guidelines, including length, format, and amount of research. Does your work meet these guidelines?

Does your writing have a clear focus?

- Does your project have an explicitly stated thesis? If not, is your thesis clearly implied?
- Is each paragraph related to your thesis?
- Do you get off track at any point by introducing other topics?

Are your main points adequately developed?

- Do you support your main points with reasons and evidence?
- Can you add more examples and details that would help to explain your main points?
- Would additional research fill in gaps or make your case stronger?

Is your organization effective?

- Is the order of your main points clear to your reader? (You may want to make a quick outline of your draft if you have not done so already.)
- Are there any places where you find abrupt shifts or gaps?
- Are there sections or paragraphs that could be rearranged to make your draft more effective?

Do you consider your potential readers' knowledge and points of view?

- Do you give enough background if your readers are unfamiliar with your subject?
- Do you acknowledge opposing views that readers might have?
- Do you appeal to common values that you share with your readers?

Do you represent yourself effectively?

- To the extent you can, forget for a moment that you wrote what you are reading. What impression do you have of you, the writer?
- Does "the writer" create an appropriate tone?
- Has "the writer" done his or her homework?
- Is the writing project visually effective? Has "the writer" selected an attractive and readable font? Does "the writer" use headings and illustrations where they are helpful?

Do you conclude emphatically?

- Conclusions that only summarize tend to bore readers. Does your conclusion offer more than a review of the ideas you have already fully discussed?
- Could you use your conclusion to discuss further implications?

- Could you conclude by making recommendations for change or improvement, or by urging readers to take action?
- Have you left your audience with a final provocative idea that might invite further discussion?

When you finish, make a list of your goals for the revision. You may have to write another draft before you move to the next stage.

4b Learn Strategies for Rewriting

Now it's time to go through your draft in detail. You should work on the goals you identified in your review.

1. Keep your audience in mind. Step back and assess your paper from a reader's perspective. Paragraphs with strong, engaging openers keep an audience's attention, establish a writer's credibility, and above all intrigue readers so that they want to read on. Reread each of your paragraph's opening sentences and ask yourself whether the language is strong and engaging enough to keep your reader interested in your argument from paragraph to paragraph.

2. Sharpen your focus wherever possible. You may have started out with a large topic but find now that most of what you wrote concerns only one aspect of it. For example, you may have started with the large topic of privacy, but your focus now is on the current practice of some retailers' selling their customer databases to companies that build junk mail lists. Revise your thesis and supporting paragraphs as needed.

3. Check that key terms are adequately defined. What are your key terms? Are they defined precisely enough to be meaningful? If your argument relies on an abstract term such as *justice*, you are obligated to define it specifically.

4. Develop where necessary. Key points and claims may need more explanation and supporting evidence. Look for opportunities to replace generalizations with specific details.

General statement	Images of nursing in the popular media present problems for the profession.
Specific details	*Nurse Jackie*, a recent television show, depicts the nurse as drug-dependent and irrational. *Grey's Anatomy* largely ignores the nursing profession with the single exception of Dell, an unfocused and unintelligent character. Shows from earlier periods are even worse, depicting nurses in a variety of subservient roles.

5. Check links between paragraphs. Carefully crafted transitions between paragraphs accomplish two things: They explain to your reader why a paragraph logically follows the previous one, and they express the twists and turns of your thinking.

If you are struggling with your transitions, try this quick diagnostic: Underline the first and last sentences of each paragraph in your paper and then read these underlined sentences aloud to a friend. Do these sentences together make a logical and coherent argument? If not, spend more time figuring out the relationships between your ideas. Often you can express these relationships more clearly by choosing accurate transitional phrases such as *although*, *for example*, *on the other hand*, *in contrast*, *similarly*, and so on (see Sections 3c and 3e).

6. Consider your title. An effective title makes the reader want to read what you have written. Be as specific as you can in your title, and if possible, suggest your stance. "Use of Anabolic Steroids" as a title is vague and bland, and it suggests a topic far too large to be handled well in a few pages. A stronger title would be "Is Andro a Food Supplement or a Steroid?"

7. Consider your introduction. In the introduction you want to get off to a fast start and convince your reader to keep reading. If your subject is climate change, consider starting with rhetorical questions such as "Does the rise in global temperature really have an impact on the earth? Do we, as humans, need to be concerned about global warming?" Then you might follow these questions with a sentence that moves toward answering them: "The movie *An Inconvenient Truth*, directed by Davis Guggenheim, follows Al Gore and his use of emotion, logic, and credibility in an effort to convince people all over the world that global warming is an issue that touches everyone and that needs to be addressed." In three sentences you have established your topic and outlined how you plan to develop your ideas about it in the rest of the paper.

8. Consider your conclusion. Restating your claim usually isn't the best way to finish; conclusions that offer only a summary tend to bore readers. The worst endings say something like "In my paper I've said this." In contrast, effective conclusions remind readers where your argument has taken them and then invite further discussion. Try to leave your reader with something interesting and provocative. Think about whether there is an implication you can draw or another example you can include that sums up your position. You might briefly discuss the implications of your argument, or you could argue why your readers' ideas or beliefs should change because of your findings. If you are writing a proposal, your ending might be a call for action.

9. Improve the visual aspects of your text. Does the font you selected look attractive? (See Section 15c.) Do you use the same font throughout? Are you consistent if you use more than one font? Do you include headings and subheadings to identify key sections of your argument? If you include statistical data, would presenting it in charts be effective? (See Section 17c.) Would illustrations help to establish key points? For example, a map could be very useful if you are arguing about the location of a proposed new highway.

4c Respond to Other Writers' Drafts

Your instructor may ask you to review your classmates' drafts. Writing a response to the work of a fellow student may make you feel uncomfortable. You may think you don't know enough to say anything useful. Remember that you are charged with letting the writer know how only you—one of many potential readers—react.

But you do have to put forth your best effort. Responding to other people's writing requires the same careful attention you give to your own draft. To write a helpful response, you should go through the draft more than once. Before you begin, number the paragraphs if the writer has not already done so.

First reading

Read at your normal rate the first time through without stopping. When you finish you should have a clear sense of what the writer was trying to accomplish.

- *Main idea:* Write a sentence that summarizes what you think is the writer's main idea in the draft.
- *Purpose:* Write a sentence that summarizes what you think the writer was trying to accomplish in the draft.

Second reading

In your second reading, you should be most concerned with the content, organization, and completeness of the draft. Make notes as you read.

- *Introduction:* Does the writer's first paragraph effectively introduce the topic and engage your interest?
- *Thesis:* Where exactly is the writer's thesis? Note in the margin where you think the thesis is located.
- *Focus:* Does the writer maintain a focus on the thesis? Note any places where the writer seems to wander to another topic.

- *Organization:* Are the sections and paragraphs ordered effectively? Do any paragraphs seem to be out of place? Do you note any abrupt shifts? Can you suggest a better order for the paragraphs?
- *Completeness:* Do any sections and paragraphs lack key information or adequate development? Where do you want to know more?
- *Sources:* If the draft uses outside sources, are they cited accurately? If there are quotations, are they used correctly and worked into the fabric of the draft?

Third reading

In your third reading, turn your attention to matters of audience, style, and tone.

- *Audience:* Who is the writer's intended audience? What does the writer assume that the audience knows and believes?
- *Style:* Is the writer's style engaging? How would you describe the writer's voice?
- *Tone:* Is the tone appropriate for the writer's purpose and audience? Is the tone consistent throughout the draft? Are there places where another word or phrase might work better?

When you have finished the third reading, write a short paragraph on each bulleted item, referring to specific paragraphs in the draft by number. Then end by answering these two questions:

1. What does the writer do especially well in the draft?
2. What one or two revisions would most improve the draft?

4d Edit for Particular Goals

In your final pass through the text of your paper, you should concentrate on style and eliminate as many errors as you can.

1. Check the connections between sentences. Notice how your sentences are connected. If you need to signal the relationship from one sentence to the next, use a transitional word or phrase.

2. Check your sentences. If you noticed that a sentence was hard to read or didn't sound right when you read your paper aloud, think about how you might rephrase it. Often you can pick up problems with verbs (see Chapters 38 and 39), pronouns (see Chapter 40), and modifiers (see Chapter 41) by reading aloud. If a sentence seems too long, you might break it into two or more sentences. If you notice a string of short sentences that sound choppy, you might combine them. If you notice run-on sentences or sentence fragments, fix them (see Chapter 37).

3. Eliminate wordiness. Writers tend to introduce wordiness in drafts. Look for long expressions that can easily be shortened (*at this point in time* to *now*) and unnecessary repetition. Remove unnecessary qualifiers (*rather, very, somewhat, little*). See how many words you can take out without losing the meaning (see Chapter 32).

4. Use active verbs. Any time you can use a verb other than a form of *be* (*is, are, was, were*) or a verb ending in *-ing,* take advantage of the opportunity to make your style more lively. Sentences that begin with *There is (are)* and *It is* often have better alternatives:

Draft It is true that when students consider post-secondary education opportunities they will generally be overwhelmed by the many different options presented to them as they are trying to focus on the right program for them.

Revised When you consider post-secondary education opportunities, start by identifying areas of primary interest to you.

Notice too that the use of active verbs often cuts down on wordiness (see Chapter 31).

5. Use specific and inclusive language. As you read, stay alert for any vague words or phrases (see Chapter 34). Check to make sure that you have used inclusive language throughout (see Chapter 35).

Example of sentence-level editing

~~It is a widely believed opinion that computers have greatly influenced the lives of the latest generation. I agree with this opinion. I remember back w~~ **W**hen I was in grade 4, we had a computer **literacy** class every Friday~~. The classroom held about~~ **in a room equipped with** 20 Apple IIe computers. Besides learning how to type correctly, we were given simple graphic programming assignments. ~~Thus, I along with m~~ **M**y fellow classmates **and I** were assigned to input VLIN (Vertical Line) and HLIN (Horizontal Line) commands followed by a colour and coordinates~~. When we finished we would have~~ **that created** a picture on the monitor. ~~This was not a photographic quality image by any means.~~ Because the pixels were only slightly smaller than sugar cubes~~,~~ and ~~we~~ were limited to 16 colours, these images made ~~the~~ **our** Nintendo Entertainment System's graphic**s** look like the ~~graphic~~ output of a Hollywood studio production **by comparison**.

4e Proofread Carefully

To proofread effectively, you have to learn to slow down. Some writers find that moving from word to word with a pencil slows them down enough to allow them to find errors. Others read backward to force themselves to concentrate on each word.

1. Know what your spell-checker can and cannot do. Spell-checkers are the greatest invention since peanut butter. They turn up many typos and misspellings that are hard to catch. But spell-checkers do not catch wrong words (e.g., *to much* should be *too much*), missing endings (*three dog*), and other, similar errors. You still have to proofread carefully to eliminate misspellings.

2. Check for grammar and mechanics. Nothing hurts your credibility with readers more than a text with numerous errors. Many job application letters get tossed in the reject pile because an applicant made a single glaring error. Issues of grammar are treated in Chapters 36 through 41. The conventions for using punctuation, capitalization, italics, abbreviations, acronyms, and numbers can be found in Chapters 38 through 47. Get into the habit of referring to these chapters.

4f Learn to Edit the Writing of Others

Editing someone else's writing is easier than editing your own. In your own writing you know most of the time what you meant to say and often you don't notice where a reader might be stopped or jarred. But editing someone else's writing is also harder because you want to give the writer useful feedback without taking over the writer's task.

1. Make comments in the margins. If you find a sentence hard to read, let the writer know. If you think a sentence is repetitive, let the writer know. If you think a word was left out, say so in the margin. Also let the writer know when a sentence is especially successful.

> *Word missing here?*
> *Same point as sentence 1?*
> *Can you join this sentence with the previous sentence?*
> *Vivid description!*

2. Use symbols to indicate possible problems. Draw a wavy line under any phrase or sentence where you think there may be a problem. Even if you are not sure what the problem is, you can ask the writer to look carefully at a particular sentence. If you think a word is misspelled, draw a circle around it. If you think words can be deleted, put parentheses around them.

> A webcam is a web page that hosts images or even live video streams served by a digitel camera attached to a computer. Webcams serve as surveillance, entertainment, control, and many other services. Webcam technology has become quite popular (with people) since the first webcams hit the World Wide Web.

WRITING SMART

Standard proofreading symbols

Advanced editing requires learning standard proofreading symbols. Authors, editors, and printers use proofreader's marks to indicate changes. These marks are used in pairs: One mark goes in the text where the change is to be made and the other goes in the margin, close to the change.

Mark in the margin	Mark in the text
(delete mark)	Delete: take it out
⁀	Close up: foot ball
^	Caret: insert here
#	Insert a space: aword
(tr)	Transpose: the in beginning
^,	Add a comma: moreover we
'	Add an apostrophe: Ellens books
" / "	Add double quotation marks: James Joyce's Clay
:	Add a colon: 3 45 p.m.
;	Add a semicolon: concluded however, we
⊙	Add a period: last call Next we
¶	Begin a new paragraph
No ¶	No new paragraph
sp	Spell out: 7 dwarfs=>seven dwarfs
stet	Ignore correction: in the beginning

PART

2 Writing for Different Purposes

You **can learn more and do more** with MyWritingLab and with the eText version of *The Brief Penguin Handbook*. Find resources in MyWritingLab to help you successfully complete your assignment.

5 Read and View with a Critical Eye 39

6 Write to Analyze 48

7 Write to Reflect 59

8 Write to Inform 65

9 Write to Persuade 77

5 Read and View with a Critical Eye

QUICK*TAKE*

- Ask questions while you read (see below)
- Recognize verbal fallacies (see p. 42)
- Recognize visual fallacies (see p. 45)

5a Become a Critical Reader

Critical thinking begins with critical reading. For most of what you read, one time through is enough. When you start asking questions about what you are reading, you are engaging in *critical reading.*

Critical reading is a four-part process. First, begin by asking where a piece of writing came from and why it was written. Second, read the text carefully to find the author's central claim or thesis and the major points. Third, decide if you can trust the author. Fourth, read the text again to understand how it works.

Where did it come from?

- Who wrote this material?
- Where did it first appear? In a book, newspaper, magazine, or online?
- What else has been written about the topic or issue?
- What do you expect after reading the title?

What does it say?

- What is the topic or issue?
- What is the writer's thesis or overall point?
- What reasons or evidence does the writer offer?
- What does the writer assume that the intended readers know and believe?

Can you trust the writer?

- Does the writer have the knowledge and experience to write on this subject?
- Do you detect a bias in the writer's position?
- Can you trust the writer's facts? Where did the facts come from?
- How reliable are the writer's sources?

- Does the writer acknowledge opposing views and unfavourable evidence? Does the writer deal fairly with opposing views?

How does it work?

- How is the piece of writing organized? How are the major points arranged?
- How does the writer conclude? Does the conclusion follow from the evidence the writer offers? What impression does the reader take away?
- How would you characterize the style? Describe the language that the writer uses.
- How does the writer represent herself or himself?
- Is the page design attractive and correctly formatted? Are photos, tables, and graphics well integrated into the text and clearly labelled?

5b Read Actively

If you own what you are reading, read with a pencil in hand. Pens and highlighters don't erase, and often you won't remember why you highlighted a particular sentence.

Annotate what you read

Using annotating strategies will make your effort more rewarding.

- **Mark major points and key concepts.** Sometimes major points are indicated by headings, but often you will need to locate them.
- **Connect with your experience.** Think about your own experiences and how they match up or don't match up with what you are reading.
- **Connect passages.** Notice how ideas connect to each other. Draw lines and arrows. If an idea connects to something a few pages before, write a note in the margin with the page number.
- **Ask questions.** Note anything that puzzles you, including words to look up.

Critical response

Here is a small sample of the side of the debate we almost never hear:

This article appears very convincing, but it admits to being one-sided.

Appearing before the Commons Committee on Environment and Sustainable Development last year, Carleton University paleoclimatologist Professor Tim Patterson testified, "There is no meaningful correlation between CO_2 levels and Earth's temperature over this [geologic] time frame. In fact, when CO_2 levels were over ten times higher than they are now, about 450 million years ago, the planet was in the depths of the absolute coldest period in the last half billion years." Patterson asked the committee, "On the basis of this evidence, how could anyone still believe that the recent relatively small increase in CO_2 levels would be the major cause of the past century's modest warming?"

Harris is only bringing up arguments that he felt weren't emphasized enough in the media.

There could easily have been other factors 450 million years ago that are not present now.

Patterson concluded his testimony by explaining what his research and "hundreds of other studies" reveal: on all time scales, there is very good correlation between Earth's temperature and natural celestial phenomena such as changes in the brightness of the Sun.

No one disagrees with carbon dioxide's heat-retaining properties.

—Tom Harris, "Scientists Respond to Gore's Warnings of Climate Catastrophe," canadafreepress.com, Canada Free Press, 12 June 2006, Web, 9 Jan. 2012

Map of argument structure
Causes of global warming

CO_2 levels ≠ earth's temperature ······▶ 450 million years ago: CO_2 levels 10x > now, but temps = < 0°C ······▶ Instead, earth's temp ≈ sun brightness

5c Write Summaries

A summary should be concise but complete.

- **Begin your summary with the main point.**
- **Report the key ideas.** Represent the author's argument in miniature as accurately as you can. Quote or paraphrase key points, according to your discipline's conventions (see pages 257–260 for how to integrate or paraphrase an author's words into your summary).
- **Recount the author's argument.** Avoid inserting your opinion. Your aim is to focus on the author's points and the position he or she advocates.

Tom Harris raises several objections to Al Gore's film *An Inconvenient Truth*. He attacks several points made by Gore, citing experts in various fields. The scientists mentioned contend that Antarctica is gaining mass, not losing it, and that the sea level is rising at perhaps only 0.03 mm/year due to the combined effects of melting and freezing in Antarctica and Greenland. Many areas in the earth are in fact cooling; the IPCC's models gave more weight to areas that are warming, but if they had weighted everything equally, they would not have found a great difference. Perhaps most importantly, 450 million years ago the earth's climate was far colder, but CO_2 levels were 10 times higher.

5d Recognize Verbal Fallacies

Reasoning depends less on proving a claim than it does on finding evidence for that claim that readers will accept as valid. The kinds of faulty reasoning called *logical fallacies* reflect a failure to provide sufficient evidence for a claim that is being made.

Fallacies of logic

- **Begging the question.** *People who take 8:00 a.m. classes are crazy because no sane person would choose to get up that early*. The fallacy of begging the question occurs when the claim is restated and passed off as evidence.
- **Either-or.** *Either we increase corporate taxes or else individuals will have to pay higher taxes.* The either-or fallacy suggests that there are only two choices in a complex situation. Rarely, if ever, is this the case. (In this example, the writer ignores the fact that individuals may have to pay higher taxes even if the government raises corporate taxes.)
- **False analogies.** *Japan quit fighting in 1945 when the Allies dropped nuclear bombs on them. Maybe NATO should use nuclear weapons against other countries.* Analogies always depend on the degree of resemblance of one situation to another. In this case, the analogy fails to recognize that circumstances today are very different from those in 1945, and it is easy to point out how the analogy fails.
- **Hasty generalization.** *We have been in a drought for three years; that's a sure sign of climate change*. A hasty generalization is a broad claim made on the basis of a few occurrences. Climate cycles occur regularly over spans of a few years; climate trends must be observed over centuries.

- ***Non sequitur.*** *A university that can raise a billion dollars from alumni should not have to raise tuition.* A *non sequitur* (which is a Latin term meaning "it does not follow") ties together two unrelated ideas. In this case, the argument fails to recognize that the money for capital campaigns is often donated for special purposes, such as centres for excellence, and is not part of a university's general revenue.
- **Oversimplification.** *No one would run stop signs if we had a mandatory death penalty for doing it.* This claim may be true, but the argument would be unacceptable to most citizens. More complex, if less definitive, solutions are called for.
- ***Post hoc* fallacy.** *The stock market goes down when a Northeast division team plays in the Stanley Cup finals in an even year.* The *post hoc* fallacy (from the Latin *post hoc ergo propter hoc*, which means "after this, therefore because of this") assumes that things that follow in time have a causal relationship.
- **Rationalization.** *I could have finished my paper on time if my printer was working.* People frequently come up with excuses and weak explanations for their own and others' behaviour that avoid actual causes.
- **Slippery slope.** *If the government were to legalize a gateway drug such as marijuana, there would be a huge increase in the use of hard drugs such as cocaine and heroin.* The slippery slope fallacy maintains that one thing will inevitably cause something else to happen.

Fallacies of emotion and language

- **Bandwagon appeals.** *Since all the power hitters in baseball use steroids, I'll have to use them, too, if I want to be able to compete.* This argument suggests that everyone is doing it, so why shouldn't you? But on close examination, it may be that everyone really isn't doing it—and in any case, it may not be the right thing to do.
- **Name calling.** Name calling is frequent in politics and among competing groups (*radical, tax-and-spend liberal, racist, fascist, right-wing ideologue*). Unless these terms are carefully defined, they are meaningless.
- **Polarization.** *Feminists are all man haters.* Polarization, such as name calling, exaggerates positions and groups by representing them as extreme and divisive.
- **Straw man.** *Loggers won't be satisfied until they clear-cut every mountainside in British Columbia.* A straw man argument is a diversionary tactic that sets up another's position in a way that can be easily rejected. In fact, logging all the trees would put the lumber industry out of business.

 Become a Critical Viewer

Critical viewing is similar to critical reading, although it may be a skill less often practised. Usually photographs come in a context—in a book with a caption, in a family photo album, in a magazine advertisement—that tells us a great deal about why the photograph was taken and what purpose it is intended to serve. But even without the external context, there are often clues within a photograph that suggest its origins.

We could guess the approximate date of the photograph in Figure 5.1 as being late nineteenth or early twentieth century, based on the shack and accompanying tent and wagon. We see no signs of gasoline-powered vehicles or roads, suggesting this homestead predates this technology. The low scrub on the hills suggests the foothills of Alberta or the hilly country of northern Saskatchewan. In fact, this photograph was taken in 1910 by journalist Georgina Binnie-Clark for her book *A Summer on the Canadian Prairie.* She describes her homesteading efforts in Saskatchewan's Qu'Appelle Valley in this book. Single and married men got free land for their homesteads, but single women did not. Binnie-Clark had to buy her farm, which created financial hardship for her.

One approach to critical viewing is to examine a photograph in terms of its composition. In the photograph of the prairie homestead, the steep hillside and tangled brush dwarf the shack, tent, and wagon—all manufactured structures. The edge of the farm, which runs to the foot of the

Figure 5.1 A typical prairie homestead

hills, splits the picture roughly in half with nature dominating the scene. The pale grey sky and white tent contrast with the dark landscape.

Another approach to critical viewing is to analyze the content. In 1910 settlers were still breaking ground for what would become some of the world's most bountiful farm land. Many settlers left towns in eastern Canada and, like Binnie-Clark, left family and careers behind to break sod in the West. The hours were long, the work back-breaking, and the winters harsh. If we put this image of the homestead against our knowledge of Binnie-Clark as its builder (a relationship known as *juxtaposition*), we can better appreciate the sacrifice made by these settlers—including single women. The broader context for this image helps it serve as an ironic commentary: Adding to the general hardship, Binnie-Clark had to pay for what her male counterparts received as a gift.

No one set of questions can cover the great variety of images, but a few general questions can assist you in developing a critical response:

- What kind of an image or visual is it?
- Who created this image (movie, advertisement, television program, and so on)?
- What is it about? What is portrayed in the image?
- Where did it first appear? Where do you usually find images such as this one?
- When did it appear?

The following questions are primarily for still images. For animations, movies, and television, you also have to ask questions about how the story is being told:

- What attracts your eye first? If there is an attention-grabbing element, how does it connect with the rest of the image?
- What impression of the subject does the image create?
- How does the image appeal to the values of the audience? (For example, politicians love to be photographed with children.)
- How does the image relate to what surrounds it?
- Was it intended to serve purposes other than art and entertainment?

5f Recognize Visual Fallacies

Misleading images

The era of digital imaging has made it possible to create images of lifelike dinosaurs chasing humans, interactions between people now living and those long dead, and human feats that defy human limits and the laws of physics.

Figure 5.2 This photograph, showing a shark attacking a British Navy diver, is a hoax, created by combining two real but unrelated pictures.

Figure 5.3 A photograph of a great white shark taken off the coast of South Africa by Charles Maxwell.

Figure 5.4 A photograph of a helicopter from a California National Guard Reserve Unit, taken by Lance Cheung, with the Golden Gate Bridge in San Francisco in the background.

Figure 5.2 circulated on the internet for a while, purporting to show a shark attacking a British Navy diver. In fact, the photo was created by combining two unrelated pictures (see Figures 5.3 and 5.4). Figure 5.3 is a great white shark snapped by Charles Maxwell off the coast of South Africa. Figure 5.4 is an HH-60G Pave Hawk helicopter from a California National Guard unit taken by Lance Cheung. In the background is the Golden Gate Bridge in San Francisco. The two photos were combined to create the shark "attack."

Critical viewers ask questions about images similar to those they ask about texts.

Misleading charts

A special category of visual fallacies is misleading charts. For example, Glitzycorp might use the chart in Figure 5.5 to attract investors. The chart shows remarkable growth from 2009 to 2011 and projects additional sales for 2012. But is the picture accurate? Sure.

Notice that the bars in this chart start at 20, not 0. The effect makes the $22 million sales in 2010 appear to double the $21 million sales of 2009, even though the increase was less than 5 percent. Three years is also a short span to use to project a company's future profits. Figure 5.6 shows the sales of Glitzycorp over seven years, and it tells quite a different story. The big growth years were from 2005 to 2007, followed by a collapse in 2008 and slow growth ever since.

Glitzycorp's sales charts illustrate how facts can be manipulated in visual presentations.

Figure 5.5 Misleading. The starting point on the y-axis is $20 million, not $0.

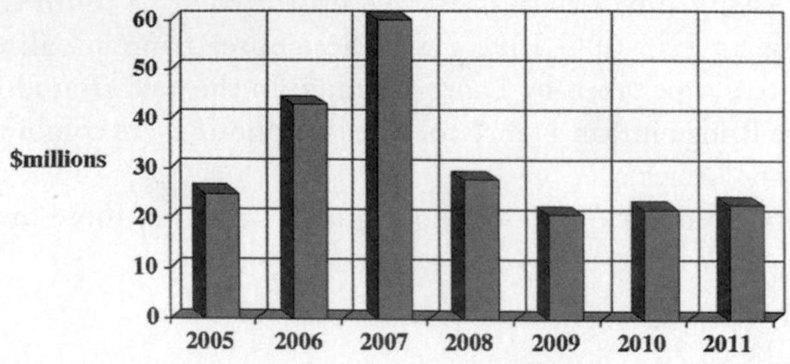

Figure 5.6 Accurate. The actual increase from 2009 to 2010 was less than 5 percent.

6 Write to Analyze

QUICK*TAKE*

- Analyze the context and the text (see p. 49)
- Organize and write a rhetorical analysis (see p. 52)
- Analyze images and other visual texts (see p. 57)

6a Understand the Goal of a Rhetorical Analysis

The goal of a *rhetorical analysis* is to understand how a particular act of writing or speaking influenced particular people at a particular time. Rhetorical analysis is not limited to speaking and writing. The tools of rhetorical analysis have been applied to understanding how meaning is made by other human creations, such as art, buildings, photographs, dance, memorials, websites, music, advertisements—any kind of symbolic communication.

Writing a rhetorical analysis (also called *critical analysis* or *textual analysis*) is frequently an assignment in post-secondary education. A rhetorical analysis requires you to step back from a text and consider it from multiple perspectives. Writing a rhetorical analysis can give you a heightened awareness of a text and a better appreciation of what the author accomplished.

Understanding how communication works or fails to work is a worthy goal by itself, but rhetorical analysis has other benefits. It enables you to think about a text in more depth, to better understand the arguments it makes, and to appreciate how it is put together. In turn, this knowledge helps you in writing your own text. You will have a much better sense of what has been said and written about your subject and where you have opportunities to contribute your own ideas.

6b Analyze the Context and the Text

A rhetorical analysis begins with a text to analyze. If your instructor does not assign a text, select a text that has significance for you, either because it was important when it was written or because it is about a subject that is important to you.

Think of your analysis as running on a continuum between considering the *context*—the relationship between the piece of writing or speaking and the larger society surrounding it—and the *text* itself—what it is about and how it is designed. We can think of the context, which lies at one end of the continuum, in two senses. First, the *immediate context* refers to where the text was written and read or heard. For example, on January 19, 1914, Nellie McClung argued for voting rights for women in Manitoba by acting as a female premier denying suffrage to a male delegation in a play staged at the Winnipeg Theatre. Second, the *broader context* refers to the larger cultural and historical circumstances in which a text is produced and read. The broader context for "The Women's Parliament" was Premier Dufferin Roblin's earlier dismissal of a female delegation petitioning for enfranchisement in the Manitoba legislature, and the larger backdrop of the women's suffrage movement in North America and England in the early 1900s. McClung's satire helped to change her contemporaries' minds about voting rights for women, contributing to a Conservative government defeat and the passage of a bill allowing women to vote in Manitoba by 1916.

At the other end of the continuum lies the text itself. We can consider a text as if it were a piece in a museum, where we closely scrutinize it. For example, Nellie McClung recounted the proceedings of "The Women's Parliament" in her novel *Purple Springs,* where, if you examine the language of Pearl Watson's speech, you begin to see how the humour highlights the contradiction in the period's sentiments about women. Watson notes to the men petitioning for suffrage,

> Man's place is to provide for his family, a hard enough task in these strenuous days. . . . Would letting politics enter the home help matters?

> Ah no! Politics would unsettle our men. Unsettled men mean unsettled bills—unsettled bills mean broken homes—broken vows—and then divorce. Man has a higher destiny than politics. What is a home without a bank account? The man who pays the grocer rules the world. (283)

She suggests that men do not need to vote because they already have power in their role as breadwinners (i.e., equal to but different from women). She then suggests that men are superior to women (i.e., they have a higher destiny than politics). These are contradictory positions, yet they are classic arguments that Premier Roblin had used to justify disenfranchising women in 1914.

Often in the back-and-forth movement between text and context, you gain surprising insights about how a text achieves certain effects. These questions will help you get started in composing a rhetorical analysis.

Analyze the immediate context

Examine the author

- What is the author's purpose: to change beliefs? to inspire action? to teach about a subject? to praise or blame? to amuse?
- What else did the author write?

Examine the audience

- Who was the intended audience?
- What were their attitudes and beliefs about the subject? the author? the society at the time?
- What does the author assume about the audience?

Analyze the broader context

Examine the larger conversation

- Why did this text appear at this particular time?
- What else has been said or written about this subject?
- What was going on at the time that influenced this text?

Examine the larger society

- What social, political, and economic influences can you find in the text?

278 PURPLE SPRINGS

The Speaker, in purple velvet, with a sweeping plume in her three-cornered hat, sat on the throne; pages in uniform answered the many calls of the members, who, on the Government side were showing every sign of being bored, for the Opposition had the floor, and the honorable member from Mountain was again introducing her bill to give the father equal guardianship rights with the mother. She pleaded eloquently that two parents were not any too many for children to have. She readily granted that if there were to be but one parent, it would of course be the mother, but why skimp the child on parents? Let him have both. It was nature's way. She cited instances of grave injustice done to fathers from having no claim on their offspring.

The Government members gave her little attention. They read their papers, one of the Cabinet Ministers tatted, some of the younger members powdered their noses, many ate chocolates. Those who listened, did so to sneer at the honorable member from Mountain, insinuating she took this stand so she might stand well with the men. This brought a hearty laugh, and a great pounding of the desks.

When the vote was taken, the House divided along party lines. Yawningly the Government members cried "No!"

Robertson Jones sniffed contemptuously; evidently this was a sort of Friday afternoon dialogue, popular at Snookum's Corners, but not likely to cause much of a flutter in the city.

■ Text

■ Broader context

■ Immediate context

Analyze the text

Examine the kind of text

- What kind of text is it: speech? essay? editorial? advertisement?
- What is the medium: print? website? voice recording?

Summarize the content

- What is the author's main claim or main idea?
- How is the main claim or main idea supported?
- How is the text organized?

Examine the appeals

- *Ethos:* How does the author represent himself or herself? How does the author build or fail to build trust?
- *Logos:* What kinds of facts and evidence does the author use?
- *Pathos:* How does the author appeal to values shared with the audience?

Examine the language and style

- Is the style formal? informal? academic?
- Does the author use humour or satire?
- What metaphors are used?

6c Organize and Write a Rhetorical Analysis

When you have completed your initial analysis, you are ready to begin writing. Expect to discover additional ideas you can use in the analysis while you are writing and to go back and forth with your analysis.

1 Before you write

Take stock of your initial analysis

- If the text you chose is not working for the assignment, find one that works better.
- Review your notes on the author, the audience, the circumstances of original publication or delivery, what other texts the author was responding to, and what else was going on at the time (the immediate context).
- Decide on the best way to organize your analysis.

Think about your readers

- How much do readers know about your text? the author? the events surrounding the text? other texts like it?
- What will readers gain from reading your analysis?

2 Write an introduction

Begin your analysis by describing the immediate context

- Inform your readers about the author and why the author selected this particular topic.
- Describe the original audience and the conversation about the topic that was going on at the time the text was written.

Make a claim

- Make a claim about how the text you are analyzing uses rhetoric for particular purposes.

3 Organize and write the body of your paper

Support your claim with your detailed analysis of the text and context

- Give examples from the text to show how the author builds credibility with the audience, appeals to their values and beliefs, and convinces them with facts and evidence.
- Analyze the author's style, tone, and language, including metaphors.
- Analyze how the author responded to the immediate context and the broader context.

4 Write a conclusion

End with more than a summary

- Draw larger implications from your analysis.
- End with a vivid example from the text.

5 Revise, revise, revise

Evaluate your draft

- Make sure your analysis meets the requirements of the assignment.
- Consider where you might provide more information about the context.
- Consider where you might provide more evidence supporting your claim about the text.
- When you have finished revising, edit and proofread carefully.

 Sample Rhetorical Analysis

Abbott 1

Kaleigh Abbott

Writing Studies 103

Dec. 9, 2012

Should we worry about exposure to medical imaging radiation? Yes, it turns out.

Introduction

Abbott's analysis places the visual argument into a broader context of scientific data on radiation exposure.

Images allow us to represent data to communicate messages and various arguments. I analyzed "Exposed: Medical Imaging Delivers Big Doses of Radiation," by Mark Fischetti from *Scientific American* magazine to determine how persuasive it was in making its argument using various techniques such as colour choices, size of shapes used to present data, and the relationship created between the viewer and the image. I also examined the broader context of information on radiation exposure to assess the visual's accuracy.

Analysis

The analysis section explains how the visual's layout and presentation of data use *ethos*, *pathos*, and *logos* to persuade viewers.

The visual "Exposed: Medical Imaging Delivers Big Doses of Radiation" (reproduced in Figure 1) claims that the increase in a person's exposure to radiation is largely due to medical imaging. It uses a black background to create a negative impression of radiation and a sombre mood, thus appealing to the emotions and suggesting that radiation has a negative effect on humans. The distressed facial expression of the cartoon person also reinforces the impression of the harmful effects of an increase in radiation

Abbott 2

exposure. The person in the visual does not make direct eye contact with the viewer, thus creating an unequal relationship that depicts the exposed individual as an object, shrinking under the weight of his radiation exposure.

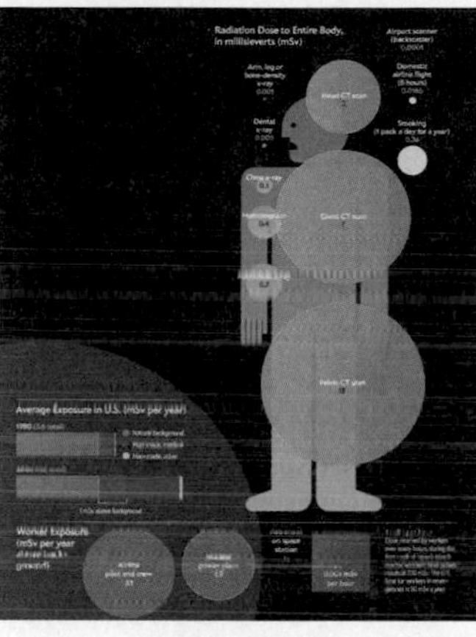

Figure 1

Abbott uses the concept of relationship between viewer and image from p. 1 as one of her tools of analysis.

The background contrasts the large orange circles that depict the ways that people are exposed to radiation. The orange, blue, yellow, and green draw the observer's attention to the statistics indicating the amount of radiation a person is exposed to from various medical imaging methods. In contrast, other situations that expose people to radiation are illustrated in shades of grey at the bottom of the image. One grey circle shows the amount of radiation an astronaut receives, an amount substantially higher than any medical imaging exposure; however, the grey circle is less noticeable and thus does not affect the main claim.

The scale to which the circles are drawn also impacts the argument. These circles are not proportional to the size of the body and thus look as if

Abbott 3

the radiation is engulfing the individual. If the scale chosen to represent the radiation exposure were not amplified, the message would be less powerful since the circles would be smaller, making the radiation seem less dangerous. The bar chart provides an alternative way for readers to access the information shown in the image.

The analysis section presents the analysis following the list of topics outlined in the introduction section.

Initially, the visual is persuasive. The brightly coloured circles organize the information, and including radiation exposure from other sources creates the impression of balanced information. The visual's credibility is reinforced by the illustrator's name and a link to more information about the subject. Lastly, the image is published in *Scientific American*, a reputable magazine that received the 2011 National Magazine Award for General Excellence.

The Broader Context

Discussion of the broader context focuses on verifying the statistical data presented in the visual.

The image communicates the dangerous consequences of radiation, while also demonstrating that medical imaging, specifically the CT scan, is a large contributor to increased radiation exposure. Robb-Nicholson reported a 50% increase in radiation exposure with 24% of it due to CT scanning; this source supports the visual's main claim [1]. Statistics relayed in the image—for example, the amount of radiation received in an X-ray of the abdominal area—is verified by Lin, who reported amounts as 0.7mSV[2]. Lin also reported the amount of radiation from a brain CT to be

Abbott 4

2 mSv, which agrees with the amount reported in the image [1,2]. This research supports the main claim of the visual, increasing its persuasiveness.

Conclusion

Illustrators rely on *pathos, ethos,* and *logos* to convince viewers of the visual argument presented. Carefully chosen colours, the layout of information, and the relationship between the viewer and the image all have an impact on how the visual persuades the observer. "Exposed" is initially convincing due to the techniques the illustrator has used. Further analysis of the broader context verified the data presented in the visual, making the argument more convincing.

Abbott 5

References

1. Robb-Nicholson C. *A doctor talks about radiation risk from medical imaging*. Harv Women's Health Watch 2010 Oct;18(2):4-5.

2. Lin EC. *Radiation risk from medical imaging*. Mayo Clin Proc. 2010 Dec;85(12):1142-1146.

6e Analyze Images and Other Visual Texts

The word *text* typically brings to mind words on a printed page. But in the sense that anything that can be "read" can be a text, then nearly everything is a text. We see hundreds of visual texts every day distributed on television, the web, films, newspapers, advertisements, product labels, clothing, signs, buildings—indeed, on nearly everything. We can analyze how these images create meaning by the same means we use to analyze verbal texts—by examining the relationship between the text and its contexts.

Consider the advertisement for CARE reprinted below. It was found in a recent issue of *Canadian House & Home*. Over 2.5 million people read this magazine per year, and 155 000 visit the website each month. According to the website, this magazine helps readers "define their own unique sense of style." As part of this effort, the magazine includes columns such as "Ask a Designer," "Food and Style," and "Before & After." Feature stories in the issue where the CARE ad appeared include an article describing how "seventy top designers give Toronto's historic McLean House a luxe top-to-toe makeover, all for a good cause." Proceeds from the makeover went to the St. Alban's Boys and Girls Club and Sunnybrook Hospital's Women & Babies program. The CARE advertisement, then, may well connect with philanthropically minded readers.

This advertisement speaks to the readers of this magazine, and this issue of it, specifically. The largest image in the ad is of a woman, possibly from Central America, who is looking directly at the camera. Her direct gaze means that we must engage with her as a person—if she had been looking away, for example, we could treat her as an object. Across the woman's left arm is the handwritten phrase "I am powerful." Her folded arms, ramrod-straight stance, and direct gaze reinforce that statement. Behind her is a field of lush green plants and a child kneeling between the rows of plants.

■ CARE advertisement

The main text of the ad occupies the bottom quarter of the page and starts with this argument: "She can plant the seeds of change. If she can get the seed." The logical appeal here is clear—a small investment from the reader can help women in other countries buy land and seeds in order to realize their dreams of creating a better life for themselves and their families. The largely female readers of *Canadian House & Home* will identify with this dream—they, too, believe in the right to own land, the inherent power of women, and the dignity of work. This ad reaches out to these readers in terms that will resonate with them and with images that demand their attention.

Write to Reflect

QUICK*TAKE*

- Find a reflective topic (see below)
- Identify a focus (see p. 60)
- Determine your organization, write an introduction, write a title (see p. 60)

Find a Reflective Topic

Reflecting on experience

Reflections are often assumed to deal primarily with personal and private experiences, but many disciplines use reflective writing to help students draw links between theoretical knowledge in a textbook and their own experiences. This kind of reflection aims not to vent feelings or expose secrets but to think about an idea or theory in the context of your own life experience. For example, after examining the scientific evidence about tanning beds, Sarah Liu discovered that the UVB rays that stimulate human vitamin D production are absent from tanning beds. She realized that she and her friends had been damaging their skin with the UVA rays in tanning beds, not receiving the health benefits that they thought.

Instructors may also use reflective writing to help students analyze their experiences.

Choosing a self-reflective topic

If your instructor asks you to write a reflective essay based on memories, listing possible topics is a good way to start.

- List five people who have been significant in your life.
- List five events that have been important in your life. Think about one-time events, such as getting a scholarship, and recurring events, such as a yearly family get-together.
- List five places that have been important in your life.
- Now look through your lists and check the items that are especially vivid.

Once you have selected a topic, try freewriting to stimulate your memories and explore your present perspective (see Section 2b). Take five to ten minutes to write about the event, person, or place as you remember it. Then write for five to ten minutes about how you think about the event, person, or place today. What has changed from your first experience? Why do you feel differently now?

Not all reflective topics are about the past. You can visit a place or go to an event and focus on your interaction with the place or event instead of on the place or event itself.

7b Identify a Focus

Reflections about your personal experience may not have a formal thesis, but they typically have a **focus** that makes the reflection coherent by communicating a central idea to readers. Why is this experience important? Why is it memorable? In short, why is it worth writing about?

Often the focus comes not in the big idea but in the small details that call for reflection. A reflective paper that asks you to research a topic and then evaluate the research based on your experience generally does need a formal thesis and an argument centred on your response to the research. How does your experience compare with the theoretical perspective?

7c Organize and Write a Reflection

When you have a topic and a focus that communicates the importance of the experience or event to your readers, then it's time to write your reflection. You might not follow this order, as writing is often a back-and-forth process.

1 Before you write

Think about your readers

- What attitudes are your readers likely to have about your subject?
- How can you make readers care about your subject?
- What will readers gain from reading your reflection?

Write an introduction

Engage your readers quickly
- Choose a title that will interest readers.
- Start with the incident, place, or person that is the focus.

Organize and write the body of your paper

Should you use a chronological organization?
- Use chronological order to let readers relive events with you.

Should you use a conceptual organization?
- Use conceptual order to show connections and links between ideas.

Communicate experiences with details
- Refer to research sources, where appropriate.
- Give specifics such as dates and names to provide background information.
- Augment visual details with other sensory details (smells, sounds, tastes, tactile feelings).
- Choose specific words to convey details.

Consider your voice and tone
- Your writing should sound like you. Be yourself.
- If your writing sounds like the voice that makes announcements in the airport, try rewriting as you would talk.
- Let yourself go in the first draft. If you become excessive, you can adjust the language when you revise.

Write a conclusion

End by inviting further reflection
- Share any discoveries you made in the process of reflecting.
- Avoid a simple moral lesson, but your conclusion should help your readers to make sense of your reflection.

Revise, revise, revise

Evaluate your draft
- Make sure your reflection meets the requirements of the assignment.
- Consider how you might sharpen the focus and significance of your reflection.
- Make sure you explain how your experience compares with the theoretical ideas, as appropriate.
- When you have finished revising, edit and proofread carefully.

7d Sample Reflective Essay

In his English class, Eric Graves was asked to write a reflective essay on a situation or an event that was important to him. For this assignment, Graves decided to write about his experiences as a Canadian attending high school in Chicago. The focus of Graves's reflection is that the beating he received could be seen as part of a larger cultural context.

Graves 1

Eric Graves

Professor Thomas

Introduction to English

25 April 2013

Apartness

Graves begins with a dramatic retelling of the incident.

Crack. That's the sound of the starter pistol firing at track practice half an hour earlier. Crack. That's the sound of the locker-room door slamming open a minute before. Crack. That's the sound of a fist violently impacting with my face, three seconds after I realize I'm in trouble.

The end of this paragraph sets up the epiphany that will be described in the rest of the essay.

That instant, as you pulled my arms together from behind me, a window of insight was opened before me. In the split second it took for my brain to recognize that you were not closing your gym locker, but rather closing your arms around mine to prevent retaliation for the blow your friend would deliver, I reached an epiphany.

Perhaps the fact that I have never seen you around school before, let alone wronged you in any way, is the problem. Why have we never met before? Because you are black, and I am white.

Maybe if I had not accepted the self-segregated society into which I had moved, I would know you.

Graves 2

Maybe if I had not conformed to the apartheid culture of the Chicago public school system, you would recognize me as a person instead of as an anonymous white punching bag. Maybe you would have gotten to know me, realized that I am from Canada, that I like basketball and video games, and that we are very much alike. Maybe if I had reached out to you, tried to get to know you, we could have been friends.

But I didn't.

And now I am paying for it with the blood running from my nose. Blood. It is one and the same for both of us, so why do we pretend that there's some monumental wall between us? Because we've both been programmed to think so.

Details such as the blood help to communicate the experience.

In a culture that promotes a segregated lifestyle, it is no wonder that we are in this situation. Turn on the TV, and watch Chris Rock equate white people to the devil. Change the channel, and watch Dave Chappelle portray white people as vicious racists. Don't get me wrong, I think these guys are hilarious. The problem arises when you turn off the TV, and the negative stereotypes and exaggerations that are constructed on the tube work their way into the viewer's off-air perceptions. You go to school, and this depiction of hateful, malicious "white people" gets projected onto some white kid you've never seen before. Why would you want to talk to some white kid who seems racist and malevolent? So you ignore him.

This and the next paragraph mirror each other and give both sides of the story.

Graves 3

Now, the same thing happens to that unknown white kid when he returns home to his mostly white suburban Chicago neighbourhood, turns on the TV, and watches a news report on Kobe Bryant's rape trial. He changes the channel and watches news coverage of a Senate hearing without seeing a black senator. What happens when he connects the negative media image of black people, his whitewashed neighbourhood, and the seemingly hostile black kids at school?

He probably doesn't get a very good perception of black people. His logical response: ignore them. We are subtly taught to ignore each other, to live apart, instead of reconciling our differences. Instead of healing, our historical wounds fester. And we model this behaviour for our children. Generations later the hatchet that caused these injuries lies unburied. But we still pretend everything is fine.

But everything is not fine. You showed me this first-hand. And I thank you for it. Because now that I realize what is wrong, I can help to fix it. I can help to dismantle the wall.

The final image connects the physical actions with the intellectual insights.

Crack. Is that the sound of this illusion fracturing, or is it just my nose?

8 Write to Inform

QUICKTAKE

- Find a topic that explains or one that explores questions and problems (see below)
- Write a title and an introduction that puts the reader's interest in the foreground (see p. 66)
- Identify your main points and decide how to best present them (see p. 67)

 Find an Informative Topic

Many of the writing tasks assigned in university and college are informative—from lab reports and essay exams to analyses of literature, research papers, and case studies. Look at your assignment for keywords such as *study, analyze, explain*, and *explore*, which indicate what kind of writing you are expected to produce. Informative writing has four primary functions: to report new or unfamiliar information; to analyze for meaning, patterns, and connections; to explain how to do something or how something works; and to explore questions and problems.

Reporting information

Reporting information takes many forms, ranging from reports of experimental research and reports of library research to simple lists of information. Writing to reflect (discussed in Chapter 7) and writing to persuade (Chapter 9) also report information. The main difference is that the focus of a report and other informative kinds of writing is on the subject, not on the writer's reflections or on changing readers' minds or on getting them to take action. Writers of reports usually stay in the background and keep their language neutral, giving the impression of an objective, impartial observer.

Analyzing meaning, patterns, and connections

Writers do more than report what they read and observe. They often construct meaning through selecting what and what not to include and in organizing that information. Sometimes this construction of meaning is made explicit as *analysis*. The complexity of the world we live in requires making connections. For example, scientists now agree that the earth has become warmer over the last few decades, but to what extent this warming has been caused by the burning of fossil fuels remains controversial. Historians debate the importance of certain historical events (for example, the Treaty of Versailles following World War I) and how those events led to subsequent events (World War II).

Explaining how

Often what you know well is difficult to explain to others. You may know how to solve certain kinds of difficult problems, such as how to fix a malfunction in your car's electrical system, but if you have to tell someone else how to do it over the phone, you may quickly become very frustrated. Often you have to break down a process into steps that you can describe in order to explain it. Explaining a process sometimes requires you to think about something familiar in a new way.

Exploring questions and problems

Not all informative writing is about topics with which you are familiar or those that you can bring to closure. Often post-secondary writing involves issues or problems that perplex us and for which we cannot come to a definitive conclusion. The goal in such writing is not the ending but the journey. Tracing the turns of thought in a difficult intellectual problem can result in writing far beyond the ordinary. Difficult issues often leave us conflicted; readers appreciate it when we deal honestly with those conflicts.

Finding a topic

When your general subject is specified in your assignment, you can make your work more enjoyable by choosing a specific topic that is either more familiar to you or that you find particularly interesting. If you choose a topic that you find interesting, your enthusiasm increases your readers' interest too. Here are guidelines you can use when choosing a topic:

- Choose a topic you will enjoy writing about.
- Choose a topic that you know something about or can readily find information about.
- Choose a topic for which you can make a contribution of your own, perhaps by viewing something familiar in a new way.
- If you choose an unfamiliar topic, you must be strongly committed to learning more about it.

8b Narrow Your Topic and Write a Thesis

A central difficulty with writing to inform is determining where to stop. For any large subject, even a lifetime may be insufficient. The key to success is to limit the topic. Find a topic you can cover thoroughly in the space you have. Broad, general topics are nearly impossible to cover in an essay of five pages. Look for ways of dividing large topics such as *the use of steroids among post-secondary students* into smaller categories and select one that is promising. *Why post-secondary athletes ignore the risks of steroids* is a topic that you are more likely to be able to cover in a short paper.

Often your readers will lack initial interest in your topic. If you ignore their lack of interest, they in turn will likely ignore you. Instead, you can take your readers' knowledge and interest into account when you draft your thesis. For example, someone who knows a lot about birds in the parks of your city might write this informative thesis:

> Watching birds in urban areas is interesting because unusual birds often show up in city parks.

It doesn't sound like a topic that most post-secondary students would find as interesting as the writer does. But if the writer puts the audience's attitude in the foreground, challenging them to consider a subject they have likely not thought much about, a post-secondary audience might read beyond the title:

> Although most post-secondary students think of bird watching as an activity for retired people, watching birds gives you a daily experience with nature, even in urban areas.

This thesis also gives the writer a stance from which to approach the topic.

8c Organize and Write an Informative Essay

Successful reporting of information requires a clear understanding of the subject and clear presentation. How much information you need to include depends on your readers' knowledge of and potential interest in your topic. You might not follow this order, as writing is often a back-and-forth process.

1 Before you write

Think about your readers

- What do your readers already know about the subject?
- What questions or concerns might they have about your subject?
- What is their attitude toward the subject? If it is different from yours, how can you address the difference?

Review your thesis and scope

- When you learn more about your topic, you should be able to identify one aspect or concept that you can cover thoroughly.

2 Write an introduction

Engage your readers quickly
- Write a title and an introduction that will make readers take an interest in your topic.

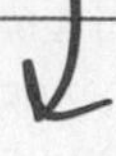

3 Organize and write the body of your essay

Think about your main points
- Use an idea map to organize your main points (see Section 2b).
- Make a working outline to identify your main points and the relationships among them.

Decide how your points are best ordered
- Chronological organization often works best for a topic that occurs over time.
- Conceptual organization focuses on how important concepts are related.
- Compare-and-contrast organization helps to show how two things are similar or different.

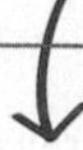

4 Write a conclusion

End with more than a summary
- Make a point that readers can take away.
- Raise an interesting question.
- End with a vivid example.

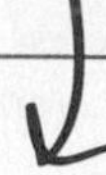

5 Revise, revise, revise

Evaluate your draft
- Make sure your informative essay meets the requirements of the assignment.
- Examine the order of your ideas and reorganize them if necessary.
- Add detail or further explanation where needed.
- When you have finished revising, edit and proofread carefully.

WRITING SMART

Use visuals to report information

Complex statistical data can often be presented effectively in a table or a chart. Other visuals such as maps and photos can help readers to understand your subject. Be sure to provide the sources of your data and the source of any visual that you do not create.

Carbon Emissions Increase

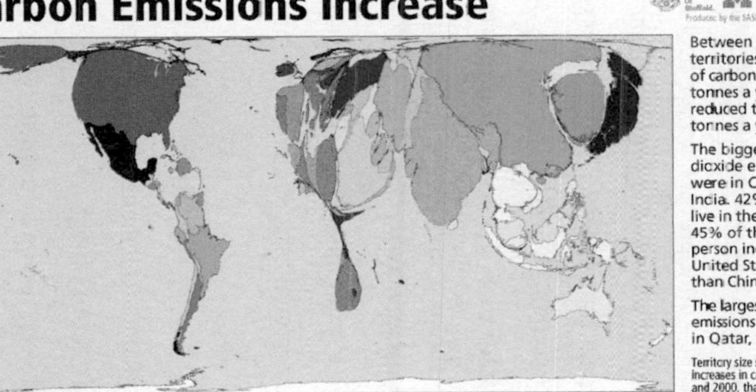

Between 1980 and 2000, 72% of territories increased their emissions of carbon dioxide, totalling 6.6 billion tonnes a year. Other territories reduced their emissions by 1.9 billion tonnes a year.

The biggest increases in carbon dioxide emissions over this period were in China, the United States and India. 42% of the world population live in these 3 territories, they caused 45% of the world increases. The per person increase in emissions from the United States was over 3 times larger than China's, and over 4 times India's.

The largest increases in carbon dioxide emissions per person living there were in Qatar, then Bahrain.

Territory size shows the proportion of all territory level increases in carbon dioxide emissions between 1980 and 2000, that occurred there.

Land area

Technical notes
- Data are from the United Nations Development Programme's 2004 Human Development Report.
- "The denominator used is population in 2002, so that the change shown is simply in emissions.
- See website for further information.

HIGHEST INCREASES IN CARBON DIOXIDE EMISSIONS

Rank	Territory	Value	Rank	Territory	Value
1	Qatar	41.1	11	Libyan Arab Jamahiriya	5.7
2	Bahrain	15.6	12	Oman	5.4
3	Kuwait	11.7	13	[illegible]	[illegible]
4	Saudi Arabia	11.2	14	Malaysia	4.7
5	United Arab Emirates	10.1	15	[illegible]	[illegible]
6	Trinidad & Tobago	7.7	16	Cyprus	[illegible]
7	Australia	7.1	17	Greece	[illegible]
8	Singapore	6.4	18	New Zealand	3.4
9	Republic of Korea	6.3	19	Turkmenistan	3.4
10	Israel	6.3	20	Portugal	[illegible]

increase in carbon emitted between 1980 to 2000, in tonnes per person per year*

CHANGE IN CARBON EMISSIONS 1980 TO 2000

"... *emissions of carbon dioxide – the most important cause of climate change – continue to rise in many parts of the world ...*"
Michel Jarraud, 2005

Map 297

www.worldmapper.org

Produced by the SASI group (Sheffield) and Mark Newman (Michigan)

Source: SASI Group and Mark Newman, "Carbon Emissions Increase" 2006, Web, 10 Jan. 2009.

8d Sample Informative Essay

Gray 1

Trent Gray

Professor Graves

WRS 103

29 November 2011

Will Time Travel Ever Be Possible?

The thesis occurs early in the paper.

Time travel into the future is possible through the use of dilation [1]. This can be achieved through the use of high velocity or low mass. It is not as clear whether travelling to the past is possible. Simple paradoxes, like the grandfather paradox, are used to dispute the possibility of reverse time travel. Novikov's self-consistency principle [2] can be used to ensure that paradoxes that would prevent time travel cannot occur. Wormhole theory also provides a method to achieve reverse time travel [3]. If self-transport into the past is not possible, it is still possible to use particles travelling faster than the speed of light to send signals into the past and future [4]. Sending signals into the past would be a futile effort because there would not be a civilization able to receive these signals; however, future civilizations could communicate with us.

Dilation

Headings are used to organize the different theories of time travel.

Time is a linear element of the universe that can be manipulated. An object experiences the passage of time subjectively, depending on its velocity and mass, through a natural phenomenon called dilation [1]. Dilation states that the faster an object travels, the

Gray 2

slower time acts on it. This means that if an object were to travel faster than the Earth it would age more slowly than the Earth. If this object were to return to Earth it would have aged less than its surroundings and appear as though it had travelled forward in time. If an object could travel fast enough for long enough, it could travel past entire centuries without aging more than a few years.

Dilation also assesses the impact that mass has on time. The closer a body is to a massive object, the faster time acts on that particular body. This means that time acts more slowly on satellites orbiting thousands of kilometres above the Earth's surface than it does on objects at sea level. This has been measured and confirmed by precise clocks that can detect time in thousandths of a second on both Earth and satellites in orbit [1].

Reverse Time Travel

Going back into the past could cause many paradoxes. One such paradox is the grandfather paradox. This paradox asks what would happen if a person were to travel to a time before the birth of his or her parents and kill their grandfather. If a person's grandfather died before fathering one of his or her parents, that person could never have been created to travel into the past and kill his or her grandfather. Simple paradoxes like this one suggest time travel is not possible because nature does not allow paradoxes.

Gray gives examples to illustrate complex concepts.

Gray 3

Novikov's self-consistency principle states that general relativity could be used to create closed timelike curves (CTC) [2]. These curves would prevent anyone who is travelling into the past from doing anything that could alter the future and create a paradox.

An experiment that involves using a billiard ball as a projectile has been proposed to test Novikov's principle [2]. In this experiment, a billiard ball is fired into a primary time travelling machine, then exits through a secondary time machine. This test would be set up so that the ball will exit the secondary time machine just before it enters the primary machine and at an angle that will deflect the ball so that it will not enter the primary time machine. If Novikov's theory is correct, this test will not be able to occur because the ball cannot exit the secondary time machine if it has never entered the primary time machine. Instead, the self-consistency principle states that the ball exiting the secondary time machine will never be able to hit itself in the present from an angle that would deflect the ball in a way that would cause it to miss the primary time machine. If successful, this experiment would prove that CTCs do exist and ensure that paradoxes cannot occur.

Wormholes

Another theory that supports time travel states that time machines could use wormholes to travel between points in time [3]. Wormholes have never been

To report information effectively, Gray combines analysis with a fuller description of the problem.

Gray 4

observed but are considered theoretically possible in some scenarios created using the theory of general relativity. Fundamentally, wormholes are objects that allow for the passage of matter instantaneously through time and are broken into two general groups: Schwarzschild and traversable wormholes. Schwarzschild wormholes are theorized as developing at the centre of black holes, but as collapsing before anything could pass through them. This means that they could not be used by humankind. Traversable wormholes could be generated and maintained for a useful period of time if a matter with a negative energy density could be found. This matter could be used to stabilize traversable wormholes and allow reverse travel time. These theories far outpace modern experimental science and technology, but are theoretically possible. Future technology could possibly be developed to test modern theories.

Faster-Than-Light Communication

Another train of thought concerning travelling back in time does not involve actually sending living beings through time, but instead using particles travelling faster than the speed of light to cross time. This theory basically works in the reverse of the method that astronomers use to read into the history of our universe. When we look at stars, we see light that was emitted millions of years ago, so we see events that occurred millions of years ago that

A conceptual organization was chosen to elaborate the different possible theories of time travel.

Gray 5

produced this light. This allows astronomers to see what different parts of our universe looked like millions of years ago. If particles were to move faster than the speed of light, then they could move faster than time; so, depending on the reference frame of the particle, it would either move forward or backward in time [4]. These particles could then be used as signals in inter-time communication. The theory of general relativity states that particles cannot be accelerated to the speed of light without becoming infinitely massive, but it is possible for particles that are already travelling the speed of light to exist. These particles are called *tachyons* [4]. If we could develop a method to deflect and manipulate tachyons, we could send them on paths where they could be received by beings in another time. Sending tachyons into our past would not be useful to us because nobody would be able to receive them. However, we could send them into the future and communicate with our future selves. This could also lead to an incredible jump in science and technology because people in the future will very likely be more advanced than we are. If these people shared their knowledge with us, they could possibly help us develop other forms of time travel.

Conclusion

The conclusion assesses which of the theories is most probable.

Dilation has been used to reason that travelling into the future is possible and is the only part of time travel that we are able to test. This has convinced

Gray 6

many scientists that forward time travel is possible. Travelling back in time is a much less likely possibility. Nobody from the future has ever travelled back to any period of time that we have been alive to witness. This suggests that nobody can travel backwards in time, otherwise they certainly would have wanted to meet Jesus or Einstein. Believers in wormhole time travel consider this fact a non-issue because wormhole travel requires a wormhole in both the initial and final times that are travelled to. We have not yet invented a wormhole time machine, so nobody in the future who has invented such a machine could come back and visit us. The idea that we could communicate with people in the future is also unproven because nobody has discovered a tachyon yet. This means that even if signals are beaming past us at this moment, we are unaware and unaffected. There are many unknowns associated with time travel, and there is a lot of research that still needs to be done to determine if it could be possible. If sustainable wormholes could be created, then travelling into the past would appear to be more probable but not certain. Using today's knowledge and logic, travelling into the past appears unlikely, mainly due to the many paradoxes that could occur and the unlikelihood that we could create and sustain a transverse wormhole.

Gray summarizes the main theories of time travel here at the start of his conclusion.

Gray 7

References

1. Editors of thebigview.com. Time dilation. thebigview.com [Internet]. 2011 [cited 2011 Nov 3]. Available from: http://www.thebigview.com/spacetime/timedilation.html
2. Carlini A, Frolov V, Mensky M, Novikov I, Soleng H. Time machines: the Principle of Self-Consistency as a consequence of the Principle of Minimal Action. Mod Phys. 1997;99:23–34.
3. Lovgren S. Are wormhole tunnels for time travel? Natl Geogr [Internet]. 2005 [cited 2011 Nov 3]. Available from: http://news.nationalgeographic.com/news/2005/09/0916_050916_timetravel_2.html
4. Chiao R. What is known about tachyons, theoretical particles that travel faster than light and move backward in time? Is there scientific reason to think they really exist? Sci Am [Internet]. 1999 [cited 2011 Nov 3]; 77:1254. Available from: http://www.scientificamerican.com/zarticle.cfm?id=what-is-known-about tachy

9 Write to Persuade

QUICK*TAKE*

- Find and narrow a topic (see below)
- Make sure you support arguments with evidence (see p. 79)
- Acknowledge opposing viewpoints (see p. 79)

9a Position Arguments

When you imagine an argument, you might think of two people, or two groups of people, with different views, engaged in a heated debate. In post-secondary courses, public life, and professional careers, written arguments are meant to persuade readers who refuse to accept a **claim** when it is expressed as an assertion. Extended written arguments attempt to change people's minds by convincing them that a new idea or point of view is valid, or that a particular course of action is the best one to take.

Written arguments

- offer evidence and reason,
- examine the assumptions on which the evidence and reason are based,
- explore opposing arguments, and
- anticipate objections.

How you develop a written argument depends on your goals. You may want to convince your readers to change their way of thinking about an issue or perhaps get them to consider the issue from your perspective.

In a position argument you make a claim about a controversial issue. To do this you must

- define or rebut the issue,
- take a clear position,
- make a convincing argument, and
- acknowledge opposing views.

9b Develop a Topic and Take a Position

Most instructors will give you a topic (or a list of topics), ask you to do some research on the topic (you choose) using credible sources, and then take a position and argue for your perspective on that topic.

One strategy for writing a position argument is to examine the definitions of key terms associated with your topic (e.g., How do the media define *nurses*? How does the Canadian Nurses Association define *nurses*?) and to evaluate the consequences or implications of those definitions. The definition strategy requires matching a concept with a series of criteria to assess how well they fit.

The media (e.g., TV programs) define *nurses* as	Criteria 1	unintelligent
	Criteria 2	unimportant
	Criteria 3	subordinate
Something is or is not true because [criteria 1, 2, 3, 4] of the Canadian Nurses Association defines *nurses* as	Criteria 1	self-regulated
	Criteria 2	professional
	Criteria 3	autonomous
	Criteria 4	educated

As the above table indicates, a Registered Nurse (RN) in Canada is not like the nurses depicted in the media. RNs are self-regulated and autonomous (not subordinate), professional and educated (not unintelligent and unimportant).

Claim: The Canadian Nurses Association's definition of an RN is directly opposed to that offered by depictions of nurses in the media such as television programs.

Another strategy for writing a position argument is to rebut—or take an opposing viewpoint on—the stated position. You might challenge the criteria that a writer uses to define a concept (as in the example above) or you might challenge the evidence offered to support a claim. Often the evidence presented is incomplete or wrong. Sometimes you can find counter-evidence to support your refutation.

9c Support Claims with Reasons

The difference between an *assertion* (e.g., media depictions of nurses are destined to negatively impact the field of nursing) and a *claim* (e.g., media depictions of nurses are destined to negatively impact the field of nursing because they undermine the public's belief that nurses are capable of making worthwhile contributions to a healthcare team) is the presence of a reason linked to the claim. A reason often occurs in a *because* clause, a statement that begins with the word *because* and provides a supporting reason for the claim. The word *because* signals a *link* between the claim and the reason.

Supporting reasons are a good beginning to solid evidence to support your claim. In addition, examples, scholarly research, data, and statistics are other types of evidence that transform an assertion into a claim and a claim into an argument.

Make an Arguable Claim

Media depictions of nurses will negatively impact the field of nursing	because	they undermine the public's belief that nurses can make worthwhile contributions to a healthcare team.
CLAIM ··········▶	**LINK** (***because*** **clause)** ··········▶	**REASON**

The problem lies in convincing readers to accept that the reason provided is linked to the claim. Reader might challenge the writer's assertion that media depictions of nurses can affect the public's perception of that profession by asking How? So what? Why?

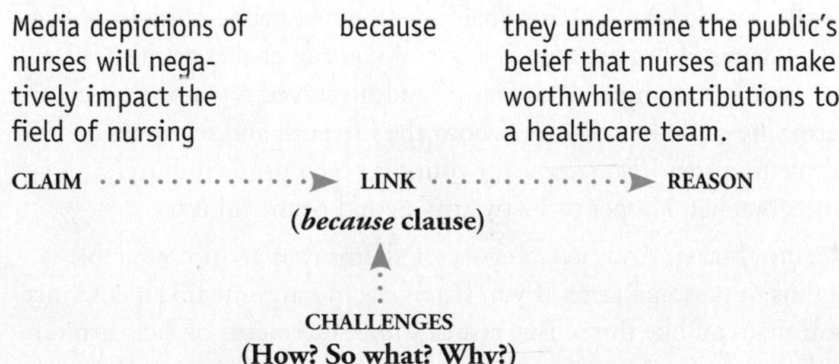
Media depictions of nurses will negatively impact the field of nursing
because
they undermine the public's belief that nurses can make worthwhile contributions to a healthcare team.
CLAIM
LINK
REASON
(because clause)
CHALLENGES
(How? So what? Why?)

The argument should not end just because it is challenged. Instead, you must generate a series of claims, each of which is supported by evidence your readers will accept:

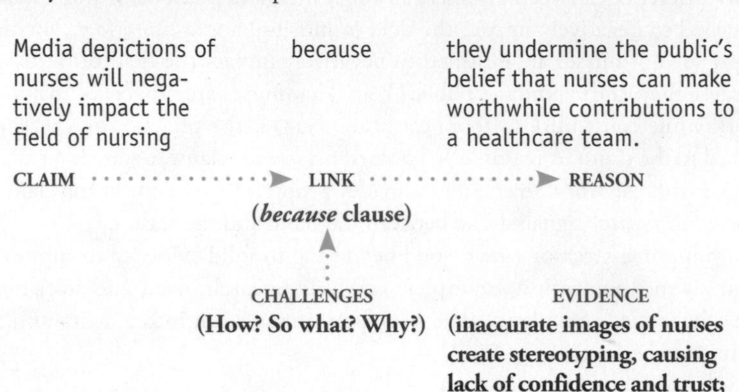
Media depictions of nurses will negatively impact the field of nursing
because
they undermine the public's belief that nurses can make worthwhile contributions to a healthcare team.
CLAIM
LINK
(*because* clause)
REASON
CHALLENGES
(How? So what? Why?)
EVIDENCE
(inaccurate images of nurses create stereotyping, causing lack of confidence and trust; lead to deteriorating relationships between patients and nurses)

A claim must have one or more supporting reasons, and the reasons must be linked to the claim in order to be accepted by readers. An argument in post-secondary writing, therefore, consists of a claim and a series of appropriately linked supporting reasons.

STAYING ON TRACK

Recognize what is not arguable

Certain topics can be argued only in limited ways.

- **Statements of fact.** Statements of fact are usually not considered arguable since they can usually be verified by research. You can easily verify that Sir John A. Macdonald was the first prime minister of Canada. Claims of fact are arguable only if you can challenge the basis of the fact. For example, since Pierre Trudeau served two non-consecutive terms, he could be considered both the fifteenth and seventeenth prime minister. If you argue for counting each prime minister only once, Stephen Harper is the twenty-second prime minister.
- **Personal taste.** Another category of claims that are not arguable is claims of personal taste. If you hate peas, no argument can convince you that you like them. But just as some statements of fact turn out to be arguable, so too do many claims of personal taste turn out to be value judgments based on arguable criteria.

STAYING ON TRACK *(Continued)*

- **Claims of belief.** Many claims rest on *belief* or *faith*. If a person accepts a claim as a matter of faith or religious belief, that claim is true for that person and cannot be refuted. Of course, people still argue about the existence of God, and which (if any) religion reflects the will of God. But those who hold to irrefutable beliefs will not be convinced by those arguments.

9e Organize and Write a Position Argument

Thinking of reasons to support a claim is not hard. What *is* hard is convincing your audience that your reasons are good ones. Imagine you will have critical readers—people who are going to listen carefully to what you have to say but who are not going to agree with you automatically. Whenever you put forward a reason, they will ask *So what?* You will have to have evidence, and you will have to link that evidence to your claim in ways they will accept if they are to agree that your reason is a good reason. Be open to new ideas while you are writing. Often you will go back and forth in developing a position argument.

1 Before you write

Think about your readers

- What do your readers already know about the subject?
- What is their attitude toward the subject? If it is different from your position, how can you address the difference?
- What are the chances of changing the opinions and beliefs of your readers? If your readers are unlikely to be moved, can you get them to acknowledge that your position is reasonable?
- Are there any sensitive issues you should be aware of?

2 Write an introduction

Engage your readers quickly

- Get your readers' attention with an example of what is at stake.
- Define the subject or issue.
- State your thesis to announce your position.

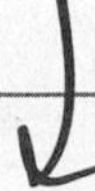

3 Organize and write the body of your paper

Develop reasons

- Can you argue from a definition? Is _____ a _____?
- Can you refute an opposing viewpoint?
- Can you compare and contrast? Is _____ like or unlike _____?
- Can you argue that something is good (better, bad, worse)?
- Can you argue that something caused (or may cause) something else?
- Can you refute objections to your position?

Support reasons with evidence

- Can you support your reasons by going to a site and making observations?
- Can you find facts, statistics, or statements from authorities to support your reasons?

Consider opposing views

- Acknowledge other stakeholders for the issue, and consider their positions.
- Explain why your position is preferable.
- Make counter-arguments if necessary.

4 Write a conclusion

End with more than a summary

- Think of a strong way to end by offering more evidence in support of your thesis, reinforcing what is at stake, or giving an example that gets at the heart of the issue.

5 Revise, revise, revise

Evaluate your draft

- Make sure your position argument meets the requirements of the assignment.
- Can you sharpen your thesis to make your position clearer?
- Can you add additional reasons to strengthen your argument?
- Can you supply additional evidence?
- Examine your language for bias and emotionally loaded words and reword if needed.
- When you have finished revising, edit and proofread carefully.

9f Sample Position Argument

NURSE: INCOMPETENT LACKEY? 1

Nurse: Incompetent Lackey?

Chelsea Chambers

University of Alberta

Faculty of Nursing

Nursing 190, Section E09

October 3, 2011

Chambers states her position clearly in the first paragraph.

Popular media have undoubtedly had an immense influence on the way that the public perceives nurses and nursing as a career. Over time, many of the same stereotypes and perceptions about what a nurse is and does have been recycled and maintained as the status quo (Gordon & Nelson, 2005). Popular media do the opposite of what professional nursing organizations want to achieve and portray to the public. Popular media constantly misinform the public of the value of nurses and the nursing profession. Furthermore, this miscommunication clearly has a negative effect on the way nurses feel about their jobs and affects their ability to do their jobs (Cabaniss, 2011). The effects of popular media on nursing are far-reaching and inevitably meld into nursing practice. The purpose of this paper is to describe how popular media wrongly characterize nurses as subordinate, incompetent, and unimportant, and to discuss how this affects nursing practice.

How Popular Media Portray Nurses

Then Chambers describes how popular media distort images of the nursing profession.

Popular media's distortion of the nursing profession is long-standing (Gordon & Nelson, 2005). How the public interprets this information will impact the way in which nurses can do their jobs. A direct result of this warped representation of nursing is the widely held opinion that being a nurse requires no intellectual challenge or demand (Cabaniss, 2011). Nurses are too often conventionalized as being far less

NURSE: INCOMPETENT LACKEY? 3

knowledgeable than doctors, reliant on doctors, and incapable of any autonomous practice (Takase et al., 2006, as cited in Stanley, 2008). This has led to nurses being represented as followers rather than leaders, unskilled servants rather than intelligent innovators, and doting caregivers rather than caring health professionals (Stanley, 2008).

According to Benner, Sutphen, and Leonard (2010, as cited in Cabaniss, 2011), portraying nurses as being poorly educated and doting physician assistants is hardly a modern depiction of a profession that requires post-secondary education and countless numbers of skills. The media are recycling this trivial and ridiculous image all the time. The craft and skills of nurses are grossly underappreciated and undervalued in TV sitcoms and Hollywood movies.

Examples of the Misrepresentations of Nurses in Popular Media

The representations of nurses on TV and in movies are foremost derogatory and archetypal. More often than not, nurse characters serve merely as props and doormats to other "more important" characters (Cabaniss, 2011). An example of this can be seen as early as the 1950s when *Dr. Hudson's Secret Journal* aired. Ann Talbot was the most prominent nurse character in the series, but she served no other purpose than to be Dr. Hudson's personal assistant (Kalisch & Kalisch, 1982). She most frequently

Chambers provides evidence from numerous television programs to support her conclusions about how nurses are misrepresented.

appeared doing clerical work and menial office tasks. The character of Ms. Wills in *Ben Casey*, a series that began in 1961, is another example of the nurse as glorified receptionist. It appeared as though Ms. Wills's most important task was to answer the phone and deliver messages (Kalisch & Kalisch, 1982). This undermines a nurse's intelligence, skill set, and purpose.

Temperatures Rising aired in the early 1970s, and the nurses featured in this sitcom all shared the most noteworthy trait of being superb followers (Kalisch & Kalisch, 1982). These characters were incapable of making any decisions on their own and completely depended on the doctor for everything. The principal nurse character on *Trapper John* only had one purpose—to be the chief surgeon's lackey (Kalisch & Kalisch, 1982).

A more modern example of the nurse as glorified receptionist can be found on *Grey's Anatomy*. The nurse characters are only seen in the background, forever poised at the nurses' station (Cabaniss, 2011). The surgeons are portrayed as the heroes who are always saving lives. The actual role that nurses serve and their true professional purpose are totally missing. At least nurses are seen in the background of *Grey's Anatomy*. Nurses are not seen in any form on the Fox drama *House* (Cabaniss, 2011). The surgeons on the show *Private Practice* mock the only nurse character,

NURSE: INCOMPETENT LACKEY? 5

Dell. He is depicted as flighty, unintelligent, and far less important than any of the surgeons he works with (Cabaniss, 2011). The principal character on the show *Nurse Jackie* does not help the image of nursing when she is the epitome of a completely dysfunctional and irrational person (Cabaniss, 2011). Her behaviour and actions thoroughly belittle and misrepresent the nursing profession.

It is these sorts of images the public is presented with on a day-to-day basis that are destined to negatively impact the field of nursing. These images seriously undermine the public's belief that nurses are of any importance or that they are capable of making worthwhile contributions to a healthcare team.

Professional Nursing Literature

These fictional and derogatory images of nurses are in stark contrast to what the Canadian Nurses Association (2007) describes a nurse to be. Their definition of a Registered Nurse includes the terms *self-regulated, professional, autonomous, education, collaboration, and research* (CNA, 2007, p. 6). These terms do not coincide with the unintelligent, unimportant, and subordinate portrayals of nurses in popular media. A baccalaureate degree is generally the standard level of education for entering this profession; however, many nurses in Canada have continued their education and have achieved master's degrees and doctorates in nursing (CNA, 2007). This

This section includes the Canadian Nurses Association definition of *nurses*, highlighting the disparities between media representation and reality.

level of education clearly belongs to a profession that should be considered intellectually demanding and challenging. RNs are expected to keep up with ever-changing technologies, systems, and client needs. That is why making education a continually important facet throughout their careers is critical to enhance their knowledge and practical skills (CNA, 2007).

The nursing profession makes up the larger part of the healthcare provider population, but nurses are consistently being thrown into subordinate roles in workplaces (McKinnon, 1999). Nurses are too often denied the chance to advocate about issues relating to client care (Gordon & Nelson, 2005). According to McKinnon (1999), to make the role of nurses more recognized by the public and peers, it is up to nurses to make their contributions more visible. As stated by Whyte (2008), surveys have proven that the public is unclear about what it is that nurses do and that nursing does not appear to be a desirable career choice anymore. These findings pose serious concerns for nursing shortages and the well-being of clients who depend on nurses.

The Effects on Nursing Practice

Chambers works out the details of her position, showing how the negative portrayals may impact Canadian nursing practice.

If the public is constantly bombarded with inappropriate and inaccurate images of nursing, then it is certain that these images will lead them to misunderstand a nurse's job. The public can't be blamed for misunderstanding or stereotyping the

NURSE: INCOMPETENT LACKEY? 7

nurse's role. However, this misunderstanding may lead to a lack of trust and confidence in nurses that will eventually lead to the deterioration of the relationship between nurses and clients. Confidentiality, dignity, and accountability are just three of the eight values that the Canadian Nurses Association has identified as being integral to nursing practice (CNA, 2007, p. 28). These values would be compromised if a client does not feel as though he or she can trust his or her nurse. Clients may also react negatively if their nurse does not act the way they see nurses acting on TV or in movies (Cabaniss, 2011).

The public must be made aware of the enormous changes that have occurred in the field of nursing (Whyte, 2008). More is being asked of nurses than ever before; consequently, nurses have had to adapt by expanding their skill set and knowledge base (Whyte, 2008). The public must be informed of the indispensable contributions that nurses are making to clients' well-being.

The lack of factual representations of nurses in the media can be held responsible for much of the public's misunderstanding of what a nurse does. Nurses and the nursing community must work more closely with forms of popular media in order to ensure that the public is properly educated about the nursing profession (Stanley, 2008). The entire profession must

NURSE: INCOMPETENT LACKEY? 8

find its united voice and make itself more visible to and heard by the public (Cabaniss, 2011).

Conclusion

Chambers concludes by considering the implications of these misrepresentations on the profession of nursing.

There should be major concern regarding how popular media constantly represent nurses as subordinate, incompetent, and unintelligent. The general public is constantly battered with images that belittle and misrepresent a profession that professional nursing literature correctly depicts as intellectually taxing and vital to the care of clients. Initiatives must be made to educate the public about the significance of nursing practice and the contributions that nurses make to a functioning healthcare team. What will be the fate of the nursing profession if changes do not take place and the truth about nurses is left unsaid?

References

Cabaniss, R. (2011). Educating nurses to impact change in nursing's image. *Teaching and Learning in Nursing, 6*, 112–118. doi:10.1016/j.teln.2011.01.003

Canadian Nurses Association. (2007). *Framework for the practice of Registered Nurses in Canada.* Retrieved from http://www.cna-aiic.ca

Gordon, S., & Nelson, S. (2005). An end to angels. *American Journal of Nursing, 105*(5), 62–69.

Kalisch, P. A., & Kalisch, B. J. (1982). Nurses on prime-time television. *American Journal of Nursing, 82*(2), 264–270. Retrieved from http://www.jstor.org/stable/3463069

McKinnon, B. (1999). Student's corner. Leadership: A means of empowering the nursing profession. *Contemporary Nurse: A Journal for the Australian Nursing Profession, 8*(1), 252–254.

Stanley, D. J. (2008). Celluloid angels: A research study of nurses in feature films 1900–2007. *Journal of Advanced Nursing, 64*(1), 84–95. doi:10.1111/j.1365-2648.2008.04793.x

Whyte, A. (2008). What is going on? *Nursing Standard, 22*(23), 18–22.

PART 3 Writing in the Disciplines

You **can learn more and do more** with MyWritingLab and with the eText version of *The Brief Penguin Handbook*. Find resources in MyWritingLab to help you successfully complete assignments in other disciplines and in your business writing.

10 Learn to Write in Academic Disciplines 93

11 Write in Specific Genres 98

12 Write About Literature 123

13 Write About Film and New Media 136

10 Learn to Write in Academic Disciplines

QUICK*TAKE*

- Become an academic writer (see below)
- Know the purposes and genres of academic disciplines (see p. 94)
- Know the types of evidence required in each discipline (see p. 96)

10a Become an Academic Writer

In any discipline, good writing is likely to exhibit similar qualities: It will be clear, concise, and logical, supplying appropriate evidence in sufficient amounts to persuade the audience. But because disciplines have different purposes, they use different vocabularies, formats, and evidence to make and support claims. What kinds of questions does a botanist ask? How does a sociologist solve problems? What kinds of evidence will be most convincing to a banker or a stockbroker? Learning to communicate with professionals in your field helps you think like a professional in that field.

In post-secondary education, the many fields and majors are organized into disciplines. These groupings can vary from one institution to another, but the chart on pages 94 and 95 shows the most common divisions. Note, however, that there is significant overlap and sharing of knowledge among various fields. For example, archaeology is often housed in humanities programs, yet the study of ancient civilizations combines many of the scientific methods used in natural sciences such as paleontology.

It is also becoming more and more common for researchers to collaborate with experts in other fields to solve problems. Thus a sociologist might work with a professional in business administration to study the group dynamics of a large organization.

Ask your instructor for advice and for examples of the writing genres common in your field. Some genres, such as lab reports and case studies, vary considerably from discipline to discipline, so locate an example from your field.

DISCIPLINES, PURPOSES, AND GENRES				
Discipline	**Common fields or majors**	**Purposes**	**Genres**	**Preferred documentation style**
Fine Arts	Theatre, dance, studio art, art history, music	Creation of artwork; history and reception of art	Essay, critique, review, visual analysis, iconography, research paper, grant proposal, creative writing	MLA and CMS (see Ch. 26 and 28)
Humanities	Literature, history, classics, political science, languages, philosophy, law, education	Interpreting, appreciating, and imagining the human experience	Essay, research paper, abstract, case study, grant proposal, oral history, ethnography	Primarily MLA, but also APA and CMS (see Ch. 26, 27, and 28)
Education	Curriculum and instruction, education administration	Training teachers and developing effective teaching methods	Lesson plan, literature review, abstract, case study, grant proposal	APA (see Ch. 27)
Social Sciences	Psychology, sociology, anthropology, geography, social work, human ecology	Exploring human behaviour in individuals and groups—both in the past and the present—with a strong desire to learn to predict human behaviour in the future	Literature review, abstract, case study, oral history, grant proposal, poster presentation	Primarily APA (see Ch. 27)
Natural Sciences	Physics, math, astronomy, biology (botany, zoology, marine science), geology, ecology, chemistry. Also health science fields such as nursing, pharmacy, kinesiology	The study of living things, inanimate matter, systems, and processes	Literature review, lab report, abstract, grant proposal, poster presentation	APA and CSE (see Ch. 27 and 29); some sciences, such as chemistry and physics, have their own style guides

DISCIPLINES, PURPOSES, AND GENRES

Discipline	Common fields or majors	Purposes	Genres	Preferred documentation style
Business	Finance, business administration, management, accounting, marketing, public relations	Building and maintaining healthy businesses and markets	Summary, letter, email, memo, business plan, speech/presentation, marketing plan, case study, market analysis	CMS and APA (see Ch. 28 and 27)
Media/ Communications	Journalism, radio/television/film studies, advertising, information management	Informing and entertaining the public, promoting commerce, and effecting the exchange of information	Article, analysis, advertising, scripts, screenplays	APA and CMS (see Ch. 27 and 28)
Engineering	Civil, industrial, chemical, petroleum, aerospace, biomedical, mechanical, electrical (including computer science)	Practical application of science and technology to improve human civilization	Case study, design report, progress report, lab report, proposal	Primarily IEEE, CSE, and APA (see Ch. 30, 29, and 28)
Health Sciences	Nursing, pharmacy, kinesiology, premed, veterinary medicine	Improving health and well-being	Lab report, case study, poster presentation	APA and CSE (see Ch. 27 and 29)
Computer Science and Technology	Information management, technical communications, computer engineering	Building, maintaining, and optimizing electronic communications systems and databases	User manuals, support documentation, technical reports, journal articles	CSE and IEEE (see Ch. 29 and Ch. 30)
Political Science	Law, government, public affairs, economics	Creating and interpreting laws and policies	Legal briefs, policy and position papers, analyses, journal articles	APA and CMS (*Canadian Guide to Legal Citation*) (see Ch. 27 and 28)

10b What Counts as Evidence in the Disciplines?

Experts in most fields prefer certain types of evidence. Though any kind of logical evidence can be, and is, used in almost any field, the types noted below are those that carry the most weight. If you have any doubts about the kind of evidence to use, you should always check with your instructor.

FIELDS OF STUDY AND TYPES OF EVIDENCE

Field	Controlled experimental data	Non-participatory observation	Participatory observation	Material data (fossil records, human artifacts, material properties)	Historical records (letters, maps)	Literary texts	Man-made artifacts (buildings, paintings)	Pre-existing, gathered statistics	Interviews, surveys	Articles by other experts
Literature					✓	✓				✓
Classics					✓	✓	✓			✓
Archaeology				✓	✓	✓	✓			✓
History		✓			✓	✓	✓	✓	✓	✓
Political Science		✓			✓			✓	✓	✓
Geography	✓		✓	✓	✓			✓		✓
Astronomy	✓	✓		✓	✓			✓		✓
Chemistry	✓			✓				✓		✓
Biology	✓	✓		✓				✓		✓
Psychology	✓	✓	✓	✓	✓			✓	✓	✓
Sociology		✓	✓		✓			✓	✓	✓
Economics		✓			✓			✓	✓	✓
Business		✓	✓					✓	✓	✓
Engineering	✓	✓	✓	✓				✓		✓
Fine Arts		✓	✓		✓	✓	✓			✓
Geology	✓	✓		✓	✓			✓		✓

Experts in the various disciplines look for different kinds of evidence because they are trying to solve different problems. For example, here are questions the experts in 16 fields might ask in beginning to explore the topic of global climate change:

Field	Possible questions
Geography	What constitutes a "normal" range of global climate conditions?
Geology	What do worldwide coal deposits tell us about the global paleolithic climate?
Astronomy	What can humans' impact on earth's atmosphere and climate teach us about making other planets habitable?
Biology	Is recent deforestation responsible for an increase in CO_2 in the earth's atmosphere?
Chemistry	To what extent has the reduced production of chlorofluorocarbons "solved" the problem of ozone depletion?
Psychology	How has the "clean energy" movement changed individuals' norms regarding fossil fuels?
Sociology	How does a community's assumptions about socio-economic value affect its response to the threat of global climate change?
Economics	What burdens do carbon dioxide emissions controls impose on large versus small businesses?
Business	Which "clean" energy sources are most likely to become profitable in the next 20 years?
Engineering	How can engineers protect coastal urban areas from the stronger hurricanes associated with global warming?
Political Science	How might rising sea levels affect the stability of governments in coastal developing nations?
History	What percentage of recorded famines might be attributable in part to global climate change?

Field	Possible questions
Archaeology	What effect did global climate change have on ancient human population and migration patterns?
Classics	What ancient texts describe possible effects of global climate change, and what can these texts tell us about humans' responses to such change?
Literature	How do literary descriptions of climate-related catastrophes (floods, drought, hurricanes) change over time?
Fine Arts	How might a performance piece utilizing dance and music demonstrate the impact of global climate change on human beings?

11 Write in Specific Genres

QUICK*TAKE*

- Recognize the elements of popular academic and workplace writing

11a Write an Essay Exam

Instructors use essay exams to test your understanding of course concepts and to assess your ability to analyze ideas independently.

Elements of an exam essay

Introduction	Briefly restate the question, summarizing the answer you will provide. **Example** The letter Lydia Bennett leaves after eloping highlights several of her most important character traits: her failure to take her own mistakes seriously, her casual attitude toward morality, and her disregard for the pain she causes others.

Body paragraphs	Each paragraph should address a major element of the question. Order them so that the reader can tell how you are responding to the question. **Example** Of the many factors leading to the downfall of Brian Mulroney's government, implementing the GST was the most important.
Conclusion	*Briefly* restate your answer to the question, not the question itself. **Example** Thus, the three things all responsible creditors assess before making a loan are the borrower's capacity, credit history, and collateral.

What you need to do

- Make sure you understand the question. Actively respond with the kinds of information and analysis the question asks you to provide; don't just write generally about the topic.
- Plan your response before you begin writing, with an outline, list, or diagram. Note how much time you have to write your response.
- Respond to each element of the question, providing support and being as specific as possible.
- Save a few minutes to read over your essay, correcting errors and adding information where needed.

Sample exam essay

HIS 210 Pre-Confederation History of Canada Describe the political, economic, and cultural variables that led to the establishment and then abolition of slavery in Canada.

Amy Zhao began her response to the essay question by jotting down ideas for each of the three categories mentioned. Her outline also served as a map for the structure of her essay.

political	*economic*	*cultural*
Established first in Quebec by Louis XIV	*Slaves used to relieve labour shortage in New France*	*Canadians called them servants, not slaves*
Opposition to slavery in courts in BNA led to its decline	*Slaves worked as domestic servants, skilled artisans, and farmhands*	*Treatment was as bad as in the U.S.*

political	*economic*	*cultural*
Strict proof of ownership required, which limited slavery	*Many slaves brought by Loyalists escaping U.S. after American Revolution*	*Disobeying led to whipping, torture, and sometimes murder*
Slavery abolished first by Upper Canada in 1793		*Many black people left Canada in late eighteenth century because of poor treatment and returned to Africa*
All slaves freed in 1834		

Political, economic, and cultural variables enabled the development of slavery in Canada, and they also served to phase it out. It originated to solve an economic problem—a shortage of labour in New France in the 1600s—when Louis XIV allowed ownership of African slaves. Slaves initially carved settlements from the wilderness. Later they worked as domestic servants, skilled artisans, and farmhands. Canadian slaves were not a threat to their masters, but they still suffered whipping, torture, and murder by their owners. The slave population in Canada grew after the American Revolution when thousands of Loyalists brought their slaves with them. Many freed slaves left Canada in the late 1700s to escape discrimination, returning to Africa. Political variables such as court rulings that imposed, for example, strict proof of ownership, led to the decline of slavery. It was abolished first in Upper Canada in 1793, and all slaves were finally freed in 1834.

Amy uses key terms from the question to show where she is addressing that element of the question.

11b Write an Observation

Observations are common in the natural sciences and in social science disciplines such as psychology, sociology, and education. They begin as notes taken first-hand by the writer as he or she observes an event, phenomenon, or place. Observations should include as many relevant and specific details as possible.

Elements of an observation

<table>
<tr><td>Title</td><td>Include a precise title.
EXAMPLE
Alfvén Wave Activity near Trapper Lake, NWT, on 29 Nov. 2010</td></tr>
<tr><td>Background and context</td><td>Be specific about what or whom you are observing. How did you limit your site or subject? What background information do readers need? How will a deeper understanding of your subject help people?
EXAMPLE
The closer a body is to a massive object, the faster time acts on that particular body. This means that time acts more slowly on satellites orbiting thousands of kilometres above the Earth's surface than it does on objects at sea level. This effect has been measured and confirmed by precise clocks that can detect time in thousandths of a second on both Earth and satellites in orbit.</td></tr>
<tr><td>Record of observations</td><td>Report what you observed in some logical order: chronologically, from most obvious features to least obvious, or some other pattern.
EXAMPLE
On the second day of observation, between 8:00 and 11:00 a.m., a significantly higher number of migratory birds was seen in the feeding area.</td></tr>
<tr><td>Conclusion or summary</td><td>Give your readers a framework in which to understand your observations. What conclusions can you draw from them? What questions are left unanswered?
EXAMPLE
It appears that the toddlers observed were often aware of social expectations even when they were unable to meet those expectations in their own behaviour. This indicates that an awareness of norms probably develops independently from an individual's ability to control impulsive behaviour.</td></tr>
</table>

What you need to do

- Carry a notebook and make extensive field notes. Provide as much information as possible about the situation in which your observations occurred.
- Record in your notebook exactly when you arrived and left, where you were, and exactly what you saw and heard.
- Analyze your observations before you write about them. Identify patterns, and organize your report according to those patterns.

Sample observation

Hee 1

D. Hee

GEO 206L Fall 2011

October 3, 2011

The Karst System in Maligne Canyon in Jasper, Alberta

Background and Context

"Background and Context" section provides specific details that describe the topic in great detail.

Visuals such as photographs, tables, and charts provide more details.

Maligne Canyon is an amazing natural gorge located in Jasper National Park. Many people believe that the canyon is a series of both above-ground and underground caves, which could explain the rounded, concave form of the canyon walls. The walls have many horizontal lines created by varying colours of grey that differentiate the layers of limestone at Maligne Canyon. In addition, the aqua blue water is very powerful and has eroded a winding path through the limestone that leaves rocks with a smooth, bowl-shaped appearance. Furthermore, in the depression in the rocks, there is a light beige pile of sediment. This pile of sediment, composed of larger rocks and fine-grain sand, is attributed to the water wearing down the limestone into finer particles, a process commonly known as erosion. At the top of the

Hee 2

photograph included on page 1, the canyon is very narrow, which gives the water passing through it a calm, stream-like appearance. When progressing downward, the canyon's depth increases as it widens into a circular shape. The water appears to be very peaceful while it meanders through most of the canyon, but as it flows through the last crevasse, the water explodes over the edge of the limestone, creating a white mist. Similar to the Grand Canyon, the vegetation near the edge of the water is sparse. As a result of the steep rocky landscape, many plants and trees are not able to grow in these conditions. Therefore, only a few various shades of green can be found on the limestone. Mostly, mosses and coniferous trees grow on the canyon walls. Nevertheless, on the edge of the canyon the flat landscape creates a more advantageous growing environment, resulting in more diversity in vegetation, for instance, the mixture of coniferous and deciduous trees and other plants that grow along the edge.

Record of Observations:

The Karst Topography in the Maligne Canyon

Created by the powerful force of water, Maligne Canyon is a series of caves and sinkholes found above and beneath the surface. This is a karst landscape, which means that soluble rocks have been dissolved to form sinkholes and caves. The karst system is created by the

This section links the description to the natural processes that created the features.

Hee 3

erosion of limestone. Limestone, composed of calcite, is one of the most abundant rocks found in the canyon. In addition, it is very soluble in water. These two factors (abundance and solubility) facilitate the erosion of the rock by the flowing water. The erosion is due to carbonic acid, which is formed through the solution of carbon dioxide from the atmosphere and water. The water flows through the fractures in the rock, dissolving the limestone and creating a network of passageways [1,2,3].

Note the use of headings to communicate the organization of the observations.

Solution Caves

As the rock becomes more eroded it allows for a larger volume of water to pass through, resulting in the enlargement of the fractures. This process of erosion is continuous, and at some point, the passages become so large that they create caves and sinkholes. Because these caves are formed by the chemical reaction between the limestone and the carbonic acid (i.e., a solution), they are called *solution caves* [4].

Sinkholes

Sinkholes are formed when the area beneath the rock surface has been eroded so much that a large space develops under the rock surface. Soon the rock surface cannot withstand the external forces (e.g., gravity, atmospheric pressure) any longer and the surface collapses. Sinkholes can unite with one another and form larger depressions in the limestone called *poljen*. These

Hee 4

particular sinkholes typically have flat floors, which are sometimes covered by a layer of soil that has been transported by the water flowing between the fractures of the limestone. The soil on the bottom of the poljen can be a place for vegetation to grow; however, the amount of vegetation growth also depends on other variables such as the water level and the intensity of the sunlight [1].

Drainage System

The interconnected caves allow for the water to flow underground in the cave systems rather than flowing on the surface like a typical river. This creates an underground drainage system rather than a surface drainage system and further enhances the erosion of the limestone. The drainage system is extensive, demonstrated by the fact that when trace dyes are put in the water, the time it takes for the water to travel from Medicine Lake to Maligne Canyon ranges from half a day to seven days [2].

Conclusion

While the high peaks of the Rockies are often the obvious attraction, the mountain canyons provide a unique geography that is amazing to both scientists and tourists. Maligne Canyon rewards those visitors with a spectacle that is both amazing and mysterious.

Hee 5

References

1. Ford DC. Karst landform. The Canadian Encyclopedia [Internet]. 2011 [cited 2011 Oct 3]. Available from: http://encyclopediacanadienne.ca/index.cfm?PgNm=TCE&Params=A1ARTA0004237
2. What is karst? The University of Texas at Austin [Internet]. [cited 2011 Oct 3]. Available from: http://www.esi.utexas.edu/outreach/caves/karst.php
3. Ward C. Understanding the geology of canyons. MountainNature.com [Internet]. 2005 [cited 2011 Oct 2]. Available from: http://www.mountainnature.com/geology/Canyons.htm
4. White WB. Cave. Encyclopædia Britannica Online Academic Edition [Internet]. 2011 [cited 2011 Oct 3]. Available from: http://www.britannica.com/EBchecked/topic/100583/cave/49697/Karst-topography?anchor=ref524558

11c Write a Case Study

Case studies are used in a wide range of fields such as nursing, psychology, business, and anthropology. Their exact structure can vary from discipline to discipline, so be sure to get instructions from your professor. Case studies are narrow in focus. Rather than giving the "big picture" about phenomena, they provide a rich, detailed portrait of a specific event or subject.

Elements of a case study

Introduction	Explain the purpose of your study and how or why you selected your subject. Use language appropriate to your discipline, and specify the boundaries of your study.
Methodology	Explain the theories or formal process that guided your observations and analysis during the study. **EXAMPLE** A face-to-face survey methodology was used, where interviewers asked respondents a set of prepared questions and noted answers on the survey sheet.
Observations	Describe the "case" of the subject under study by writing a narrative, utilizing interviews, research, and other data to provide as much detail and specificity as possible. **EXAMPLE** The subject reported a lengthy history of heart trouble, beginning at age 37, involving multiple trips to the emergency room.
Discussion	Explain how the variables in your case might interact. Don't generalize from your case to a larger context; stay within the limits of what you have observed.
Conclusion	What does all this information add up to? What is implied, suggested, or proven by your observations? What new questions arise?
References	Using the appropriate format, cite all the outside sources you have used. (See Ch. 27 for APA documentation and Ch. 29 for CSE documentation.)

What you need to do

- Understand the specific elements of your assignment. Ask your instructor if you aren't sure about the focus, context, or structure your case study should have.
- Use careful observation and precise, detailed description to provide a complex picture with a narrow focus.
- Write your observations in the form of a narrative, placing yourself in the background (avoid using *I* or *me*).
- Analyze your findings and interpret their possible meanings, but draw your conclusions from the observed facts.

Sample case study

Some disciplines require title pages. See page 334 for an example of an APA title page.

Underage Drinking Prevention Programs

in the Radisson School District

INTRODUCTION

The introduction identifies both the problem and the particular subject of the case study.

This study examines the effect of Smith and Bingham's drinking-prevention curriculum on drinking rates in the Radisson School District, 2000–2006. Prior to 2002, the Radisson School District offered no formal drinking-prevention education. In 2000, as part of a state initiative, the district proposed several underage drinking education curricula for possible adoption. After substantial debate and input from parents, Smith and Bingham's curriculum was chosen for implementation in ninth through twelfth grades. This study tracks student drinking rates from 2000 to 2006, and compares the results after introduction of the curriculum to district rates prior to implementation.

DISCUSSION

The data from this study showed no correlation between the curriculum and student drinking rates. Drinking rates remained unchanged before, during, and after the implementation of the curriculum. Additionally, survey data indicate that levels of student drinking remained constant as well. Therefore, in this case, it cannot be said that Smith and Bingham's curriculum had any measurable effect on changing students' drinking behaviour.

CONCLUSION

The conclusion sums up what has been observed. Many case studies do not give definitive answers but rather raise further questions to explore.

In terms of reducing student drinking, Smith and Bingham's curriculum does not appear to be any more effective than no drinking-prevention education at all. Since no measurable results were obtained, the strong administrative support for the curriculum in the school district cannot be attributed to its success. A possible explanation for that support may be the approval expressed by parents who preferred it to the other curricula proposed. Further studies might usefully expand the scope of this study and compare multiple school districts' use of Smith and Bingham's curriculum to identify variables that might alter its effectiveness.

 Write a Lab Report

Lab reports follow a strict structure, enabling specialists in a given field to quickly assess the experimental methods and findings in any report. Though the basic elements are usually the same, details of formatting can vary among disciplines in the sciences. Check with your instructor for the specific elements needed in your report.

Elements of a lab report

Title	The title of a lab report should state exactly what was tested, using language specific to the field.
Introduction	The introduction gives the full context of the problem, defining the hypothesis being tested.
Methods	Describe the materials used, as well as the method of investigation. Your methods and procedure sections should be specific enough to allow another researcher to replicate your experiment. **Example** A double-blind structure was used so that the investigators would not know which subjects received placebos.
Procedure	Step by step, narrate exactly what you did and what happened. In most fields, you will use the passive voice to avoid distracting the reader with references to yourself. **Example** The salts were dissolved in distilled water to achieve a salinity level of 3%.
Results	State the outcomes you obtained, providing well-labelled charts and graphics as needed. **Example** The tempered glass plates resisted fracture 2.3 times better than the standard glass plates.
Discussion	State why you think you got the results you did, using your results to explain. If there were anomalies in your data, note them as well. **Example** Since all the plants grew normally, it appears that the high acidity levels in the soil were not harmful to their early development. However, the low fruit yields indicate that high acidity is detrimental to reproduction.

Conclusion	Briefly, what was learned from this experiment? What still needs to be investigated?
References	Using the appropriate format, cite all the outside sources you have used. (See Ch. 27 for pyschology lab reports and Ch. 29 for science lab reports.)

What you need to do

- Understand the question you are researching and the process you will use before you begin. Ask your instructor if you need clarification.
- Take thorough notes at each step of your process. You may be asked to keep a lab notebook with a specific format for recording data. Review your notes before you begin drafting your report.
- Don't get ahead of yourself. Keep methods, procedure, discussion, and conclusion sections separate. Remember that other scientists will look at specific sections of your report expecting to find certain kinds of information. If that information isn't where they expect it to be, your report will not make sense.
- Write your abstract last. Writing all the other sections of the report first will give you a much clearer picture of your findings.

Sample lab report

Brodie 1

Erin Brodie

CHEM 265L Winter 2009

January 31, 2009

Experiment 2: Synthesis of Acetanilide

Introduction

The synthesis of acetanilide was carried out by the addition-elimination mechanism of nucleophilic acyl substitution. This type of reaction involves the nucleophile (in this reaction the aniline) attacking the carbonyl bond on the carboxylic acid derivative and attaching [3]. This causes the double bond with the oxygen to become a single bond, and the carbon itself to form a tetrahedral intermediate. The electrons pair that was forced out of the carbonyl double bond then reforms this bond with the carbon, causing the elimination of the leaving group [3]. The product formed is the carbonyl with the nucleophile attached in place of the leaving group [3].

This mechanism applies to the reactions of most carboxylic acid derivatives, but the rate depends on the reactivity of the carboxylic acid derivate with the specific nucleophile and the structure of the acid derivative [3]. Generally, more reactive carboxylic acid derivatives have less basic leaving groups [3]. Another property that affects the reactivity of these acid derivatives is their degree of resonance [3]. The little amount of resonance stabilization in acid chlorides makes them quite reactive [3]. The weak resonance stabilization in anhydrides, because the stabilization is shared between two carbonyl groups, makes these species reactive as well [3].

State context of problem and hypothesis being tested.

Methods

This experiment was carried out as described in the CHEM 265L manual.

Refer to appropriate section in the lab manual or describe methods in detail.

Brodie 2

Results and Observations

When the concentrated HCl was added to the initial mixture of aniline and water, it evolved steam immediately and produced some heat. After the charcoal was added, it stuck more to the sides of the test tube than did the rest of the solution, which led to it separating out of the mixture. This caused a lot of the charcoal to remain in the tube (even after it was washed) and not make it into the Pasteur pipette filter.

Immediately after the acetic anhydride and sodium acetate trihydrate solutions were added to the sample, a white precipitate began to form. It quickly made the solution murky enough that the stirring vane was no longer visible.

Text describes results and observations. Table tabulates results and observations.

Compound	Actual yield	% yield	Published melting point	Observed melting point	Appearance
Acetanilide	0.0387 g	2.60%	114.3°C (Lide, 3–4)	104°C	Pearly, off-white, granulated crystals that form lumps

Table 1 Results from experiment

Discussion

The overall yield of this reaction was very small compared to the theoretical yield. One reason for this may have been the charcoal sticking to the side of the test tube after it was added to the acidic aniline and water solution. The solution was mixed well after the charcoal was added, and so it is likely that some of the aniline was stuck with the charcoal on the side of the test tube. The test tube was rinsed with DI water and shaken vigorously to try to dislodge some of this charcoal and anything that was stuck

Brodie 3

with it, but this did not work very well. The test tube was cleaned well with soap, water, and a test tube brush before this experiment, but the soap was difficult to rinse out completely because of the test tube's small size. After the test tube was rinsed with tap water seven or eight times, it was rinsed with acetone and dried with an air valve.

Account for any anomalies in the data.

Another possible reason for the small yield was the filtering. The product was transferred quantitatively to the funnel, but after it was allowed to dry for the directed amount of time, the filter paper had also dried and moved around in the bottom of the funnel, allowing some of the crystals to fall through the funnel. The crystals also stuck to both the funnel and the filter paper, making them hard to collect. This aspect may have been improved by doing the experiment under slightly more humid conditions, which would decrease the static charge in the air.

The purity of the product produced was fairly high. The crystals appeared homogeneous, with the same structure and similarly sized granules. The colour was also uniform throughout the sample. The observed melting point of the acetanilide was 104°C, which is about 10 degrees lower than the published melting point of 114.3°C[2]. This difference indicates that there are some impurities in the product, but that they make up relatively little of the product.

Use your results to explain the outcome of the experiment.

It is likely that the reaction went to completion, because the precipitate began to form as soon as the solutions were combined and the solutions were stirred thoroughly throughout the formation of the precipitate. Also, when the precipitate was transferred to the funnel, it was a very thick paste. Most of the vial was filled with the solid precipitate and it was caked onto the stirring vane. The reaction also produced acetic acid, which would account for the liquid component of the final solution. Side reactions are unlikely, because of the reactivity of aniline and acetic anhydride.

Brodie 4

Acetanilide has a variety of uses. It is currently used in rubber accelerator, dyes, and camphor synthesis [1]. Previously it has been used in pharmaceuticals as both an intermediate in drug synthesis but also as a drug itself [1]. It was found to be toxic to the liver and kidneys, and so was replaced by other, less toxic drugs that could also reduce pain and fever [1].

Conclusions

State what was learned from the experiment.

This reaction mechanism is common to almost all carboxylic acid derivatives, making it generally useful in a variety of reactions. It is also important as a possible side reaction that could occur in other reactions that involve carboxylic acid derivatives [3]. The more reactive acid derivatives are quite readily converted to less reactive species, based on the various stabilities and reactivities of the reactants involved [3].

While this particular reaction was not very successful in producing a high yield of product, it is an important reaction to understand and be aware of.

References

Cite outside references. This report uses in-text CSE style (see Chapter 29).

1. Acetanilide. Wikipedia [Internet]. 2007 [cited 2008 Jan. 28]. Available from: http://en.wikipedia.org/w/index.php?title=Acetanilide&oldid=36368098
2. Lide DR, editor. CRC handbook of chemistry and physics. Boca Raton (FL): CRC; 2003. 2608 p.
3. Wade LG. Organic chemistry. Upper Saddle River (NJ): Pearson Education; 2006. 1320 p.

For another example of a lab report, see pages 390–391.

11e Write a Letter of Application

Successful letters of application place the reader's needs first and show why you are the best candidate. Great jobs attract many applicants. Convince your readers that you are worthy of an interview. A well-written letter of application is the way you get your foot in the door.

Elements of a letter of application

Inside address and salutation	Use the name and title of the person doing the hiring whenever possible. If you don't know the person, call the organization for the person's name and official title.
First paragraph	Name the position for which you are applying.
Body	Explain why your education, experience, and skills make you a good candidate for the position.
Conclusion	Mention that you've enclosed your resumé and your contact information.

What you need to do

- Limit yourself to one page.
- Find out as much as you can about the organization or company.
- Don't fall into the trap of emphasizing why the job would be good for you; instead, show why you are well suited for the employer's needs.
- List in your resumé the qualifications and work experience that make you well suited for the position, then describe them in your letter and remember to bring them up if you get an interview.
- Close your letter with a paragraph that summarizes your strengths. In your last sentence, say thank you and sound confident. For example, "I appreciate your time in reviewing my application, and I look forward to hearing from you."
- If you are applying by email, name the position you are applying for in the subject line (*Application for production assistant position*).

Sample Job Advertisement and Letter of Application

The letter of application should be tailored to the job advertisement. Figure 11.1 reproduces the advertisement to which the sample letter and resumé respond.

PAID INTERNSHIP

Employer: Digital Workshop Inc.

Job title: Junior System/Network Administrator

Work location: Edmonton, AB

Successful applicant must grasp knowledge of network infrastructure to resolve users' issues quickly without interrupting company operations. He or she must meet project-oriented deadlines and accept additional assignments to improve his or her professional development. After three weeks of training in Edmonton, candidate will be placed in St. Louis, Missouri, for the rest of the term. Must have a Canadian passport.

Required skills:

- Excellent communication, both oral and written
- Able to learn technical and professional skills
- Able to act calmly in critical situations
- Self-motivated

Preferred requirements: Knowledge of these operating systems:

- MS Windows
- Oracle Solaris
- CISCO IOS
- Linux

Knowledge of the following network protocols:

- TCP/IP
- HTTP(s)
- (t)FTP
- SSH

Knowledge of the following hardware platforms:

- Intel x86
- Sun SPARC

Email resumé to Fergus Blackwell, fblackwell@dwi.com

Figure 11.1 A sample job advertisement. Target your application letter to the qualifications described in the advertisement.

Sample letter of application

937 2nd Ave. NW
Calgary, AB T2N 0E7

5 April 2012

Fergus Blackwell
Digital Workshop Inc.
7914 59th St.
Edmonton, AB T6B 3C3

Dear Mr. Blackwell:

Please consider my application for the internship position of junior network administrator at Digital Workshop advertised on the University of Calgary's website. My major qualifications for your position include experience managing a secure wireless network, my coursework on a BSc in computer engineering, excellent communication skills, and work authorization for the U.S.

Apply for and identify the position, explain where you saw the advertisement, and list two or three of your major qualifications.

I have some experience with managing a network, having set up secure wireless networks for friends and family members, which has acquainted me with knowledge of TCP/IP, SSH, (S)FTP, and HTTP(s). I also have experience with Linux and Windows operating systems from classes in my program. My communication skills are strong: In my last year of high school I was awarded the Senior Prose English Award for an essay titled "Experience." Although I am a Canadian citizen, I grew up in Chicago and have retained my permanent residency while attending post-secondary school in Canada. I am authorized to work in the U.S., as mentioned in the ad.

Explain your qualifications and add evidence to show your strength as a candidate.

My interest in computer hardware and software is ongoing; I have read and experimented with computer components and software for years. This experience has equipped me to respond effectively to the kinds of problems encountered by a network administrator at Digital Workshop. I am persistent in finding out what is needed to create innovative solutions, so I could contribute to the kinds of achievements that helped Digital Workshop win recognition as one of the top 200 fastest-growing companies in Canada.

List other qualifications and show your knowledge of the company.

I look forward to discussing with you at an interview other qualifications in my resumé that may be useful in helping Digital Workshop develop additional database management applications. Please email me at tspark@yahoo.ca or call my cellphone at 403-123-4567 to schedule an interview.

Request an interview, refer to your resumé, and include contact information.

Sincerely,

Terrence S. Park

11f Write a Resumé

Finding the right job depends on writing a successful resumé, one of the most important pieces of writing you will ever compose. The secret of a successful resumé is understanding its purpose: place you in the small group of candidates to be interviewed.

Elements of a resumé

Objective section	Target the objective section to the position you are applying for. Be as specific as possible. **Example** Managing a continuing care unit to which I can bring my extensive nursing skills, which include active CARNA registration and Heart and Stroke Foundation for BLS Healthcare Providers (Level C).
Overview section	List your education in reverse chronological order, beginning with certificates or degrees earned. List work experience in reverse chronological order, focusing on your more recent jobs and including details of your duties. **Example** Reviewed real-estate investments and loan portfolios for documentation, structure, credit analysis, risk identification, and credit scoring.

What you need to do

- Focus on the employer's needs. Imagine you are the person hiring. List the qualifications and work experience an ideal candidate would have.
- Make a list of your qualifications and work experience.
- Compare the two lists. What qualifications and work experience do you have that make you well suited for the position? Put checks beside the items on your list that you find are most important for the position.
- Create a printed resumé that you can attach as an electronic file onto a web form. Cut and paste your information from the resumé into the web form, where it is stored in an electronic database.
- Include keywords (nouns) on your resumé to ensure that your application comes up when the employer searches the database.

- Create two printed resumés—a scannable resumé and a traditional resumé. Many companies now scan resumés and store the information in a database. Make your scannable resumé simple and clean, and avoid any graphics such as bulleted points and lines.
- Similarly, since formatting is often lost when you are required to cut and paste your resumé into an online form, make this version as simple and free of formatting as possible.

Sample resumé

Terrence S. Park
937 2nd Ave. NW
Calgary, AB T2N 0E7
tspark@yahoo.ca
403-123-4567

SKILLS

Extensive knowledge regarding PC hardware quality, installation, maintenance, etc.
Quick and efficient learner
Self-motivated and able to work well both independently and in groups
High level of experience with Windows 98/2000/XP/7/2008
Knowledge of Ubuntu Linux
High degree of experience with Microsoft Office, including Excel and Word
Object-oriented C# programming experience and interest
Experience with wireless and local area networking

EDUCATION

2008–2012 BSc (Applied), Computer Engineering
University of Calgary, Calgary, AB

EXPERIENCE

2011–2012 Help Desk, University of Calgary
Stationed at help desk 10–15 hours a week, solving users' problems as quickly and efficiently as possible. Also troubleshot issues with LAN, computer classrooms, and public labs.
2009–2010 Wait Staff, Swiss Chalet, Calgary, AB
Waited on tables, some food preparation, cleaning as necessary. Won "Wait Person of the Year" in 2010.

AWARDS

Senior Prose English Award for non-fiction essay (high school)
Placed seventh in high jump at the 2010 Canadian Junior Track and Field Championships in Saskatoon, SK

INTERESTS

High jump: dedicated year-round training 3 days a week. Will continue training for the high jump with the goal of representing Canada at the 2016 Olympic Games in Rio de Janeiro.
Computer hardware: recently built personal computer with heavy emphasis on performance-to-cost ratio, which required extensive research into every hardware component
Electronics: including radios, televisions, small appliances, wireless devices, modified video game consoles and how they work
Writing: mostly prose essays, with occasional short stories

WORK AUTHORIZATION

Citizenship: Canadian
Other: U.S. Permanent Resident Card holder

11g Write a Business Memo

Memoranda, or memos, are a type of internal communication and are one of the most common forms of workplace writing. Memos are circulated internally, meaning within a company or among members of a team working on a particular project. While email is quickly replacing memos for day-to-day communication in many workplaces, the memo remains the preferred method for more formal communication. In particular, memos are valued for creating a paper trail that can be used later to confirm information and process. The primary purpose of a memo is to distribute information. Typical uses for a memo include summarizing the results of an important meeting, announcing a new policy, and updating team members on the progress of a project.

Elements of a Memo

Date	Include date that the memo is distributed.
To	List all recipients.
From	List yourself and any other authors.
Subject	Create a subject line that offers a brief preview of the memo's contents.
Introduction	Provide any necessary background information as briefly as possible. Include only the background information that your readers are likely to *need* in order to understand the memo.
Body	Detail all necessary information as clearly and concisely as possible. Many memos use design elements such as short paragraphs or bulleted lists to make the content easy for a busy reader to absorb at a glance.
Conclusion	If appropriate, use a brief conclusion to suggest any necessary follow-up steps.

What you need to do

- Use your company memo template (if available). If your company does not have a template, basic templates are available within most word processing programs.
- Begin with a header that includes each of the following on a new line: *Date, To, From, Subject.*
- Determine your purpose and stick to it. Focus on a single topic within your memo.

- Be brief and direct. Busy readers need to be able to absorb the information in your memo as quickly as possible.
- Use a professional tone.
- Format your memo for easy skimming. Provide ample white space, and make use of bulleted or numbered lists to make important information stand out.
- Conclude with a call to action, if appropriate to your purpose.
- All of these points also apply when you are creating a business memo which will be sent by email.

Game*Place* Canada

Memo

Date: October 1, 2012
To: Erica, JeeSu, Devon, Josh, and Olivia (New Product Sales Team)
From: Melanie (Human Resources)
Subject: Twitter Policy @ GamePlace Canada

This is a quick refresher on some important company policies as you head to Las Vegas on Friday for our new product trade show. GamePlace UK has asked that we highlight our new product lines using frequent Twitter posts throughout the show. Mark Tinsdale requests that you keep the following guidelines in mind before you click "send" each time:

- Highlight a different product with each post.
- Aim for a positive and enthusiastic tone.
- Keep it interesting, but remember that you're an ambassador for Game*Place* Canada, so all postings should always be professional.
- No posts should engage or identify the competition (see previous point).

We encourage all of you to have a great week in Las Vegas and to connect and network with as many of the other gaming companies and personnel as you can. And remember, what happens on Twitter in Las Vegas will not stay in Las Vegas!

12 Write About Literature

QUICK*TAKE*

- Read literature critically (see below)
- Analyze literature and develop an interpretation (see p. 125)
- Write a literary analysis (see p. 127)

12a Become a Critical Reader of Literature

Reading literature requires a set of practices different from those you might use while reading the Sunday paper or a magazine article. Think of yourself as an active critical observer. Carry on a dialogue with the text using marginal notes. Although writing in the margins as you read may seem like extra work at first, you will soon discover that it saves time and, before long, sharpens your reading skills. Keeping a record of your reading will force you to engage with a text; being an active reader is practice toward being a thoughtful reader. And marginal comments will be your best source from which to generate a paper topic.

As you read, make notes using the following list as a guide:

- Study the plot of the story. Determine how the events in the story relate to one another. What is the conflict and how is it resolved?
- Examine the principal characters in the story. What are their most defining characteristics? Are there minor characters? What purpose do they serve?
- Describe the setting of the story. What role does it play?
- Identify the point of view—that is, the perspective from which the story is told. Does a major character relay the events? A minor character? A fly on the wall?
- Look for shifts in the tone, style, and language of the story.
- Look for symbols, imagery, and interesting metaphors. Are sounds, images, or motifs repeated? What role do they play?
- Identify the story's central theme or main idea. Consider the title of the story and how the main characters fit the theme.

When reading poetry, also pay attention to the following:

- Identify the rhyme scheme. For example, when the first and third lines rhyme and the second and fourth, the rhyme scheme is *abab*.

- Listen to the metre. The most common metre in English is *iambic*, where an unstressed syllable is followed by a stressed syllable (for example, "To swell the gourd, and plump the hazel shells," from John Keats, "To Autumn").
- Listen for alliteration, the repetition of initial consonant sounds (for example, *b*aby *b*oomer, *C*razy *C*anuck, *r*oad *r*age, *W*orld *W*ide *W*eb).
- Note the stanza, the unit of poetry. The shortest stanza is the two-line couplet.

12b Be an Active Reader

Investigate words and references that are unfamiliar. Note connections among ideas in the text that will help you develop a strong thesis.

Ruins of a Great House

though our longest sun sets at right declensions and makes but winter arches, it cannot be long before we lie down in darkness, and have our light in ashes . . .

—BROWNE, *Urn Burial*

Dismembered parts: the house is in ruins

Stones only, the disjecta membra of this Great House,
Whose moth-like girls are mixed with candledust,
Remain to file the lizard's dragonish claws.
The mouths of those gate cherubs shriek with stain;
Axle and coach wheel silted under the muck
Of cattle droppings.
Three crows flap for the trees
And settle, creaking the eucalyptus boughs.

Limes: limey = Englishmen

Imperialism is a disease that "killed" England?

A smell of dead limes quickens in the nose
The leprosy of empire.
"Farewell, green fields,
Farewell, ye happy groves!"

Faulkner = American novelist

Marble like Greece, like Faulkner's South in stone,
Deciduous beauty prospered and is gone,
But where the lawn breaks in a rash of trees

Dead slaves buried like animals in the grounds around the plantation house

A spade below dead leaves will ring the bone
Of some dead animal or human thing
Fallen from evil days, from evil times.

It seems that the original crops were limes
Grown in the silt that clogs the river's skirt;
The imperious rakes are gone, their bright girls gone,

The river flows, obliterating hurt.
I climbed a wall with the grille ironwork
Of exiled craftsmen protecting that great house
From guilt, perhaps, but not from the worm's rent
Nor from the padded cavalry of the mouse.
And when a wind shook in the limes I heard
What Kipling heard, the death of a great empire, the abuse
Of ignorance by Bible and by sword.

House feels no guilt but suffers physical decay

A green lawn, broken by low walls of stone,
Dipped to the rivulet, and pacing, I thought next
Of men like Hawkins, Walter Raleigh, Drake,
Ancestral murderers and poets, more perplexed
In memory now by every ulcerous crime.
The world's green age then was a rotting lime
Whose stench became the charnel galleon's text.
The rot remains with us, the men are gone.
But, as dead ash is lifted in a wind
That fans the blackening ember of the mind,
My eyes burned from the ashen prose of Donne.

Hawkins: first Englishman to sell slaves in Caribbean

Poet rages about Elizabethan poets who exploited African slaves, then remembers England was a colony of Rome, and also exploited

Ablaze with rage I thought,
Some slave is rotting in this manorial lake,
But still the coal of my compassion fought
That Albion too was once
A colony like ours, "part of the continent, piece of the main,"
Nook-shotten, rook o'erblown, deranged
By foaming channels and the vain expense
Of bitter faction.
All in compassion ends
So differently from what the heart arranged:
"as well as if a manor of thy friend's . . ."

All share pain, guilt, exploitation, and misery

Albion = England

Nook-shotten = many angled or cornered

All people are victims and oppressors

—Derek Walcott, from *Selected Poems*

12c Develop an Interpretation

Assignments for English classes tend to be more open-ended than writing assignments in other disciplines, so you can focus on an aspect of the text that interests you. Develop an original idea. Ideally your audience will see the text differently after reading your interpretation.

Opinion versus interpretation

Papers about literature are often called *critical analyses*. Don't let the term trip you up. *Critical* in this sense doesn't mean judgmental. The fact is, your understanding of the text is much more interesting to a reader than whether you like it or not. Avoid making an argument about your opinion of a text unless the assignment specifically asks for one. Instead, develop an interpretation that illuminates some aspect of the text.

WRITING SMART

Electronic resources for writing about literature

While libraries are still the best places for literary research, you can find a number of handy resources online.

- **Bartleby.com** (www.bartleby.com) features free e-texts of well-known poetry, prose, and reference works, including the *Cambridge History of English and American Literature*.
- **Library and Archives Canada** (www.collectionscanada.ca) has a searchable collection of texts and criticism featuring Canadian literature.
- **MLA Bibliography** is a searchable bibliography of literary criticism available on your library's website.
- **Oxford English Dictionary**, available on your library's website, records the history of a word's meaning, tracking where it first appeared and how its definition has changed through the years.
- **Project Gutenberg** (www.gutenberg.org) offers free e-texts of hundreds of works of literature.

Develop your thesis

Ask *what*, *how*, and *why* questions. These questions will lead you from observation, to exploration, to an interpretation.

Observation: What's going on in the text?

What did you observe in the text that was unexpected, odd, powerful, or central? What questions did you ask? Wonderful interpretations frequently evolve from a question or confusion about the text.

> Why does the concluding scene of *Pride and Prejudice* feature the Gardiners, two secondary characters?

Although you won't have an interpretation yet, answering *why* questions will help you narrow your focus to a potentially fruitful topic for interpretation.

Exploration: How does the text do what it's doing?

The answer to this question may consider technical, stylistic, or thematic aspects of the text. At this point you'll begin to develop the first stages of your interpretation.

> How does Austen feature the Gardiners in the last scene of *Pride and Prejudice*? Throughout the novel Austen shows us strained or broken marriages, but the Gardiners are an exception. She presents them as a well-matched, well-adjusted couple.

Analysis and Interpretation: Why does the text do what it's doing?

Consider to what end or for what purpose the text functions as it does. What are the ultimate implications of a particular feature of the text? Answers will frequently fall into one of the following lines of inquiry:

1. It advances or complicates a major theme of the text.
2. It engages in commentary about larger political, social, philosophical, or literary issues of the author's day.
3. It reflects the influence of another writer or text.
4. It advances the plot or adds depth to a character.
5. It's attempting to be technically innovative. It highlights a capability or limitation in the author's choice of theme, genre, structure, stylistic elements, or narrative technique.

> Why does the end of *Pride and Prejudice* feature such secondary characters as the Gardiners? The Gardiners exemplify successful marriage. By ending the novel with them, Austen lends a note of hope for Elizabeth and Darcy's union. The novel, then, is not a condemnation of marriage as an institution but of the social forces that promote bad matches. We can analyze Austen's characterization of the Gardiners to better understand the kind of marriage making she wants to advocate.

12d Write a Literary Analysis

Keep your audience in mind when writing a literary analysis. Those who have already read the work will be bored by plot summary. Quote or paraphrase passages that advance your interpretation. Never use the text as evidence without analyzing it. Your analysis should be a close reading of the text that explains how the text you've chosen illustrates your interpretation.

1 Before you write

Read and analyze closely

- Go through your text line by line, annotating your responses.
- Develop a thesis for your interpretation that might start with a question and turn into a claim.
- When you have a thesis, reread the text to look for evidence.

2 Write an introduction

Engage your reader

- Raise what is at stake in your literary text. Many literary texts speak to large issues, whether about art or life. What issues does your text raise?

3 Organize and write the body of your paper

Use literary concepts to examine your text

- Take into account literary concepts such as character, setting, theme, motif, symbol, point of view, and imagery to express your ideas.
- Your analysis will likely answer such questions as who are the characters, what is the setting and what role does it play, what are themes or motifs in the text, from what point of view is the work told, what language choices are made, and what is the significance of the title?

Support your interpretation

- Cite the precise passages in the text that support your interpretation.
- Attribute every direct quotation and explain its significance.
- If your instructor asks you to use secondary sources, either literary criticism or biographical information about the author, decide where these sources are relevant.

4 Write a conclusion

End with more than a summary

- Draw larger implications from your analysis.
- End with a vivid example from the text.

5 Revise, revise, revise

Evaluate your draft

- Make sure your analysis meets the requirements of the assignment.
- Make sure your thesis is specific and significant. If you identify a pattern but say nothing about why it is important, your reader will ask "So what?" What does the pattern contribute to an overall interpretation?
- Make sure your evidence and examples are relevant to your thesis. Explain the significance of the evidence for your thesis.
- When you have finished revising, edit and proofread carefully.

Incorporating critical strategies

Your instructor might ask you to use particular critical strategies, such as to consider a literary work from a feminist approach. Ask your instructor to recommend major critical books and articles that deal with your topic. Then consider ways you can advance or revise the conversation about your topic. Does your interpretation of the text advance or complicate an existing critical perspective? Is there a scene or an aspect of the text that the critics don't consider but should? By developing original responses to these questions, you enter the critical conversation.

STAYING ON TRACK

Use the literary present tense

The disciplinary convention in English is to employ the *literary present tense*. This convention requires the use of present tense when analyzing any literary text such as a poem, a play, a work of fiction, an essay, or a sermon. Also use the present tense when discussing literary criticism.

Incorrect
Past tense

In *Song of Myself* Walt Whitman **tempered** his exuberant language with undercurrents of doubt about whether language **could** do all he **asked** of it.

Correct
Present tense

In *Song of Myself* Walt Whitman **tempers** his exuberant language with undercurrents of doubt about whether language **can** do all he **asks** of it.

However, you should employ the past tense when discussing literary history. The author's life, the creation of the text, the text's publication,

(Continued on next page)

STAYING ON TRACK *(Continued)*

and the critical reception of the text all exist outside the work itself and require the past tense. The following passage uses the past tense to discuss the publication history and critical reception of *Leaves of Grass*.

Correct
Past tense

Beyond doubting whether his audience would understand the spirit of his verse, Whitman **worried** that *Leaves of Grass* would never reach an audience at all. He **was** so concerned, in fact, that he **published** reviews of the book under false names to drum up publicity.

12e Sample Literary Analysis

The following student paper responds to the assignment topic "Analyze an extended metaphor in Derek Walcott's 'Ruins of a Great House.' In your analysis show how the speaker uses this metaphor to think through his ideas about colonialism and imperialism."

Charles 1

Eric Charles

Professor Ugor

English 113 E15

10 October 2012

Walcott, Extended Metaphors, and "Ruins of a Great House"

In "Ruins of a Great House," Derek Walcott uses extended metaphors to describe the legacy of English imperialism in the Caribbean, and to explore his conflicted feelings about colonialism. First, he employs the image of a derelict plantation manor to mirror the deterioration of English imperialism in the Caribbean. His second extended metaphor explores his conflicted feelings about colonialism through the conflict of fire and coal, and through it he comes to a realization. By using these extended metaphors, Walcott conveys his ideas in a vivid, poignant way that leaves the reader thinking about them after the poem has finished.

The first stanza of "Ruins of a Great House" describes the house and surrounding area, and it begins drawing parallels to the legacy left by the British Empire. Several colonial references are interspersed with descriptive phrases about the house to connect the two ideas. In lines 5 and 6, Walcott juxtaposes artifacts of affluent English colonial lifestyle with elements of poor island life: "Axle and coach wheel silted under the muck / Of cattle droppings." This juxtaposition shows that the British colonial society broke down and decayed, much like the

Charles 2

grounds of the plantation, and was replaced by the more natural lifestyle of subsistence farming (as was the lifestyle of the slaves who were then free). The author draws another connection between the grounds of the house and the empire it represents when he writes, "A smell of dead limes quickens in the nose / The leprosy of empire" (9, 10). The rotting of the "original crops" of the plantation occurs because the plantation is now abandoned due to the rotting of the imperialist English society that once ran the plantations (19).

Walcott further ties the idea of the decayed empire and the decayed house together when he says, "Deciduous beauty prospered and is gone" (14). The use of the word *deciduous* implies the cycle of seasons, and the fact that the beauty has prospered and gone indicates that the British Empire is in the winter of its reign. The author also suggests this in lines 27–29: "And when a wind shook in the limes I heard / What Kipling heard, the death of a great empire, the abuse / Of ignorance by Bible and by sword." By connecting the death of a great empire with the sound of the wind shaking the limes of the plantation, Walcott creates another parallel and strengthens the extended metaphor of the manor house as the British Empire. He then uses this metaphor as a basis for the rest of the poem, and he goes on to explore his conflicted emotions through a second metaphor.

The second extended metaphor that Walcott creates in "Ruins of a Great House" is the internal

Charles 3

conflict he feels about colonialism presented as the conflict between a fire and its fuel. The sudden introduction of a first-person narrator halfway through moves the poem away from description and sets the stage for the speaker's battle of emotions. New emotions begin to appear coinciding with the introduction of the speaker in line 23: "I climbed a wall with the grille ironwork / Of exiled craftsmen protecting that great house / From guilt, perhaps, but not from the worm's rent" (23–25). The speaker suggests that the craftsmen were decorating the great house using grille ironwork to reassure themselves of their superiority over the slaves who worked their plantations and to stave off guilt. Next he considers the pioneers of colonialism:

> Dipped to the rivulet, and pacing, I thought next
> Of men like Hawkins, Walter Raleigh, Drake,
> Ancestral murderers and poets, more perplexed
> In memory now by every ulcerous crime. (31–34)

While pacing in agitation, he describes the pioneers of colonialism as "ancestral murderers and poets," a phrase that highlights his internal conflict. Walcott himself is a poet and descended from both an Englishman and slaves (Damrosch et al. 949). He accuses them of being murderers, yet he would not be alive were it not for their actions.

The conflict he feels gives way to anger and frustration when he further reflects on their twisted, rotten legacy:

Charles 4

> The world's green age then was a rotting lime
> Whose stench became the charnel galleon's text.
> The rot remains with us, the men are gone.
> But, as dead ash is lifted in a wind
> That fans the blackening ember of the mind,
> My eyes burned from the ashen prose of Donne.
> (35–40)

Walcott's first use of combustion as a metaphor for the speaker's emotions occurs in line 39. "Blackening ember" indicates that the fire of hatred has been slowly burning out, but when the speaker remembers Donne's writings regarding compassion among fellow humans and witnesses the flagrant contradiction of that compassion by Donne's contemporaries, represented by the plantation house, the flames grow. Walcott continues, "Ablaze with rage I thought, / Some slave is rotting in this manorial lake," (41–42). The "blackening ember" of the speaker's hatred is now "ablaze," representing how strongly he feels. However, Walcott states, "But still the coal of my compassion fought / That Albion too was once / A colony like ours, 'Part of the continent, piece of the main,' " (43–45). The coal opposing the fire of the speaker's anger is his compassion for his fellow man. He recognizes that Britain was once a colony of the Roman Empire, just as the Caribbean became a colony of Britain. He realizes that his "vain expense of bitter faction" will do no good, and that the "ancestral murderers and poets" that he reviles were in a situation similar to his

Charles 5

(47–48, 33)—descendants of the oppressors. He ultimately recognizes that he cannot change history, and so he must rely on the river of time to continue to flow and obliterate his anger (22). Walcott concludes, "All in compassion ends / So differently from what the heart arranged: / 'as well as if a manor of thy friend's . . .'" (49–51). The speaker's compassion overrules the anger of his heart, yet his compassion is a different kind from that described by John Donne. Walcott expresses the kind of bitter empathy the speaker has for the British colonialists by using a John Donne quote to ironically refer to them as "friends" and to refer back to the plantation manor/British Empire metaphor he constructed earlier in the poem.

By using these extended metaphors in "Ruins of a Great House," Derek Walcott is able to effectively communicate the post-colonial condition of the Caribbean and the conflicted emotions of anger and empathy that the speaker feels regarding the British colonialists in a piercing way that provokes thought. His first extended metaphor serves to accurately describe the post-colonial state of the Caribbean, and it provides the background against which the rest of the poem plays out. His second extended metaphor serves to viscerally communicate his emotional conflict in a way that resonates with the reader. Through Walcott's use of extended metaphors, readers are able to gain insight into an important historical period and, possibly, into their own emotions.

Charles 6

Works Cited

Damrosch, David, et al. *The Longman Anthology of World Literature.* New York: Pearson, 2009. Print.

Walcott, Derek. *Ruins of a Great House.* English 113 Assignment Description Handout, 2012. Print.

13 Write About Film and New Media

QUICK*TAKE*

- Respond to new media critically (see p. 137)
- Learn the genres of film and new media criticism (see p. 139)
- Write a film analysis of a video game (see p. 149)

In many ways, writing about film and new media is a lot like writing about literature: You need to develop a critical perspective on the film, game, or website that you are writing about. Just as good readers of literature will reread a text (or parts of a text) several times, so, too, will film critics view a film more than once. They might even re-view related films by the same director or involving some of the same actors if they feel that this would help them write a more nuanced and informative critique. Critical essays based on games and other new media demand that the writer have extensive experience with the game and perhaps with similar games on the market now or games from the previous generation or competing platforms. This kind of research helps writers build context for their comments and extends the scope of their writing beyond the instance of the particular film, game, or media product under consideration. Ultimately, this kind of knowledge makes your writing more sophisticated and informative.

13a Become a Critical Viewer

To view films or new media critically requires you to create distance between yourself and the film or media you are evaluating. How do you do that? One way is to view a film several times; after the second or third viewing, you become less conscious of the plot because you know what is going to happen. You then become more conscious of other aspects of the film, such as the acting, wardrobes, sets, camera angles, and so on. Reviewing a film allows you to step outside the flow of action that tends to dominate a first viewing. The same can be said for video games: the first few times you play, your attention probably focuses on trying to stay alive (in the case of first-person shooter games) or active. After you've become adept at the game, you can attend to other aspects of it: the quality of the graphics, the cleverness of the plot and storyline, and the relative challenges that the game poses for various levels of players. If you have had experience with previous versions of a particular game—or similar games from other manufacturers that are in the same genre—then you can draw upon that experience, too, when you evaluate or comment.

13b Learn the Genre: Film Reviews

One way to learn what makes for a good review of films and media is to read the reviews others have written. To find reviews of films, visit these internet sites:

- Rotten Tomatoes (www.rottentomatoes.com)
- Internet Movie Database (www.imdb.com)
- Movie Review Query Engine (www.mrqe.com)
- Yahoo! Movie Reviews page (dir.yahoo.com/Entertainment/Movies_and_Film/Reviews)
- UC Berkeley library film studies resource page (www.lib.berkeley.edu/MRC/filmstudies/reviewslist.html)
- Roger Ebert (rogerebert.suntimes.com)
- Fast Forward Weekly: Film Reviews (www.ffwdweekly.com/screen/film-reviews; see Figure 13.1)
- your library's website; see Figure 13.2

Criticism and analysis tend to differ from film reviews, however, so you should be aware of the distinctions your professors may make between these kinds of writing assignments.

You've probably read film reviews when trying to decide whether or not to see a film or when deciding which film to watch. The reviews tend to be short—between 500 and 1000 words—and to focus pretty much exclusively on the movie being reviewed, although they sometimes include brief

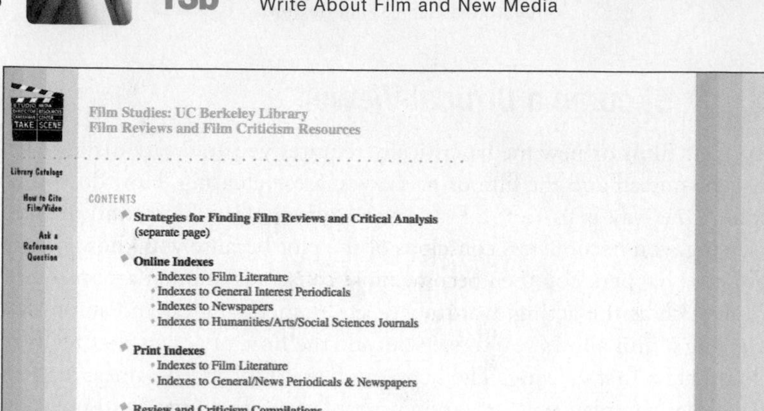

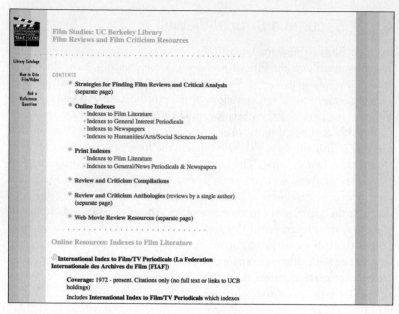

Figure 13.1 UC Berkeley library film studies resource page.

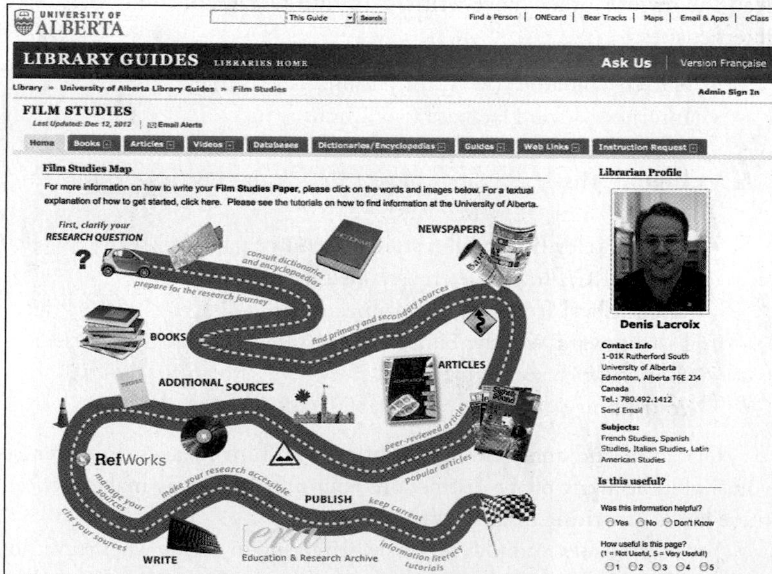

Figure 13.2 Consult your library site for a similar reference page.

references or comparisons to sequels or movies from the same genre. Reviews also tend to be specific, personal evaluations of one particular film. Another key point about reviews is that they are written for readers who have not yet seen the film. Readers read movie reviews to evaluate whether they should spend their time and money viewing this particular film.

In writing about a horror movie such as *Slither,* for example, reviewers will comment only on that film. While reviewers may mention other films that the director worked on or that some of the actors appeared in, these references are brief, often parenthetical, notes. The introduction to a review takes some innovative aspect of the film—in *Slither*'s case, the word itself—and then places the film in the genre of horror films by alluding to previous classic films. A plot summary appears early in the review, followed by comments evaluating some important aspects of the film, such as pacing, character development, plot development, and special effects. Generally, a film review does not "give away" the ending.

13c Learn the Genre: Film Criticism

As a student in a film course, you may be asked to respond to films in a variety of ways besides reviews. An important component of these responses will be analysis. An analysis differs from a review in that you assume the reader has seen and understood the film and is interested in a new interpretation (which your analysis offers). Since your reader is familiar with the film, you can reduce the amount of plot summary in your analysis to include just the details needed to provide a context for your points of analysis. There are a number of genres in which you may be asked to write, depending on what your instructor feels is important in understanding a film. They tend to fall into the categories discussed below.

In a film class, you may be asked to write a *mise en scène* analysis. *Mise en scène* refers to analyzing a particular scene or cut in a film using established criteria. Some of the criteria that may be used in a *mise en scène* analysis are as follows:

- Production design (sets, props, costumes)
- Colour (production design and lighting)
- Lighting
- Actors' movement/blocking
- Framing (depth of field, height, angle)
- Sound
- Black and white or colour film, fine-grain or grainy texture

If you were writing a *mise en scène* analysis of a scene—for example, the opening of *Pride & Prejudice* (2005)—you might decide to discuss the details of the costume worn by Keira Knightley as she finishes reading her book and arrives home. You might also assess the framing of the book, over her shoulder, and the final page before she closes it. As you can see, *mise en scène* analysis parallels "close reading" in literary analysis because both techniques ask you to focus on what is in the scene or the text. In your *mise en scène* analysis, you would take each (or some) of the characteristics above and comment on how each one contributes to your understanding of a particular scene in the film and its significance.

One complication that may come up is that *mise en scène* can also refer to a style of filmmaking in which the entire film is made up of scenes, and each scene is one shot. This style contrasts with the montage style, a style dominated by frequent cuts to different angles, the sort of style associated with many fast-paced music videos. Check with your instructor to confirm that the assignment is limited to *mise en scène* analysis or that *mise en scène* style is just one of several aspects you are being asked to evaluate.

Sequence analysis asks you to focus specifically on a set of shots within a smaller part or sequence within a film. In this kind of analysis, you would begin the process of researching the essay by identifying all the shots within a sequence. You would then write an essay explaining how these shots make sense or are joined together for viewers as the sequence proceeds. Why does one shot lead to the next? What does each shot add to the narrative of the sequence—does it provide a reaction, a confirmation, a contrast? What are the borders of this sequence? How is this sequence related to other sequences in the film? How is sound used both within the sequence itself and as a transition into and out of the sequence?

Critical analysis essays take the specific techniques within a film—the *mise en scène* and sequence techniques described above—and add to them an understanding of the cultural context of the film. Here are some of the key questions that a critical analysis attempts to answer:

- When was the film made? What was going on economically and politically?
- What other films were made at that time? Is this film part of a genre or a specific kind of film?
- What is the quality of the screenwriting? Is the dialogue realistic or didactic?
- Who made the film? What other films did this person make?
- How was the film received by critics and the public when it was first released?
- Does the film make connections to other films, to historical events, and/or to people?

This kind of essay resembles the kind of researched essay described in Chapter 12, Write About Literature, and in Part 5, Planning Research and Finding Sources (Chapters 19–22). You will need to find out something

about the film in question. Look for information about these types of related subjects:

- Reviews of the film at the time it was released
- Some news stories pertaining to cultural, economic, and political events at the time
- Biographical information about who made it
- Other films made at the time that may have influenced the director

Consider starting your research process with these sources:

- *Critical Dictionary of Film and Television Theory*
- *Cinema Studies: The Key Concepts*
- Film Literature Index (webapp1.dlib.indiana.edu/fli/advancedSearch.jsp)
- FIAF International Federation of Film Archives
- International Index to Performing Arts (iipa.chadwyck.com/marketing.do)
- FIAF International Index to Film Periodicals (fiaf.chadwyck.com)
- *Retrospective Index to Film Periodicals*
- Canadian Film Encyclopedia (tiff.net/canadianfilmencyclopedia; see Figure 13.3)

View the films you are studying several times, making notes about the structure, themes, techniques, and your own reactions to them. Do some research about the directors, producers, and actors, and the cultural, political, and economic events at the time the film was made and shown. As you read,

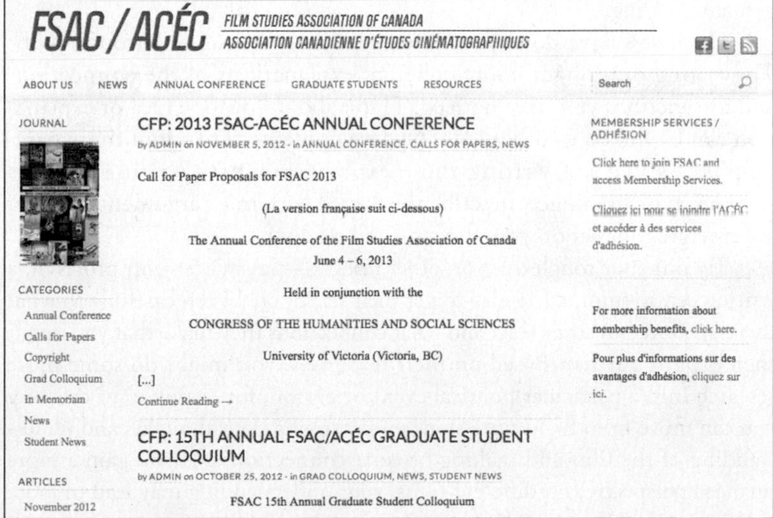

Figure 13.3 http://www.filmstudies.ca

WRITING SMART

Electronic resources for writing about film

Here is a list of post-secondary writing programs that offer useful advice to students on writing about films. Visit some of them to help you get started.

- Dartmouth Writing Program: www.dartmouth.edu/~writing/materials/student/humanities/film.shtml
- University of Richmond: http://writing2.richmond.edu/writing/wweb/filmstudies/terms.html
- Emily Carr Institute of Art + Design: http://blogs.eciad.ca/wc/all-posts/writing-reviews-film
- Hunter College, City University of New York: http://rwc.hunter.cuny.edu/reading-writing/on-line/writing-about-film.pdf

look for connections or disjunctions between techniques, for example, and technological developments. When did colour become possible for films? When were hand-held cameras developed? How did these (or other) technological developments affect what ended up on the screen? These are just some of the kinds of connections you could make as you try to put the film you viewed into a critical context for your reader. By making these kinds of connections, you are creating new knowledge and a new perspective on the film you are studying.

Once you have done your research, start working on a rough draft. Try writing out longer, more coherent explanations of the connections and disjunctions you have noticed. Think about how one idea or explanation can be linked to other ideas or developments. Then join those paragraphs. As you are writing these explanations, try writing a thesis statement. In a sentence, describe the overall pattern or argument that you see emerging, based on your viewing and reading.

Try out your rough draft on other readers—classmates, your professor, a writing centre tutor, a friend—to get their reactions. Listen carefully to what they say. Note how they react and what connections they make that you might then explore further. Based on their responses, you might do some more research into a particular political event or person, for example. In this way you can move from first impressions to developing your thoughts and understanding of the film and making broader connections. As you gain a more nuanced perspective on different films, your understanding may lead to more sophisticated claims (i.e., thesis statement) about the film you are analyzing.

At this point in your writing process, pay attention to editing your draft and crafting your sentences (see Part 7, Effective Style and Language; Part 8, Understanding Grammar; and Part 9, Understanding Punctuation and Mechanics).

 Sample Analysis of *The Woman in the Window*

The following paper presents an analysis of Fritz Lang's *The Woman in the Window* (1944). It uses many of the techniques drawn from *mise en scène* analysis to argue that the thematic movement in the film proceeds from an initially voyeuristic relationship between Wanley and Alice's portrait to a fetishistic relationship.

Kamal 1

Justin Kamal

Professor Graves

FS 312: Film Noir

24 February 2009

From Fear to Fetishism: Voyeurism in *The Woman in the Window*

Fritz Lang's *The Woman in the Window* (1944) presents a complicated portrayal of feminine objectivity as a result of masculine crisis of identity. In "The Man's Melodrama," Florence Jacobowitz states that "the anxiety which *film noir* desperately tries to lay to rest revolves around the male protagonist's crisis of identity and fears of not living up to the responsibilities of domination, power and achievement so central to masculinity" (153). Though the film's male protagonist, Professor Wanley, fails to live up to the ideals of masculine dominance, it is his fear of the idealized beautiful woman and not his sadistic impulses that leads him to objectify her. While he attributes an idealized identity to the woman in the portrait, at no

Kamal 2

point does he attempt to make her his possession or to dominate her. Contrarily, it is she who takes control of his actions and eventually leads him to his imagined death. Aware of his masculine deficiencies and inability to attract a woman of Alice's beauty, Wanley resorts to voyeurism as a safe means by which to observe her without the fear of impotence associated with meeting her in person. This voyeuristic relationship becomes fetishistic as he indulges in his fantasy of courting her, which eventually leads to disaster and reaffirms his initial fears and apprehensions.

Wanley's masculine shortcomings foreground his fear of Alice and motivate his voyeuristic behaviour. His friends Dr. Barkstane and District Attorney Lalor jest at his admiration of the portrait and assert their ownership of the woman portrayed by referring to her as their "dream girl." The men do not know Alice but attribute to her an idealized identity based on their masculine preconceived notions of attractive women. Wanley, on the other hand, is content admiring the portrait itself and not the subject it represents. While he states that it is an extraordinary portrait, Lalor adds that the portrait's subject is probably an extraordinary woman as well. Wanley does not claim ownership of Alice as the other men do because he does not wish to have her. It is not a lack of attraction that hinders him but a fear of the responsibility associated with masculine ideals of domination and charisma, both of which he does not have. Though the other men are arguably no more masculine or attractive than he is, they exhibit a sadistic behaviour in reducing Alice to an object serving their personal interests.

Kamal 3

While the other men exercise sadistic control over Alice and her portrait, Wanley acknowledges the inaccessibility of both. He admires the portrait and its subject from afar as he would marvel at an ornate sword, knowing his inability to handle it and its ability to destroy him. Alice does not own the portrait either, nor, by association, her own image. As such, the portrait exists as a separate entity ensnaring an idealized image while remaining out of the reach and the control of anyone. Upon first meeting Alice, Wanley expresses his admiration for the artist before briefly complimenting her. Alice responds to his compliment by questioning how he could make an assumption about her personality before meeting her in person. Wanley switches focus once again to the portrait, explaining that if he were the artist, he would be very happy about it. Wanley and Alice are framed in a medium long shot with the portrait centred between them representing the shared object on which their meeting is based. Alice then moves closer to the painting as the camera zooms in to a medium shot framing Alice and her portrait on one side and Wanley on the other. This shot represents the duality of Alice's identity, portraying both her actual self and her idealized counterpart. However, while the portrait is out of Wanley's reach, Alice is well within it and proves it to him by holding his arm and asking him for a drink.

Prior to his meeting with Alice, Wanley resorts to voyeurism as his only means by which to observe her without having to actually meet her. Protected by a glass barrier and the confines of the portrait itself, Wanley is

Kamal 4

safe from the expectations of masculine performance. This security is shattered as he sees Alice's reflection in the window. His discomfort level becomes apparent as he struggles, flustered, to articulate his thoughts. Alice, on the other hand, is calm and collected as she observes his reaction. She supplants his voyeuristic power, as he becomes the object of her gaze just as she was the object of his. Whatever control he may have had is disrupted as he is faced with the fear of confronting the living manifestation of the harmless object in the portrait. Alice becomes a voyeur as well: the objects of her fascination are the men who attempt to objectify her through their gazes. Wanley nervously asks her if he reacted "normally," which calls into question the masculine norms of behaviour on which he bases his assumptions of normality. She explains that there are two ways people generally observe the portrait: one is a "solemn stare" and the other is a "long low whistle." The quiet admiration of the solemn stare and the fetishizing lustfulness of the long low whistle are combined in Wanley's "long low solemn whistle," which Alice finds attractive since he does not look like "a man much given to whistling." This preconception mirrors that of Lalor in which he assumes that she is an extraordinary woman. Wanley expresses his apprehension by stating that she must not misunderstand his admiration, which further reveals his fear of her.

As Alice takes control of the situation and actively expresses interest in him, Wanley transitions from voyeurism to fetishism. His fantasy is not necessarily to be with her but for her to find him attractive. Alice makes

Kamal 5

several suggestive remarks indicating her desire to spend the night with him; she tells him that she was alone that night and does not like to be alone. Taken aback by her advances, Wanley quickly changes the subject by asking her if she had looked at his face as he admired the portrait. The shot/reverse shot depicting Wanley on one side and Alice and her portrait on the other is disrupted as Alice steps forth and makes her intentions clear. At this point, they are shown in a medium shot with their arms crossed and the portrait is no longer visible in the frame; this signals the end of the voyeuristic power of Wanley as well as Alice. As they walk away, the camera returns to the portrait, which is left powerless as it has lost its admirer in favour of its flesh and blood counterpart. Alice's enthusiasm about venturing off with a man she has never met is unrealistic and highly suspicious. Considering that she observes several men's reactions to the portrait, there is no indication as to why she chose Wanley—that is, if she does not do the same with all of them. This dubious situation suggests that she does in fact have alternative intentions. Dumbfounded that a beautiful woman desires his company, Wanley is grateful to her for facilitating the situation and indulges in his fetish.

Wanley ignores the warning signs and flirts with disaster as he abandons his mundane lifestyle in favour of a more exciting one. At several points in the film, primarily involving his conversations with the police, he repeats this imprudent behaviour, leading himself closer to disaster. Though the initial social barrier between him

Kamal 6

and Alice has been removed, his interactions with her remain cautiously distant. This is largely due to his confusion resulting from Alice's transcendence from a controlled medium into a seductive physical manifestation. As his world radically changes, Wanley is unsure whether he is still the conservative, domestic man he was the day before or something entirely different. This confusion results in a crisis of identity, forcing him to take on a charismatic masculine role that he is unable to achieve due to his innate simplicity. Though he never has sex with Alice, his willingness to spend the night with her implies that his intentions are far from innocent. There is nothing to suggest that they would not have slept together had Mazard not arrived. In addition to committing—or at least leaning toward—adultery, Wanley embraces masculine aggression by murdering Mazard. Both of these actions are highly unusual for a domestic family man. His attempts at transcending his masculine limitations lead him to his imagined death.

Though the encounter with Alice and the subsequent events turn out to be nothing but a dream, Wanley learns the important lesson that his mundane world is where he belongs. After he awakens from his nightmare, he revisits the portrait and laughs at the ridiculousness of his imaginings. This is quickly interrupted by the reflection of a woman's face in the exact same location on the portrait as that of Alice. This parallelism triggers his renewed sense of caution in a way that would not have had the same effect if framed differently. When the woman asks him for a light, he refuses and runs away like a frightened

Kamal 7

child, which indicates his return to a domestic state. Though his indulgence in his fantasy implies his sense of masculine inferiority, he does not acquire masculine traits as a result of his experience. On the contrary, having seen the undesirable results of his indulgence, his masculinity is diminished as he becomes more fearful of beautiful women. By revisiting the portrait, he exhibits a return to voyeurism but not to fetishism, which as his experience has shown, leads to disaster. As the film's final words foretell, he will never again allow himself to succumb to his fetish, "not for a million dollars."

Kamal 8

Works Cited

Jacobowitz, Florence. "The Man's Melodrama: Woman in the Window and Scarlet Street." *The Movie Book of Film Noir*. Ed. Ian Cameron. London: Studio Vista, 1992. 152–64. Print.

 13e Write About New Media

In the same way you might be asked to write about films or literature, you may be asked to write about new media: video games, web-based information sites, art installations, blogs, bots, and (cy)borgs. New media attempt to create an experience in ways similar to a film or literary work. They aim to create an intellectual or emotional viewing or reading experience. The new media—computer-based CDs, internet-based multiple-player games, television-based gaming consoles—often combine elements of the "old" media to create these new experiences. For example, World of Warcraft, an internet-based multi-player dungeon (MUD), combines rich visual imagery with text-based chat features and real-time voice-over internet chat using an earpiece and microphone. Players meet online to organize "instances" or quests that the group will undertake together at a certain time and place. Each player brings the character that he or she has created and built by gathering items and defeating robots (bots) that the creators of the game have deployed throughout it. By combining the ability to speak as well as write to other players in real time, the creators of this game have created a new experience.

How can we talk about the relative quality or success of these new media? In this part of the chapter, we will focus on how to write an essay critiquing a video game experience.

Write a video game review

Before reviewing a video game, one of the first things you should do is read a variety of reviews. Online sources for reviews are available at these sites:

- Game Rankings.com (www.gamerankings.com)
- Video Game Review (www.videogamereview.com)
- AMG All Game Guide (www.allgame.com)
- Yahoo! Video Game Reviews (http://dir.yahoo.com/Recreation/Games/Video_Games/Reviews)
- GameSpot.com (www.gamespot.com/reviews.html)
- Metacritic.com (www.metacritic.com/game; see Figure 13.4)

Reviews tend to vary widely from a fill-in-the-blank type form to full-blown essays topping 4000 words. Make sure that the requirements for the assignment you are asked to write differentiate between these two kinds of reviews.

The general criteria for evaluating new media experiences include these concepts:

- Difficulty level (first-time player; experienced player of previous versions)
- Gameplay and strategy (character development, environments, gear)
- Graphics (realistic; smoothly transforming during play)
- Sound (quality, variety, appropriateness)
- Narrative (consistency within and across storylines)
- Authenticity (the degree to which the virtual world is consistent within itself)
- Transparency (the degree to which players can lose themselves in the virtual world and look through the interface rather than noticing it)

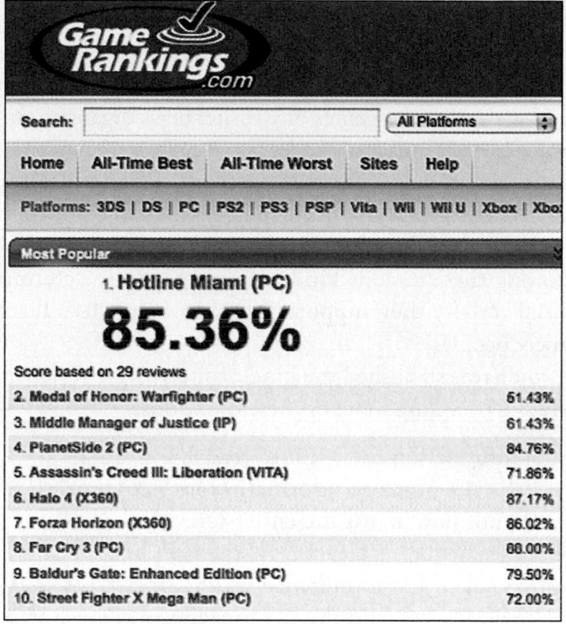

Figure 13.4 www.gamerankings.com

Structure your review

Video game reviews generally address the same kind of audience as film reviews: readers who have not tried the game but are wondering whether it is worth the investment to buy. Game reviews also follow the same general pattern as film reviews. The introductory paragraph offers an overview of the game's strengths, identifies the genre of game (e.g., role-playing, shooter, racing), establishes brief links to the other games that this company has published, and evaluates the experience of playing it. The next paragraphs take readers through strategies for getting the game started. For example, many games offer a variety of choices for players as they build their virtual characters. These paragraphs help readers understand the implications that these choices may have when they are 100 hours into playing the game and it is too late to change their minds.

The next paragraphs describe some of the different paths that players could take through the game. Many games create a virtual geography or landscape that players move through; these paragraphs describe how these landscapes are distinct and what kinds of encounters you are liable to find there. Finally, these reviews end with one or two paragraphs that detail improvements in the game.

Write a website review

Another kind of text you might be asked to create is a review or analysis of a specific website or kind of website. Just as there are classes or kinds of films and games, there are various genres of website: news organization–sponsored websites (www.cbc.ca), educational sites (www.ontariosciencecentre.ca), social organizations and online communities (www.facebook.com), educational organization sites (www.uwo.ca), personal sites (www.ualberta.ca/~graves1), blogs (www.blogscanada.ca), and more. Your first task is to distinguish among these various kinds of web pages by determining what kind of social activity they support. Are they help sites? Teaching sites? Places to meet people?

Once you have established the kind of site you are reviewing, you can evaluate the site by asking some of these questions:

- Is the information broken into readable chunks?
- Does the site organize information into columns so that lines of text do not flow across the entire screen?
- Does the site have a clear visual theme?
- Can you identify the audience for the site?
- Can you move around the site easily?
- How deep or how much content is provided on the site?
- How useful and how many links are on the site?

Once you have evaluated the site for both formal (design) and content aspects, start writing your analysis or review. As in film and literature essays, the scope of your essay will depend on the assignment. Are you asked to review a newspaper site only in the context of that site alone (as a kind of *mise en scène* analysis) or are you asked to critically review it in the context of newspaper sites within Canada or across the U.S. (http://dir.yahoo.com/News_and_Media/Newspapers/By_Region/Countries/Canada)? Should you be comparing the different ways the same story is represented in Calgary and Ottawa? Halifax and Houston? What you might say about each site will depend on the scope of the assignment that your instructor provides.

13f Sample Game Review

The review below was written in response to the following assignment:

> Select a computer-based video game that has been released in the last year. Write a review of that game using the criteria listed above. In your review, make sure you comment on previous games by the same creative group or company and indicate how this game fits with the other games that this group or company has produced.

Park 1

Terrence Park

Professor R. Brown

Media Studies 120

27 April 2006

Review of The Elder Scrolls IV: Oblivion by Bethesda Softworks LLC, a ZeniMax Media Company

Oblivion is the fourth game of the Elder Scrolls series from Bethesda Softworks. Like its predecessors (Arena, Daggerfall, and Morrowind), Oblivion is a single-player role-playing game (RPG) set in the massive medieval world of Tamriel. However, each game takes place in a different province with a different plot and characters. Oblivion is set in the capital of the empire, Cyrodiil. This works nicely for the central plot, which involves the assassination of the emperor and his heirs, throwing the empire into disarray and creating a very interesting environment to explore. The most remarkable aspect of Oblivion (aside from the amazing graphics) is that it is entirely open-ended, allowing players unlimited freedom to explore the detailed world and complete quests as they see fit, or to focus on the main quest line immediately, something that has rarely been done in other series.

Introduction identifies the game, outlines its genre and related games by Bethesda, and evaluates the game's unique features.

The reason most linear RPGs avoid an open-ended structure is that they depend on killing creatures for the player to gain "experience," "level up," and become more powerful. Oblivion uses a refined version of the innovative levelling system from previous Elder Scrolls games that allows players to go up a level by increasing their skills. Each character class (the game has 21 predefined classes and the option to create your own custom class) is

Outlines game's unique features and how they improve the quality of the game experience.

Park 2

specialized in Combat Arts, Magic Arts, or Stealth Arts. The chosen specialization is the overall focus of the class, but unlike most RPGs it does not lock the player in to one particular play style. Each specialization has seven skills, and those skills start off higher, and are easier to increase, than skills outside the chosen specialization. Each class has seven major skills, which start significantly higher, and are easier to increase, than the other skills (minor skills). Ten increases in any combination of major skills allow the player to level up, regardless of how many monsters have been killed. Going up a level allows the character to increase attributes (which govern skills), health, and overall power. This innovative levelling system can take some getting used to, especially when creating a custom class, but overall it is much more rewarding than choosing a stock class and slaughtering creatures mindlessly in order to level.

Another interesting aspect of character creation is race. There are 10 unique races (including lizardlike Argonians, catlike Khajiit, 3 types of elves, and 4 types of humans), each with different skill bonuses and unique abilities. Each race has a different look and flavour (fully customizable, via the use of copious amounts of sliders and options) and different starting attribute scores, something lacking in almost all other games of this genre.

What is truly amazing about Oblivion is the incredible detail and realism of the graphics, which are evident during character creation. On the higher visual settings, hair looks lifelike. This is the first video game I have ever played that accurately portrays such minute detail. This

Park 3

multitude of options makes for some very interesting gameplay combinations and allows for some truly unique characters.

The graphical strength of Oblivion evident in character creation carries over to the environment. The trees and grass of the forests and the architecture of the buildings in the environment are amazingly detailed. This attention to background detail seems like a minor feature, but when compared to other video games it becomes huge. Most video games have trouble creating believable trees and natural scenery, because they are not naturally composed of straight lines. When a video game does create a believable model of natural objects, too often there are about three tree models used, which really detracts from the experience. Oblivion uses an engine specifically for creating natural foliage and curving, believable trees. When in town, the effects are just as stunning. Buildings are architecturally believable for the time period and extremely well done (the buildings on a rural farm are one storey, with grass-thatched roofs, surrounded by a low wall made of rocks to keep the wandering sheep in). Non-player characters (NPCs) look almost lifelike and have realistic facial expressions and mouth movement during dialogue. In fact, Oblivion uses a new artificial intelligence system called Radiant AI, developed by Bethesda, that gives each NPC individual priorities and a daily schedule. It is common to walk by and witness two NPCs engaged in small talk, before one excuses himself and heads to the pub for a drink. This system could still use refining, as there are disjointed

Explains the improved graphics and character behaviours that make the game more realistic.

Park 4

conversations that do not make total sense and break the experience of the game. However, I would rather witness occasional bizarre behaviour in NPCs than have them behave in a uniformly dull manner all the time. All in all, the Radiant AI system is an improvement, but still not quite ready for prime time.

This paragraph elaborates further improvements to the game.

The gameplay itself is improved over Oblivion's predecessors. In Morrowind, melee fighting consisted of beating something until it died, using only one button. The melee fighting in Oblivion has been reworked, with new moves and a blocking button added. In addition, parries and power attacks are now possible, greatly changing the melee experience. In Morrowind, skills were simply static modifiers that changed the chance of successfully completing an action. In Oblivion, new skill perks are obtained upon reaching certain skill levels. For example, when characters obtain skill level 25 in Armourer (repairing weapons and armour), repair hammers last twice as long before breaking. When they reach skill level 50, they gain the ability to repair magic items. Upon reaching skill level 75, they can fortify weapons and armour, making them more effective. When characters reach skill level 100 (the highest level), repair hammers never break for them. This skill perk mechanism provides further incentive to increase skill levels and adds interesting flavour to each character. Further gameplay improvements include a new fast travel option (to eliminate much of the horrible "fetch these" quests that other RPGs rely on), the ability to ride horses, and more guilds and organizations than previous games.

Park 5

Despite all of the innovative ideas in Oblivion, it is not perfect. There are a lot of reported glitches (although less than its predecessors), and the interface is kind of cluttered. The font size of the inventory window may seem too big to some, and it causes a lot more scrolling than needed. In order to achieve the amazing graphics with no in-game load screens, the draw radius for grass and high-quality texture is somewhat small. This means distant objects are poorly rendered, and the grass suddenly appears 30 metres away from the character. Because every line in the game is spoken by voice actors (including Patrick Stewart and Sean Bean), a lot of the characters sound the same. Also, some of the lines spoken by the beggars exhibit perfect English while others have thick lowbrow accents. This discontinuity is startling and takes away from the experience.

This paragraph summarizes flaws or areas in the game that need some improvement.

All in all, The Elder Scrolls IV: Oblivion is an incredibly innovative game with great graphics and gameplay but is not without its flaws. Most of its flaws are minor and excusable, but they do tend to detract a little from the overall experience.

PART

4 Designing and Presenting

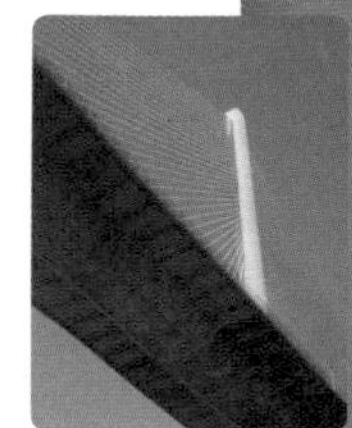

You **can learn more and do more** with MyWritingLab and with the eText version of *The Brief Penguin Handbook*. Find resources in MyWritingLab to help you successfully complete your assignment.

14 Compose Using Standard Designs 159

15 Design for Print 166

16 Communicate with Words and Images 171

17 Compose Images 180

18 Design Presentations 189

14 Compose Using Standard Designs

QUICK*TAKE*

- Compose using standard academic designs for MLA and APA papers (see below)
- Consider using templates for resumés and web pages (see p. 162)
- Design web pages for impact and navigation (see p. 164)

14a Design Essays and Reports in MLA or APA Style

Many instructors will identify the format or structure that they want you to use when submitting an essay or report. Many job application websites also require applicants to submit the information on their resumés in text boxes that limit the number of words or characters applicants can include. Grant proposal writers also face limitations like this: Some funding agencies now use a question-and-answer format for applicants with text boxes that limit the information a writer can provide.

MLA essays

The last section in Chapter 26 details how to format a research paper in MLA style. Here are some of the design considerations that MLA style specifies:

- Do not use a title page (unless requested by your instructor).
- Double-space all text.
- Apply a 1-inch margin on all four sides of the page.
- Ensure that the end of each line in a paragraph is unjustified (uneven).
- Begin each paragraph with a ½-inch indentation.
- Use one typeface throughout the document.
- Begin the "Works Cited" section, which lists all references cited, on a new page at the end of your paper.

The emphasis in MLA style is on standardization: Each essay should have the information that the instructor wants to see in the same place and formatted in the same way. See Figure 14.1 for an example of the first page in an MLA paper.

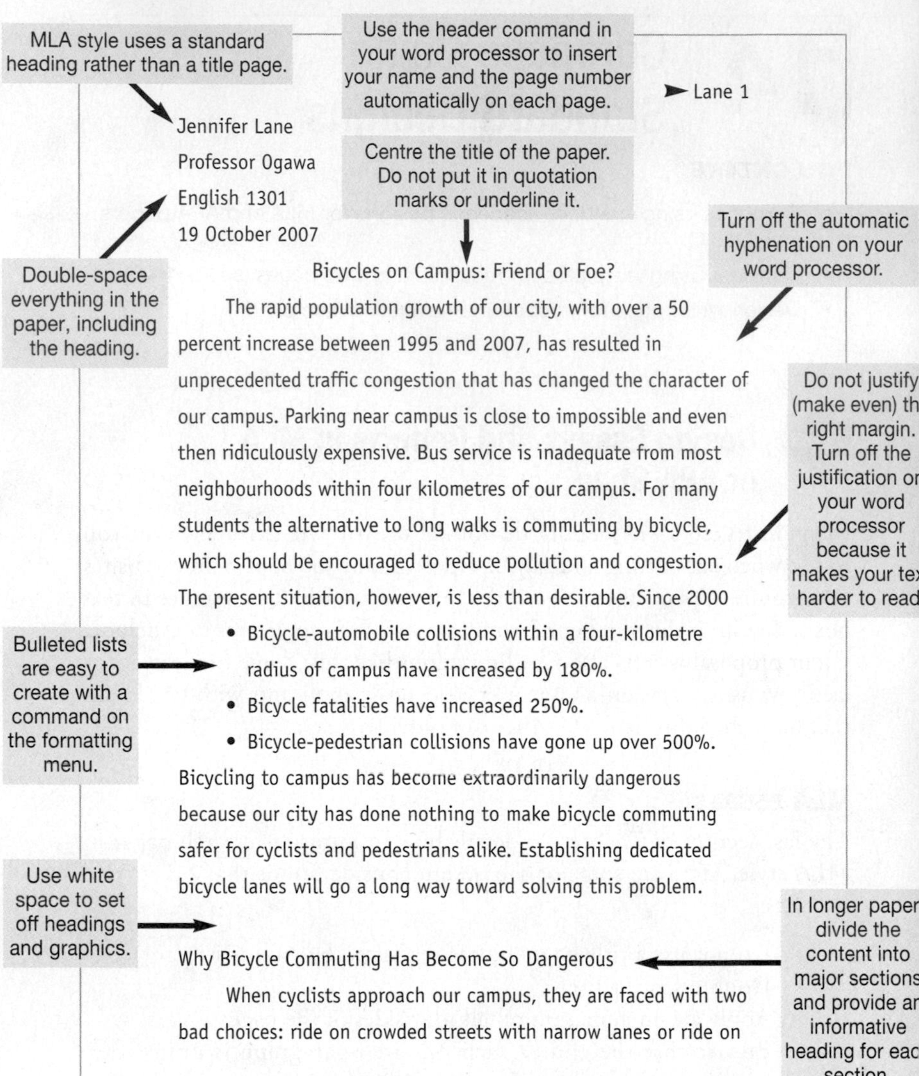

Figure 14.1 The first page of a paper in standard MLA format. Your instructor may have specific formatting requirements. Ask your instructor for formatting instructions if they are not specified in the assignment.

APA papers

The last section in Chapter 27 details how to format a research paper in APA style. While APA style and MLA style share the goal of standardization, the rules for APA differ in the details:

APA style uses a title page.

BODY OBJECTIFICATION 1

Include page header and page number, beginning with the title page.

Body Objectification: Relationship with
Fashion Magazines and Weight Satisfaction
Michael Moshenrose and Keli A. Braitman
York University

Centre the title, name of author(s), and name of school.

Figure 14.2 The first page of a paper in standard APA format.

- Use a title page (see Figure 14.2).
- Begin with an abstract (titled "Abstract"), which appears on the page after the title page and before the main report.
- Format and name tables and figures according to APA conventions.
- Use the heading "References" for the section that lists all references cited.
- Use the headings "Abstract," "Methods," "Results," "Discussion," and "References" for research reports.

The emphasis in APA style is on breaking up the text into recognizable and easy-to-find chunks. Headings help readers find the section they are looking for, and they also help readers keep track of where they are in longer documents.

Technical and scientific genres

Reports of all kinds tend to use headings to enable readers to see the structure of a document. For example, the sample case study in Chapter 11 uses the headings "Discussion" and "Conclusion." Lab reports often use the headings "Methods," "Results," and "Discussion" (the acronym MRaD can help you remember these headings).

14b Consider Using Templates for Resumés and Web Pages

Some writing genres, such as resumés, combine structure with choice: They follow a standard format but give you the opportunity to make some design decisions. The options for formatting a resumé are quite varied, and some follow the conventions of a particular profession or field. Academic resumés, for example, are called CVs (curriculum vitae) and tend to document the person's academic career through time. Chapter 11 presents an example of a student resumé, with the typical headings and information included. See Figure 14.3 for a standard template for a resumé.

Templates help writers create well-organized and attractive documents. Many word processing and presentation slide programs offer writers a variety of templates for many different genres. Microsoft Word, for example, offers over 40 different categories of templates, and within each category there are many sample templates.

Templates offer several advantages. First, they speed up the writing process by making design decisions for the writer. Second, they often look

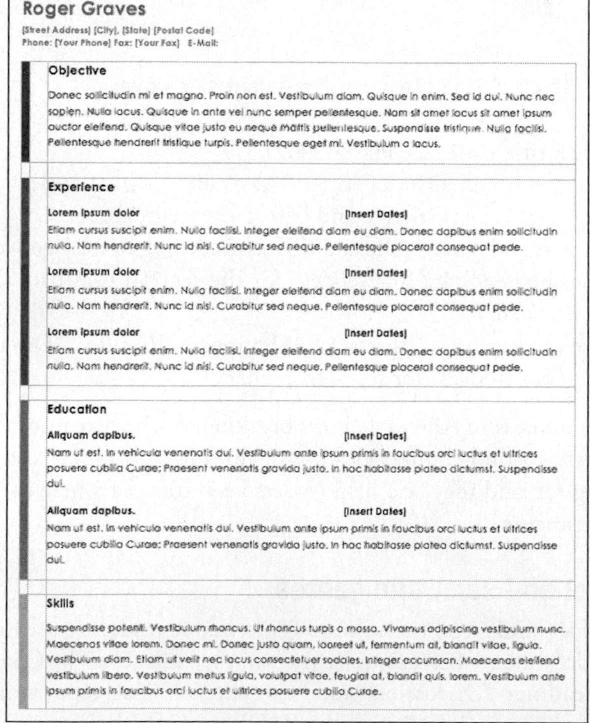

Roger Graves

[Street Address] [City], [State] [Postal Code]
Phone: [Your Phone] Fax: [Your Fax] E-Mail:

Objective

Donec sollicitudin mi et magna. Proin non est. Vestibulum diam. Quisque in enim. Sed id dui. Nunc nec sapien. Nulla lacus. Quisque in ante vel nunc semper pellentesque. Nam sit amet lacus sit amet ipsum auctor eleifend. Quisque vitae justo eu neque mattis pellentesque. Suspendisse tristique. Nulla facilisi. Pellentesque hendrerit tristique turpis. Pellentesque eget mi. Vestibulum a lacus.

Experience

Lorem ipsum dolor [Insert Dates]
Etiam cursus suscipit enim. Nulla facilisi. Integer eleifend diam eu diam. Donec dapibus enim sollicitudin nulla. Nam hendrerit. Nunc id nisi. Curabitur sed neque. Pellentesque placerat consequat pede.

Lorem ipsum dolor [Insert Dates]
Etiam cursus suscipit enim. Nulla facilisi. Integer eleifend diam eu diam. Donec dapibus enim sollicitudin nulla. Nam hendrerit. Nunc id nisi. Curabitur sed neque. Pellentesque placerat consequat pede.

Lorem ipsum dolor [Insert Dates]
Etiam cursus suscipit enim. Nulla facilisi. Integer eleifend diam eu diam. Donec dapibus enim sollicitudin nulla. Nam hendrerit. Nunc id nisi. Curabitur sed neque. Pellentesque placerat consequat pede.

Education

Aliquam dapibus. [Insert Dates]
Nam ut est. In vehicula venenatis dui. Vestibulum ante ipsum primis in faucibus orci luctus et ultrices posuere cubilia Curae; Praesent venenatis gravida justo. In hac habitasse platea dictumst. Suspendisse dui.

Aliquam dapibus. [Insert Dates]
Nam ut est. In vehicula venenatis dui. Vestibulum ante ipsum primis in faucibus orci luctus et ultrices posuere cubilia Curae; Praesent venenatis gravida justo. In hac habitasse platea dictumst. Suspendisse dui.

Skills

Suspendisse potenti. Vestibulum rhoncus. Ut rhoncus turpis a massa. Vivamus adipiscing vestibulum nunc. Maecenas vitae lorem. Donec mi. Donec justo quam, laoreet ut, fermentum at, blandit vitae, ligula. Vestibulum diam. Etiam ut velit nec lacus consectetuer sodales. Integer accumsan. Maecenas eleifend vestibulum libero. Vestibulum metus ligula, volutpat vitae, feugiat at, blandit quis, lorem. Vestibulum ante ipsum primis in faucibus orci luctus et ultrices posuere cubilia Curae.

Figure 14.3 An example of a standard template for a resumé.

professional and are consistent in their design choices. Third, they help remind writers of categories of information that they should include under specific headings. In essence, MLA style and APA style create templates for academic writing. However, templates lack individual style and constrict the kind of information that can be included in a document.

Popular social networking sites use templates to organize information on the web. Facebook, for example, has a left-hand column of information about friends, a middle column with updates, and a right-hand column with suggested friends and advertising links. LinkedIn has a main column of updates with a right-hand column with boxes for suggested people to link to, statistics about your profile, ads, and jobs you might be interested in. The website developers generate this template and make design decisions about what colours to use and what fonts to use to display the text. WordPress offers a series of templates to organize blogs like the Inkshed.ca blog in Figure 14.4.

Beyond templates: Making genre-driven design choices

Most post-secondary writing assignments, however, are not the standard essay or report. They often challenge you to decide how to organize the document you create in response to the assignment. For that reason, you need to know some basics about how to design documents. In the chapters that follow in this Part, you'll read about how to use visuals in your documents and presentations, how to choose typefaces, and how to organize information in and make presentations.

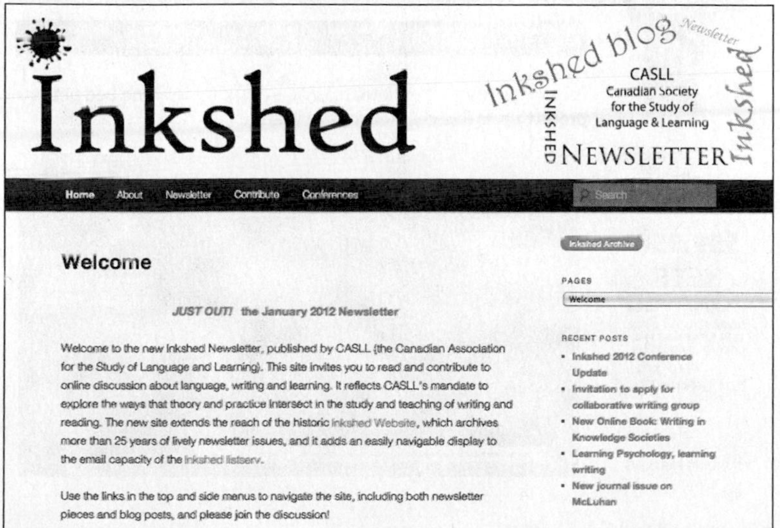

Figure 14.4 A blog based on a WordPress template.

14c Design a Website

Web authoring software makes it easy to compose web pages, but the software doesn't tell you how to design an effective website. Visitors to websites often don't read pages one after the other as they do in books. Visitors expect to be able to move through your site according to their own interests.

Determine your structure

Think in advance about the structure of your site. Decide on the major topics that should be on separate pages. Draw a map of your site that shows the pages and the links to other pages.

Consider the screenshot from the Spread the Net site (Figure 14.5). Note the navigation bar on the right side. The use of one-word links—"Learn," "Donate," "Spread"—that are easily and immediately understood encourages readers to click deeper into the site.

Make your site visually effective

A consistent look and feel makes a website appear unified and supports the content. A website does not need a loud background or flashy animations to achieve a visual theme. Instead, little things such as selecting a simple set of

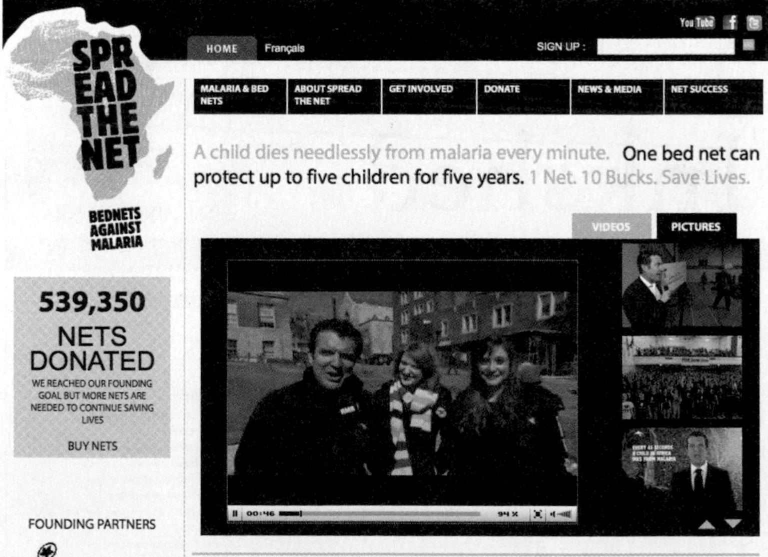

Figure 14.5 Home page of Spread the Net.

colours for the text, headings, links, and background do more to create a consistent visual theme than an attention-grabbing image. Similar graphics and images should be the same size, and often their placement can be repeated from page to page.

Make the text readable

Long stretches of text on the web tend not to get read. You can make your text more readable on the web if you do the following.

- **Divide your information into chunks.** If your information runs longer than a screen, consider placing it on two web pages.
- **Use shorter paragraphs when possible.** Long paragraphs are harder to read on the screen than in print.
- **Use a sans serif typeface.** You can specify typefaces using the font command on your web editing software.
- **Control for line width.** Lines of type that run across the entire page are often difficult to read. Divide your page into columns.
- **Use white space to separate elements** and to give visual relief.

Make navigation easy

People typically scan a website quickly and move around a lot. They are likely to click on links, following their interests. If you put content on more than one page, provide a navigation bar so that readers can navigate easily. A navigation bar can be a simple text bar or icons that are easy to create with image editing software.

WRITING SMART

Evaluate the design of a website

You can learn a great deal about effective web design by keeping these criteria in mind when you visit websites. Some will be more critical than others, depending on the site. For example, good navigational tools become more important on extensive sites.

1. **Audience and purpose.** How does the site identify its intended audience? Why was the site created?
2. **Content.** How informative is the content? Has the site been updated recently? What do you want to know more about? Are there any mechanical, grammatical, or style problems?

(Continued on next page)

WRITING SMART *(Continued)*

3. **Readability.** Is there sufficient contrast between the text and the background to make it legible? Are the margins wide enough? Are there paragraphs that go on too long and need to be divided? Are headings inserted in the right places, and if headings are used for more than one level, are the levels indicated consistently? Is high-contrast text, including text in boldface and all caps, kept short?
4. **Visual design.** Does the site have a consistent visual theme? Where is the focal point on each page? Do the images contribute to the visual appeal or do they detract from it?
5. **Navigation.** Does the first page indicate what else is on the site? How easy or difficult is it to move from one page to another on the site? Is a consistent navigation scheme used throughout the site? Are there any broken links?
6. **Accessibility.** Web accessibility means that people with disabilities and people with slow internet connections can access the information and interaction available on the web. W3C, the World Wide Web Consortium, offers guidelines and tools for assessing web accessibility (see www.w3.org/WAI/eval/Overview.html).

15 Design for Print

QUICK*TAKE*

- Design for readers (see below)
- Design brochures and flyers (see p. 167)
- Choose effective typefaces (see p. 169)

15a Start with Your Readers

Imagine yourself in the shoes of your reader. What do you, the reader, want from the writer?

Tell your reader what you are writing about

An accurate and informative title is critical for readers to decide if they want to read what you have written. Some genres require *abstracts*, which are short summaries of the overall document. Abstracts are required for scholarly articles in the sciences and social sciences as well as for dissertations. Business reports and other reports often have executive summaries, which are similar to abstracts but often briefer.

Make your organization visible to readers

Most longer texts and many shorter ones include *headings*, which give readers an at-a-glance overview and make the text easier to follow and remember. Some genres have specific formats for organization, such as the APA-style report of research that is divided into four parts: introduction, method, results, and discussion. If you are writing in a genre that requires a specific format, follow it. Readers will be irritated if you don't. (For more information on academic genres, see Chapter 11.)

A writer's scarcest resource is the reader's attention. Sidebars and pull quotes can be effective for creating interest.

Help your reader to navigate your text

Do the little things that help readers. Use headings and subheadings to enable readers to skim and scan your document to find the sections that have the information they want. Remember to include page numbers—something that word processing software can insert for you. Make cross references to other parts of your document when a subject is covered elsewhere. In reports, consider including a table of contents and list of figures. On websites, consider including a site map and a search box.

 15b Design Brochures and Flyers

Word processing and other easy to use software allow you to achieve what required a team of designers to accomplish just a few years ago. Use templates as a basis for designing brochures and flyers. These templates take advantage of designs that use typefaces and white space well. They often indicate where to place visuals and how to arrange text around those visuals.

Use colour effectively

Colour can provide contrast to draw attention to headings and emphasize words (see Figure 15.1). Colour printing is now affordable, and colour is expected on websites. We are surrounded by so much colour that

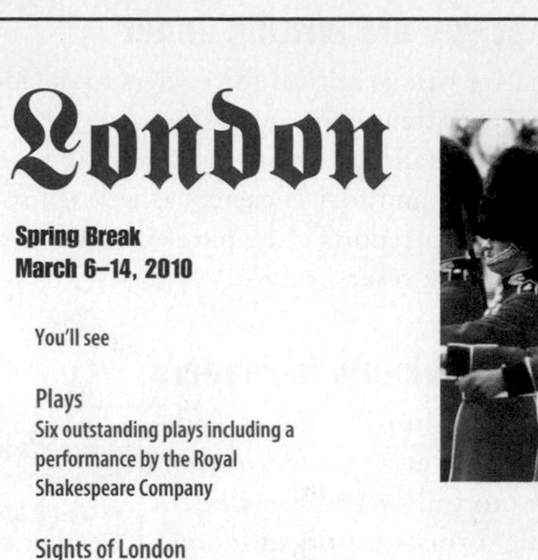

London
Spring Break
March 6–14, 2010
You'll see
Plays
Six outstanding plays including a performance by the Royal Shakespeare Company
Sights of London
Buckingham Palace, the Tower of London, Westminster Abbey, St. Paul's Cathedral, the Houses of Parliament, Big Ben, 10 Downing Street—the residence of the Prime Minister
Museums
National Gallery of Art, the new Tate Modern, the restored Globe Theatre, the British Museum
Sponsored by the Drama Club
For information contact
Karen Clark, President
Drama Club
405 Student Union
482-1564

Figure 15.1 In this sample flyer, note how the red used in the titles and headings both matches and balances the red uniforms in the image.

sometimes the strongest effects are created by using colour in minimal ways. Limited use of warm colours—yellow, orange, and especially red—can make an impact.

Make your documents look professional

With today's word processing and other easy-to-use software, you can produce a professional-looking project. Attractive brochures are one example. Templates take care of the basic layout, allowing you to focus on the content. If you are creating a brochure, select the size of paper you want, fold the sheet of paper, and number the panels. Make a sketch of what you want to appear on each panel, including headings, text, images, and graphics. Figure 15.2 shares a few tips on how to design a brochure.

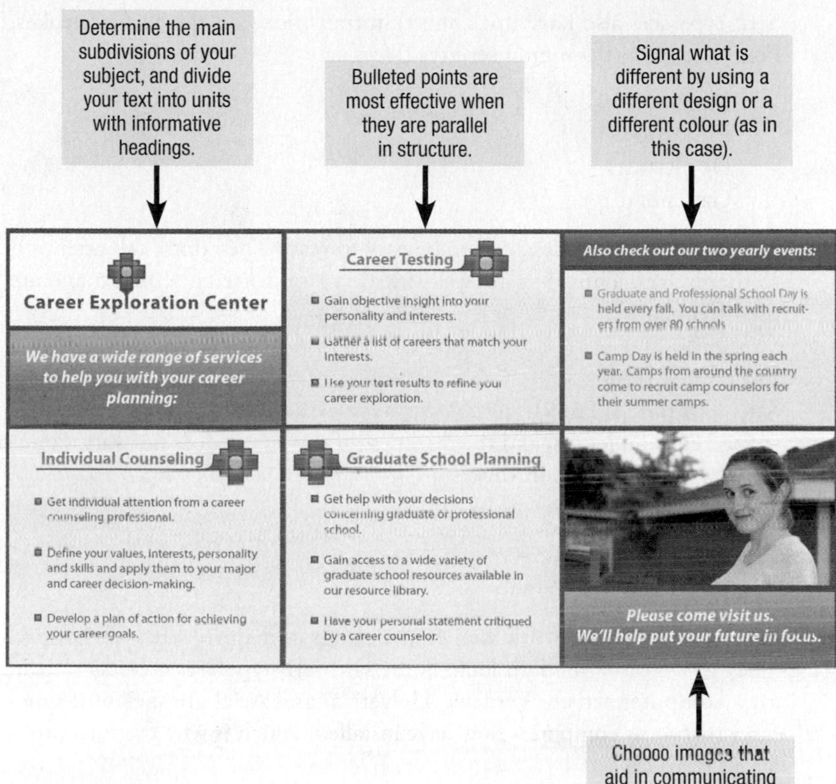

Determine the main subdivisions of your subject, and divide your text into units with informative headings.
Bulleted points are most effective when they are parallel in structure.
Signal what is different by using a different design or a different colour (as in this case).
Career Exploration Center
We have a wide range of services to help you with your career planning:
Career Testing
Gain objective insight into your personality and interests.
Gather a list of careers that match your interests.
Use your test results to refine your career exploration.
Also check out our two yearly events:
Graduate and Professional School Day is held every fall. You can talk with recruiters from over 80 schools.
Camp Day is held in the spring each year. Camps from around the country come to recruit camp counselors for their summer camps.
Individual Counseling
Get individual attention from a career counseling professional.
Define your values, interests, personality and skills and apply them to your major and career decision-making.
Develop a plan of action for achieving your career goals.
Graduate School Planning
Get help with your decisions concerning graduate or professional school.
Gain access to a wide variety of graduate school resources available in our resource library.
Have your personal statement critiqued by a career counselor.
Please come visit us.
We'll help put your future in focus.
Choose images that aid in communicating the content.

Figure 15.2 The inside panels of a three-panel brochure fold out to show the services offered by this career planning centre.

15c Choose Type

Writing on a computer enables you to use dozens of different typefaces and fonts. (A particular style of type is called a *typeface*, such as Times New Roman or Arial. A specific kind of typeface, such as Verdana bold, is called a *font*.) At first, typefaces may all appear similar, but when you pay attention to various typefaces, you will notice how they differ.

Use typefaces effectively

Serif type

Serif and *sans serif* are major categories of typefaces. Serif (rhymes with *sheriff*) typefaces were developed first. Serifs are the little wedge-shaped ends on letter forms, which scribes produced with wedge-tipped pens.

Serif typefaces also have thick and thin transitions on the curved strokes. Four of the most common serif typefaces are

Times
Palatino
Bookman
Garamond

Serif typefaces were designed to be easy to read. They don't call attention to themselves. Thus they are well suited for long stretches of text and are used frequently.

Sans serif type

Sans serif (*sans* is French for *without*) typefaces don't have the little wedge-shaped ends on letters, and the thickness of the letters does not vary. Popular sans serif typefaces include

Helvetica
Arial
Verdana

Sans serif typefaces work well for headings and short stretches of text. They give a crisp, modern look. Some sans serif typefaces are easy to read on a computer screen. Verdana, Helvetica, and Arial are sans serif typefaces that most computers now have installed, which is why they are popular on websites.

Script and decorative type

There are many script and decorative typefaces. These typefaces tend to draw attention to themselves. They are harder to read, but sometimes they can be used for good effects. Script typefaces imitate handwriting or calligraphy, which is why they often appear on diplomas, formal invitations, and similar documents.

Popular script typefaces include Nuptial Script and Dorchester Script:

When you want only the very best

Snead, Potter, and Jones, Attorneys at Law

Some decorative typefaces, including Freestyle and Beesknees, are informal, almost irreverent:

That's a no brainer.

TOTALLY AWESOME!

Use a readable type size

It's easy to change the size of type when you compose on a computer. For long stretches of text, use at least 10- or 12-point type. Use larger type for headings and for text that will be read on a screen.

Use other effects as needed

Finally, word processing programs allow you to use type fonts such as **boldface**, *italics*, and underlining. All three are used for emphasis.

16 Communicate with Words and Images

QUICK*TAKE*

- Use images and words effectively (see below)
- Organize your text and images (see p. 172)
- Decide when to use words and when to use images (see p. 179)

16a Use Images to Enhance Text

Computer technologies now make it possible for individuals to create texts that permit you to control type styles and size but also allow you to insert pictures, add tables and other graphics, print in colour, and prepare sophisticated visuals for presentations.

The problem today is not whether you can add images and graphics but *when* to add them and for what effects. Just as for other rhetorical situations, it finally comes down to what you hope to accomplish—your purpose for communicating.

■ Sometimes images are used in place of words.

■ Sometimes words bring images to mind.

Think about what an image communicates

What are the expectations of your audience?

- Most essays don't use images. Most websites, brochures, and instructions do.
- Think about the purpose of including an image. Does it communicate a concept? Does it show something that's hard to explain in words alone?
- Think about the focus of the image. You may need to crop the image.
- Provide an informative caption for the images you include and refer to them in your text.

Organization in Verbal Texts

Organization is the path the writer creates for readers to follow. Even in a reference book like this one, in which readers consult particular chapters and sections according to their needs, there is still a path from beginning to end.

Titles, headings, and paragraphs

Titles and headings combine verbal and visual indicators of levels of importance and major divisions in subject matter. Paragraphs give visual cues to the progression of ideas in verbal texts. Other visual indicators such as boldface and italics provide emphasis at the level of words and phrases. Print, after all, is a visual as well as a verbal medium.

Organization in Visual Texts

Organization is often called *composition* by photographers, artists, and designers. Both of the pictures below are of the same subject, but they are composed differently.

Static versus dynamic

The image on the left is a typical snapshot. The person is placed at the exact centre, and the horizon is about at the midpoint. Putting the subject in the exact centre is what happens when people take snapshots without thinking about how they are composed. The effect is static.

The image on the right moves the person away from the centre and places him in relation to a large rock illuminated by the setting sun. Instead of focusing on the man, we now see him in relation to objects on the beach and the sea and sky behind.

Point of View in Verbal Texts

At the most basic level, *point of view* means selecting among first person (*I, we*), second person (*you*), and third person (*he, she, it*) when you write about your subject. Using *I* emphasizes the writer or the teller of the story in fiction. Using *you* puts the relationship between writer and reader in the foreground. Using *he, she,* or *it* keeps the focus more on the subject and diminishes the prominence of the writer.

Point of view is also determined by how you locate yourself in relation to your subject. Whether you write in first or third person, you can write about a subject from close, first-hand experience or you can place yourself at a distance from your subject, giving the sense of being an impartial observer offering an overview.

You can write about Niagara Falls as if you were looking across the gorge.

Niagara Falls actually consists of three falls: the American, the Bridal Veil, and the Canadian or Horseshoe Falls. The American Falls descends between 21 and 34 metres to the rock at the base. The Horseshoe Falls descends 52 metres into the Maid of the Mist Pool below. More than 168 000 cubic metres of water go over the brink every minute during daytime hours. The flow is reduced at night, after peak tourist hours, to generate electricity. Water is removed from the river upstream to generate hydroelectricity for both Canada and the U.S. The total power-generating capacity at the falls is about 4.4 million kilowatts.

You can write about Niagara Falls from the bottom.

Once the *Maid of the Mist* reached the foot of the falls, the spray had blotted out the sun, and we felt a steady, soaking mist on everything. Now we understood why the crew had insisted we all wear huge black raincoats: otherwise we would have been drenched. The thundering of the water was deafening. We could see each other's lips move but heard only water. We caught magical glimpses of the secret world behind the waterfall.

Point of View in Visual Texts

Where we choose to stand when we take a photograph makes all the difference in how the audience sees the subject. The photographer gives the audience a vantage point to take in the subject by allowing the audience to see what the photographer sees, creating an effect comparable to the use of *I* in writing.

Photographers also create a *you* relationship with their subjects. Photographing at close range creates a sense of interaction between subject and photographer.

Focus and Frame in Verbal Texts

When you write, maintain focus on one subject at a time. You achieve focus by what you choose to include and what you choose either to leave out or to postpone until later.

When you write about a complex subject, often you think about many things at once and try to get them all into your prose

Our era is not unique as a time of uncertainty. In the past the Four Horsemen of the Apocalypse—war, disease, famine, and death—represented uncertainty. Today much of the risk is produced by humans. Science and technology are both the cause of and the solution to our problems. In the past spirits or demons took the blame for catastrophes; today the blame circles back on us. The media tell us that things go wrong because we choose the wrong lifestyle or the wrong partner or the wrong kind of food or the wrong occupation, and that it's our responsibility to fix what is wrong.

When you write about a complex subject, sort the issues and present them one at a time

Our era is not unique as a time of uncertainty. The Four Horsemen of the Apocalypse—war, disease, famine, and death—have been the daily reality for most humans in times before modernity and for many living now. There are two major differences between uncertainty today and in the past.

First is the degree to which risk is produced by humans. Science and technology are both the cause of and the solution to our present risks. Every new technology brings associated risks: trains brought the risk of train wrecks, airplanes brought plane crashes, automobiles brought traffic accidents and smog, nuclear power brought radiation leaks, the internet brought rapidly spreading computer viruses.

Second is the absence of traditions to account for risks. In the past spirits or demons took the blame for catastrophes. Today the blame circles back on us. We chose the wrong lifestyle or the wrong partner or the wrong kind of food or the wrong occupation. When things go wrong, it is the individual's responsibility to seek counselling, to retrain herself, to pull himself up by his bootstraps.

Focus and Frame in Visual Texts

Just as in writing, make the subject of your images clear to the viewer. Beginning photographers tend to see only what is at the centre of the viewfinder. More experienced photographers pay attention to the edges of the frame because they know the frame is critical to how the viewer sees the subject.

Most of the time you should aim for simplicity in images.

Interest in Verbal Texts

Readers will plow through pages of boring writing if they have a strong purpose for reading, such as investigating a financial report for a company they plan to invest in. Most of the time, however, you have to create and hold readers' interest if you expect them to finish reading what you write. When you create interest, you also build your credibility as a writer.

Details make writing lively

Tavistock is typical of the small farming communities of southwestern Ontario: well kept, prosperous, a curious blend of past and present. The sprawling farms give way to city lots with neat houses—nineteenth-century yellow brick, twentieth-century vinyl-sided split- or bi-levels, and twenty-first-century cement brick two storeys. No malls or box stores: only houses and a convenience store, a gas station, a Tim Hortons, a hardware store. At the only stoplight, County Road 26 intersects 24, 59, and Maria Street. Beyond the light, residential streets cross CR 26, but one or two blocks down the houses give way again to corn and soybean fields.

Dialogue brings people to life

In the cramped waiting room of Xiaolan Zhao's Toronto clinic, boxes of herbs vie for space with stacks of old-fashioned file folders. Nothing is high-tech here. Patients sit on mismatched, straight-backed chairs waiting for acupuncture or massage. . . . After a brief consultation with Xiaolan . . . she had a close look at my puffy kneecap. "Have you ever had acupuncture?" she asked. "No, but one of my horses did," I said. "Ahh, you take better care of your animals than you do yourself." Bingo. In one treatment, my knee was better. "One hundred per cent!" I enthused. "No," Xiaolan said patiently, "80 percent."

—Barbara Righton, *Maclean's*

Humour rewards readers and can make points memorable

Large, naked, raw carrots are acceptable as food only to those who live in hutches eagerly awaiting Easter.

Inhabitants of underdeveloped nations and victims of natural disasters are the only people who have ever been happy to see soybeans.

—Fran Lebowitz, *Metropolitan Life*

Interest in Visual Texts

Interest in visual texts is created by composition and subject matter. Some subjects possess inherent interest, but the photographer or artist must build on that interest. Kittens and puppies are cute, but viewers' interest fades quickly if the images are predictable.

Even potentially interesting subjects can be rendered boring if they are photographed in stereotypical ways.

Children often express a spontaneity lacking in adults, which provides visual interest.

Lines

Lines create interest in photographs. Strong diagonal lines can create dynamic photographs. Curved lines can produce graceful images.

 16b Know Where Images and Graphics Work Best

"A picture is worth a thousand words" is an old cliché. It's not that images are necessarily more powerful than words but that images and words are different media. Our eyes and brains are able to take in a great deal of visual information and sort that information for relevance.

Visuals are typically used in combination with text. Visuals work well when they

- deliver spatial information, especially through maps, floor plans, and other graphic representations of space;
- represent statistical relationships;
- produce a strong immediate impact, even shock value; and
- emphasize further a main point you've made in words.

16c Know Where Words Work Best

Words can do many things that images cannot. Written words work best when they

- communicate abstract ideas,
- report information,
- persuade using elaborated reasoning,
- communicate online using minimal bandwidth, and
- adapt to specific users' needs. (Computers can convert words from spoken to written language for those who are hearing impaired, or from written to spoken for those who are visually impaired.)

17 Compose Images

QUICK*TAKE*

- Compose images purposefully (see below)
- Edit images for impact (see p. 182)
- Create tables and charts to emphasize ideas (see p. 184)

17a Compose Images Purposefully

Format images for the medium you are using

Images that you want to print need to be of higher quality than those intended for the web or the screen. Pay attention to the settings on your camera or scanner.

> **STAYING ON TRACK**
>
> **Scanning and the law**
>
> Images in books and magazines published in the last 75 years are almost always owned by someone. If you copy an image for redistribution of any kind, including putting it on a website, you must find out who holds the copyright and obtain permission to use the image. Always give credit for any image that you copy, even if it is in the public domain.

Digital cameras frequently make images with 72 dpi (dots per inch), which is the maximum you can display on the screen. Most printers use a resolution from 300 to 600 dpi. Use the high-quality setting on your camera for images you intend to print.

Scanners typically offer a range of resolution from 72 to 1600 dpi. The higher the number, the finer the image, but the file size becomes larger. Images on the web or a screen display at 72 dpi, so higher resolutions do not improve the quality but do make the images slow to load.

Take pictures that aren't boring

No matter how easy it is now to take photographs, the great majority of pictures look alike. Why? It's because most people hold their cameras at eye level and put the subject in the centre. Figures 17.1 to 17.4 provide tips on taking interesting photographs.

Learn what your camera can do

Many digital cameras have special features, such as the macro setting that captures much more detail than the standard setting when photographing at close range. Read the manual that came with your camera, and try the different settings.

Fill the frame

Most people include too much in their photographs. Decide what is essential and concentrate on getting those elements in the frame.

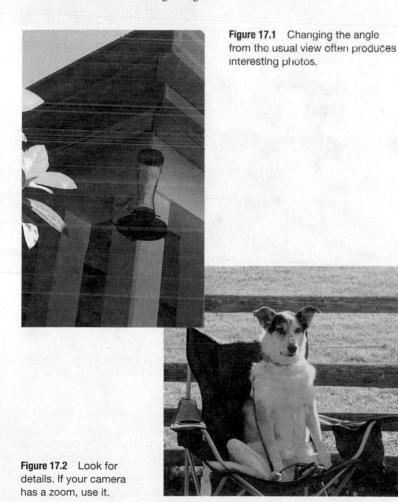

Figure 17.1 Changing the angle from the usual view often produces interesting photos.

Figure 17.2 Look for details. If your camera has a zoom, use it.

Figure 17.3 The macro setting on a camera (usually a flower symbol) allows you to take finely detailed photos from several centimetres away.

Figure 17.4 Usually the closer you can get to your subject, the better.

17b Edit Images

No matter which image editor you use, there are a few manipulations that you will need to use frequently. It's always a good idea to copy an image first and work on the copy.

- **Cropping.** Most images can be trimmed to improve visual focus and file size. To crop an image, select the rectangle tool, draw the rectangle over the area you want to keep, and select the *Crop* or *Trim* command (see Figure 17.5). The part of the image outside the rectangle will be discarded. Every pixel you can squeeze out of an image intended for use on the web makes the image display faster on a user's screen.

Figure 17.5 Cropping often improves the image by emphasizing details. Smaller images use less memory and thus are able to load faster on the screen.

- **Rotating images.** Often you'll find that you held your camera at a slight angle when taking pictures, especially if your subjects were moving. You can make small adjustments by using the *Rotate Image* command. You can also rotate images 90 degrees to give them a vertical orientation.
- **Sizing images.** All photo editing programs will tell you the height and width of an image. You can resize images to fit in a particular area of a web page or printed page. You can also change the resolution in the dpi window. Remember that if the image is intended for the web, 72 dpi is the maximum the screen will display. Higher resolution images look no better and are slower to load.
- **Adjusting colours.** Often the colours in photographs that you scan appear "off" when you view the image on a computer monitor. The image may appear too dark or lack contrast. Sometimes the colour balance appears off and you want to correct it. The basic controls for brightness, contrast, and colour saturation are similar to those on your colour television. Be aware that colours look different on different monitors and that what you print may not show the colours you saw on your screen.

WRITING SMART

Save a copy of an image before editing it

Always keep a copy of your original scan or digital photo. Once you change an image and save it, you cannot restore what you changed. Use the *Save As* command to save a copy before you start editing an image.

17c Create Tables, Charts, and Graphs

Tables, charts, and graphs are easy to create in word processing programs, spreadsheet applications, presentation software, and web-page editors, and they can be imported from one program (e.g., Excel) to another (e.g., Word). While software does much of the formatting of tables, charts, and graphs, you still have to supply the labels for the different parts of the graphic and an accurate title or caption.

Like any graphic, tables, charts, and graphs can be used to mislead readers. Small differences can be exaggerated, for example, or relevant differences concealed (see Section 5f). You have an ethical responsibility to create accurate tables, charts, and graphs.

STAYING ON TRACK

Use and evaluate tables

When to use tables

- To present a summary of several factors
- To present exact numbers
- To give an orderly arrangement so that readers can locate and compare information

Evaluating tables

- Does the table have a clear purpose?
- Does the title indicate the purpose?
- What units do the numbers represent (dollars, people, voters, percentages, and so on)?
- What is the source of the data?
- Is the table clearly organized?
- Is the table clearly labelled?

Name of item	Factor 1	Factor 2	Factor 3
AAA	000	00	0
BBB	00	0	000
CCC	0	000	00

Tables

Extensive statistical data can be dull or cumbersome to communicate in sentences and paragraphs. Readers can more quickly and easily grasp data when they are displayed in a table. A table allows readers to view an entire set of data at once or to focus only on relevant aspects (see Table 17.1).

Table 17.1 Average Earnings by Highest Level of Schooling in Atlantic Provinces, Age 15 and Older, 2001

	Canada	N.L.	P.E.I.	N.S.	N.B.
			$		
All levels	**31 757**	**24 165**	**22 303**	**26 632**	**24 971**
Less than high school graduation certificate	21 230	15 922	15 058	18 251	17 074
High school graduation certificate and/or some postsecondary	25 477	16 860	18 236	20 553	20 395
Trades certificate or diploma	32 743	26 118	24 090	27 595	27 694
College certificate or diploma	32 736	28 196	25 613	26 930	27 178
University certificate diploma or degree	48 648	41 942	37 063	41 146	40 375

Source: Statistics Canada, *Average Earnings of the Population 15 Years and Over by Highest Level of Schooling, by Province and Territory (2001 Census),* 1 Sept. 2004, Web, 15 June 2006.

Bar charts

Bar charts are useful for comparing data. Multiple bars can be combined, as shown in Figure 17.6, to emphasize comparison—in this case between the numbers of men and women employed in different fields.

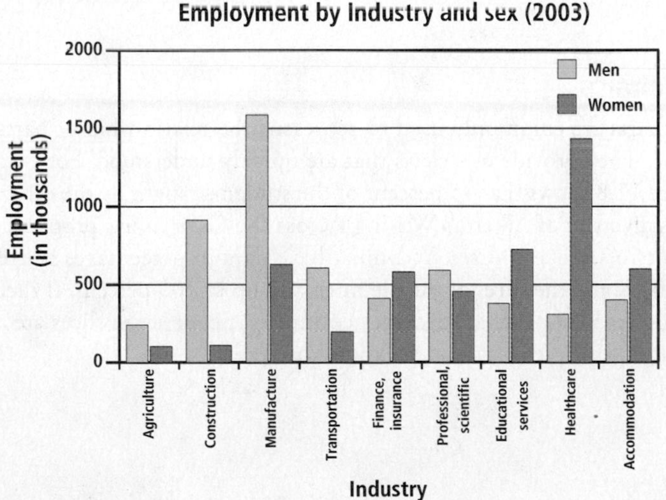

Figure 17.6 Bar charts are useful for comparing data.

Source: Statistics Canada, *Employment by Industry and Sex,* 5 Jan. 2006, Web, 5 Jan. 2006.

Line graphs

Line graphs are well suited for displaying changes in data across time. Line graphs can have one line, or two or more sets of data can be displayed on different lines, emphasizing the comparative rates of change (see Figure 17.7).

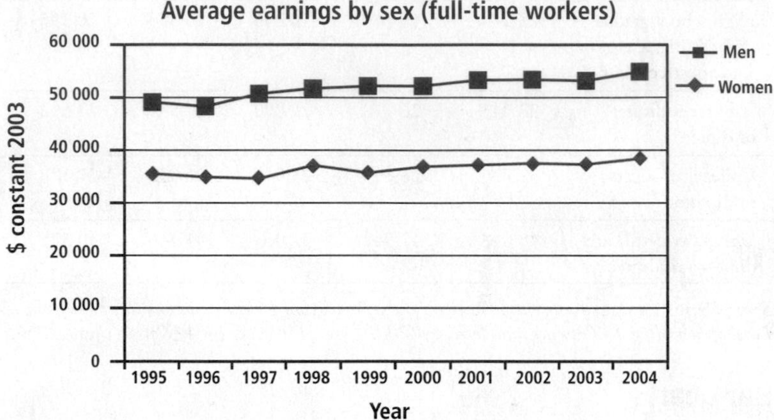

Figure 17.7 Line graphs are useful for displaying data across time.
Source: Statistics Canada, *Average Earnings by Sex and Work Pattern (Full Time Workers)*, 28 Mar. 2006, Web, 5 Apr. 2006.

Pie charts

Pie charts are commonly used to represent the relationship of parts to a whole. They provide overviews that are quickly understood. For example, Figure 17.8 shows that 85 percent of the students taught by the director of the University of Alberta's Writing Across the Curriculum program came from two science courses. You must have data in percentages to create a pie chart, and the slices of the pie must add up to 100 percent. If the slices are too small, a pie chart becomes confusing. Six or seven slices are about the limit for a pie chart that is easy to interpret.

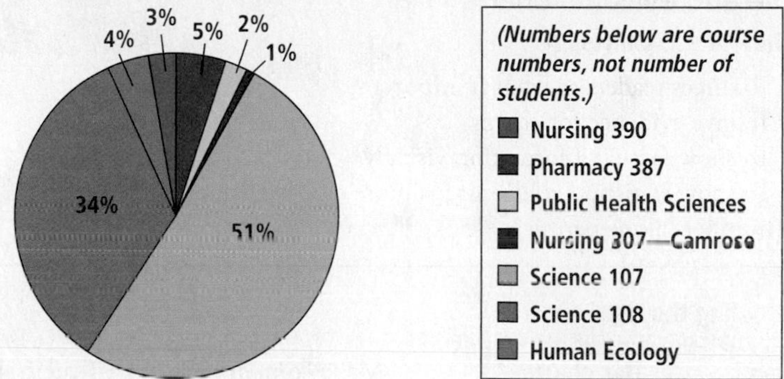

Figure 17.8 Pie charts display the relationship of parts to a whole.

Source: Roger Graves, Writing Across the Curriculum Program, University of Alberta, 2010, Web, 15 Nov. 2011.

Organizational charts and flow charts

Presentation software and the drawing module in word processing programs allow you to create organizational charts and flow charts. You can make organizational and flow charts by selecting shapes and arrows on the drawing module and by inserting them. Select the text tool for typing labels on the shapes (see Figure 17.9).

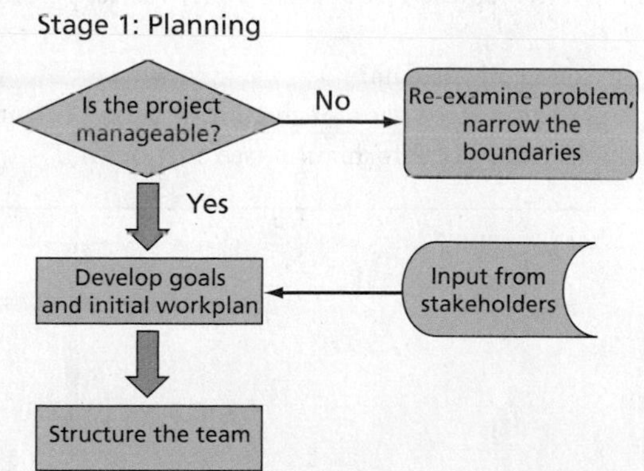

Figure 17.9 Flow charts are useful for representing steps in a process.

STAYING ON TRACK

Use and evaluate charts

When to use charts

- To direct readers to what is important
- To give evidence for claims
- To show factual information visually
- To show statistical relationships more clearly than either words or numbers alone permit

Selecting the right chart

	Bar charts	Make comparisons in particular categories
	Line graphs	Show proportional trends over time
	Pie charts	Show the proportion of parts in terms of the whole
	Flow charts	Show the steps in a process

Evaluating charts

- Does the chart have a clear purpose?
- Does the title indicate the purpose?
- What do the units represent (dollars, people, voters, percentages, and so on)?
- What is the source of the data?
- Is the type of chart appropriate for the information presented?
- Is there any distortion of information (see Section 5f)?

18 Design Presentations

QUICK*TAKE*

- Plan your presentations carefully (see below)
- Create visuals that communicate (see p. 191)
- Practise your presentations to maximize impact (see p. 193)

18a Plan a Presentation

The key to success is remembering that your purpose is to communicate effectively. Look closely at what you are being asked to present and how long you will have. Decide early on what kind of presentation you will give and what visuals you will incorporate. If you want to use visual elements, make sure the presentation room has the equipment you need.

If your presentation requires research, you will need to document the sources of your information just as you would for a research paper (see Chapters 19–22 on planning and conducting research). Provide your audience with those sources either in your talk or in a handout.

Organize your presentation

After you have done your research and analyzed your audience, it's time to organize your presentation.

- **Make a list of key points.** Think about the best order for your major points. If you use visuals, they should indicate your major points.
- **Plan your introduction.** Your success depends on your introduction. You must gain the attention of your audience, introduce your topic, indicate why it's important, and give a sense of where you are headed. It's a tall order, but if you don't engage your audience in the first two minutes, you will lose them.
- **Plan your conclusion.** You want to end on a strong note. Stopping abruptly or rambling on only to tail off leaves your audience with a bad impression. Give your audience something to take away, a compelling example or an idea that captures the gist of your presentation.

Support your presentation

When you have organized your main points, you need to decide how to support those points. Look at your research notes and think about how best to incorporate the information you found. Consider a strategy based on one or more of these elements:

- **Facts.** Speakers who know their facts build credibility.
- **Statistics.** Effective use of statistics can give the audience the impression that you have done your homework. Statistics can also indicate that a particular example is representative.
- **Statements by authorities.** Quotations from credible experts can support key points.
- **Narratives.** Narratives are brief stories that illustrate key points. Narratives can hold the attention of the audience—but keep them short or they will become a distraction.
- **Humour.** Humour is one of the best ways to convince an audience to share your point of view. You have to know the audience well, however, to predict with confidence what they will think is funny.

Organize a group presentation

Changing speakers is a distraction for the audience in a group presentation. For the group presentation to succeed, each speaker must have a clear role and the transition from one speaker to the next should be smooth.

- **Determine the roles and the goals.** Each member of the group must understand his or her role in the presentation and the goal of that segment. For example, the first speaker may serve as the host and provide transitions from one speaker to the next.
- **Coordinate research.** Each speaker should be well informed on the subtopic he or she is to present. The audience will expect answers to in-depth questions.
- **Coordinate visuals.** An advantage of group presentation is that a person not speaking can handle the visuals, allowing the speaker to focus on the delivery. This advantage is gained by practising in advance.
- **Rehearse.** Groups that try to make a presentation on the fly rarely succeed. Timing is critical. Pausing to read notes is a sure way to lose the audience.

WRITING SMART

Home field advantage

Athletes know that the home field advantage involves much more than having the crowd behind them. Each field and court has its own special characteristics. In many cases small bits of knowledge acquired from playing on the field (such as a position from which the sun is blinding at a certain time of day) can mean the difference between winning and losing. Visiting teams practise on the opponent's field or court before the game to learn as much as possible.

In post-secondary institutions many or all presentations will be in your classroom, which can give you your own home field advantage. You'll know whether the acoustics are good, whether it is easy to see visuals from everywhere in the room, and so on. In the workplace, you may be required to give presentations in unfamiliar places such as a client's site. You will have to work a little harder to ensure success.

Practise your presentation in the room where you will deliver it. Bring a friend who can tell you whether you can be heard in the back of the room and whether your visuals can be read at that distance. Make sure any equipment you need is working.

Have a backup plan for visuals. If your presentation depends on a projector, think about what you will do if it unexpectedly stops working and you suddenly cannot use the visuals you brought. For example, you can write a few main points on a whiteboard or flipchart if necessary.

Remember that the audience is with you. Most people are patient when something goes wrong. They have been in similar situations themselves. If, for example, a projector bulb burns out and another one is available, ask the audience to give you a minute or two.

18b Design Visuals for a Presentation

Visuals focus the attention of the audience and can keep your audience oriented throughout your presentation while providing you with memory aids. Charts, pictures, and diagrams can help you emphasize major points and provide information that would be tedious to describe verbally.

Current Crosswalks
Incidents Reported
• May 2012–September 2012
Auto-bike collision: 2
Auto-pedestrian collision: 14
Auto-motorcycle collision: 1
Aggravated assault with a motor vehicle: 11
Pedestrian crossing illegally: 7

■ Effective presentations explain ideas and problems with both words and images. These slides show and tell why temporary crosswalks on a busy street are inadequate.

Visuals also give your audience something to look at besides you, which helps you relax. At a minimum, consider putting an outline of your talk on an overhead transparency or a slide. Visuals take time to prepare, so start planning them early.

Guidelines for creating and using visuals effectively

Visuals can make or break a presentation. Poor-quality visuals destroy your credibility.

- **Keep the text short.** In general, put no more than six words on a line and have no more than six lines on a single slide.
- **Always proofread.** Typos and misspelled words make you appear careless and can distract the audience from your point.
- **Use a readable type size (at least 18-point type).** You have probably been in the audience for a presentation where the type size was too small to read. And you probably found it annoying.
- **Use dark text on a white or light-coloured background.** Light text on a dark background is often hard to read.

- **Focus on one element per slide.** Outlines, charts, photographs, and maps are all easy to create.
- **Keep the design simple.** Use a consistent style and colour scheme.
- **Plan your timing when using visuals.** Usually you can leave a slide on the screen for one to two minutes, which allows your audience time to read the slide and connect it to what you are saying.

STAYING ON TRACK

Present ideas—not fluff

The major drawback of presentation software is perhaps that it is too easy to use. An attractive presentation can be empty of content. Remember that your goal is to communicate information and ideas, not to dazzle your audience with special effects. Presentations heavy on special effects often come off as heavy on style and light on substance.

18c Deliver an Effective Presentation

Team Guidelines

From "me" to "we"

Agree on team roles and behaviour

- Discuss how the team will choose a leader
- Determine roles
- Recognize the importance of communication
- Agree on what is acceptable team behaviour

Nervousness

Nervousness is usually invisible. If you make a mistake, remember that your audience will understand. Stage fright is normal, and often you can draw on that energy to make a more forceful presentation. Take a deep breath before you begin, and smile.

Practice

There is no substitute for rehearsing your speech several times.

- You will become more confident.
- You will be able to focus more on your audience and on maintaining eye contact.
- You will be more comfortable using your visuals.
- You will know how long your presentation will take.

Effective techniques

- Practise in advance.
- Talk, don't read.
- Stand, don't sit.
- Make eye contact.
- Signal main points with gestures.
- Speak loudly and not too quickly.
- Use effective visuals.
- Focus on main points.
- Give an overview in the introduction.
- Give a conclusion that ends with a key idea or example.
- Believe in what you say; enthusiasm is contagious.
- Finish on time.

STAYING ON TRACK

Avoid death by PowerPoint

PowerPoint and similar slideware programs have become prevalent in businesses, organizations, and post-secondary institutions alike, yet there are many critics of PowerPoint culture. And it's no mystery why. Think about all the bad presentations you have sat through. Write down what you don't like. Your list may look like the following:

What I don't like about PowerPoint presentations
Data-dump presentations—too much information
Too much text on the slides, making it hard to read it all
Text too small to read
One bulleted point after another
Cutesy clip art and distracting transitions
Presenter reading word for word off the slides

STAYING ON TRACK *(Continued)*

The basic problem is that presenters don't acknowledge the difference between an oral presentation and a written document. PowerPoint, Apple Keynote, and other slideware were designed to support presentations with graphics, not to be the focus of the presentation. Why should an audience take the time to come to a presentation when they are asked to read the slides? Your audience expects to be informed and motivated by you.

PART 5 Planning Research and Finding Sources

You **can learn more and do more** with MyWritingLab and with the eText version of *The Brief Penguin Handbook*. For help with planning your research project and finding and evaluating your sources successfully, click on "Resources," then select "Research." Review the tutorials (Read, Watch, Listen) within each topic, then complete the Exercises and click on the Gradebook to measure your progress.

Research Map 1: Conducting Research

Post-secondary research writing requires that you

- determine your goals,
- find a topic,
- ask a question about that topic,
- find out what has been written about that topic,
- evaluate what has been written about that topic, and
- make a contribution to the discussion about that topic.

Here are the steps in planning research and finding sources.

1 | Plan the research project

First, analyze what you are being asked to do and set a schedule; go to Sections 19a and 19b.

Ask a question about a topic that interests you and narrow that topic. Go to 19c.

Determine what kinds of research you will need; go to 19d.

Conduct field research if it is appropriate for your project. See strategies for

- **CONDUCTING INTERVIEWS**; go to 22b.
- **ADMINISTERING SURVEYS**; go to 22c.
- **MAKING OBSERVATIONS**; go to 22d.

2 | Draft a working thesis

Draft a working thesis. Go to 19e.

Create a working bibliography. Go to 19f.

If you are asked to create an annotated bibliography, go to 19g.

You'll see in Parts 5 and 6 the process Joshua LaGrange used to produce his research project.

See Research Map 2 (page 251) for guidance on incorporating and documenting sources.

3 Find and track sources

Consult with a research librarian if possible, and determine where and how to start looking.

Find sources online and in print:

- for sources in **DATABASES**, go to 20b.
- for sources on the **WEB**, go to 20c.
- for **VISUAL** sources, go to 20d.
- for **PRINT** sources, go to 20e.

Keep track of sources. Go to 20f.

4 Evaluate sources

Decide which sources are going to be useful for your project. For each source you'll need to determine the

- **RELEVANCE** to your research question; go to 21a.
- **QUALITY** for your purposes; go to 21b.

Evaluate the different types of sources you are using:

- **DATABASE and PRINT SOURCES**; go to 21c.
- **WEB SOURCES**; go to 21d.

19 Plan Your Research

QUICK*TAKE*

- Analyze the assignment first (see below)
- Find and narrow a topic (see p. 201)
- Draft a working thesis (see p. 204)

19a Analyze the Research Task

Research is a creative process, which is another way of saying it is a messy process. Even though the process is complex, your results will improve if you keep the big picture in mind while you are immersed in research. If you have an assignment that requires research, look closely at what you are being asked to do.

Look for keywords

Often the assignment will tell you what is expected.

- An *analysis* or *examination* asks you to look at an issue in detail, explaining its history, the people and places affected, and what is at stake.
- A *review of scholarship* requires you to summarize what key scholars and researchers have written about the issue.
- An *evaluation* requires you to make critical judgments.
- An *argument* requires you to assemble evidence in support of a claim you make.

Identify your potential readers

- What are readers likely to know about your subject?
- What background information will you need to supply?
- What is your purpose in writing?
- If readers disagree with you, how might you convince them?

Assess the project's length, scope, and requirements

- What kind of research are you being asked to do?
- What is the length of the project?
- What kinds and number of sources or field research is required?
- Which documentation style—such as MLA (see Chapter 26) or APA (see Chapter 27)—is required?

Writer at Work

Joshua LaGrange made notes on his assignment sheet.

WRS 103: Writing for Undergraduate Students in Science Research Report (Objective Argument)

Choose a science-based topic that interests you and for which you can find scientific evidence to support at least two sides of a controversy about that topic (e.g., Have researchers found enough evidence of materials on Mars to conclude that the planet at one time sustained life?). Examine the existing evidence (find at least four different sources) and decide which side of the controversy makes sense to you, given your research findings.

Argue one side clearly

Review the evidence for both sides of the controversy and use that evidence to show how it supports one side of the story better than the other. In other words, write a position argument on how you see the evidence fitting together to show that one side of the controversy seems a better explanation for the data than the opposing viewpoint. Argue your position using the structure used in science disciplines. That is, show readers the case in favour of one explanation over the other so that readers can follow your thinking and arrive at a conclusion similar to the one you reached about this topic.

Purpose: Your purpose in writing this paper is to practise thinking and writing like a scientist. Assemble the evidence, decide on the best explanation for the evidence, and then write a report in which you explain it to readers so that they will understand the case and accept your explanation. Your goal is to use the objective style of argument followed in science disciplines to make this case for readers (see Section 11b).

Audience: Write for other science students and professors who are interested in scientific controversies but unfamiliar with the details of your particular topic. Assume that they have the background to understand the technical aspects but lack the particular background on your topic.

Length: 750–1000 words, excluding references

3 or 4 pages + references

Genre: Research report. See Section 27g for how to format a research report in APA style. Format your research report according to APA style guidelines. Use CSE style for your references (see Chapter 29).

Include at least four credible sources (two for each side of the controversy). Use scientific style to argue your position.

Due Dates:
Oct. 18: Hand in a paragraph outlining your topic.
Oct. 22: Hand in a critical summary of two of the sources that you will use in this paper.
Nov. 1: Bring an electronic draft of assignment 3 to class for in-class peer review.
Nov. 8: Final draft due of assignment 3 (include your first draft, plus the workshop comments).

One week to revise

19b Set a Schedule

Writer at Work

Joshua used the assignment to create a work schedule.

TASK	DATE
Find topic and locate credible research sources	Oct. 16
Start a working bibliography	Oct. 16–22
Hand in paragraph outlining my topic	Oct. 18
Read and evaluate sources and write critical summaries/annotations	Oct. 17–22
Hand in critical summaries/annotations	Oct. 22
Plan organization of report, write a draft	Oct. 22-30
Review and revise draft	Oct. 31
Bring electronic copy of draft to class	Nov. 1
Revise, edit, and check formatting and documentation	Nov. 1–7
Submit final draft	Nov. 8

19c Find a Topic

If you ask meaningful questions, research will be enjoyable. Your courses may give you ideas about questions to ask, or you may simply want to pursue an interest of your own. One good way to begin is by browsing, either in your library or on the web.

You might begin browsing by doing one or more of the following:

- **Visit "Research by Subject" on your library's website.** Clicking on a subject such as "African and African Canadian Studies" will take you to a list of online resources. Often you can find an email link to a reference librarian who can assist you.
- **Look for topics in your courses.** Browse your course notes and readings. Are there any topics you might want to explore in greater depth?
- **Browse a web subject directory.** Web subject directories, including Yahoo! Directory (dir.yahoo.com), are useful when you want to narrow a topic or learn what subcategories a topic might contain. In addition to the web subject directories, the Library of Congress Virtual Reference Shelf (www.loc.gov/rr/askalib/virtualref.html) may help you identify sites relevant to your topic.
- **Consult a specialized encyclopedia.** Specialized encyclopedias focus on a single area of knowledge, go into more depth about a subject, and often include bibliographies. Check if your library database page has a link to the Gale Virtual Reference Library, which offers entries from many specialized encyclopedias and reference sources.
- **Look for topics as you read.** When you read actively, you ask questions and respond to ideas in the text. Review what you wrote in the margins or the notes you have made about something you read that interested you. You may find a potential topic.

Writer at Work

Joshua did a quick search on the internet using "scientific controversy" as his search title and quickly located a number of possible topics. He evaluated these topics' benefits and obstacles to determine which one might best fit the assignment requirements.

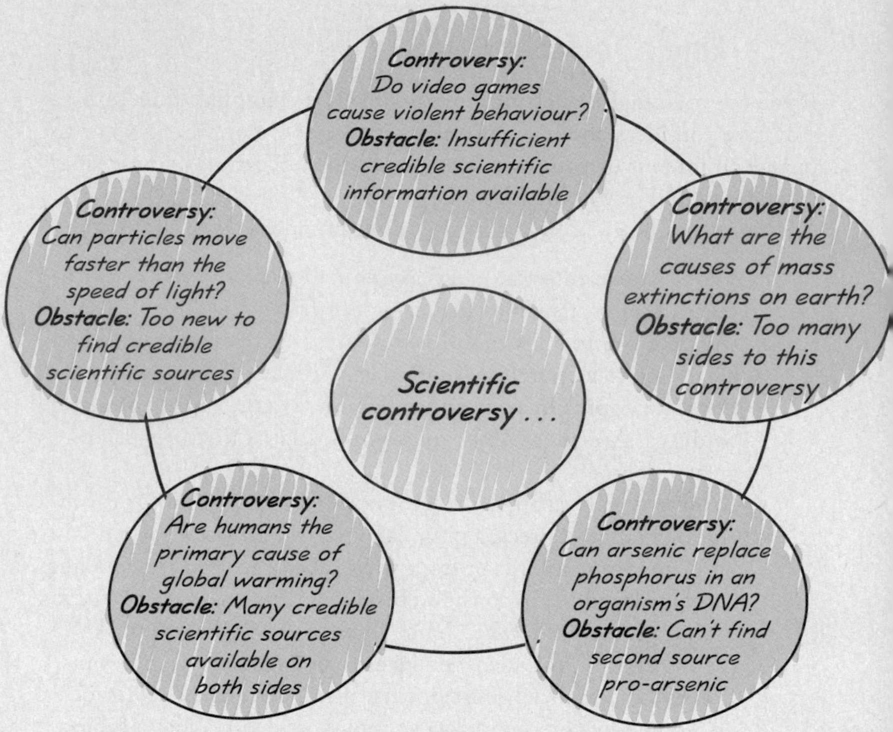

Scientific controversy . . .

Controversy: Do video games cause violent behaviour? **Obstacle:** Insufficient credible scientific information available

Controversy: What are the causes of mass extinctions on earth? **Obstacle:** Too many sides to this controversy

Controversy: Can arsenic replace phosphorus in an organism's DNA? **Obstacle:** Can't find second source pro-arsenic

Controversy: Are humans the primary cause of global warming? **Obstacle:** Many credible scientific sources available on both sides

Controversy: Can particles move faster than the speed of light? **Obstacle:** Too new to find credible scientific sources

Two possibilities looked promising—examining the causes of mass extinctions (such as the dinosaurs') on earth and evaluating humans as the primary cause of global warming. Joshua decided to choose global warming because there was lots of research published on this topic.

STAYING ON TRACK

Decide if a topic is manageable

It can be tricky to find a balance between what you want to say about a topic and the amount of space you have to say it in. Usually your instructor will suggest a length for your project, which should help you decide how to limit your topic. If you suspect your topic is becoming unmanageable and your project may be too long, look for ways to narrow your focus.

Off track A 5-page paper on European witch hunts

On track A 5-page paper tracing two or three major causes of the European witch hunts of the fifteenth and sixteenth centuries

Off track A 10-page paper on accounting fraud

On track A 10-page paper examining how a new law would help prevent corporate accounting fraud

19d Determine What Kind of Research You Need

When you begin your research, you will have to make a few educated guesses about where to look. Ask these questions before you start.

- How much information do you need? The assignment may specify the number of sources you should consult.
- Are particular types of sources required? If so, do you understand why those sources are required?
- How current should the information be? Some assignments require you to use the most up-to-date information you can locate.
- Do you need to consider point of view? Argument assignments sometimes require you to consider opposing viewpoints on an issue.

Secondary research

Most people who do research rely partly or exclusively on the work of others as sources of information. Research based on the work of others is called *secondary research*. In the past this information was contained almost exclusively in collections of print materials housed in libraries, but today enormous amounts of information are available on the internet and in various recorded media. Chapters 20 and 21 explain in detail how to find and evaluate database, web, and print sources.

Primary research

Much of the research done at a university creates new information through *primary research:* experiments, data-gathering surveys and interviews, detailed observations, and the examination of historical documents. If you are researching a campus issue such as the problem of inadequate parking for students, you may need to conduct interviews, make observations, and take a survey. Or, if you are training in a field where primary research is important, you may be required to conduct research in order to learn research methods. Chapter 22 explains how to plan and conduct three types of field research: interviews (22b), surveys (22c), and observations (22d).

 Draft a Working Thesis

If you ask a focused and interesting research question, your answer will be your *working thesis.* This working thesis will be the focus of the remainder of your research and ultimately your research project.

Ask questions about your topic

When you have a topic that is interesting to you, manageable in scope, and possible to research using sources or doing field research, then your next task is to ask researchable questions.

Explore a definition

- While many (most) people think X is a Y, can X be better thought of as a Z?

  While many people think a tanning bed will increase their vitamin D levels, most tanning beds produce only UVA rays that cause skin to change colour but do not stimulate vitamin D production.

Evaluate a person, activity, or thing

- Can you argue that a person, activity, or thing is either good, better, or best (or bad, worse, or worst) within its class?

  Fender Stratocasters from the 1950s remain the best electric guitars ever made because of their versatility, sound quality, and player-friendly features.

Compare or contrast

- Can you think of items, events, or situations that are similar or dissimilar to the one you are writing about?

Television viewing in Great Britain is not plagued by frequent commercials because television programming is financed through a flat-rate fee rather than through advertising.

Examine why something happened

- Can you argue that while there were obvious causes of Y, Y would not have occurred had it not been for X?

  Rising atmospheric temperatures and an increasing number of fires in Canadian forests may be due to increased carbon levels in the atmosphere that trigger a "positive feedback loop." That is, as more carbon enters the atmosphere (from forest fires and pollution), conditions evolve that promote more fires.

- Can you argue for an alternative cause rather than the one many people assume?

  The defeat of the Confederate Army at the Battle of Gettysburg in July 1863 is often cited as the turning point in the Civil War, but in fact the South was running out of food, equipment, and soldiers, and it lost its only real chance of winning when Great Britain failed to intervene on its side.

Counter objections to a position

- Can the reverse or opposite of an opposing claim be argued?

  New medications that relieve pain are welcomed by runners and other athletes, but these drugs can mask signals that their bodies send, increasing the risk of serious injury.

Argue why something matters

- Can you challenge commonly held attitudes to show why something that many people haven't considered actually matters a great deal?

  Although most people think of wind- and solar-generated electricity as the main alternatives to coal, oil, and gas, increasing nuclear-generated power and reducing electricity consumption are alternatives that have the potential to reduce greenhouse gas emissions.

Turn your answers into a working thesis

Topic	Reading disorders
Researchable question	Why do some people learn to read top-to-bottom Chinese characters more easily than left-to-right alphabetic writing?
Working thesis	The direction of text flow may be an important factor in how an individual learns to read.

Writer at Work

Joshua's working thesis answered (and complicated) his research question.

TOPIC	*What is the primary cause of global warming? There are two sides: one contends that human activities are warming the atmosphere (and discredits critics as having interests in the oil and gas industry), and the other side argues that human activities are not a significant factor (and discredits critics as trying to be politically correct).*
RESEARCHABLE QUESTION	*What is the major scientific evidence offered to support each side of the controversy over the cause of global warming?*
WORKING THESIS	*Until we determine how human carbon dioxide emissions affect the feedback mechanisms that regulate carbon dioxide concentrations in the earth's atmosphere, we cannot clearly determine causation.*

19f Create a Working Bibliography

When you begin to collect your sources, make sure you get full bibliographic information for everything you might want to use in your project: articles, books, websites, and other materials. Decide which documentation style you will use. If your instructor does not tell you which style is appropriate, ask. (The major documentation styles—MLA, APA, CMS, CSE, and IEEE—are dealt with in detail in Chapters 26–30.)

Find the necessary bibliographic information

Chapter 20 gives instructions on what information you will need to collect for each kind of source. In general, as you research and develop a working bibliography, you should write down more information rather than less. You can always delete unnecessary information when it comes time to format your citations according to your chosen documentation style (APA, MLA, CMS, CSE, or IEEE), but it is time-consuming to go back to sources to find missing bibliographic information.

Record bibliographic information

There are many ways to record and organize your sources. You can record each source's bibliographic information on individual notecards; you can print out or photocopy relevant pages from each source; you can email articles to yourself from library databases; and you may be able to use your library's bibliographic software to manage citations (e.g., Endnote or RefWorks). Whichever way you choose, always check that you have complete and accurate publication information for each source.

If you want to quote text from these sources, be sure to use quotation marks around copied material to ensure you don't plagiarize unintentionally. Don't forget to record page numbers for quoted material if you will need it for your documentation style (e.g., MLA, APA, and CMS all use page numbers). Keep in mind that quotations build your credibility in some disciplines, but paraphrasing and summarizing are better in others.

Writer at Work

Joshua formatted the following citation using CSE style because he was writing a scientific report on the Spruce Grouse, a bird that he had photographed on a field trip to Jasper National Park. He paraphrases rather than quotes from the original source because in science disciplines direct quotations undercut (rather than build) the writer's credibility.

Beaudoin E, Schondube J. Spruce grouse: Canachites canadensis. University of Michigan [Internet]. 2002 [cited 2011 Sept 20]. Available from: http://www.biokids.umich.edu/critters/Canachites_canadensis

Male Spruce Grouses use their exaggerated characteristics to attract females. Males will mate with several females each season and do not help raise their young. Their mating procedure begins with facing the female, giving her a view of all their exaggerated characteristics: their breast feathers, eye combs, tail feathers, and mane-like feathers around the neck. They will also utilize strutting and aerial actions to impress the female. The male will then approach the female several times, each time squatting to the ground and stretching out his neck. Finally, when he is close enough, he will make a challenging noise and then mount the female from behind.

19g Create an Annotated Bibliography

A working bibliography is an alphabetized list of sources with complete publication information that a writer has used to research a specific topic. An *annotated bibliography* builds on the basic citations of a working bibliography by adding a brief summary or evaluation of each source. Annotated bibliographies must include

- a complete citation in the documentation style you are using (MLA, APA, CMS, CSE, IEEE), and
- a concise summary of the content and scope.

In addition, your instructor may ask you to include one or more of the following:

- A comment on the relevance of the source to your research topic
- An assessment of the background and qualifications of the author
- A comparison to another work on your list

Writer at Work

LaGrange 1

Joshua LaGrange

Professor Graves

WRS 103

September 30, 2011

Annotated Bibliography

Harris, T. Scientists respond to Gore's warnings of climate catastrophe. Canada Free Press [Internet]. 2006 [cited 2011 Sep 20]. Available from http://www.canadafreepress.com/2006/harris061206.htm

Tom Harris, in 2006, raises several objections to Al Gore's film *An Inconvenient Truth*. The article is from Canada Free Press, and so cannot be relied upon as a scientific article. Also, due to its journalistic nature, it lacks citations that can be verified. Harris attacks several points made by Gore, citing experts in various fields. The scientists mentioned contest that Antarctica is gaining mass, not losing it, and that the sea level is rising at perhaps only 0.03 mm/year due to the combined effects of melting and freezing in Antarctica and Greenland. Many areas in the earth are in fact cooling; the IPCC's models gave more weight to areas that are warming, but if they had weighted everything equally, they would not have found a great difference. Perhaps most importantly, 450 million

LaGrange 2

years ago the earth's climate was far colder, but CO_2 levels were ten times higher.

This article appears very convincing, but it admits to being one-sided. It does not accurately portray the scientific community, but only brings up arguments that the author felt were not emphasized enough in the media. A lot of these data do not contradict the idea of anthropogenic global warming anyway. While they may refute some of Gore's arguments, they only really show that things are not as dramatic as he said. As for the last argument, that 450 million years ago there was more CO_2 but the earth was much cooler, there could easily have been other factors then that are not present now; no one disagrees with carbon dioxide's heat-retaining properties.

The New Party. Inaccuracies in Al Gore's An inconvenient truth. The New Party [Internet]. 2009 [cited 2011 Sep 20]. Available from http://www.newparty.co.uk/articles/inaccuracies-gore.html

The New Party (a UK political party) website offers a factual page referencing a court case concerning Al Gore's film *An Inconvenient Truth*. It states that to show the film in class, UK teachers must inform students that it is a political film intended to show only one side of an argument and that there are

nine inaccuracies, as determined by a court expert. The court expert contested the following claims: (1) that the melting of glaciers on Mount Kilimanjaro is evidence of global warming; (2) that Hurricane Katrina, the drying of Lake Chad, the drowning of several polar bears, and coral reef bleaching could be attributed to global warming; (3) that sea levels will rise by seven metres or that Europe will lose the gulf stream; (4) that global warming caused sea levels to rise and necessitated the evacuation of some Pacific islands near New Zealand (in fact, this did not occur); and finally, (5) that the graph showing temperature and atmospheric CO_2 concentration over the last 600 000 years explains the cause of the temperature fluctuations with reference to CO_2 concentration. In this last case, the expert notes that CO_2 concentration lags behind temperature by 800–2000 years.

This article is reliable; however, it documents only a court case, not a widespread scientific consensus. It also only argues against some of Gore's evidence; it does not disprove his point.

20 Find Sources

Quick*Take*

- Find sources in library databases (see p. 215)
- Find sources on the web (see p. 220)
- Find multimedia sources (see p. 225)
- Keep track of sources (see p. 230)

 20a Develop Strategies for Finding Sources

Libraries still contain many resources not available on the web. Even more important, libraries have professional research librarians who can help you locate sources quickly.

Determine where to start looking

Searches using Google or Yahoo! turn up thousands of items, many of which are often not useful for research. Considering where to start is the first step.

Scholarly books and articles in scholarly journals are often the highest-quality sources, but the lag in publication time makes them less useful for very current topics. Newspapers cover current issues, but often not in the same depth found in books and scholarly journals. Government websites and publications are often the best for finding statistics and are also valuable for researching science and medicine.

Learn the art of effective keyword searches

Keyword searches take you to the sources you need. Start with your working thesis and generate a list of possible keywords for researching your thesis.

First, think of keywords that make your search *more specific*. For example, a search for sources related to youth voter participation might focus more specifically on young adults *and*

voter registration
historical participation rates
voter turnout

WRITING SMART

Find the right kinds of sources

Type of Source	Type of Information	How to Find Them
Scholarly books	Extensive and in-depth coverage of nearly any subject	Library catalogue
Scholarly journals	Reports of new knowledge and research findings by experts	Online library databases
Trade journals	Reports of information pertaining to specific industries, professions, and products	Online library databases
Popular magazines	Reports or summaries of current news, sports, fashion, and entertainment subjects	Online library databases
Newspapers	Recent and current information; foreign newspapers are useful for international perspectives	Online library databases
Government publications	Government-collected statistics, studies, and reports; especially good for science and medicine	Library catalogue and city, province/territory, and federal government websites
Videos, audios, documentaries, maps	Information varies widely	Library catalogue, web, and online library databases

Also think about *more general* ways to describe what you are doing—what synonyms can you think of for your existing terms? For example, instead of relying on "young adult," try keywords like

under 30
Generation Y
post-secondary students

You can even search using terms that refer to related people, events, or movements that you are familiar with:

women's suffrage
Aboriginal voters

Many databases have a thesaurus that can help you find more keywords.

WRITING SMART

Adjust searches to improve results

If your search turns up hundreds or thousands of hits, consider the following options:

- Try more specific search terms.
- Use a phrase within quotation marks or specify "the exact phrase."
- Specify NOT for terms you are not interested in finding.
- Limit your search by a date range.
- Limit the search by domain name (site:.edu, site:.gc.ca).

If your search turns up fewer than 10 hits, you could use these options.

- Check your spelling.
- Try broader search terms.
- Try another index or search engine.

Writer at Work

Joshua LaGrange wanted to assess the volume of publications on the causes of global warming, so he began with Web of Science, a science-based database. He first used "global warming" and "causes" as keywords, but this search produced over 2000 sources, most of which were off-topic. So he refined his search by limiting it to articles in meteorology and atmospheric sciences related to glaciation and sorted them by relevance rather than most recent, which resulted in 14 sources.

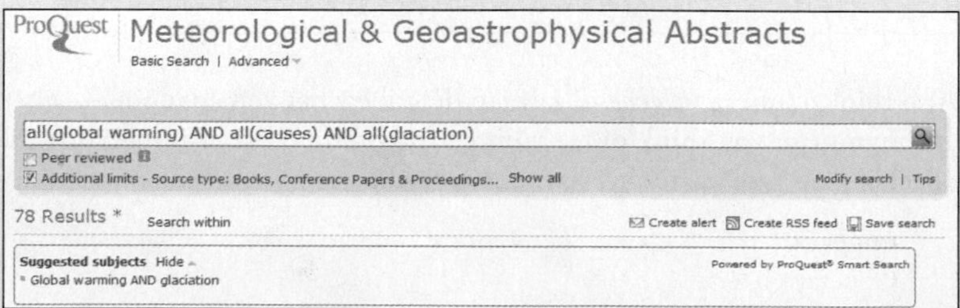

Find Sources in Databases

Sources found through library databases have already been filtered for you by professional librarians. They will include some common sources like popular magazines and newspapers, but the greatest value of database sources are the many journals, abstracts, studies, e-books, and other writing produced by specialists whose work has been scrutinized and commented upon by other experts. When you read a source from a library database, chances are you are hearing an informed voice in an important debate.

Locate databases

You can find databases on your library's website (see Figure 20.1 for an example). Sometimes you will find a list of databases. Sometimes you select a subject, and then you are directed to databases. Sometimes you select the name of a database vendor such as EBSCO or ProQuest. The vendor is the company that provides databases to the library.

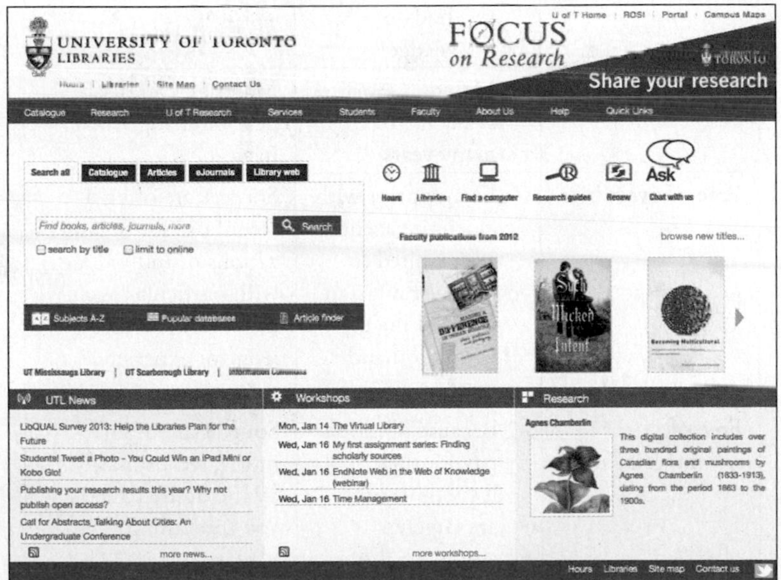

Figure 20.1 You can find a link to your library's database collection on the library's home page.

WRITING SMART

Know the advantages of database versus web sources

	Library database sources	Web sources
Speed	✓ Users can find information quickly	✓ Users can find information quickly
Accessibility	✓ Available 24/7	✓ Available 24/7
Organization	✓ Materials are organized for efficient search and retrieval	User must look in many different places for related information
Consistency and quality	✓ Librarians review and select resources	Anyone can claim to be an "expert," regardless of qualifications
Comprehensiveness	✓ Collected sources constitute a wide and representative body of knowledge	No guarantee that the full breadth of an issue will be represented
Permanence	✓ Materials remain available for many years	Materials can disappear or change in an instant
Free of overt bias	✓ Even sources with a definite agenda are required to meet certain standards of documentation and intellectual rigour	Sources are often a "soapbox" for organizations or individuals with particular agendas and little knowledge or experience
Free of commercial slant	✓ Because libraries pay for their collections, sources are largely commercial-free	Sources are often motivated primarily by the desire to sell you something

Use databases

Your library has a list of databases and indexes by subject. If you can't find this list on your library's website, ask a reference librarian for help. Follow these steps to find articles.

1. Select a database appropriate to your subject. (For example, if you are researching multiple sclerosis, you might start with Health Reference Center, MEDLINE, PsycINFO, or PubMed.)
2. Search the database using your list of keywords. (You could start with *multiple sclerosis* and then combine *MS* with other terms to narrow your search.)
3. Once you have chosen an article, print or email to yourself the complete citation for the article. Look for the email link after you click on the item you want.
4. Print or email to yourself the full text if it is available. The full text is better than cutting and pasting because you might lose track of which words are yours, leading to unintended plagiarism.
5. If the full text is not available, check the online library catalogue to see if your library has the journal.

Your library will probably have printed handouts or information on the web that tells you which database to use for a particular subject. Ask a librarian who works at the reference or information desk to help you.

If you wish to get only full-text articles, you can check that option. Full-text documents give you the same text you would find in print. In HTML versions, images are sometimes not reproduced and page numbers are not usually included. Get the PDF version if it is available, since articles in PDF format are scans of the printed text with page numbers.

Writer at Work

Joshua did a full-text search of "climate change" on Academic Search Complete.

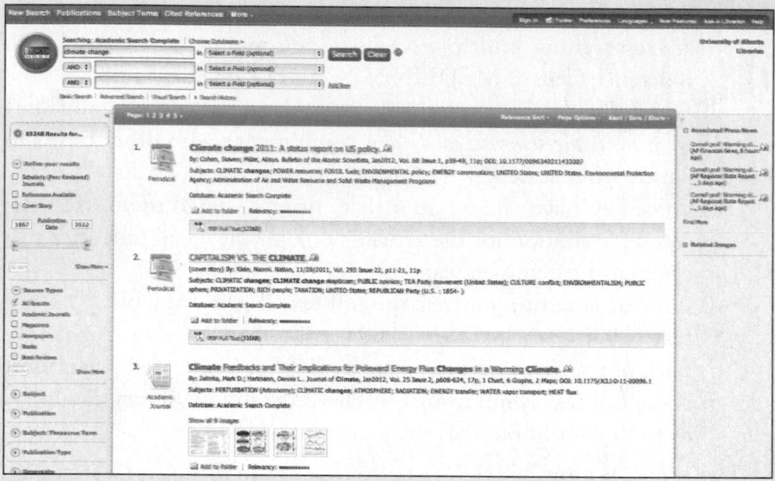

Common Databases

Academic OneFile (formerly Expanded Academic ASAP)	Indexes periodicals from the arts, humanities, sciences, social sciences, and general news, with full-text articles and images.
Academic Search Premier and Complete	Provides full-text articles for thousands of scholarly publications, including social sciences, humanities, education, computer sciences, engineering, language and linguistics, literature, medical sciences, and ethnic-studies journals.
ArticleFirst	Indexes journals in business, the humanities, medicine, science, and social sciences.
Business Search Premier	Provides full-text articles in all business disciplines.
EBSCOhost Research Databases	Gateway to a large collection of EBSCO databases, including Academic Search Premier and Complete, Business Source Premier and Complete, ERIC, and Medline.

Factiva	Provides full-text articles on business topics, including articles from the *Wall Street Journal.*
Google Books	Allows you to search within books and gives you snippets surrounding search terms for copyrighted books. Many books out of copyright have the full text. Available for everyone.
Google Scholar	Searches scholarly literature according to criteria of relevance. Available for everyone.
General OneFile	Contains millions of full-text articles about a wide range of academic and general-interest topics.
JSTOR	Provides scanned copies of scholarly journals.
LexisNexis Academic	Provides full text of a wide range of newspapers, magazines, government and legal documents, and company profiles from around the world.
ProQuest Databases	Like EBSCOhost, ProQuest is a gateway to a large collection of databases with over 100 billion pages, including the best archives of doctoral dissertations and historical newspapers.

WRITING SMART

Why database searches are often better than the first 10 hits on Google

If you did a Google search for *oil spill* in summer 2010, the first link on the list would have been www.BP.com/OilSpillNews, a site that issued BP press releases giving the company's spin on the oil spill. BP paid Google a large sum to have its site show up first. A search for *oil spill lawsuits* would have produced three law firms at the top of the list for the same reason—the law firms, looking for business, had paid to be first.

There's nothing wrong with Google making money through advertising, but the first hits on Google searches are often of limited value for research. Library databases are supported by subscriptions from libraries, not through advertising, and you don't have to wade through the commercial clutter.

20c Find Sources on the Web

Because anyone can publish on the web, there is no overall quality control and there is no system of organization—two strengths we take for granted in libraries. Nevertheless, the web offers you some resources for current topics that would be difficult or impossible to find in a library. The key to success is knowing where you are most likely to find current and accurate information about the particular question you are researching, and knowing how to access that information.

Use search engines wisely

Search engines designed for the web work in ways similar to library databases and your library's online catalogue, but with one major difference. While databases typically do some screening of the items they list, search engines potentially take you to everything on the web—millions of pages in all. Consequently, you have to work harder to limit searches on the web or you can be deluged with tens of thousands of items.

Kinds of search engines

A search engine is a set of programs that sort through millions of items at incredible speed. There are four basic kinds of search engines.

1. **Keyword search engines** (e.g., Bing, Google, Yahoo!). Keyword search engines give different results because they assign different weights to the information they find.
2. **Meta-search engines** (e.g., Dogpile, MetaCrawler, Surfwax). Meta-search engines allow you to use several search engines simultaneously. While the concept is sound, meta-search agents are limited because many do not access Google or Yahoo!
3. **Web directories** (e.g., Britannica.com, Yahoo! Directory). Web directories classify websites into categories and are the closest equivalent to the cataloguing system used by libraries. On most directories professional editors decide how to index a particular website. Web directories also allow keyword searches.
4. **Specialized search engines** are designed for specific purposes:
   - regional search engines (e.g., Baidu for China)
   - medical search engines (e.g., WebMD)
   - legal search engines (e.g., Lexis)
   - job search engines (e.g., Monster.com)
   - property search engines (e.g., Realtors.ca)
   - comparison-shopping search engines (e.g., Froogle)

Advanced searches

Search engines often produce too many hits and are therefore not always useful. If you look only at the first few items, you may miss what is most valuable. The alternative is to refine your search. Most search engines offer you the option of an advanced search, which gives you the opportunity to limit numbers.

The advanced searches on Google and Yahoo! give you the options of using a string of words to search for sites that contain (1) all the words, (2) the exact phrase, (3) any of the words, or (4) that do not contain certain words. They also allow you to specify the site, the date range, the file format, and the domain. For example, if you want to limit a search for climate change to government websites such as Natural Resources Canada, you can specify the domain as .gc.ca (.gov would limit a search for American government websites). (See Figure 20.2.)

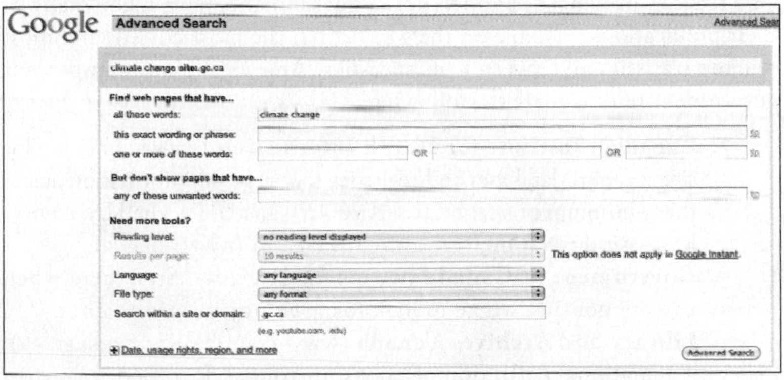

Figure 20.2 Limiting the domain to .gc.ca (or .gov) eliminates commercial sites from the search.

The OR operator is useful if you don't know exactly which term will get the results you want, especially if you are searching within a specific site. For example, you could try this search: "face-to-face OR f2f site:webworkerdaily.com."

You can also exclude terms with the minus sign (–) operator. If you want to search for social network privacy, but not Facebook, try "social network privacy –Facebook."

WRITING SMART

Keep track of web research

One of the easiest ways to return to websites you find useful for your research is to use the **Add to Favorites** or **Add Bookmark** command on your browser. You can arrange the sites you mark in folders and even download them onto a keychain drive or other storage device so that you can retrieve the websites on other computers.

You can also use the **History** menu on your browser to obtain a list of sites you have visited. Most allow you to go back a few days, so if you remember a site you visited but didn't add to your favourites list, you can probably find it again.

Find online government sources

The federal, provincial, and territorial governments have made many of their publications available on the web. Often the most current and most reliable statistics are government statistics. Among the more important government resources are the following:

- **Canadian Institute for Health Information** (www.cihi.ca). This site contains databases and registries that capture information across the continuum of healthcare services in Canada. For the U.S. equivalent, visit the **National Institutes of Health** (www.nih.gov).
- **Government of Canada** (www.canada.gc.ca). Start here when you are not sure where to look for government information.
- **Library and Archives Canada** (www.collectionscanada.gc.ca). The national collection of books, historical documents, government records, photos, films, and music. Many of the resources of the largest library in the world are available on the web at the **Library of Congress** (www.loc.gov).
- **Parliament of Canada** (www.parl.gc.ca). The major source of legislative information in Canada, including bills, committee reports, and links to House of Commons voting records.
- **Public Health Agency of Canada** (www.phac-aspc.gc.ca). A trustworthy source for health statistics in Canada. For authoritative information about health statistics in the U.S. and worldwide, see the **Centers for Disease Control and Prevention** (www.cdc.gov).
- **Science.gc.ca** (www.science.gc.ca). The official source for science and technology information from the government of Canada. Additional information on U.S. scientific discovery and space exploration is available at **NASA** (www.nasa.gov).

- **Statistics Canada** (www.statcan.gc.ca). The source for official Canadian government statistics for economic, social, and census data. For U.S. government statistics on employment, wages, and consumer prices, see the **Bureau of Labor Statistics** website (www.bls.gov). For U.S. census and other statistical information, see the **U.S. Census Bureau** website (www.census.gov).

Find online reference sources

Your library's website has a link to *reference sites*, either on the main page or under another heading like *research tools.*

Reference sites are usually organized by subject, and you can find resources under the subject heading.

- **Business information** (links to business databases and sites like Hoover's that profile companies)
- **Dictionaries** (including *The Oxford English Dictionary* and various subject dictionaries and language dictionaries)
- **Education** (including *The College Blue Book* and others)
- **Encyclopedias** (including Britannica Online and others)
- **Government information** (links to federal, provincial/territorial, and local websites)
- **Reference books** (commonly used books like atlases, almanacs, biographies, handbooks, and histories)
- **Statistics and demographics** (links to federal, provincial/territorial, and local government sites; Statistics Canada [www.statcan.gc.ca] is a good place to start)

Find and explore archives

An archive is traditionally a physical place where historical documents, such as manuscripts and letters, are stored. Recently the term has come to mean any collection of documents, typically preserved for educational purposes, and many are now available online.

For example, if you want to do a research project on Pier 21 and the war brides' immigration to Canada, you will need to look at documents written at the time—letters, diaries, newspaper articles, passenger lists, and border entry records. The Pier 21 Research Department (www.pier21.ca/research) is a good place to start research on this topic. Here are three other excellent electronic archive sites where you can find documents, films, photographs, and news clippings from the period.

- **CBC Digital Archives** (www.cbc.ca/archives). A selection of radio and television clips from more than 60 years of broadcasting by the Canadian Broadcasting Corporation.

- **JSTOR: The Scholarly Journal Archive** (www.jstor.org). Electronic archive of the back issues of over 100 scholarly journals, mainly in the humanities and social sciences fields.
- **Library and Archives Canada** (www.collectionscanada.gc.ca). Huge repository of texts, photographs, and documents related to Canada's cultural, social, and political development. Combines the collections of the National Library of Canada and the National Archives of Canada.

Search interactive media

The internet allows you to access other people's opinions on thousands of topics. Millions of people post messages on discussion lists and groups, Facebook groups, blogs, RSS feeds, Twitter, and so on. Much of what you read on interactive media sites is undocumented and highly opinionated, but you can still gather important information about people's attitudes and get tips about other sources, which you can verify later.

Several search engines have been developed for interactive media. Facebook and Twitter also have search engines for their sites.

Discussion list search engines

- **Big Boards** (www.big-boards.com). Tracks over 2000 of the most active discussion forums

> **WRITING SMART**
>
> **Know the limitations of Wikipedia**
>
> Wikipedia is a valuable resource for current information and for popular culture topics that are not covered in traditional encyclopedias. You can find out, for example, that SpongeBob SquarePants's original name was "SpongeBoy," but that it had already been copyrighted.
>
> Nevertheless, many instructors and the scholarly community in general do not consider Wikipedia a reliable source of information for a research project. The fundamental problem with Wikipedia is stability, not whether the information is correct or incorrect. Wikipedia and other wikis constantly change. The underlying idea of documenting sources is that readers can consult the same sources that you consulted. To be on the safe side, treat Wikipedia as you would a blog. Consult other sources to confirm what you find on Wikipedia and cite those sources.

- **Google Groups** (groups.google.com). Archives discussion forums dating back to 1981
- **Yahoo! Groups** (ca.groups.yahoo.com). A directory of groups by subject

Blog search engines

- **Google Blog Search** (www.google.ca/blogsearch). Searches blogs in several languages besides English
- **IceRocket** (blogs.icerocket.com). Searches blogs, MySpace, and Twitter
- **Technorati** (www.technorati.com). Searches blogs and other user-generated content

20d Find Multimedia Sources

Massive collections of images; audio files including music, speeches, and podcasts; videos; maps; charts; graphs; and other resources are now available on the web. For example, the Hubble Space Telescope discovered a planet being devoured by a star in 2010. A search for "hubble star eats planet" on NASA's website turns up the image shown in Figure 20.3.

Figure 20.3 The Hubble Space Telescope finds a star eating a planet (www.nasa.gov/mission_pages/hubble/science/planet-eater.html).

Find images

The major search engines for images include the following:

- **Bing Images** (www.bing.com/images)
- **Google Image Search** (images.google.ca)
- **Picsearch** (www.picsearch.com)
- **Yahoo! Image Search** (ca.images.search.yahoo.com)

Libraries and museums also offer large collections. The Archives Canada collection includes virtual exhibits of historical items associated with Canada's history (www.archivescanada.ca/english/virtual/search.asp).

Find videos

- **Bing Videos** (www.bing.com/videos)
- **blinkx** (www.blinkx.com)
- **Google Videos** (video.google.com)
- **Yahoo! Video Search** (video.search.yahoo.com)
- **YouTube** (www.youtube.com)

Find podcasts

- **iTunes Podcast Resources** (www.apple.com/itunes/podcasts)
- **PodcastDirectory.com** (www.podcastdirectory.com)

Find charts, graphs, and maps

You can find statistical data represented in charts and graphs on many government websites.

- **Statistics Canada** (www40.statcan.gc.ca/l01/cst01)
- **Google Earth** (earth.google.com)
- **National Geographic Map Machine** (mapmachine.nationalgeographic.com)
- **Atlas of Canada** (atlas.gc.ca/sites/english/index.html)
- **Perry Casteñada Map Collection, University of Texas** (www.lib.utexas.edu/maps/map_sites/map_sites.html)

Respect copyright

Just because images, videos, and other multimedia files are easy to download from the web does not mean that everything is available for you to use. Look for the creator's copyright notice and suggested credit line. This notice will tell you if you can reproduce the multimedia file.

For example, the Cascades Volcano Observatory makes its images available to all: "The maps, graphics, images, and text found on our website, unless stated otherwise, are within the Public Domain. You may download and use them. Credit back to the USGS/Cascades Volcano Observatory is appreciated." Most images on government websites can be reproduced, but check the copyright restrictions. You should acknowledge the source of any image you use.

In many cases you will find a copyright notice that reads, "Any use or retransmission of text or images in this website without written consent of the copyright owner constitutes copyright infringement and is prohibited." You must write to the creator to ask permission to use an image from a site that is not in the public domain, even if you cannot find a copyright notice.

 20e Find Print Sources

Print sources may seem "old fashioned" if you grew up with the internet. You might even feel a little bit intimidated by them. But they are the starting point for much of the research done by experts. In college or university and beyond, they are indispensable. No matter how current the topic you are researching, you will likely find information in print sources that is simply not available online.

Print sources have other advantages as well.

- Books are shelved according to subject, allowing easy browsing.
- Books often have bibliographies, directing you to other research on the subject.
- You can search for books in multiple ways: author, title, subject, or call letter.
- The majority of print sources have been evaluated by scholars, editors, and publishers, who decided whether they merited publication.

Find books

Nearly all libraries now shelve books according to the Library of Congress Classification System, which uses a combination of letters and numbers to give you the book's unique location in the library. The Library of Congress call number begins with a letter or letters that represent the broad subject area into which the book is classified.

Writer at Work

Joshua's subject search for climate change identified this book.

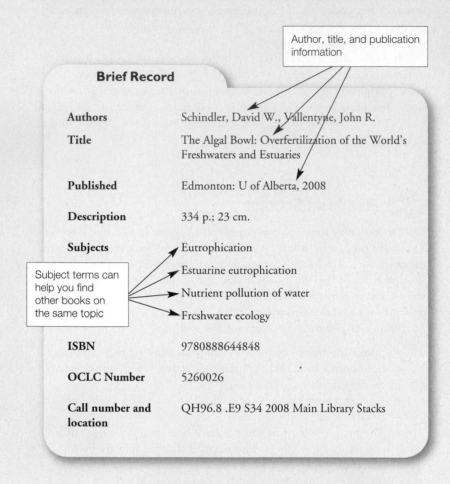

Author, title, and publication information

Brief Record

Authors	Schindler, David W., Vallentyne, John R.
Title	The Algal Bowl: Overfertilization of the World's Freshwaters and Estuaries
Published	Edmonton: U of Alberta, 2008
Description	334 p.; 23 cm.
Subjects	Eutrophication Estuarine eutrophication Nutrient pollution of water Freshwater ecology
ISBN	9780888644848
OCLC Number	5260026
Call number and location	QH96.8 .E9 S34 2008 Main Library Stacks

Subject terms can help you find other books on the same topic

Locating books in your library

The floors of your library where books are shelved are referred to as the stacks. The call number will enable you to find the item in the stacks (see Figure 20.4). You will need to consult the locations guide for your library, which gives the level and section where an item is shelved.

Figure 20.4 The signs in the stacks guide you to the books you are looking for.

Locating e-books

Use your library's online catalogue to find e-books in the same way you find printed books (see Figure 20.5). You'll see on the record "e-book" or "electronic resource." Click on the link and you can read the book and often download a few pages.

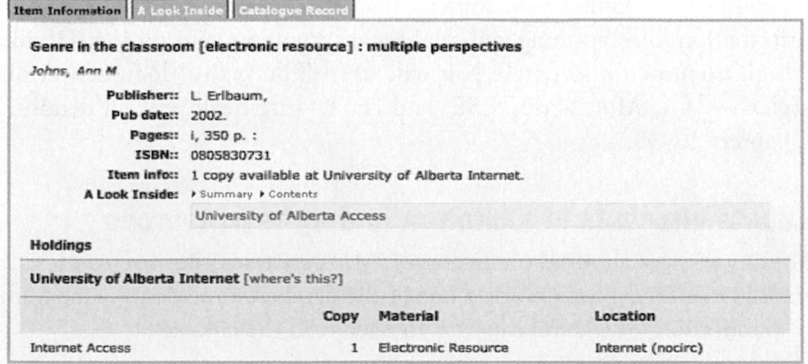

Item Information | A Look Inside | Catalogue Record

Genre in the classroom [electronic resource] : multiple perspectives

Johns, Ann M

Publisher:: L. Erlbaum,
Pub date:: 2002.
Pages:: i, 350 p. :
ISBN:: 0805830731
Item info:: 1 copy available at University of Alberta Internet.
A Look Inside: ▸ Summary ▸ Contents
University of Alberta Access

Holdings

University of Alberta Internet [where's this?]

	Copy	Material	Location
Internet Access	1	Electronic Resource	Internet (nocirc)

Figure 20.5 Books are increasingly becoming available in electronic form through your library's online catalogue.

Locating book reviews

Book Review Digest will be available in the print version in your library's reference room, or your library's website will have a link to the online version, Book Review Digest Plus. Library databases also contain reviews.

- **Academic OneFile** (Search for the title or author and add the word "review" [for example, *The Algal Bowl* and review].)
- **Academic Search Complete** (Enter the title of the book and limit the *Document Type* to "Book Review.")

Find journal articles

Like books, scholarly journals provide in-depth examinations of subjects. The articles in scholarly journals are written by experts, and they usually contain lists of references that can guide you to other research on a subject.

Popular magazines are useful for gaining general information. Articles in popular magazines are usually short, with few, if any, source references, and are typically written by journalists. Some instructors frown on using popular magazines, but these journals can be valuable for researching current opinion on a particular topic. (See Section 21b for more on scholarly journals and popular magazines.)

Many scholarly journals and popular magazines are available on your library's website. Find them the same way you look for books, using your library's online catalogue. Databases increasingly contain the full text of articles, allowing you to read and copy the contents onto your computer. If the article you are looking for isn't available online, the paper copy will be shelved with the books in your library.

 20f Keep Track of Sources

As you begin to collect your sources, make sure you get full bibliographic information for everything you might want to use in your project. Decide which documentation style you will use. (The major documentation styles—MLA, APA, CMS, CSE, and IEEE—are dealt with in detail in Chapters 26–30.)

Locate elements of a citation in database sources

For any sources you find on databases, MLA style requires you to provide the full print information, the name of the database in italics, the medium of publication (*Web*), and the date you accessed the database.

If page numbers are not included, use *n. pag.* Do *not* include the URL of the database.

Author's name	Lavoie, Judith
Title of article	"Coal bigger threat to climate change than oilsands: Study"
Publication information	
Name of periodical	*Times Colonist* [Victoria]
Date of publication (and edition for newspapers)	21 Feb. 2012
Section and page number	B5
Database information	
Name of database	NewspaperDirect Library PressDisplay
Date you accessed the site	21 Feb. 2012

The citation would appear as follows in an MLA-style works-cited list (see Section 26g).

Lavoie, Judith. "Coal Bigger Threat to Climate Change Than Oilsands: Study." *Times Colonist (Victoria)* 21 Feb. 2012: B5. *NewspaperDirect Library PressDisplay*. Web. 21 Feb. 2012.

APA style no longer requires listing the names of common databases or listing the date of access, unless the content is likely to change (see Section 27e). If you name the database, do not list the URL.

Lavoie, J. (2012, February 21). Coal bigger threat to climate change than oilsands: Study. *Times Colonist* [Victoria], p. B5. Retrieved from http://www.pressdisplay.com

Locate elements of a citation in web sources

As you conduct your online research, make sure to collect the necessary bibliographic information for everything you might want to use as a source. Because of the potential volatility of web sources (they can and do disappear overnight), their citations require extra information. Depending on the citation format you use, you'll arrange this information in different ways.

Collect the following information about a website:

Author's name, if available (if not, use the associated institution or organization)	Horne, Matt
Title of article	"Claims of climate leadership in B.C.'s Natural Gas Strategy leave much to be desired"
Publication information	
Name of site or online journal	Pembina Blogs
Publisher or sponsor of the site (for MLA style)	The Pembina Institute
Date of publication (for an article) or of site's last update	15 Feb. 2012
Date you accessed the site	21 Feb. 2012
URL (for some APA formats including blogs)	http://www.pembina.org/blog/611
Document Object Identifier (DOI) if available, in preference to URL, for APA	(See Chapter 27)

An MLA works-cited entry for this article would look like this:

Horne, Matt. "Claims of Climate Leadership in B.C.'s Natural Gas Strategy Leave Much to Be Desired." *Pembina Blogs*. The Pembina Institute, 15 Feb. 2012. Web. 21 Feb. 2012.

In an APA references list, the citation would look like this:

Horne, M. (2012, February 15). Claims of climate leadership in B.C.'s natural gas strategy leave much to be desired [Web log post]. Retrieved from http://www.pembina.org/blog/611

You can find more examples of how to cite web sources in MLA style (Section 26h) and APA style (Section 27e).

Locate elements of a citation in print sources

For books you will need, at minimum, the following information, which can typically be found on the front and back of the title page.

Author's name	Stovell, Bruce
Title of the book	*Jane Austen & Company: Collected Essays*
Publication information	
Place of publication	Edmonton
Name of publisher	University of Alberta Press
Date of publication	2011
Medium of publication	Print

Here's how the book would be cited in an MLA-style works-cited list.

Stovell, Bruce. *Jane Austen & Company: Collected Essays. Edmonton:* U of Alberta P, 2011. Print.

Here's the APA citation for the same book.

Stovell, B. (2011). *Jane Austen & company: Collected essays.* Edmonton, AB: University of Alberta Press.

You will also need the page numbers if you are quoting directly or referring to a specific passage, and the title and author of the individual chapter if your source is an edited book with contributions by several people.

For journals, you will need the following:

Author's name	Afros, Elena, and Catherine F. Schryer
Title of article	"The genre of the syllabus in higher education"
Publication information	
Name of journal	*Journal of English for Academic Purposes*
Volume number and issue number	28.2
Date of publication (and edition for newspapers)	2011
Page numbers of the article	147–171
Medium of publication	Print

An entry in an MLA-style works-cited list would look like this:

> Afros, Elena, and Catherine F. Schryer. "The Genre of the Syllabus in Higher Education." *Journal of English for Academic Purposes* 28.2 (2011): 147-71. Print.

And in APA style, like this:

> Afros, E., & C.F. Schryer. (2011). The genre of the syllabus in higher education. *Journal of English for Academic Purposes, 28,* 147–171.

21 Evaluate Sources

Quick*TAKE*

- Determine the relevance of sources (see below)
- Determine the quality of sources (see p. 235)
- Evaluate database and print sources (see p. 238)
- Evaluate web sources (see p. 239)

21a Determine the Relevance of Sources

Whether you use print or online sources, a successful search will turn up many more items than you can expect to use in your final product. You have to make a series of decisions as you evaluate your material. Use your research question and working thesis to create guidelines for yourself about importance and relevance.

For example, if your research question asks why the Roman Empire declined rapidly at the end of the fourth and beginning of the fifth centuries CE, you may find older sources as valuable as new ones. Edward Gibbon's three-volume history, *The Decline and Fall of the Roman Empire*, remains an important source even though it was published in 1776 and 1781.

But if you ask a research question about contemporary events—for example, why Chinese businesses are thriving in African nations at a time when the Western presence is dwindling—you will need to find current information. Statistics such as the growth of Chinese trade with Africa to $106 billion in 2008 or the fact that over a million Chinese live and work in Africa describes the trend, but statistics alone do not explain why. An article on the new popularity of Chinese food in some African cities might be interesting, but it is not relevant. Relevant articles will discuss China's willingness to invest in factories and businesses in Africa while Western investment in the continent has decreased.

Use these guidelines to determine the importance and relevance of your sources to your research question.

- Does your research question require you to consult primary or secondary sources?
- Does a source you have found address your question?
- Does a source support or disagree with your working thesis? (You should not throw out work that challenges your views. Representing opposing views accurately enhances your credibility.)
- Does a source add significant information?
- Is the source current? (For most topics try to find the most up-to-date information.)
- What indications of possible bias do you note in the source?

21b Determine the Quality of Sources

In the internet era, we don't lack for information, but we do lack filters for finding quality information. Two criteria will help you make a beginning assessment of quality: individual versus edited sources and popular versus scholarly sources.

Distinguish individual and anonymous sources from edited sources

Anyone with a computer and access to the internet can put up a website. Furthermore, anyone can put up sites anonymously or under an assumed name. It's no wonder that there are so many sites that contain misinformation or are intentionally deceptive.

In general, sources that have been edited and published in scholarly journals, scholarly books, major newspapers, major online and print magazines, and government websites are considered of higher quality than what an individual might put on a personal website, a Facebook page, or in a user review or a blog. Nevertheless, people tend to believe reports from individuals. Corporations are well aware that blogs and user reviews on sites like Amazon are now more trusted than newspaper and magazine articles, and they regularly send bloggers information about new products and pay them for favourable mentions. Some corporations have gone even further, hiring public relations firms to write favourable reviews and favourable blogs.

Edited sources can have biases, and indeed some are quite open about their perspectives. The *Globe and Mail* offers a conservative perspective, the

National Post is pro-business, and the *Toronto Star* is a liberal voice. The difference between such sources and individual and anonymous sites is that we know the editorial perspectives of these newspapers, and we expect the editors to check the facts. On self-published websites and in self-published books, anything goes.

Distinguish popular sources from scholarly sources

Scholarly books and *scholarly journals* are published by and for experts. Scholarly books and articles published in scholarly journals undergo a *peer review* process in which a group of experts in a field reviews them for their scholarly soundness and academic value. Scholarly books and articles in scholarly journals include

- author's name and academic credentials, and
- a list of works cited.

Newspapers, *popular books*, and *popular magazines* vary widely in quality. Newspapers and popular magazines range from highly respected publications such as the *Globe and Mail*, *Discover*, and the *New York Times* to the sensational tabloids at grocery-store checkouts. Popular sources are not peer reviewed and require more work on your part to determine their quality.

POPULAR VERSUS SCHOLARLY SOURCES

	Popular books and magazines	Newspapers	Scholarly books and journals
Author	staff writers, journalists	journalists	scholars, researchers
Audience	general public	general public	scholars, college and university students
Reviewed by	professional editor	professional editor	other scholars and researchers
Purpose	entertain, express an opinion	entertain, express an opinion, inform	share information with the scholarly community
Documentation	usually none	usually none	extensive, with lists of works cited or footnotes
Advertisements	frequent in magazines	frequent	a few ads for scholarly products
Evidence of bias	usually some bias	usually some bias	little bias

	Popular books and magazines	Newspapers	Scholarly books and journals
Examples	[magazines] *Canadian Living*, *GQ*, *Rolling Stone*, *Sports Illustrated*, *Maclean's*; [book] Elizabeth Gilbert, *Eat, Pray, Love*	*New York Times*, *Toronto Star*, *Globe and Mail*, *The Independent* (London), *Washington Times*	[journals] *College English*, *JAMA*: *Journal of the American Medical Association*; [book] David Schindler & John Vallentyne, *The Algal Bowl: Overfertilization of the World's Freshwaters and Estuaries*

Distinguish primary sources from secondary sources

Another key distinction for researchers is primary versus secondary sources. In the humanities and fine arts, *primary sources* are original, creative works and original accounts of events written close to the time they occurred. *Secondary sources* interpret creative works and primary sources of events.

In the sciences, *primary sources* are the factual results of experiments, observations, clinical trials, and other factual data. *Secondary sources* analyze and interpret those results.

PRIMARY VERSUS SECONDARY SOURCES

Examples	Humanities and fine arts	Sciences
Primary sources	• Novels, short stories, poems, plays, music • Paintings, sculpture, photographs, maps • Speeches • Diaries, letters, journals • Interviews with witnesses and participants • Government records	• Published results • Collections of data • Collections of observations
Secondary sources	• Histories • Biographies • Literary criticism • Reviews	• Publications interpreting the results of experiments and clinical trials • Reviews of several studies or experiments

Read sources critically

Evaluating sources requires you to read critically, which includes the following:

- Identifying the source, which is not always easy on the web
- Identifying the author and assessing the author's credentials
- Understanding the content—what the text says
- Recognizing the author's purpose—whether the author is attempting to reflect, inform, or persuade
- Recognizing how the purpose influences the choice of words, examples, and structure
- Recognizing biases in the choice of words, examples, and structure
- Recognizing what the author does not include or address
- Developing an overall evaluation that takes into account all of the above

(For more on critical reading, see Chapter 5.)

Evaluate the quality of visual sources

Evaluating the quality of visual sources involves skills similar to those of critical reading. As you do in critical reading, you should

- identify and assess the source,
- identify the creator,
- identify the date of creation,
- describe the content,
- assess the purpose, and
- recognize how the purpose influences the composition of the image or graphic.

For graphics including charts and graphs, pay attention to the source of any data presented and whether the data are presented fairly. (For more on the evaluation of visual sources, see Sections 5e and 5f.)

21c Evaluate Database and Print Sources

Books are expensive to print and distribute, so book publishers generally protect their investment by providing some level of editorial oversight. Printed and online materials in your library undergo another review by professional librarians, who select them to include in their collections. Library database collections, which your library pays to access, are also screened, which eliminates many poor-quality sources.

This initial screening doesn't free you, however, from the responsibility of evaluating the quality of the sources. Many printed and database sources contain their share of inaccurate, misleading, and biased information. Also, all sources carry the risk of becoming outdated if you are looking for current information.

WRITING SMART

Checklist for evaluating database and print sources

Over the years librarians have developed a set of criteria for evaluating sources, and you should apply them in your research.

1. **Source.** Who published the book or article? Enter the publisher's name on Google or another search engine to learn about the publisher. Scholarly books and articles in scholarly journals are generally more reliable than popular magazines and books, which tend to emphasize what is sensational or entertaining at the expense of accuracy and comprehensiveness.
2. **Author.** Who wrote the book or article? What are the author's qualifications? Enter the author's name on Google or another search engine to learn more about him or her. Does the author represent an organization?
3. **Timeliness.** How current is the source? If you are researching a fast-developing subject such as treating ADHD, then currency is very important, but even historical topics are subject to controversy or revision.
4. **Evidence.** Where does the evidence come from—facts, interviews, observations, surveys, or experiments? Is the evidence adequate to support the author's claims?
5. **Biases.** Can you detect particular biases of the author? How do the author's biases affect the interpretation offered?
6. **Advertising.** For print sources, is advertising a prominent part of the journal or newspaper? How might the ads affect the credibility or the biases of the information that gets printed?

21d Evaluate Web Sources

Researching on the web has been compared to drinking from a fire hose. The key to success is not only getting the torrent down to the size of a glass, but also making sure the water in the glass is pure enough to drink.

Pay attention to domain names

Domain names can give you clues about the quality of a website.

- **.com** Commercial site. The information on a .com site is generally about a product or company. While the information may be accurate, keep in mind that the purpose of the site is to sell a product or service.
- **.edu** Educational institution. The suffix tells you the site is on a school server, ranging from kindergarten to higher education. If the information is from a department or research centre, it is generally credible, but if the site is an individual's, treat it as you would other kinds of self-published information.
- **.gc.ca** or **.gov** Government. If you see either of these suffixes you're viewing a federal government site. Most government sites are considered credible sources.
- **.org** Non-profit organization. Initially, nonpartisan organizations like the Red Cross used this domain, but partisan political groups and commercial interests have increasingly taken the .org suffix. Treat this domain with scrutiny.
- **.mil** Military. This domain suffix is owned by the various branches of the American armed forces.
- **.net** Network. Anyone can use this domain.

Be alert for biased websites

Nearly every large company and political and advocacy organization has a website. We expect these sites to represent the company or the point of view of the organization. Many sites on the web, however, are not so clearly labelled.

For example, if you do a search for "Sudden Infant Death Syndrome (SIDS)" and "vaccines," you'll find near the top of the list an article titled "Vaccines and Sudden Infant Death Syndrome (SIDS): A Link?" (www.thinktwice.com/sids.htm). The article concludes that vaccines cause SIDS. If you look at the home page—www.thinktwice.com—you'll find that the site's sponsor, Global Vaccine Institute, opposes all vaccinations of children.

Always look for other objective sources for verification of your information. The Public Health Agency of Canada website addresses the proposed link between immunizations and SIDS in its list of frequently asked questions (FAQ) by emphasizing that recent research from around the world has shown that vaccines do not cause SIDS (see Figure 21.1). The website notes that research has revealed factors other than vaccines that are linked to SIDS, including sleeping position and second-hand smoke.

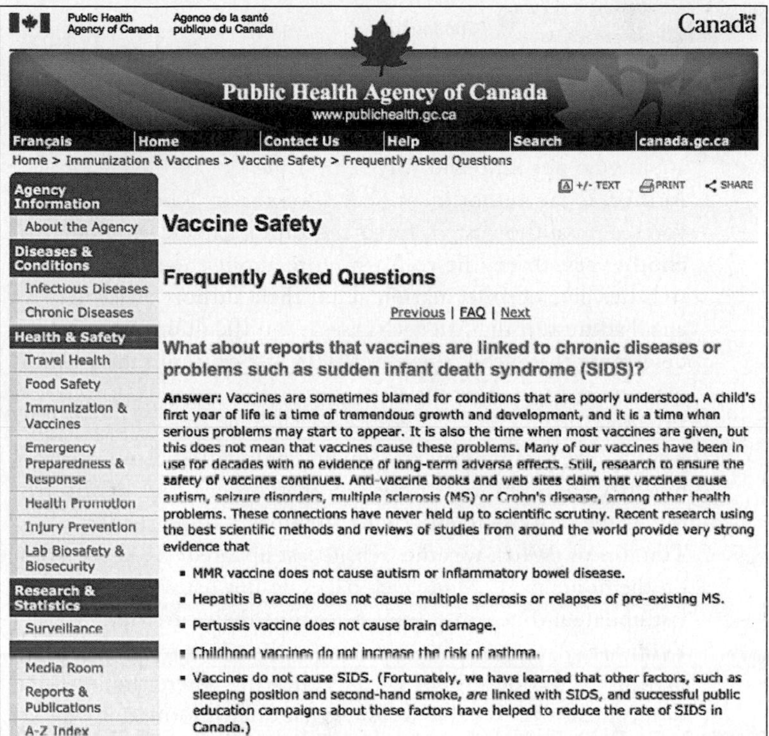

Public Health Agency of Canada | Agence de la santé publique du Canada | Canada

Public Health Agency of Canada
www.publichealth.gc.ca

Français | Home | Contact Us | Help | Search | canada.gc.ca

Home > Immunization & Vaccines > Vaccine Safety > Frequently Asked Questions

Agency Information
About the Agency
Diseases & Conditions
Infectious Diseases
Chronic Diseases
Health & Safety
Travel Health
Food Safety
Immunization & Vaccines
Emergency Preparedness & Response
Health Promotion
Injury Prevention
Lab Biosafety & Biosecurity
Research & Statistics
Surveillance
Media Room
Reports & Publications
A-Z Index

+/- TEXT PRINT SHARE

Vaccine Safety

Frequently Asked Questions

Previous | FAQ | Next

What about reports that vaccines are linked to chronic diseases or problems such as sudden infant death syndrome (SIDS)?

Answer: Vaccines are sometimes blamed for conditions that are poorly understood. A child's first year of life is a time of tremendous growth and development, and it is a time when serious problems may start to appear. It is also the time when most vaccines are given, but this does not mean that vaccines cause these problems. Many of our vaccines have been in use for decades with no evidence of long-term adverse effects. Still, research to ensure the safety of vaccines continues. Anti-vaccine books and web sites claim that vaccines cause autism, seizure disorders, multiple sclerosis (MS) or Crohn's disease, among other health problems. These connections have never held up to scientific scrutiny. Recent research using the best scientific methods and reviews of studies from around the world provide very strong evidence that

- MMR vaccine does not cause autism or inflammatory bowel disease.
- Hepatitis B vaccine does not cause multiple sclerosis or relapses of pre-existing MS.
- Pertussis vaccine does not cause brain damage.
- Childhood vaccines do not increase the risk of asthma.
- Vaccines do not cause SIDS. (Fortunately, we have learned that other factors, such as sleeping position and second-hand smoke, *are* linked with SIDS, and successful public education campaigns about these factors have helped to reduce the rate of SIDS in Canada.)

Figure 21.1 FAQ on vaccines and SIDS from the Public Health Agency of Canada (www.phac-aspc.gc.ca/im/vs-sv/vs-faq13-eng.php).

WRITING SMART

Checklist for evaluating web sources

Web sources present special challenges for evaluation. When you find a web page by using a search engine, you will often go deep into a complex site without having any sense of the context for that page. To evaluate the credibility of the site, you would need to examine the home page, not just the specific page you get to first.

Use these criteria for evaluating websites.

1. **Source.** What organization sponsors the website? Look for the site's owner at the top or bottom of the home page or in the

(Continued on next page)

WRITING SMART *(Continued)*

web address. Enter the owner's name on Google or another search engine to learn about the organization. If a website doesn't indicate ownership, then you have to make judgments about who put it up and why.

2. **Author.** Is the author identified? Look for an "About Us" link if you see no author listed. Enter the author's name on Google or another search engine to learn more about the author. Often websites give no information about their authors other than an email address, if that. In such cases it is difficult or impossible to determine the author's qualifications. Be cautious about information on an anonymous site.
3. **Purpose.** Is the website trying to sell you something? Many websites are infomercials that might contain useful information, but they are no more trustworthy than other forms of advertising. Is the purpose to entertain? To inform? To persuade?
4. **Timeliness.** When was the website last updated? Look for a date on the home page. Many web pages do not list when they were last updated; thus you cannot determine their currency.
5. **Evidence.** Are sources of information listed? Any factual information should be supported by indicating where the information came from. Reliable websites that offer information will list their sources.
6. **Biases.** Does the website offer a balanced point of view? Many websites conceal their attitude with a reasonable tone and seemingly factual evidence such as statistics. Citations and bibliographies do not ensure that a site is reliable. Look carefully at the links and sources cited, and peruse the "About Us" link if one is available.

Writer at Work

Joshua LaGrange's topic, climate change, focuses on disputes among scientists and has been the subject of extended heated debate. He decided to explore some of the newest ideas being developed to "green" the economy. One of the books he found was Andrew Heintzman's *The New Entrepreneurs: Building a Green Economy for the Future.* Here is his evaluation:

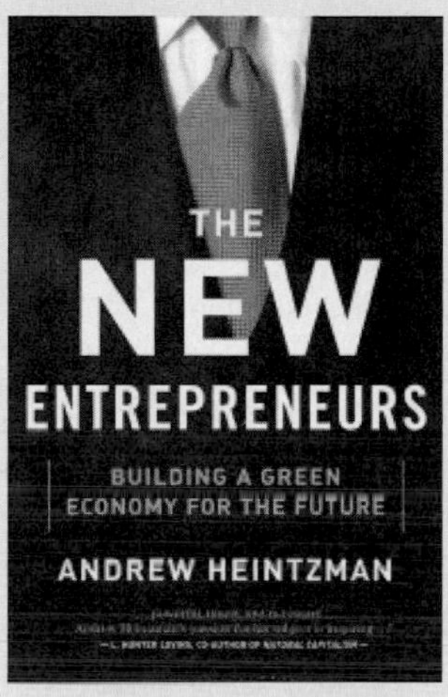

Source	good reviews; House of Anansi is a 45-year-old Canadian publisher of important authors who have won international awards for writing
Author	Andrew Heintzman is president of Investeco Capital and invests in companies like the ones he talks about in the book
Purpose	to describe new innovative companies helping to "green" the economy
Timeline	published in 2010
Evidence	based on the author's experience
Biases	author strongly committed to his method but isn't trying to sell anything
Conclusion	because he is a venture capitalist himself, author is convincing about the subject; published reviews and user reviews on Amazon are strongly favourable

22 Plan Field Research

QUICK*TAKE*

- Conduct informative interviews (see p. 245)
- Design and administer focused surveys (see p. 245)
- Make detailed observations (see p. 248)

22a Know What You Can Obtain from Field Research

Even though much of the research you do for university or college courses will be secondary research conducted at a computer or in the library, some topics do call for primary research, requiring you to gather information on your own. Field research of this kind can be especially important for exploring local issues. It is also used extensively in professions that you may be joining after post-secondary school.

Remember, you're not a huge polling organization with thousands of employees and unlimited resources. The data you collect will necessarily be limited in scope. You won't be able to sample a wide range of people in a survey, and you can't spend years observing wildlife in a distant location. But you can use field research to provide concrete evidence about attitudes, environments, and opinions in your immediate location. If you are making an argument about a local issue, local opinions or conditions are an important part of that argument. Field research that directly measures those opinions or conditions will give your argument much more credibility.

Be aware that the ethics of conducting field research requires you to inform people about what you are doing and why you are gathering information. If you are uncertain about the ethics of doing field research, talk to your instructor.

Three types of field research that can usually be conducted in post-secondary education are *interviews, surveys,* and *observations.*

- **Interviews.** Post-secondary school campuses are a rich source of experts in many areas, including those on the faculty and in the surrounding community. Interviewing experts on your research topic can help build your knowledge base. You can use interviews to discover what the people most affected by a particular issue are thinking and feeling.

- **Surveys.** Extensive surveys that can be projected to large populations, such as those used in political polls, require the effort of many people. Small surveys, however, can often provide insight on local issues.
- **Observations.** Local observation can be a valuable source of data. For example, if you are researching why a particular office on your campus does not operate efficiently, observe what happens when students enter and how they are handled by the staff.

22b Conduct Interviews

Before you contact anyone to ask for an interview, think carefully about your goals; knowing what you want to find out through your interviews will help you determine whom you need to interview and what questions you need to ask.

- Decide what you want or need to know and who can best provide that for you.
- Schedule each interview in advance, and let the person know why you are conducting the interview.
- Plan your questions in advance. Write down a few questions and have a few more in mind. Listen carefully so that you can follow up on key points.
- Come prepared with a notebook and pencil for taking notes and jotting down short quotations. Record the date, time, place, and subject of the interview. A digital recorder can sometimes intimidate the person you are interviewing. If you want to use a digital recorder, ask for permission in advance.
- When you are finished, thank your subject and ask his or her permission to get in touch again if you have additional questions.
- When you are ready to incorporate the interview into a paper or project, think about what you want to highlight from the interview and which direct quotations to include.

22c Administer Surveys

Use surveys to find out what large groups of people think about a topic (or what they are willing to admit they think). Surveys need to be carefully designed. There are two important components: the survey instrument itself—which is the list of questions you will ask—and the place, time, and way in which the survey will be administered.

- Write a few specific questions. Make sure that they are unambiguous—people will fill out your survey quickly, and if the questions are confusing, the results will be meaningless. To make sure your questions are clear, test them on a few people before you conduct the survey.
- Include one or two open-ended questions, such as "What do you like about X?" and "What don't you like about X?" Open-ended questions can be difficult to interpret, but sometimes they turn up information you had not anticipated.
- Decide whom you need to survey and how many people to include. If you want to claim that the results of your survey represent the views of residents of your dormitory, your method of selecting respondents should give all residents an equal chance to be selected. Don't select only your friends.
- Decide how you will contact participants in your survey. If you are going to mail or email your survey, include a statement about what the survey is for and a deadline for returning it. You may need to get permission to conduct a survey in a public place.
- Think about how you will interpret your survey. Multiple-choice formats make data easy to tabulate, but often they miss key information. Open-ended questions will require you to figure out a way to analyze responses.
- When writing about the results, be sure to include information about who participated in the survey, how the participants were selected, and when and how the survey was administered.

An example of a survey on study habits that a student could administer in the student union or library appears on page 247.

STAYING ON TRACK

Keep survey language impartial

Writers of effective surveys must take into account people's subconscious biases, reading, writing, and listening patterns, and other subtle factors. For a small survey, you probably won't be able to control many of the variables important in large polls. Still, you want your survey results to be as accurate and credible as possible. That means you have to let people make up their own minds. So take care that the questions you ask don't actively encourage people to give the answers you may want to hear.

STAYING ON TRACK *(Continued)*

Off track Would you like the library to stop closing at the ridiculous hour of 9:00 p.m.?

On track Would you like the library to stay open later at night?

Off track Do you want the Student Council spending your student fees on things like chips and soda?

On track Do you think the Student Council should have discretion to use student fees for entertainment costs?

Study Habits Survey

Your answers to these questions will help me determine whether the library's schedule ought to be altered.

1. How often do you use the library?	• Daily • Three or more times a week • Once a week • Once a month • Once a semester • Never
2. At what time do you most often use the library?	• 8:00 a.m.–noon • Noon–4:00 p.m. • 4:00 p.m.–8:00 p.m. • After 8:00 p.m.
3. Have you ever had to leave the library because it was closing?	• Yes • No
4. Have you ever had to wait to use the library because it wasn't yet open?	• Yes • No
5. In general, how well do the library's current hours meet your study needs?	• Not at all well • Somewhat well • Quite well • Extremely well
6. What for you would be the ideal hours for the library to be open?	

■ Students in a marketing class at Ryerson University conducted a survey at a ski resort in Georgian Bay to test whether simulated trading could predict consumer trends.

 Make Observations

Simply observing what goes on in a place can be a very effective research tool. Your observations can inform a controversy or topic by providing a vivid picture of real-world activity. For example, you might observe a local swimming pool to see what age groups use it the most and at what times of day. Or you might observe a drainage pond to see what forms of wildlife it attracts. Here are some tips on making observations.

- Choose a place where you can observe with the least intrusion. The less people wonder about what you are doing, the better.
- Carry a notebook and write extensive field notes. Get down as much information as you can, and worry about analyzing it later.
- Record the date, exactly where you were, exactly when you arrived and left, and important details such as the number of people present.
- Write on one side of your notebook page and use the other side to note key observations and analyze your data later.

A sample page of observations of a preschool classroom might look like this.

Observations	*Analysis*
8 a.m.	
Dimonte and Lilly	*Lilly's teacher says she always*
dropped off. Lilly	*cries when her mother drops her*
cries when her	*off, but not when her father*
mother leaves.	*does. Some of the other children*
	also exhibit this pattern.

Observations	Analysis
8:15	
Carissa tries to take the scissors outside onto the playground and is stopped by a teacher.	
8:30	
All the children are playing outside; the noise level has gradually increased.	It's interesting that the morning starts off fairly quietly, then gets louder and louder until snack time. Are the kids getting reacquainted with one another every morning, or just waking up?
8:40	
Carissa has managed to sneak the scissors outside again. The teacher takes them away.	Carissa does this over and over again during the day; does anyone know what she wants to do with the scissors outside?
8:45	
Snack time. Carissa shares her goldfish crackers with Lilly.	The girls are sharing more often now, although they also use "not sharing" as a way to punish others or show their displeasure.

Once you begin taking extensive notes about what you observe, you will collect a great deal of data. At some point you have to interpret the data. When you analyze your observations, think about what constitutes normal and unusual activities for this place. What can you determine about the purposes of these activities?

PART 6

Incorporating and Documenting Sources

You **can learn more and do more** with MyWritingLab and with the eText version of *The Brief Penguin Handbook*. For help with avoiding plagiarism and documenting your sources successfully, click on "Resources," then select "Research." Review the tutorials (Read, Watch, Listen) within each topic, then complete the Exercises and click on the Gradebook to measure your progress.

Research Map 2: Working with Sources

Using sources effectively requires that you

- avoid plagiarism in taking notes, summarizing, and paraphrasing,
- employ sources to provide evidence and points of departure,
- integrate quotations, summaries, paraphrases, and visuals,
- write and revise your research project, and
- document all sources using the format of a major documentation style.

Here are the steps in incorporating and documenting sources.

1 Understand plagiarism

First, understand exactly how plagiarism is defined; go to Section 23b.

Avoid patch plagiarism when taking notes by distinguishing source words from your own words; go to 23c.

Avoid patch plagiarism when quoting sources by putting words from the source within quotation marks; go to 23d.

Avoid patch plagiarism when summarizing and paraphrasing by putting ideas from the source into your own words; go to 23e.

2 Integrate sources

Use sources to provide evidence; go to 24a.

Use sources as points of departure; go to 24b.

Integrate quotations, summaries, and paraphrases into your research project; go to 24d and 24e.

Integrate visuals into your research project; go to 24f.

You'll see in Parts 5 and 6 the process Joshua LaGrange used to produce his research project. Joshua's annotated bibliography appears on pages 209–211.

See Research Map 1 (on the back of the divider for Part 5) for guidance on planning research and finding sources.

3 | Write and revise

Take stock of your research to determine which sources are critical to your project and what further research you may need to do; go to 25a.

Plan your organization by creating a working outline; go to 25b.

Begin your draft by writing a specific title, an introduction, and a conclusion; go to 25c.

Review your project and revise, beginning with high-level issues of content and organization; go to 25d.

4 | Document sources

Decide which documentation style you will use:

- **MODERN LANGUAGE ASSOCIATION (MLA):** go to Chapter 26.
- **AMERICAN PSYCHOLOGICAL ASSOCIATION (APA):** go to Chapter 27.
- **CHICAGO MANUAL OF STYLE (CMS):** go to Chapter 28.
- **COUNCIL OF SCIENCE EDITORS (CSE):** go to Chapter 29.
- **INSTITUTE OF ELECTRICAL AND ELECTRONIC ENGINEERS (IEEE):** go to Chapter 30.

23 Understand and Avoid Plagiarism

QUICK*TAKE*

- What is plagiarism? (see p. 253)
- Avoid plagiarism when taking notes (see p. 255)
- Avoid plagiarism when quoting sources (see p. 257)
- Avoid plagiarism when summarizing and paraphrasing (see p. 258)

23a Understand the Purposes of Sources

From a student's point of view, documenting sources can seem like learning Latin—something obscure and complicated that has little use in daily life. You don't see footnotes or lists of works cited in magazines and newspapers, so you may wonder why they are so important in post-secondary writing. Careful documentation of sources, however, is essential to developing knowledge and allows scholars and researchers to build on the work of other scholars and researchers.

Sources build knowledge

Knowledge is built through ongoing conversations that take place in writing as well as talking. The practice of citing sources provides a disciplinary map, indicating the conversation in which the writer is participating and how that writer responds to what has been said before. Often knowledge building does not move in a straight line, but rather reflects wrong turns and backtracking. Tracing these movements would be extremely difficult if writers did not acknowledge their sources.

Sources must be accurate

Accurate referencing of sources allows you or any reader the opportunity to consult those sources. For example, historians who write about the distant past must rely on different kinds of evidence, including letters, records, public documents, newspaper articles, legal manuscripts, and other material from that time; they also take into account the work of contemporary scholars. Other historians working in the same area must be able to find and read these primary sources to assess the accuracy of the interpretation. Research using sources requires that summaries and paraphrases be accurate, that words taken from the original be set off in quotation marks, and that full information be provided to locate the source.

Sources and fairness

Another basic issue is fairness. When historians draw on the interpretations of other historians, they should give those historians credit. In this respect citing sources builds community with writers of both the present and the past. When you begin to read the published research in an academic discipline, your awareness of that community takes shape. But the issue of fairness is also part of the much larger issues of intellectual property and scholastic honesty—issues that need to be considered carefully when you use sources.

 23b What Is Plagiarism?

Plagiarism means claiming credit for someone else's intellectual work, whether it's to make money or get a better grade. Intentional or not, plagiarism has dire consequences. Reputable authors have gotten into trouble through carelessness by copying passages from published sources without acknowledging those sources. A number of famous people have had their reputations tarnished by accusations of plagiarism, and several prominent journalists have lost their jobs and careers for copying the work of other writers and passing it off as their own.

Deliberate plagiarism

If you buy a paper on the web, copy someone else's paper word for word, or take an article off the web and turn it in as yours, it's plain stealing, and people who take that risk should know that the punishment can be severe—usually failure for the course and sometimes expulsion. Deliberate plagiarism is easy for your instructors to spot because they recognize shifts in style, and it is easy for them to use search engines to find the sources of work stolen from the web.

Patch plagiarism

The use of the web has increased instances of plagiarism in college and university. Some students view the internet as a big free buffet where they can grab anything, paste it in a file, and submit it as their own work. Other students intend to submit work that is their own, but they commit patch plagiarism because they aren't careful in taking notes to distinguish the words of others from their own words (see Section 20f).

What you are not required to acknowledge

Fortunately, common sense governs issues of academic plagiarism. The standards of documentation are not so strict that the source of every fact you cite must be acknowledged. You do not have to document the following.

- **Facts available from many sources.** For example, many reference sources report that the death toll of the sinking of the *Titanic* on April 15, 1912, was around 1500.
- **Results of your own field research.** If you take a survey and report the results, you don't have to cite yourself. You do need to cite individual interviews.

What you are required to acknowledge

The following sources should be acknowledged with an in-text citation and an entry in the list of works cited (MLA style) or the list of references (APA style).

- **Quotations**. Short quotations should be enclosed within quotation marks, and long quotations should be indented as a block. See Section 24d for how to integrate quotations with signal phrases.
- **Summaries and paraphrases**. Summaries represent the author's argument in miniature as accurately as possible (see Section 24e). Paraphrases restate the author's argument in your own words.
- **Facts that are not common knowledge**. For facts that are not easily found in general reference works, cite the source.
- **Ideas that are not common knowledge**. The sources of theories, analyses, statements of opinion, and arguable claims should be cited.
- **Statistics, research findings, examples, graphs, charts, and illustrations**. As a reader you should be skeptical about statistics and research findings when the source is not mentioned. When a writer does not cite the sources of statistics and research findings, there is no way of knowing how reliable the sources are or whether the writer is making them up.

STAYING ON TRACK

Plagiarism in post-secondary writing

If you find any of the following problems in your academic writing, you may be guilty of plagiarizing someone else's work. Because plagiarism is usually inadvertent, it is especially important that you understand what constitutes using sources responsibly. Avoid these pitfalls.

STAYING ON TRACK *(Continued)*

- **Missing attribution.** Make sure the author of a quotation has been identified. Include a lead-in or signal phrase that provides an attribution of the source, and identify the author in the citation.
- **Missing quotation marks.** You must put quotation marks around material quoted directly from a source.
- **Inadequate citation.** Give a page number to show where in the source the quotation appears or where a paraphrase or summary is drawn from.
- **Paraphrase relies too heavily on the source.** Be careful that the wording or sentence structure of a paraphrase does not follow the source too closely.
- **Distortion of meaning.** Don't allow your paraphrase or summary to distort the meaning of the source, and don't take a quotation out of context, resulting in a change of meaning.
- **Missing works-cited entry.** The works-cited page must include all the works cited in the project.
- **Inadequate citation of images.** A figure or photo must appear with a caption and a citation to indicate the source of the image. If material includes a summary of data from a visual source, an attribution or citation must be given for the graphic being summarized.

 23c Avoid Plagiarism When Taking Notes

The best way to avoid unintentional plagiarism is to take care to distinguish source words from your own words. Don't mix words from the source with your own words. Create a folder for your research project and clearly label the files.

- **Create a working bibliography and make separate files for content notes.** Create a file for each source. If you work on paper, use a separate page for each source. Also write down all the information you need for a list of works cited or a list of references in your working bibliography (see Section 20f).
- **If you copy anything from a source when taking notes, place those words in quotation marks and note the page number(s) where those words appear.** If you copy words from an online source, take special care to note the source. You could easily copy online material and later not be able to find where it came from.

- **Print out the entire source so that you can refer to it later.** Having photocopies or complete printed files allows you to double-check later that you haven't used words from the source by mistake and that any words you quote are accurate.

Writer at Work

Joshua LaGrange printed a copy of Tom Harris's article and made notes in the margin of the photocopy.

Harris, Tom. "Scientists Respond to Gore's Warnings of Climate Catastrophe." Canada Free Press. Tom Harris, 12 June 2006. Web. 30 Oct. 2011.

Not a reliable website

"Scientists have an independent obligation to respect and present the truth as they see it," Al Gore sensibly asserts in his film "An Inconvenient Truth," showing at Cumberland 4 Cinemas in Toronto since Jun[e] 2. With that outlook in mind, what do world climate experts actually think about the science of his movie?

This is an important issue—who counts as an expert?

Professor Bob Carter of the Marine Geophysical Laboratory at James Cook University in Australia gives what, for many Canadians, is a surprising assessment: "Gore's circumstantial arguments are so weak that they are pathetic. It is simply incredible that they, and his film, are commanding public attention."

Citation missing for the source

But surely Carter is merely part of what most people regard as a tiny cadre of "climate change skeptics" who disagree with the "vast majority of scientists" Gore cites?

No; **Carter is one of hundreds of highly qualified non-governmental, non-industry, non-lobby group climate experts** who contest the hypothesis that human emissions of carbon dioxide (CO_2) are causing significant global climate change. "Climate experts" is the operative term here. Why? Because what Gore's "majority of scientists" think is immaterial when only a very small fraction of them actually work in the climate field.

Asserts this but offers no proof

23d Quote Sources Without Plagiarizing

Most people who get into plagiarism trouble lift words from a source and use them without quotation marks. Where the line is drawn is easiest to illustrate with an example. In the following passage, Nell Irvin Painter discusses the African Diaspora, the dispersion of African people from their native lands in Africa. She describes the cultural differences that distinguish contemporary African Americans and Canadians from their ancestors.

■ Nell Irvin Painter

> The three centuries separating African Americans from their immigrant ancestors profoundly influenced their identity. A strong case can be made for seeing **African Americans as a new, Creole people, that is, as a people born and forged in the Western Hemisphere.** Language provides the most obvious indicator: **people of African descent in the Diaspora do not speak languages of Africa as their mother tongue. For the most part, they speak Portuguese, Spanish, English, and French as a mother tongue, although millions speak Creole languages (such as Haitian Creole and South Carolinian Gullah) that combine African grammars and English vocabulary.**
>
> As the potent engine of culture, language influences thought, psychology, and education. Language boundaries now divide descendants whose African ancestors may have been family and close neighbors speaking the same language. One descendant in Nashville, Tennessee, may not understand the Portuguese of her distant cousin now living in Bahia, Brazil. Today, with immigrants from Africa forming an increasing proportion of people calling themselves African American, the woman in Nashville might herself be an African immigrant and speak an African language that neither her black neighbors in Tennessee nor her distant cousin in Brazil can understand. Religion, another crucial aspect of culture, distinguishes the different peoples of the African Diaspora. Millions of Africans are Muslims, for instance, while most African Americans see themselves as Christian. They would hardly agree to place themselves under the Sharia, the legal system inspired by the Koran, which prevails in Northern Nigeria.
>
> —Nell Irvin Painter, *Creating Black Americans: African-American History and Its Meanings, 1619 to the Present*, New York: Oxford UP, 2006, 5, print

If you were writing a paper or creating a website that concerned Canadians of African cultural heritage, you might want to refer to Painter's arguments about cultural differences resulting from different languages. Your options are to paraphrase the source or to quote it directly.

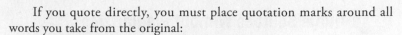

If you quote directly, you must place quotation marks around all words you take from the original:

> One scholar notes the numerous linguistic differences among Canadians of African descent: "**[P]eople of African descent in the Diaspora do not speak languages of Africa as their mother tongue. For the most part, they speak Portuguese, Spanish, English, and French as a mother tongue**" (Painter 5).

Notice that the quotation is introduced and not just dropped in. This example follows Modern Language Association (MLA) style, where the citation goes outside the quotation marks but before the final period. In MLA style, source references are made according to the author's last name, which refers you to the full citation in the works-cited list at the end. Following the author's name is the page number where the quotation can be located. (Notice also that there is no comma after the name.) If you want to cite a newspaper article without a byline or another anonymous source, you use the first important word or two of the title to make the reference. This system allows you to find the reference easily in the list of works cited, since the list is arranged alphabetically by author and title.

If the author's name appears in the sentence, cite only the page number, in parentheses:

> According to Nell Irvin Painter, "**people of African descent in the Diaspora do not speak languages of Africa as their mother tongue**" (5).

If you want to quote material that is already quoted in your source, use single quotes for that material:

> Nell Irvin Painter traces a long history of African descendants' interest in Egyptian culture. Speaking of African Americans, she notes, "Hoping that past greatness portended future gloy, [they] often recited a verse from the Bible that inspired this hope: 'Princes shall come out of Egypt; Ethiopia shall soon stretch forth her hands unto God' (Psalms 63:31)" (7).

 Summarize and Paraphrase Sources Without Plagiarizing

Summarize

When you summarize, you cite your source, but instead of quoting it directly you state the major ideas of the entire source, or part of the source, in a paragraph or perhaps even a sentence. The key is to put the summary in your own words.

Plagiarized

Nell Irvin Painter's argument in *Creating Black Americans* implies that we should consider Canadians of African descent **as a new Creole people, born and forged in the Western Hemisphere.**

Most of the words are lifted directly from the original.

Acceptable summary

Nell Irvin Painter argues in *Creating Black Americans* that the experiences of African descendants in the Western Hemisphere made them so culturally different from their ancestors that we can think of them as a separate people.

Paraphrase

When you paraphrase, you represent the idea of the source in your own words at about the same length as the original. You still need to include the reference to the source of the idea. The following example illustrates what is not an acceptable paraphrase.

Plagiarized

Nell Irvin Painter contends that cultural factors such as language and religion divide African Americans from their ancestors. **People of African descent** no longer speak the **languages of Africa** as their first language. Since language is a **potent engine of culture**, the **thought, psychology, and education** of contemporary African Americans is radically different from that of their ancestors. **Religion, another crucial aspect of culture**, also divides African Americans from Africans. **Sharia, the legal system inspired by the Koran**, may **prevail in Northern Nigeria**, but it is foreign to Christian African Americans (5).

Even though the source is listed, this paraphrase is unacceptable. Too many of the words in the original are used directly here, including much or all of particular phrases. When a string of words is lifted from a source and inserted without quotation marks, the passage is plagiarized. Changing a few words in a sentence is not a paraphrase. Compare these two sentences:

Source

People of African descent in the Diaspora do not speak languages of Africa as their mother tongue.

Unacceptable paraphrase

People of African descent no longer **speak the languages of Africa** as their first language.

The paraphrase keeps the structure of the original sentence and substitutes a few words. It is much too similar to the original.

A true paraphrase represents an entire rewriting of the idea from the source.

Acceptable paraphrase

> Nell Irvin Painter contends that cultural factors such as language and religion divide African descendants in North America from their ancestors. Black North Americans speak a wide variety of languages, but usually these are not African. Painter notes how important language is in shaping cultural identity; it dictates in large part how people think and feel. Linguistic differences create significant boundaries between people. Religion, like language, is a fundamental part of how many people identify themselves. Many black Canadians identify as Christians, and they would probably see sharp contrasts between their faith and the Muslim faith common in much of Africa (5).

Even though there are a few words from the original in this paraphrase, such as *identity* and *language*, these sentences are original in structure and wording while accurately conveying the meaning of the source.

24 Use Sources Effectively

QUICK*TAKE*

- Use sources to provide evidence (see below)
- Use sources as points of departure (see p. 261)
- Integrate quotations into your project (see p. 267)
- Integrate summaries and paraphrases into your project (see p. 269)
- Integrate visuals into your project (see p. 270)

24a Use Sources to Provide Evidence

It's often been joked that a certain percentage (depending on the commentator) of all statistics are made up on the spot, which of course is an example of the error it describes. Readers expect to see evidence to support claims, and they want to know where the evidence came from. For example, polls and studies are often funded by those who have an interest in the outcome.

Your obligation is to find the most reliable evidence and to document the sources of that evidence. Let's consider an example of a student, George Abukar, writing on the topic of identity theft. Abukar had a friend whose driver's licence was stolen. The thief then applied for a credit card in George's friend's name and made thousands of dollars of fraudulent purchases. None of the people who could have stopped the thief did so: The credit card company did not bother to verify the friend's identity, and the three major credit card reporting agencies did not remove the information about unpaid bills from her file, leaving her with a bad credit rating. Abukar's thesis proposes that the federal government pass legislation making credit-reporting agencies liable for damages when their negligence leads to loss from identity theft.

Sources can help you build a case for why your claim matters. To argue for his thesis, Abukar had to establish first that the problem affected many more people besides his friend. He cites an RCMP report that estimates the cost of credit card fraud.

Readers expect evidence to support claims and reasons.

> The RCMP set counterfeiting and credit card losses for 2007 at more than $300 million from over 350 000 different accounts. The same report notes that 70 percent of dollar losses through credit card fraud arise from counterfeit cards (41 percent) and no-card fraud (33 percent)—deceptive telemarketers and fraudulent websites charging for nonexistent products and services.

24b Use Sources as Points of Departure

All good research writing responds to sources. Every significant issue has an extensive history of discussion with various points of view.

Maintain your voice when using sources

Your task as a researcher is to enter ongoing discussions by "talking" to your sources. Just as you would in a conversation with several people who hold different views, you may disagree with some people, agree with some, and agree with others only up to a point and then disagree.

Think about assuming roles in relation to your sources:

- The *skeptic*, who disagrees with a source,
- The *contributer*, who agrees with a source and has another point to add,
- The *analyst*, who agrees with a source up to a point but has reservations.

George Abukar uses all three strategies to position his sources in relation to his argument.

Take the role of the skeptic

You can use this template.

A common way of thinking about this issue is ____________________, but this view is mistaken because ____________________.

George Abukar argues that there are inadequate safeguards against identity theft because credit card companies and reporting agencies have no financial interest in preventing this theft and in some ways even profit from it. He needed to establish that it is individuals who are commonly viewed as responsible for this theft. He found a tip sheet published online by the Financial Consumer Agency of Canada (www.fcac-acfc.gc.ca) that implies this view and included a quotation from the site in his paper.

Abukar quotes common-sense advice from the FCAC website.

Mostly, consumers are told to protect themselves. The Financial Consumer Agency of Canada (among other government and business-sponsored organizations) offers a tip sheet that tells consumers how to protect themselves. Some of the advice is obvious, such as "Keep your wallet or purse out of reach—in public places, crowds and while on public transportation." Some tips are more obscure: "Put other ID documents (SIN, birth certificate, passport) in a safe place." Some tips assume that people have a lot more time, patience, and knowledge than they really do:

> Shred documents with personal information (including your name and address) . . . When on the Internet, make sure the web site you are using is secure before transmitting personal information . . . Don't leave personal information lying around at home, in your vehicle or at the office. (Financial Consumer Agency of Canada)

Abukar points out how impractical the FCAC advice is.

While this advice seems useful on the surface, most people don't have time to shred every document they receive with their name and address on it. Similarly, this advice warns people against leaving personal information in their homes, but it does not suggest safe places to store this information.

Take the role of the contributor

You can use this template.

I agree with ________________________ *because my experience confirms that* ________________________.

Sources should not make your argument for you. Indicate exactly how they support your position by making an additional point.

The credit reporting agencies are not content with letting consumers and banks foot the bill for their sloppy handling of our digital identities. They want to make more money off the insecurity they have created. Kevin Drum reports in *Washington Monthly*:

> For their part, the major credit-reporting bureaus—Experian, Equifax, and TransUnion—don't seem to care much about the accuracy of their credit reports. In fact,

he source escribes how redit card eporting gencies make noney off the ear of identity heft, supporting bukar's claim.

they actually have a positive incentive to let ID theft flourish. Like mobsters offering "protection" to frightened store owners, credit-reporting agencies have recently begun taking advantage of the identity-theft boom to offer information age protection to frightened consumers. For $9.95 a month, Equifax offers "Credit Watch Gold," a service that alerts you whenever changes are made to your credit report. Experian and TransUnion offer similar services. In effect, customers are being asked to pay credit agencies to protect them from the negligence of those same agencies.

bukar makes n additional oint that builds n his source.

Unlike consumers, who usually at least try to act responsibly to protect their credit rating, credit-reporting agencies avoid responsibility for, and profit from, identity theft. Therefore, the most important step to take in reducing identity theft is to implement legislation that holds credit-reporting agencies responsible for the damage their actions or inactions cause consumers.

Take the role of the analyst

You can use this template.

I agree with ______________________ up to a point, but I disagree with the conclusion ______________________ because ______________________.

Incorporating sources is not a matter of simply agreeing or disagreeing with them. Often you will agree with a source up to a point, but you will object to the conclusions. Or you may agree with the conclusions but not with the reasoning. In other words, you may find that someone's views are correct but not for the reasons put forth.

Abukar used a source with which he was in basic agreement, but he found one part of the argument in the source much stronger than the other part.

bukar summarizes he position of is source.

In his book *The Digital Person: Technology and Privacy in the Information Age*, Daniel J. Solove proposes that the way to reduce identity theft is to change the structure, or "architecture," of the systems we use to collect and store personal information. He recommends giving individuals more control over their personal information, and requiring the companies that use that information to inform people whenever something unusual happens to their files. While Solove's plan sounds good, he neglects the key for implementing the solution. Solove says that any new system should be "premised on the notion that the collection and use of personal information is an activity that carries duties and responsibilities" (121). This statement is an indirect way of saying, "Companies that handle personal information ought to be held

bukar goes n to argue hat the source misses now the solution proposed might be implemented.

liable for damages caused by identity theft." I would argue that if you make companies responsible to consumers by making them liable (the second half of Solove's plan), then they will automatically give consumers more control over their own information (the first half).

WRITING SMART

Determine the relationship of each source to your thesis

Gather the list of sources you have found in your research. You may have assembled these sources in a working bibliography or an annotated bibliography. Examine each source in relation to your working thesis. Note beside each source how it relates to your argument, using the "skeptic," "contributor," and "analyst" strategy.

- Does the source provide evidence for your claim or your reasons?
- Do you disagree with the source and can you use it as a jumping-off point for your argument?
- Do you agree with the source and find you can expand on it?
- Do you agree with the source up to a point and can you use it to show how your argument is different and perhaps better?

24c Decide When to Quote and When to Paraphrase

Use sources to support what you say; don't expect them to say it for you. Next to plagiarism, the worst mistake you can make with sources is to string together a series of long quotations. This strategy leaves your readers wondering whether you have anything to say. Relying too much on quotations from others also makes for a bumpy read. Think about how each source relates to your thesis (see Section 24b).

When to quote and when to paraphrase

In deciding when to include direct quotations and when to paraphrase, the general rule is to consider the importance of the original wording.

- If you want to refer to an idea or fact and the original wording is not critical, make the point in your own words.
- Save direct quotations for language that is memorable or conveys the character of the source.

Writer at Work

For background to his analysis of Al Gore's use of rhetorical appeals in *An Inconvenient Truth*, Joshua LaGrange wanted to cite two criticisms from Tom Harris's critique of the logical arguments used to support androgenic theories of global warming in "Scientists Respond to Gore's Warnings of Climate Catastrophe."

Harris, Tom. "Scientists Respond to Gore's Warnings of Climate Catastrophe." Canada Free Press. Tom Harris, 12 June 2006. Web. 30 Oct. 2011.

Professor Bob Carter of the Marine Geophysical Laboratory at James Cook University in Australia gives what, for many Canadians, is a surprising assessment: "Gore's circumstantial arguments are so weak that they are pathetic. It is simply incredible that they, and his film, are commanding public attention." . . .

QUOTE SENTENCE "Gore's circumstantial arguments are so weak that they are pathetic."

Carter is one of hundreds of highly qualified non-governmental, non-industry, non-lobby group climate experts who contest the hypothesis that human emissions of carbon dioxide (CO_2) are causing significant global climate change. "Climate experts" is the operative term here. Why? Because what Gore's "majority of scientists" think is immaterial when only a very small fraction of them actually work in the climate field.

Even among that fraction, many focus their studies on the impacts of climate change; biologists, for example, who study everything from insects to polar bears to poison ivy. "While many are highly skilled researchers, they generally do not have special knowledge about the causes of global climate change," explains former University of Winnipeg climatology professor Dr. Tim Ball. "They usually can tell us only about the effects of changes in the local environment where they conduct their studies." . . .

PARAPHRASE Harris quotes two scientists who dispute the qualifications of Gore's "experts" on climate change. Point is that Gore quotes researchers who can assess "climate impact" but not rule on androgenic causes of global warming.

Among experts who actually examine the causes of change on a global scale, many concentrate their research on designing and enhancing computer models of hypothetical futures. "These models have been consistently wrong in all their scenarios," asserts Ball. "Since modelers concede computer outputs are not 'predictions' but are in fact merely scenarios, they are negligent in letting policy-makers and the public think they are actually making forecasts."

Second point is that predictions about future climate outcomes are based on computer modelling, and models are often wrong.

WRITING SMART

Use quotations effectively

Quotations are a frequent problem area in research projects. Review every quotation to ensure that each is used effectively and correctly.

- **Limit the use of long quotations.** If you have more than one block quotation on a page, look closely to see if one or more can be paraphrased or summarized. Use direct quotations only if the original wording is important.
- **Check that each quotation is supporting your major points rather than making major points for you.** If the ideas rather than the original wording are what's important, paraphrase the quotation and cite the source.
- **Check that each quotation is introduced and attributed.** Each quotation should be introduced and the author or title named. Check for verbs that signal a quotation: Smith *claims*, Jones *argues*, Brown *states*.
- **Check that each quotation is properly formatted and punctuated.** Prose quotations longer than four lines (MLA) or forty words (APA) should be indented one inch in MLA style or one-half inch in APA style. Shorter quotations should be enclosed within quotation marks.
- **Check that you cite the source for each quotation.** You are required to cite the sources of all direct quotations, paraphrases, and summaries.
- **Check the accuracy of each quotation.** It's easy to leave out words or mistype a quotation. Compare what is in your project to the original source. If you need to add words to make the quotation grammatical, make sure the added words are in brackets. Use ellipses to indicate omitted words.
- **Read your project aloud to a classmate or a friend.** Each quotation should flow smoothly when you read your project aloud. Put a check beside rough spots as you read aloud so that you can revise later.

 Integrate Quotations

All sources should be well integrated into the fabric of your project. Introduce quotations by attributing them in your text:

> Even those who fought for the United States in the U.S.–Mexican War of 1846 were skeptical of American motives: "We were sent to provoke a fight, but it was essential that Mexico should commence it" (Grant 68).

The preceding quotation is used correctly, but it loses the impact of the source. Compare it with the following:

> Many soldiers who fought for the United States in the U.S.–Mexican War of 1846 were skeptical of American motives, including Civil War hero and future president Ulysses S. Grant, who wrote: "We were sent to provoke a fight, but it was essential that Mexico should commence it" (68).

Use signal phrases

Signal verbs often indicate your stance toward a quotation. Introducing a quotation with "X says" or "X believes" tells your readers nothing. Find a livelier verb that suggests how you are using the source. For example, if you write "X contends," your reader is alerted that you likely will disagree with the source. Be as precise as possible.

Signal phrases that report information or a claim

X argues that . . .
X asserts that . . .
X claims that . . .
X observes that . . .
As X puts it, . . .
X reports that . . .
As X sums it up, . . .

Signal phrases when you agree with the source

X affirms that . . .
X has the insight that . . .
X points out insightfully that . . .
X theorizes that . . .
X verifies that . . .

Signal phrases when you disagree with the source

X complains that . . .
X contends that . . .
X denies that . . .
X disputes that . . .
X overlooks that . . .
X rejects that . . .
X repudiates that . . .

Signal phrases in the sciences

Signal phrases in the sciences often use the past tense, especially for interpretations and commentary.

X described . . .
X found . . .
X has suggested . . .

Introduce block quotations

Long direct quotations, called *block quotations*, are indented from the margin instead of being placed in quotation marks. In MLA style, a quotation longer than four lines should be indented one inch. A quotation of 40 words or longer is indented one-half inch in APA style. In both MLA and APA styles, long quotations are double-spaced. You still need to integrate a block quotation into the text of your project by mentioning who wrote or said it.

- No quotation marks appear around the block quotation.
- Words quoted in the original retain the double quotation marks.
- The page number appears after the period at the end of the block quotation.

It is a good idea to include at least one or two sentences following the quotation to describe its significance to your thesis.

Double-check quotations

Whether they are long or short, you should double-check all quotations you use to be sure they are accurate and that all words belonging to the original are set off with quotation marks or placed in a block quotation. If you wish to leave out words from a quotation, indicate the omitted words with ellipses (. . .), but make sure you do not alter the meaning of the original quote (see Section 48e). If you need to add words of your own to a quotation to make the meaning clear, place your words in square brackets (see Section 48d).

24e Integrate Summaries and Paraphrases

Summaries and paraphrases likewise need introductions. The following paragraph is the summary of a book. The source is noted at the end, but the reader cannot tell exactly which ideas come from the source.

> In 2001 it became as fashionable to say the Internet changes nothing as it had been to claim the Internet changes everything just two years before. While the profit-making potential of the Internet was overrated, the social effects were not. The Internet is demolishing old castles of expertise along with many traditional relationships based on that expertise (Lewis).

In the following summary, signal phrases make it clear which ideas come from the source. The summary also indicates Lewis's stance and includes a short quotation that gives the flavour of the source.

> In 2001 it became as fashionable to say the Internet changes nothing as it had been to claim the Internet changes everything just two years before. In the midst of the gloom, one prominent contrarian has emerged to defend the Internet. Michael Lewis observes in *Next: The Future Just Happened* that it's as if "some crusty old baron who had been blasted out of his castle and was finally having a look at his first cannon had said, 'All it does is speed up balls'" (14). Lewis claims that while the profit-making potential of the Internet was overrated, the social effects were not. He sees the Internet demolishing old castles of expertise along with many traditional relationships based on that expertise.

STAYING ON TRACK

Weave sources into your paper

Sources should be well integrated into your project. A common mistake is to drop in quotations without introducing them or indicating their significance. We don't know how the following long quotation fits into the writer's argument.

Off track Cellphones and the Internet have not made the world a more harmonious place just because people have the increased potential to talk with each other.

> I see a world where people can't talk to each other in any meaningful way. Global networking will be a tool of business communication, consumerism, propaganda, banal conversations, and

(Continued on next page)

STAYING ON TRACK *(Continued)*

> mindless entertainment. We will have forgotten how to tell stories or how to hear them. The majority of the world's population will be very young people without extended families or intact cultures, with fanatical allegiances to dead religions or live dictatorships. We have what Jonas Salk called a "wisdom deficit." (Laurel 102)

Introduce each quotation and make clear its significance to your text. Compare the following paragraph with the paragraph above.

On track Cellphones and the Internet have not made the world a more harmonious place just because people have the increased potential to talk with each other. The tone of public discourse—be it in political campaigns, opinion in print and in pixels, talk radio, and discussion boards—has taken a turn toward the ugly. More information seems to have led to less understanding. Brenda Laurel, one of the more insightful commentators on the effects of digital media, fears we are moving toward "a world where people can't talk to each other in any meaningful way," a world where "we will have forgotten how to tell stories or how to hear them" (102). Laurel uses Jonas Salk's description of our culture as suffering from a "wisdom deficit" to sum up her point (103).

The second example introduces Brenda Laurel in relation to the writer's claim that more information has led to less understanding. The writer weaves Brenda Laurel's words into his own but preserves Laurel's distinctive voice.

Remember: Quotations don't speak for themselves.

24f Integrate Visuals

Like quotations, visuals should not be dropped in without introductions.

- Place all visuals as close as possible to the related text.
- Introduce each visual in your text.
- In MLA style, give each visual a figure number (abbreviated *Fig.*) and a caption.
- Give complete information about the source in the caption.
- If the source is not mentioned in the text, you do not need to include it in the list of works cited.

Although 70 countries around the world contain oil sands, the largest deposit occurs in northeastern Alberta, covering 140,000 km^2 (see fig. 3). Oil sands comprise bitumen—solid organic matter—and sediment, a mixture that is solid in its natural state. Under the hot summer sun, the bitumen liquefies and seeps out of the ground, blackening the waters of the Athabasca River, as it has done for thousands of years. Ironically, production of the oil sands will result in large-scale recuperation of the pristine wilderness it never was.

Fig. 3. "Location of the Athabasca, Cold Lake, and Peace River Oil Sands in Alberta with Regulatory Boundaries," Map, *Alberta Geological Survey*, Alberta Geological Survey, 28 Oct. 2011, Web. 15 Apr. 2012.

25 Write and Revise the Research Project

QUICK*TAKE*

- Revisit your research (see below)
- Plan your organization (see p. 272)
- Review and revise (see p. 275)

 25a Revisit Your Research

Before you begin writing your project, review the assignment and your goals (see Chapter 19). Your review of the assignment will remind you of your purpose (analysis, review, survey, evaluation, argument), your potential readers, your stance on your subject, and the length and scope you should aim for.

Take stock of your research

Gather the source material and any field research you have generated (see Chapters 20, 21, and 22). Often additional questions come up in the course of your research. Group your notes by subject. Ask yourself:

- Which sources provide evidence that supports your thesis or main points?
- Which sources turn out not to be relevant?
- Which ideas or points lack adequate sources? You may need to do additional research before starting to write your project.

Revise your working thesis

Often you will find that one aspect of your topic has turned out to be more interesting and has produced more information. If you have ample material, narrowing your subject is a benefit. At this stage in the writing process, your working thesis may be rough and may change as you write your draft, but having a working thesis will help keep your project focused (see Section 2c).

Revise or write out your working thesis.

I plan to (analyze, review, survey, evaluate, argue) that ________________.
This subject matters to my readers because ________________.

25b Plan Your Organization

After you have drafted a thesis, look back over your notes and determine how to group the ideas you researched. Decide what your major points will be, and how those points support your thesis. Group your research findings so that they match up with your major points.

Now it is time to create a working outline. Always include your thesis at the top of your outline as a guiding light. Some writers create formal outlines with roman numerals and the like; others compose the headings for the paragraphs of their project and use them to guide their draft; still others may start writing and then determine how they will organize their draft when they have a few paragraphs written (see Section 2d).

Writer at Work

Joshua LaGrange made a working outline for his project.

An Inconvenient Truth: A Lesson in Demagoguery

Section 1	*Introduction: summarize background on global warming and Al Gore's role in environmental movement*
Section 1A	*Thesis: Gore develops ethos, rather than logos, to convince his audience to listen to him and not the skeptics. However, his primary weapon in creating ethos is pathos, although he does employ secondary methods.*
Section 2	*Analysis of pathos/emotional appeals with specific examples from movie (e.g., opening montage of scenic shots, "we must never lose this beautiful planet")*
Section 3	*Discussion of how emotional appeals contribute to ethos (e.g., incidents from Gore's personal life: losing U.S. presidential election; son's injury; sister's death)*
Section 4	*Analysis of ethos: Gore attempts to build credibility as a speaker on scientific aspects of global warming*
Section 5	*Analysis of logical argument: focus on rebuttals to Gore's science, including U.K. court case that identified nine errors of fact in the film*
Section 6	*Conclusion: pathos and ethos are main argumentative methods. Emphasize the point that pathos fuels Gore's ethos to overcome those who would oppose him.*

 Write a Draft

Some writers begin by writing the title, first paragraph, and concluding paragraph.

Write a specific title

A bland, generic title says to readers that you are likely to be boring.

Generic Good and Bad Fats

Specific titles are like tasty appetizers; if you like the appetizer, you'll probably like the main course.

Specific The Secret Killer: Hydrogenated Fats

Write an engaging introduction

Get off to a fast start. If, for example, you want to alert readers to the dangers of partially hydrogenated oils in the food we eat, you could begin by explaining the difference in molecular structure between natural unsaturated fatty acids and trans fatty acids. And you would probably lose your readers by the end of the first paragraph.

Instead, let readers know what is at stake and provide some background and context (see Section 3e). State your thesis early on. Then go into the details in the body of your project.

> Canadians today are more heath conscious than ever before, yet most are unaware that they may be ingesting high levels of dangerous fat in the form of partially hydrogenated oils. Hydrogenation is the process of passing hydrogen bubbles through heated oil, which makes the oil taste like butter. Nearly all processed food contains some level of hydrogenated oils. The food tastes good, but the oil it contains will make you fat and can eventually kill you.

Write a strong conclusion

The challenge in writing ending paragraphs is to leave the reader with something provocative, something beyond pure summary of the previous paragraphs. Connect back to your thesis, and use a strong concluding image, example, question, or call to action to leave your readers with something to remember and think about (see Section 3e).

25d Review and Revise

After you've finished your first draft, you'll want to get comments from other writers. A good source of help is fellow students. Your instructor may include a peer review session as part of the assignment.

Reading another student's project

It is usually best to read through a project twice, looking at different levels (see Chapter 4). The first time you read through a project, concentrate on comprehension and overall impressions. See if you can summarize the project after reading it once.

Once you've read through the project a second time, write concluding suggestions and comments about how the writer could improve the project. Be specific. Saying "I liked your project" or "It's a good first draft" does not help the writer. Comments like "You need to cite more sources" or "You might consider switching paragraphs 2 and 4" give the writer specific areas to concentrate on in the revision. Remember that it's important to be supportive in the peer editing process, so try to offer comments that are positive and encouraging.

Reading your own project

Reading your project aloud to yourself will help you find rough places. Parts that are difficult for you to speak aloud are going to be hard for your readers to get through. Try to imagine yourself as a reader who does not know much about your subject or who holds a viewpoint different from your own. What could you add that would benefit that reader?

Revise, revise, revise

After you've gone through the peer editing process or assessed your own draft, sit down with your project and consider the changes you need to make. Start from the highest level, reorganizing paragraphs and possibly even cutting large parts of your project and adding new sections. If you make significant revisions, likely you will want to repeat the overall evaluation of your revised draft when you finish.

When you feel your draft is complete, begin the editing phase. Use the guidelines in Section 4d to revise style and grammatical errors. Finally, proofread your project, word by word, checking for mistakes (see Section 4e). After you print out the final project, check each page for formatting errors (see Section 26l for MLA-style formatting and Section 27g for APA-style formatting).

STAYING ON TRACK

Check for missing documentation

When you reach the proofreading stage, make one pass though your draft to check for missing documentation. Print your draft and your works-cited list, then place them beside each other.

1. Check that every parenthetical citation and every mention of an author's name in your text has an entry in your works-cited list. Put a check beside each when you find they match and note what is missing.
2. Read your text carefully for missing citations. For example, if you find a sentence similar to the following, you'll need to insert a parenthetical citation.

Off track One critic of the exuberance over Web 2.0 writes, "Today's amateur monkeys can use their networked computers to publish everything from uninformed political commentary, to unseemly home videos, to embarrassingly amateurish music, to unreadable poems, reviews, essays and novels."

On track One critic of the exuberance over Web 2.0 writes, "Today's amateur monkeys can use their networked computers to publish everything from uninformed political commentary, to unseemly home videos, to embarrassingly amateurish music, to unreadable poems, reviews, essays and novels" **(Keen 3)**.

3. Check for missing page numbers for sources that have pagination.

Off track Andrew Keen describes Wikipedia as "an online encyclopedia where anyone with opposable thumbs and a fifth-grade education can publish anything on any topic from AC/DC to Zoroastrianism."

On track Andrew Keen describes Wikipedia as "an online encyclopedia where anyone with opposable thumbs and a fifth-grade education can publish anything on any topic from AC/DC to Zoroastrianism" **(3)**.

Remember: Faulty documentation hurts your credibility as a researcher and can be a cause of plagiarism.

MLA

MLA Documentation 277

MLA Documentation Map (see the back of this divider)

You **can learn more and do more** with MyWritingLab and with the eText version of *The Brief Penguin Handbook*. For help with documenting your sources successfully in MLA style, click on "Resources," then select "Research." Look for the MLA Instruction and Multimedia resources within each topic, then complete the Exercises and click on the Gradebook to measure your progress.

MLA

26 MLA Documentation

Research writing requires you to document the sources of all of your information that is not common knowledge. The style developed by the Modern Language Association (MLA) requires you to document each source in two places: an in-text citation in the body of your project, and a list of all works cited at the end. Citing sources is a two-way process. If your readers want to find the source of a fact or quotation in your project, they can use your in-text citation to find the full information about a source in your works-cited list.

MLA DOCUMENTATION MAP

Here are the steps in the process of documentation.

1 | Collect the right information

For every source you need to have

- the name of the author or authors,
- the full title, and
- complete publication information.

For instructions go to the illustrated examples in Section 26d of the four major source types:

- **PRINTED ARTICLE**
- **PRINTED BOOK**
- **DATABASE PUBLICATION**
- **WEB PUBLICATION**

For other kinds of sources such as visual and multimedia sources, see the Index of Works-Cited Entries on pp. 296–297.

2 | Cite sources in two places

Remember, this is a two-part process.

You will learn **how to cite sources in your project** from a Writer at Work in Section 26a.

To create citations

a) in **the body of your paper**, go to 26a and 26c.
b) in a **list of works cited at the end of your paper**, go to 26b.

If you have questions that the examples in this chapter do not address, consult the *MLA Handbook for Writers of Research Papers*, seventh edition (2009), and the *MLA Style Manual and Guide to Scholarly Publishing*, third edition (2008).

3 Find the right model citations

You'll find **illustrated examples of sources** in 26d.

Once you match your source to one of those examples, you can move on to more specific examples:

- **PRINTED ARTICLE,** go to 26e.
- **PRINTED BOOK** or parts of a book, go to 26f.
- **ONLINE:** was the source
  a) in a **library database**? Go to 26g.
  b) from **another web source**? Go to 26h.

A complete list of examples is found in the Index of Works-Cited Entries on pp. 296–297.

4 Format your paper

You will find a **sample research paper in MLA style** and instructions on formatting the body of your paper and your works-cited list in Section 26l.

A note about footnotes:

MLA style does not use footnotes for documentation. Use in-text citations instead (see Sections 26a and 26c). The only use of footnotes in MLA style is for providing additional information, as you will see in Section 26k.

 26a Citing Sources in an MLA-Style Project

Writer at Work

Matt Loicano chose to compare two works of dystopic science fiction for his research paper. He wanted to explore the ways in which the authors satirized the economic systems in their futuristic worlds. You can see the complete paper in Section 26l at the end of this chapter.

How to quote and cite a source in the text of an MLA-style paper

Matt searched for a book using the NEOS Library Consortium Catalogue using the search term "dystopian science fiction." He found *The Cambridge Companion to Utopian Literature* in the *Cambridge Collections Online* database.

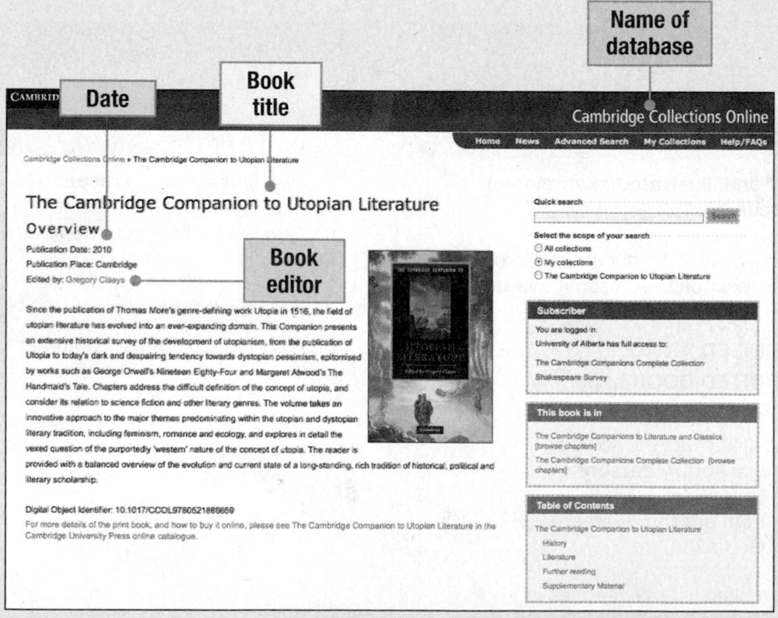

To begin his analysis, Matt decided to define *dystopia* to show how the term applied to the otherwise opposed societies (one capitalist, one communist).

Matt can either (a) use Gregory Claeys in the text of his paper with a signal phrase (see pages 267–268) or (b) place the author's name inside parentheses following the quotation. Either with or without the signal phrase, in most cases he would include the page number where he found the quotation inside parentheses.

Author's name in signal phrase

> The main difference between dystopian literature and utopian literature, according to Gregory Claeys, is that "literary dystopia utilizes the narrative devices of literary utopia . . . but predicts that inherently subjective definition of what is 'bad,' or 'less perfect.'" As Claeys later notes, "One person's utopia [is] another's dystopia" (108).

OR

Author's name in parenthetical citation

> The *Cambridge Companion to Utopian Literature* notes the main difference between dystopian literature and utopian literature is that "literary dystopia utilizes the narrative devices of literary utopia . . . but predicts that inherently subjective definition of what is 'bad,' or 'less perfect.'" Moreover, "One person's utopia [is] another's dystopia" (Claeys 108).

If Matt includes a quotation that is four lines or longer, he must double-space and indent the quotation in his paper 1 inch (see example on page 323).

Include in-text citations for summaries and paraphrases

To show the parallels between Zamyatin's One State in *We* and Soviet Russia, Matt quotes from Christopher Fern's introduction to *We*.

> Unlike H. G. Wells's futuristic world that barely resembles the source society, Zamyatin makes the parallels between the world of the One State in *We* and Soviet Russia very clear: "While depicting a society of the far future, [Zamyatin] clearly takes as his starting point Lenin's Socialist Order . . . and project[s] a world where that order is now absolute" (Fern 107).

 26b Creating the List of Works Cited

Writer at Work

Matt is ready to create an entry for the list of works cited at the end of his paper. He kept a copy of this screenshot from his search of the NEOS Catalogue and made notes about the proper information to create the works-cited entry. He used the instructions on the opposite page to form the entry.

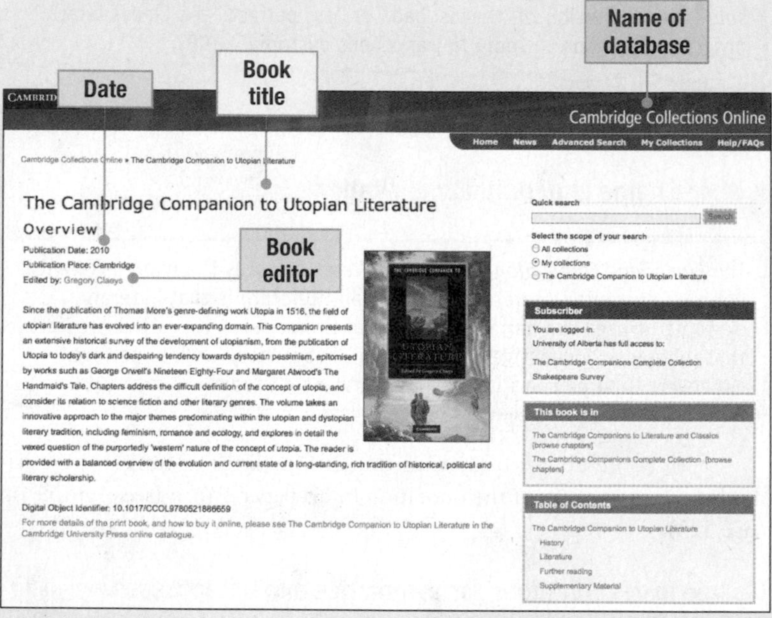

Matt asked himself a series of questions to create an entry for this source in his list of works cited.

1. What information do I need to pull from this screenshot?

For a source like this article from an online database, he needs to know five things: (1) what type of source it is; (2) the author; (3) the title; (4) the publication information; and (5) information about the online database.

2. Now how do I find the author's name?

Look for a bold heading that says something like "AUTHOR" or "BYLINE." If more than one author is listed, take note of all names listed.

3. What is the title of my source?

If the title is not immediately evident, look for a heading that says "TITLE" or "HEADLINE."

4. Where do I find the publication information?

The name and date of the periodical are usually listed at the top of the page but are sometimes found at the bottom. In this case the page number is listed beside "SECTION." Publication information for books can be found on the page after the title page at the front of the book.

5. Where do I find the name of the database?

For databases distributed by EBSCO, you have to look for the name of the database. EBSCO is the vendor who sells access to many databases such as *Academic Search Complete*. LexisNexis is the vendor that distributes access to *LexisNexis Academic* and other LexisNexis databases.

Matt listed the information.

AUTHOR	Claeys, Gregory
TITLE OF ARTICLE	"The Origins of Dystopia: Wells, Huxley and Orwell"
PUBLICATION INFORMATION	
Name of publication	The Cambridge Companion to Utopian Literature.
Date of publication	2010
Publisher	Cambridge UP
DATABASE INFORMATION	
Name of database	Cambridge Collections Online
Date the site was accessed	6 Mar. 2012

Then he used the instruction on page 307 to format his citation. You can see Matt's complete list of works cited on page 324 at the end of this chapter.

Loicano 10

Works Cited

Claeys, Gregory. "The Origins of Dystopia: Wells, Huxley and Orwell." *The Cambridge Companion to Utopian Literature*. Ed. Gregory Claeys. Cambridge UP, 2010. *Cambridge Collections Online*. Web. 6 March 2012.

26c In-text Citations in MLA Style

Paraphrase, summary, or short quotation

A short quotation takes four lines or fewer in your paper.

> While we may think that our current "information age" is unique to history, previous periods including the 18th century were also marked by "a period of 'information explosion' and long-distance transmission of data" (Giltrow 54).

Here, the author's name is provided in the parenthetical reference.

> Genre theorist and writing studies scholar Janet Giltrow answers the question "How did James Isham come to write this way?" (60).

Note that the period goes *after* the parentheses.

The author of the quotation is named in this sentence, so only a page number is needed in the parenthetical reference.

Quotations longer than four lines

The sentence introducing the quotation names the author, so only the page number needs to appear in the parenthetical reference.

> Genre theorist and writing studies scholar Janet Giltrow argues that an 18th century fur trader working for the Hudson's Bay Company learned the genre of communication from an outpost through local contexts:
>
> > The rhetorical history of this trader-writer is, inescapably, the history of his colleagues and acquaintances, too, for his ways of writing can be shown to be the outcome of social interaction, rather than schooling, or compliance with convention. As products of and contributions to social interaction, these ways of writing are not approaches to an ideal type but contingent replications, resilient but unenforceable opportunities, and incentives to other, unforeseen speech. (54)

Note that the period appears *before* the parentheses in an indented block quote.

WHEN DO YOU PROVIDE A PAGE NUMBER?

- If the source is longer than one page, provide the page number for each quotation, paraphrase, and summary.
- If an online source includes paragraph numbers rather than page numbers, use *par.* with the number.

(Cello, par. 4)

- If the source does not include page numbers, consider citing the work and the author in the text rather than in parentheses.

In a hypertext version of James Joyce's *Ulysses*, . . .

Index of In-text citations

Include in-text citations as you are writing your project rather than waiting until you finish. Use this index to determine the right format.

Sample in-text citations for sources in general

1. Author named in a signal phrase

Put the author's name in a signal phrase in your sentence.

> Lawyer and journalist Ezra Levant calls the photographs of the first open pit mines "oil sands porn" (10).

2. Author not named in your text

> According to Statistics Canada figures, women in 2003 were actually earning "slightly less—2%" than they had compared with men in 1995 (Grisson 254).

3. Work by one author

The author's last name comes first, followed by the page number. There is no comma.

> (Bell 3)

4. Work by two or three authors

The authors' last names follow the order of the title page. If there are two authors, join the names with *and*. If there are three, use a comma between the first two names and a comma with *and* before the last name.

> (Francisco, Vaughn, and Lynn 7)

5. Work by four or more authors

You may use the phrase *et al.* (meaning "and others") for all names but the first, or you may write out all the names. Make sure you use the same method for both the in-text citations and the works-cited list.

> (Abrams et al. 1653)

6. Author unknown

Use a shortened version of the title that includes at least the first important word. Your reader will use the shortened title to find the full title in the works-cited list.

> Margaret Atwood describes the literary influences that induced Alice Munro to become a writer ("Appreciations" 93).

Notice that "Appreciations" is in quotation marks because it is the shortened title of an article. If it were a book, the short title would be in italics.

7. Work by a group or organization

Treat the group or organization as the author. Try to identify the group author in the text and place only the page number in parentheses.

> According to the *Irish Free State Handbook*, published by the Ministry for Industry and Finance, the population of Ireland in 1929 was approximately 4 192 000 (23).

8. Quotations longer than four lines

NOTE: When using indented ("block") quotations that are longer than four lines, the period appears *before* the parentheses enclosing the page number.

> In her article "Art for Everybody," Susan Orlean attempts to explain the popularity of painter Thomas Kinkade:
>
> > People like to own things they think are valuable. . . . The high price of limited editions is part of their appeal: it implies that they are choice and exclusive, and that only a certain class of people will be able to afford them. (128)
>
> This same statement could also explain the popularity of phenomena like PBS's *Antiques Road Show*.

If the source is longer than one page, provide the page number for each quotation, paraphrase, and summary.

9. Two or more works by the same author

Use the author's last name and then a shortened version of the title of each source.

> The majority of books written about coauthorship focus on partners of the same sex (Laird, *Women* 351).

Note that *Women* is italicized because it is the title of a book.

10. Different authors with the same last name

If your list of works cited contains items by two or more different authors with the same last name, include the initial of the first name in the parenthetical reference. Note that a period follows the initial.

> Web surfing requires more mental involvement than channel surfing (S. Johnson 107).

11. Two or more sources within the same sentence

Place each citation directly after the statement it supports.

> Many sweeping pronouncements were made in the 1990s that the internet is the best opportunity to improve education since the printing press (Ellsworth xxii) or even in the history of the world (Dyrli and Kinnaman 79).

12. Two or more sources within the same citation

If two sources support a single point, separate them with a semicolon.

> (McKibbin 39; Gore 92)

13. Work quoted in another source

When you do not have access to the original source of the material you wish to use and only an indirect source is available, put the abbreviation *qtd. in* ("quoted in") before the information about the indirect source.

> National governments have become increasingly what Ulrich Beck, in a 1999 interview, calls "zombie institutions"—institutions that are "dead and still alive" (qtd. in Bauman 6).

Sample in-text citations for particular kinds of sources

14. One-page source

A page reference is unnecessary if you are citing a one-page work.

> Economists agree that automating routine work is the broad goal of globalization (Lohr).

15. Web sources including web pages, blogs, podcasts, wikis, videos, and other multimedia sources

MLA prefers that you mention the author in your text instead of putting the author's name in parentheses.

> Andrew Keen ironically used his own blog to claim that "blogs are boring to write (yawn), boring to read (yawn) and boring to discuss (yawn)."

If you cannot identify the author, mention the title in your text.

> The podcast "Catalina's Cubs" describes the excitement on Catalina Island when the Chicago Cubs came for spring training in the 1940s.

16. Work in an edited anthology

Cite the name of the author of the work within an anthology, not the name of the editor of the collection. For example, Melissa Jane Hardie published the chapter "Beard" in *Rhetorical Bodies*, a book edited by Jack Selzer and Sharon Crowley. Note that Hardie, not Selzer and Crowley, is named in a parenthetical citation.

(Hardie 278–79)

17. Work in more than one volume

Give the volume number in the parenthetical reference before the page number, with a colon and a space separating the two.

(Walther and Metzger 2: 647).

18. Poems, plays, and classic works

Poems

If you quote all or part of two or three lines of poetry that do not require special emphasis, put the lines in quotation marks and separate the lines using a slash (/) with a space on each side.

John Donne's "The Legacy" associates the separation of lovers with death: "When I died last, and, Dear, I die / As often as from thee I go" (1–2).

Plays

Give the act, scene, and line numbers when the work has them, the page numbers when it does not. Abbreviate titles of famous works (like *Hamlet*).

(*Ham*. 3.2.120–23).

Classic works

To supply a reference to classic works, you sometimes need more than a page number from a specific edition. Readers should be able to locate a quotation in any edition of the book. Give the page number from the edition that you are using, then a semicolon and other identifying information.

"Marriage is a house" is one of the most memorable lines in *Don Quixote* (546; pt. 2, bk. 3, ch. 19).

19. Religious texts

Cite a religious text such as the Bible or the Qur'an the first time with the name of the edition you use along with the book, chapter, and verse. In subsequent citations you need to give only the book, chapter, and verse. Abbreviate the names of books with five or more letters (*Prov.* for *Proverbs*).

The memorable phrase from the Vietnam War, "hearts and minds," actually comes from the New Testament (*New Oxford Annotated Bible*, Phil. 4.7).

26d Illustrated Samples and Index of Works Cited in MLA Style

Printed Article

You can find recent issues of printed scholarly journals and popular magazines in your library's periodicals room. Older issues are shelved on the stacks with books. Use your library's online catalogue to find the location.

Scholarly journals usually list the publication information at the top or bottom of the first page. Popular magazines often do not list volume and issue numbers. You can find the date of publication on the cover.

Name of journal, volume number, issue number, date of publication, page numbers

Ecological Applications, 17(6), 2007, pp. 1742–1751
© 2007 by the Ecological Society of America

Title of article

A CROSS-REGIONAL ASSESSMENT OF THE FACTORS AFFECTING ECOLITERACY: IMPLICATIONS FOR POLICY AND PRACTICE

Authors

SARAH PILGRIM, DAVID SMITH, AND JULES PRETTY[1]

Centre for Environment and Society, Department of Biological Sciences, University of Essex, Wivenhoe Park, Colchester CO4 3SQ United Kingdom

Abstract. The value of accumulated ecological knowledge, termed ecoliteracy, is vital to both human and ecosystem health. Maintenance of this knowledge is essential for continued support of local conservation efforts and the capacity of communities to self- or co-manage their local resources sustainably. Most previous studies have been qualitative and small scale, documenting ecoliteracy in geographically isolated locations. In this study, we take a different approach, focusing on (1) the primary factors affecting individual levels of ecoliteracy, (2) whether these factors shift with economic development, and (3) if different knowledge protection strategies are required for the future. We compared non-resource-dependent communities in the United Kingdom with resource-dependent communities in India and Indonesia ($n = 1250$ interviews). We found that UK residents with the highest levels of ecoliteracy visited the countryside frequently, lived and grew up in rural areas, and acquired their knowledge from informal word-of-mouth sources, such as parents and friends, rather than television and schooling. The ecoliteracy of resource-dependent community members, however, varied with wealth status and gender. The least wealthy families depended most on local resources for their livelihoods and had the highest levels of ecoliteracy. Gender roles affected both the level and content of an individual's ecoliteracy. The importance of reciprocal oral transfer of this knowledge in addition to direct experience to the maintenance of ecoliteracy was apparent at all sites. Lessons learned may contribute to new local resource management strategies for combined ecoliteracy conservation. Without novel policies, local community management capacity is likely to be depleted in the future.

Key words: ecoliteracy; India; Indonesia; knowledge; natural resource; oral traditions; resource management; sustainable management; United Kingdom.

Citation in the List of Works Cited

Pilgrim, Sarah, David Smith, and Jules Pretty. "A Cross-Regional Assessment of the Factors Affecting Ecoliteracy: Implications for Policy and Practice." *Ecological Applications* 17.6 (2007): 1742–51. Print.

Elements of the citation

Author's Name

The author's last name comes first, followed by a comma and the first name.

For two or more works by the same author, see page 303.

Title of Article

Use the exact title and put it inside quotation marks. If a book title is part of the article's title, italicize the book title.

Publication Information

Name of journal or newspaper
Italicize the title of the journal or newspaper.

Abbreviate the title if it commonly appears that way.

Volume, issue, and page numbers
For scholarly journals give the volume number and issue number. Place a period between the volume and issue numbers: "55.3" indicates volume 55, issue 3.

Some scholarly journals use issue numbers only.

Give the page numbers for the entire article, not just the part you used.

Medium of publication
Print.

Find the right example as your model (you may need to refer to more than one model)

What type of article do you have?

A scholarly journal article?

- For a scholarly journal, go to page 299, #27–28.

A review, editorial, or letter to the editor not in a newspaper?

- For a review, go to page 299, #29.
- For an editorial, go to page 300, #31.
- For a letter to the editor, go to page 289, #30.

A newspaper article, review, editorial, or letter to the editor?

- For a newspaper article, go to pages 300–301, #33–38.
- For a review, go to page 301, #39.
- For an editorial, go to page 301, #41–42.
- For a letter to the editor, go to page 301, #40.

A government document?

Go to pages 301–302, #43–44.

How many authors are listed?

- One, two, or more authors: go to page 300, #33–35.
- Unknown author: go to page 300, #36.

What kind of pagination is used?

- For a scholarly journal, go to page 299, #27.
- For a journal that starts every issue with page 1, go to page 299, #28.

Printed Book

Use your library's online catalogue to locate printed books on the library's shelves. Find the copyright date on the copyright page, which is on the back of the title page. Use the copyright date for the date of publication, not the date of printing.

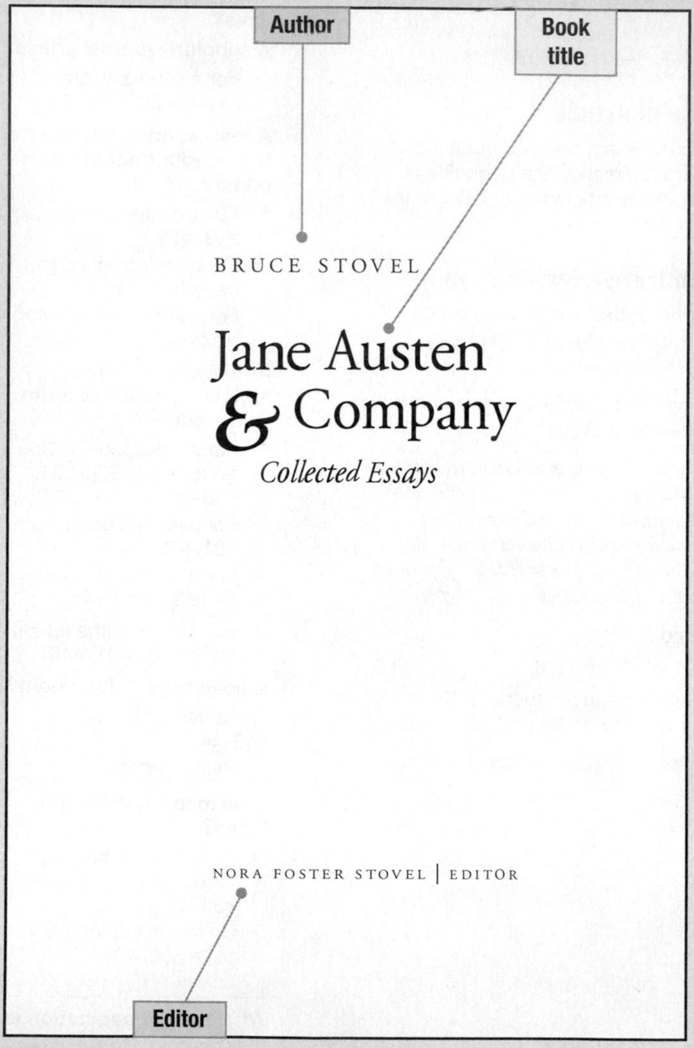

Citation in the List of Works Cited

Stovel, Bruce. *Jane Austen & Company: Collected Essays*. Ed. Nora Foster Stovel. Edmonton: U of Alberta P, 2011. Print.

Elements of the citation

Author's or Editor's Name

The author's last name comes first, followed by a comma and the first name.

For books where the editor's name takes the place of the author's name, put the abbreviation *ed.* after the name, preceded by a comma: **Kavanagh, Peter, ed.**

Book Title

Use the exact title, as it appears on the title page (not the cover).

Italicize the title.

Publication Information

Place of publication
If more than one city is given, use the first.

Publisher
Omit words such as *Publisher* and *Inc*.

For university presses, use *UP*: New York UP.

Shorten the name. For example, shorten *W. W. Norton & Co.* to *Norton*.

Date of publication
Give the year as it appears on the copyright page.

If no year of publication is given, but can be approximated, put a *c.* ("circa") and the approximate date in brackets: [c. 1999].

Otherwise, put n.d. ("no date"): Toronto: U of Toronto P, n.d.

Medium of publication
Print.

Find the right example as your model (you may need to refer to more than one model)

How many authors are listed?

- One, two, or more authors: go to page 303, #51–54.
- Unknown author: go to page 303, #55.
- Group or organization as the author: go to page 304, #57.

Do you have a book with an editor, translator, or illustrator?

- For a focus on the editor, go to page 306, #70.
- For a focus on the author of an edited book, go to page 306, #71.
- For a book with a translator, go to page 306, #72.
- For an illustrated book, go to page 306, #74.

Do you have only a part of a book?

- For an introduction, foreword, preface, or afterword, go to page 305, #64.
- For a chapter in an anthology or edited collection, go to page 305, #66.
- For more than one selection in an anthology or edited collection, go to page 305, #67.

Do you have two or more books by the same author?

- Go to page 303, #52.

Library Database Publication

You will find library databases linked off your library's website (see page 217). A few databases, including Google Scholar, are available to everyone, but most library databases are password protected if you access them off campus.

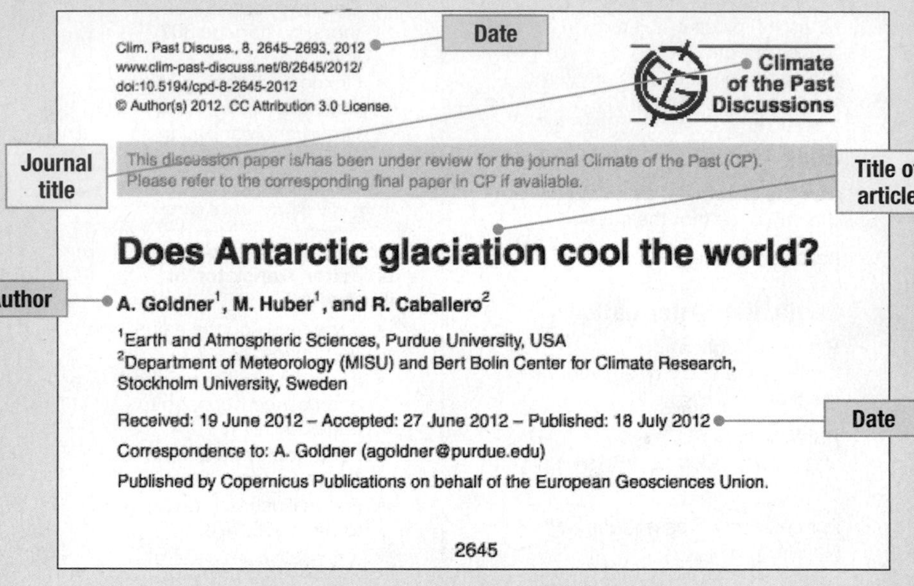
Clim. Past Discuss., 8, 2645–2693, 2012
www.clim-past-discuss.net/8/2645/2012/
doi:10.5194/cpd-8-2645-2012
© Author(s) 2012. CC Attribution 3.0 License.

Climate of the Past Discussions

This discussion paper is/has been under review for the journal Climate of the Past (CP). Please refer to the corresponding final paper in CP if available.

Does Antarctic glaciation cool the world?

A. Goldner[1], M. Huber[1], and R. Caballero[2]

[1]Earth and Atmospheric Sciences, Purdue University, USA
[2]Department of Meteorology (MISU) and Bert Bolin Center for Climate Research, Stockholm University, Sweden

Received: 19 June 2012 – Accepted: 27 June 2012 – Published: 18 July 2012

Correspondence to: A. Goldner (agoldner@purdue.edu)

Published by Copernicus Publications on behalf of the European Geosciences Union.

2645

Citation in the List of Works Cited

Goldner, A., M. Huber, and R. Caballero. "Does Antarctic Glaciation Cool the World?" *Climate of the Past* 8.4 (2012): 2645-2693. *Google Scholar*. Web. 11 Jan. 2013.

Take Note

Don't confuse the name of the vendor—the company that sells access to the database—with the name of the database. For example, EBSCO or EBSCO Host is not the name of a database but the name of the vendor that sells access to databases such as *Academic Search Complete.*

Elements of the citation

Start with the citation with the exact format of a print citation. Replace the word *Print* at the end with the name of the database, the medium (*Web*), and the date you accessed the source.

Author's Name

The author's last name comes first, followed by a comma and the first name. For two or more works by the same author, see page 303.

Title of Source

For an article in a journal or collection, use the exact title and put it inside quotation marks. If a book title is part of the article's title, italicize the book title.

Publication Information for an Article

Name of journal or newspaper
Italicize the title of the journal or newspaper. Abbreviate the title if it commonly appears that way.

Volume, issue, date, and page numbers
List the same information you would for a print item. If there are no page numbers, put *n. pag.* where the page numbers would ordinarily go.

Database Information

Name of the database
Italicize the name of the database, followed by a period.

Medium of publication
For online database sources, the medium of publication is *Web*.

Date of access
List the date you accessed the source (day, month, year).

Find the right example as your model (you may need to refer to more than one model)

Most databases allow you to search by document type, such as scholarly journal, newspaper article, financial report, legal case, or abstract. Use these categories to identify the type of publication.

What kind of publication do you have?

- For an article in a scholarly journal, go to page 307, #77
- For a magazine article, go to page 307, #78
- For a newspaper article, go to page 307, #80
- For a legal case, go to page 307, #81
- For a company report, go to page 307, #82

Do you have a publication with an unknown author?
Go to page 307, #79.

Web Publication

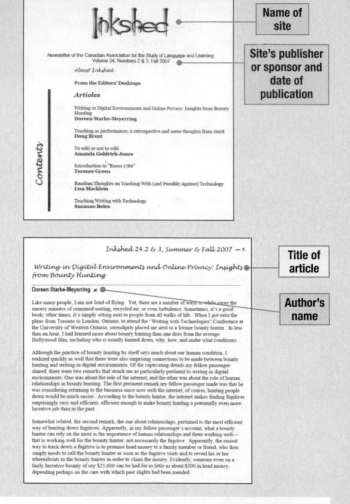

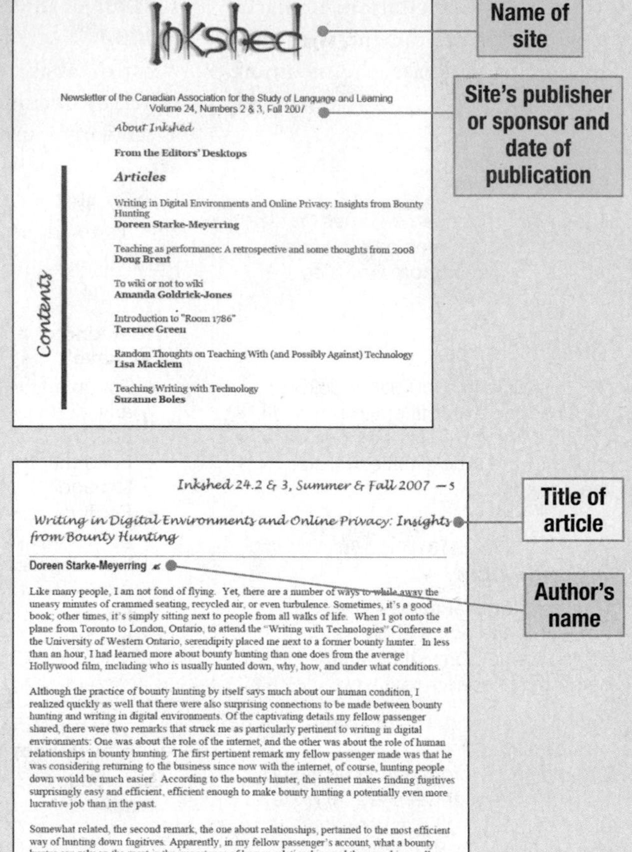

Inkshed

Newsletter of the Canadian Association for the Study of Language and Learning
Volume 24, Numbers 2 & 3, Fall 2007

About Inkshed

From the Editors' Desktops

Contents

Articles

Writing in Digital Environments and Online Privacy: Insights from Bounty Hunting
Doreen Starke-Meyerring

Teaching as performance: A retrospective and some thoughts from 2008
Doug Brent

To wiki or not to wiki
Amanda Goldrick-Jones

Introduction to "Room 1786"
Terence Green

Random Thoughts on Teaching With (and Possibly Against) Technology
Lisa Macklem

Teaching Writing with Technology
Suzanne Boles

Inkshed 24.2 & 3, Summer & Fall 2007 — 5

Writing in Digital Environments and Online Privacy: Insights from Bounty Hunting

Doreen Starke-Meyerring

Like many people, I am not fond of flying. Yet, there are a number of ways to while away the uneasy minutes of crammed seating, recycled air, or even turbulence. Sometimes, it's a good book; other times, it's simply sitting next to people from all walks of life. When I got onto the plane from Toronto to London, Ontario, to attend the "Writing with Technologies" Conference at the University of Western Ontario, serendipity placed me next to a former bounty hunter. In less than an hour, I had learned more about bounty hunting than one does from the average Hollywood film, including who is usually hunted down, why, how, and under what conditions.

Although the practice of bounty hunting by itself says much about our human condition, I realized quickly as well that there were also surprising connections to be made between bounty hunting and writing in digital environments. Of the captivating details my fellow passenger shared, there were two remarks that struck me as particularly pertinent to writing in digital environments: One was about the role of the internet, and the other was about the role of human relationships in bounty hunting. The first pertinent remark my fellow passenger made was that he was considering returning to the business since now with the internet, of course, hunting people down would be much easier. According to the bounty hunter, the internet makes finding fugitives surprisingly easy and efficient, efficient enough to make bounty hunting a potentially even more lucrative job than in the past.

Somewhat related, the second remark, the one about relationships, pertained to the most efficient way of hunting down fugitives. Apparently, in my fellow passenger's account, what a bounty hunter can rely on the most is the importance of human relationships and them working well—that is working well for the bounty hunter, not necessarily the fugitive. Apparently, the easiest way to track down a fugitive is to promise head money to a family member or friend, who then simply needs to call the bounty hunter as soon as the fugitive visits and to reveal his or her whereabouts to the bounty hunter in order to claim the money. Evidently, someone even on a fairly lucrative bounty of say $25,000 can be had for as little as about $300 in head money, depending perhaps on the care with which past slights had been mended.

> Starke-Meyerring, Doreen. "Writing in Digital Environments and Online Privacy: Insights from Bounty Hunting." *Inkshed* 24.2–3 (Fall 2007). Canadian Association for the Study of Language and Learning. Web. 7 Mar. 2012.

When Do You List a URL?

MLA style no longer requires including URLs of web sources. URLs are of limited value because they change frequently and they can be specific to an individual search. Include the URL as supplementary information only when your readers probably cannot locate the source without the URL.

Elements of the citation

Author's Name

Authorship is sometimes hard to discern for online sources. If you know the author or creator, follow the rules for books and journals.

If the only authority you find is a group or organization, list its name after the date of publication or last revision.

Title of Source

Place the title of the work inside quotation marks if it is part of a larger website.

Untitled works may be identified by a label (e.g., *Home page, Introduction*). List the label in the title slot without quotation marks or italics.

Italicize the name of the overall site if it is different from the work. The name of the overall website will usually be found on its index or home page.

Some websites are updated, so list the version if you find it (e.g., *Vers. 1.2*).

Publication Information for Web Sources

List the publisher's or sponsor's name followed by a comma. If it isn't available, use *N.p.*

List the date of publication by day, month, and year if available. If you cannot find a date, use *n.d*.

Give the medium of publication (*Web*).

List the date you accessed the site by day, month, and year.

Find the right example as your model (you may need to refer to more than one model)

Do you have a web page or an entire website?

- For an entire website, go to page 308, #84
- For a page on a website, go to page 308, #83

What kind of publication do you have, and who is the author?

- For a known author, go to page 308, #85
- For a group or organization as the author, go to page 308, #86
- For a publication with print publication data, go to page 308, #87
- For a PDF or digital file, go to page 309, #88
- For an article in a scholarly journal, newspaper, or magazine, go to page 309, #89–91
- For a government publication, go to page 310, #97

Do you have a source that is posted by an individual?

- For email or text messaging, go to page 311, #99
- For a post to a discussion list, go to page 311, #100
- For a personal home page, go to page 311, #102
- For a blog, go to page 311, #103

Index of Works-Cited Entries

26e Journals, Magazines, Newspapers, and Other Print Sources

JOURNAL AND MAGAZINE ARTICLES

20. Article by one author

Bhabha, Jacqueline. "The Child—What Sort of Human?" *PMLA* 121.5 (2006): 1526–35. Print.

21. Article by two or three authors

The second and subsequent authors' names are printed first name first.

Kirsch, Gesa E., and Jacqueline J. Royster. "Feminist Rhetorical Practices: In Search of Excellence." *CCC* 61.4 (2010): 640–72. Print.

Notice that a comma separates the authors' names.

22. Article by four or more authors

You may use the phrase *et al.* (meaning "and others") for all authors but the first, or you may write out all the names.

Breece, Katherine E., et al. "Patterns of mtDNA Diversity in Northwestern North America." *Human Biology* 76.5 (2004): 33–54. Print.

23. Article by an unknown author

Begin the entry with the title.

"UN Mission Unable to End Syria Bloodshed." *National Post* 12 Mar. 2012: A7. Print.

24. Article with a title within a title

If the title of the article contains the title of another short work, include it in single quotation marks. Italicize the title or a word that would normally be italicized.

Happel, Alison, and Jennifer Esposito. "Vampires, Vixens, and Feminists: An Analysis of *Twilight*." *Educational Studies* 46:5 (2010): 524-31. Print.

MONTHLY, WEEKLY, AND BIWEEKLY MAGAZINES

25. Monthly or seasonal magazines or journals

For magazines and journals identified by the month or season of publication, use the month (or season) and year in place of the volume. Abbreviate the names of all months except May, June, and July.

> Huang, Yasheng. "China's Other Path." *Wilson Quarterly* Spring 2010: 58–64. Print.

26. Weekly or biweekly magazines

For weekly or biweekly magazines, give both the day and month of publication, as listed on the issue.

> Toobin, Jeffrey. "Crackdown." *New Yorker* 5 Nov. 2001: 56–61. Print.

DIFFERENT TYPES OF PAGINATION

27. Article in a scholarly journal

After the title of the article, give the journal name in italics, the volume and issue numbers, the year of publication in parentheses, a colon, the inclusive page numbers, and the medium of publication.

> Duncan, Mike. "Whatever Happened to the Paragraph?" *College English* 69.5 (2007): 470–95. Print.

28. Article in a scholarly journal that uses only issue numbers

If a journal begins each issue on page 1, list the issue number after the name of the journal.

> McCall, Sophie. "Double Vision Reading." *Canadian Literature* 194 (2007): 95–97. Print.

REVIEWS, EDITORIALS, LETTERS TO THE EDITOR

29. Review

Provide the title, if given, and name the work reviewed. If there is no title, just name the work reviewed. For film reviews, name the director.

> O'Grady, Matt. Rev. of *The End of Money*. *Canadian Business* 1 Mar. 2012. Web. 20 May 2012.

30. Letter to the editor

Add the word *Letter* after the name of the author.

> Banerjee, Ron. Letter. *Maclean's* July 2011. Web. 20 May 2012.

31. Editorial

If the editorial is unsigned, put the title first. Add the word *Editorial* after the title.

"Stop Stonewalling on Reform." Editorial. *Business Week* 17 June 2002: 108. Print.

32. Published interview

Phipps, Simon. Interview. *Linux Journal* 1 June 2007: 33–34. Print.

NEWSPAPER ARTICLES

33. Article by one author

Rojas, Rick. "For Young Sikhs, a Tie That Binds Them to Their Faith." *Washington Post* 20 June 2010, final ed.: C03. Print.

34. Article by two or three authors

The second and subsequent authors' names are printed in regular order, first name first:

Chazen, Guy, and Dana Cimilluca. "BP Amasses Cash for Oil-Spill Costs." *Wall Street Journal* 26 June 2010: A1. Print.

Notice that a comma separates the authors' names.

35. Article by four or more authors

You may use the phrase *et al.* (meaning "and others") for all authors but the first, or you may write out all the names. Use the same method in the in-text citation as you do in the works-cited list.

Watson, Anne, et al. "Childhood Obesity on the Rise." *Daily Missoulian* 7 July 2003: B1. Print.

36. Article by an unknown author

Begin the entry with the title.

"Shopper Sought Who Tried to Pull Off Woman's Hijab in Grocery Store." *National Post* 10 Mar. 2012: A5. Print.

37. Article with a title in a foreign language

If the title is in a foreign language, copy it exactly as it appears on the title page, paying special attention to accent marks and capitalization.

"Iraq, Liberati gli Ostaggi Sudcoreani." *Corriere Della Sera* 8 Apr. 2004: A1. Print.

38. Article that continues to a nonconsecutive page

Add a plus sign after the number of the first page.

Blaze Carlson, Kathryn. "Bring Me My Baby." *National Post* 10 Mar. 2012: A1+. Print.

NEWSPAPER REVIEWS, EDITORIALS, LETTERS TO THE EDITOR

39. Review

List the reviewer's name and the title of the review. Then write *Rev. of* followed by the title of the work, the word *by*, and the author's name.

Eisenthal, Bram. "Stephen King Turns Cellphone Users into Zombies." Rev. of *Cell,* by Stephen King. *Montreal Gazette* 18 Feb. 2006: H1. Print.

40. Letter to the editor

Kellner, Betty. Letter. *Edmonton Journal* 12 Mar. 2012: A12. Print.

41. Editorial

Add the word *Editorial* after the title.

Pachon, Harry P. "Pricing Out New Citizens." Editorial. *Los Angeles Times* 2 Apr. 2007, home ed.: A13. Print.

42. Unsigned editorial

If the editorial is unsigned, put the title first.

"Cracking Down on Government Waste." Editorial. *National Post* 10 Mar. 2012: A16. Print.

GOVERNMENT DOCUMENTS

43. Government documents

Canada. Indian and Northern Affairs. *After Marriage Breakdown*. Ottawa: Minister of Public Works and Govt. Services Canada, 2003. Print.

Canada. House of Commons. *House of Commons Debates*. 39th Parl., 1st sess. Vol. 141, No. 9. Cat. X3-391/9E. Ottawa: Minister of Public Works and Govt. Services Canada, 2006. Print.

44. Congressional record

Cong. Rec. 8 Feb. 2000: 1222–46. Print.

BULLETINS, PAMPHLETS, AND LETTERS

45. Bulletin or pamphlet

Health Insurance for Your Pet. Winnipeg: SecuriCan General Insurance, 2005. Print.

46. Published letter

Wilde, Oscar. "To Lord Alfred Douglas." 17 Feb. 1895. In *The Complete Letters of Oscar Wilde*. Ed. Merlin Holland and Rupert Hart-Davis. New York: Holt, 2000. 632–33. Print.

47. Unpublished letter

Welty, Eudora. Letter to Elizabeth Bowen. 1 May 1951. MS. Harry Ransom Humanities Research Center, Austin.

DISSERTATIONS

48. Published dissertation or thesis

Mason, Jennifer. *Civilized Creatures: Animality, Cultural Power, and American Literature, 1850–1901*. Diss. U of Texas at Austin, 2000. Ann Arbor: UMI, 2000. Print.

49. Unpublished dissertation or thesis

Guo, Rong. "Approaching History: The Fictional Worlds of Ha Jin and Yan Gelin." Diss. U of Alberta, 2011. Print.

CONFERENCE PROCEEDINGS

50. Published proceedings of a conference

Graves, Heather, and Roger Graves, eds. *Interdisciplinarity: Thinking and Writing Beyond Borders: Proceedings of the 25th Conference of the Canadian Association of Teachers of Technical Writing, 2008*. Edmonton: CASDW, 2010. Print.

Books

ONE AUTHOR

51. Book by one author

Mayer-Schönberger, Viktor. *Delete: The Virtue of Forgetting in the Digital Age*. Princeton: Princeton UP, 2009. Print.

52. Two or more books by the same author

In the entry for the first book, include the author's name. In the second entry, substitute three hyphens and a period for the author's name. List the titles of books by the same author in alphabetical order.

Harris, Randy Allen, ed. *Rhetoric and Incommensurability*. West Lafayette: Parlor, 2005. Print.

---. *The Linguistics Wars*. London: Oxford UP, 1995. Print.

MULTIPLE AUTHORS

53. Book by two or three authors

The second and subsequent authors' names appear first name first.

Schindler, David, and John Vallentyne. *The Algal Bowl: Overfertilization of the World's Freshwater and Estuaries*. Edmonton: U of Alberta P, 2008. Print.

54. Book by four or more authors

You may use the phrase *et al.* (meaning "and others") for all authors but the first, or you may write out all the names. Use the same method in the in-text citation as you do in the works-cited list.

North, Stephen M., et al. *Refiguring the Ph.D. in English Studies*. Urbana: NCTE, 2000. Print.

ANONYMOUS AND GROUP AUTHORS

55. Book by an unknown author

Begin the entry with the title.

The Canadian Encyclopedia. Toronto: Historica-Dominion Institute, 2012. Online.

56. Book revised by a second author

Place the editor's name after the book title.

Strunk, William. *Elements of Style*. Ed. E. B. White. 4th ed. Boston: Allyn, 2000. Print.

57. Book by a group or organization

Treat the group as the author of the work.

United Nations. *The Charter of the United Nations: A Commentary.* New York: Oxford UP, 2000. Print.

TITLES WITHIN TITLES AND FOREIGN TITLES

58. Title within a title

If the title contains the title of another book or a word normally italicized, do not italicize that title or word.

Higgins, Brian, and Hershel Parker. *Critical Essays on Herman Melville's* Moby-Dick. New York: Hall, 1992. Print.

59. Title in a foreign language

If the title is in a foreign language, copy it exactly as it appears on the title page.

Fontaine, Jean. *Etudes de littérature tunisienne*. Tunis: Dar Annawras, 1989. Print.

IMPRINTS, REPRINTS, AND UNDATED BOOKS

60. Book published before 1900

You may omit the publisher for books published prior to 1900.

Rodd, Renell. *Rose Leaf and Apple Leaf*. Philadelphia, 1882. Print.

61. Book from a special imprint of the publisher

In the example below, Flamingo is a special imprint of Harper.

O'Brien, Flann. *The Poor Mouth*. London: Flamingo-Harper, 1993. Print.

62. Book with no publication date

If no year of publication is given, but it can be approximated, put a *c.* ("circa") and the approximate date in brackets: [c. 1999]. Otherwise, put *n.d.* ("no date").

O'Sullivan, Colin. *Traditions and Novelties of the Irish Country Folk.* Dublin, [c. 1793]. Print.

James, Franklin. *In the Valley of the King*. Cambridge: Harvard UP, n.d. Print.

63. Reprinted works

For works of fiction that have been printed in many different editions or reprints, give the original publication date after the title.

Wilde, Oscar. *The Picture of Dorian Gray*. 1890. New York: Norton, 2001. Print.

PARTS OF BOOKS

64. Introduction, foreword, preface, or afterword

Benstock, Sheri. Introduction. *The House of Mirth*. By Edith Wharton. Boston: Bedford-St. Martin's, 2002. 3–24. Print.

65. Single chapter by the same author as the book

Ardis, Ann. "Mapping the Middlebrow in Edwardian England." *Modernism and Cultural Conflict: 1880–1922*. Cambridge: Cambridge UP, 2002. 114–42. Print.

66. Chapter in an anthology or edited collection

Spoel, Philippa, and Chantal Barriault. "Risk Knowledge and Risk Communication: The Rhetorical Challenge of Public Dialogue." *Writing in Knowledge Societies*. Ed. Doreen Starke-Meyerring et al. Anderson: Parlor, 2011. 87–112. Print.

67. More than one selection from an anthology or edited collection

Multiple selections from a single anthology can be handled by creating a complete entry for the anthology and shortened cross-references for individual works in that anthology.

Adichie, Chimamanda Ngozi. "Half of a Yellow Sun." Eggers 1–17.

Eggers, Dave, ed. *The Best American Nonrequired Reading 2004*. Boston: Houghton, 2004. Print.

Sedaris, David. "Full House." Eggers 350–58.

68. Article in a reference work

"Utilitarianism." *The Columbia Encyclopedia*. 6th ed. 2001. Print.

THE BIBLE AND OTHER RELIGIOUS TEXTS

69. Religious texts

The New Oxford Annotated Bible. Ed. Bruce M. Metzger and Roland E. Murphy. New York: Oxford UP, 1991. Print.

Use a period to separate the chapter and verse in the in-text note: (John 3.16)

EDITIONS, TRANSLATIONS, AND ILLUSTRATED BOOKS

70. Book with an editor—focus on the editor

Lewis, Gifford, ed. *The Big House of Inver*. By Edith Somerville and Martin Ross. Dublin: Farmar, 2000. Print.

71. Book with an editor—focus on the author

Somerville, Edith, and Martin Ross. *The Big House of Inver*. Ed. Gifford Lewis. Dublin: Farmar, 2000. Print.

72. Book with a translator

Mallarmé, Stéphane. *Divagations*. Trans. Barbara Johnson. Cambridge: Harvard UP, 2007. Print.

73. Second or subsequent edition of a book

Hawthorn, Jeremy, ed. *A Concise Glossary of Contemporary Literary Theory*. 3rd ed. London: Arnold, 2001. Print.

74. Illustrated book or graphic narrative

After the title of the book, give the illustrator's name, preceded by the abbreviation *Illus.* If the emphasis is on the illustrator's work, place the illustrator's name first, followed by the abbreviation *illus.*, and list the author after the title, preceded by the word *By*.

Strunk, William, Jr., and E. B. White. *The Elements of Style Illustrated*. Illus. Maira Kalman. New York: Penguin, 2005. Print.

MULTIVOLUME WORKS

75. One volume of a multivolume work

Samuel, Raphael. *Theatres of Memory*. Vol. 1. London: Verso, 1999. Print.

76. Book in a series

Give the series name after the publishing information.

Watson, James. *William Faulkner: Self-Presentation and Performance*. Austin: U of Texas P, 2000. Print. Literary Modernism Ser.

26g Library Database Sources

Give the print citation followed by the name of the database in italics, the medium (Web), and the date you accessed the database. You do not need to list the URL of common library databases.

77. Scholarly journal article from a library database

Awano, Lisa, et al. "Appreciations of Alice Munro." *Virginia Quarterly Review* 82 (2006): 91–107. *Academic Search Complete*. Web. 13 Mar. 2012.

78. Magazine article from a library database

"The Trouble with Immortality: If We Could Live Forever, Would We Really Want To?" *Newsweek* 5 July 2010, US ed.: 78. *Academic Search Complete*. Web. 9 Dec. 2010.

79. Article with unknown author from a library database

"Dicing with Data: Facebook, Google and Privacy." *Economist* 22 May 2010, US ed.: 16. *LexisNexis Academic*. Web. 15 Sept. 2010.

80. Newspaper article from a library database

Franciane, Valerie. "Quarter Is Ready to Rock." *Times-Picayune* [New Orleans] 3 Apr. 2007: 1. *LexisNexis Academic*. Web. 23 Jan. 2010.

81. Legal case from a library database

Bilski v. Kappos. US 08-964. Supreme Court of the US 28 June 2010. *LexisNexis Academic*. Web. 28 June 2010.

82. Company report from a library database

"Nike, Inc." 3 Aug. 2010. *Factiva*. Web. 3 Aug. 2010.

 Web Sources and Other Online Sources

WEBSITES

83. Page on a website

The basic format for citing a web page includes the author or editor, the title of the page, the title of the site (in italics), the sponsor or publisher of the site, the date of publication, the medium (*Web*), and the date you accessed the site.

> "Today in Orlando." *The Orlando Project*. The University of Alberta, 2 Apr. 2010. Web. 4 Apr. 2012.

84. Entire website

> *The Orlando Project*. The University of Alberta, 2010. Web. 2 Apr. 2012.

PUBLICATIONS ON THE WEB

85. Publication by a known author

> Samadzadeh, Nozlee. "Farm Update: The Third Annual Jack Hitt Annual Last Day of Classes Pig Roast." *Yale Sustainable Food Project Student Blog*. Yale Sustainable Food Project, 3 May 2010. Web. 10 May 2010.

86. Publication by a group or organization

If a work has no author's or editor's name listed, begin the entry with the title.

> "State of the Birds." *Audubon. National Audubon Society*, 2010. Web. 19 Aug. 2010.

87. Publication on the web with print publication data

Include the print publication information. Then give the name of the website or database in italics, the medium of publication (*Web*), and the date of access (day, month, and year).

> Kirsch, Irwin S., et al. *Adult Literacy in America*. Darby: Diane, 1993. *Google Scholar*. Web. 30 Oct. 2010.

88. PDFs and digital files

PDFs and other digital files can often be downloaded through links. Determine the kind of work you are citing (e.g., article, paper, photograph, song), include the appropriate information for the particular kind of work, and list the type of file.

> Glaser, Edward L., and Albert Saiz. "The Rise of the Skilled City." Discussion Paper No. 2025. Harvard Institute of Economic Research. Cambridge: Harvard U, 2003. PDF file.

PERIODICALS ON THE WEB

89. Article in a scholarly journal on the web

Some scholarly journals are published on the web only. List articles by author, title, name of journal in italics, volume and issue number, and year of publication. If the journal does not have page numbers, use *n. pag.* in place of page numbers. Then list the medium of publication (*Web*) and the date of access (day, month, and year).

> Fleckenstein, Kristie. "Who's Writing? Aristotelian Ethos and the Author Position in Digital Poetics." *Kairos* 11.3 (2007): n. pag. Web. 6 Apr. 2010.

90. Article in a newspaper on the web

List the name of the newspaper in italics, followed by a period and the publisher's name. Follow the publisher's name with a comma. The first date is the date of publication; the second is the date of access.

> Brown, Patricia Leigh. "Australia in Sonoma." *New York Times*. New York Times, 5 July 2008. Web. 3 Aug. 2010.

91. Article in a popular magazine on the web

> Brown, Patricia Leigh. "The Wild Horse Is Us." *Newsweek*. Newsweek, 1 July 2008. Web. 12 Dec. 2010.

92. Review on the web

> Ebert, Roger. Rev. of *Gran Torino*, dir. Clint Eastwood. *rogerebert.com*. Chicago Sun-Times, 17 Dec. 2008. Web. 28 Jan. 2010.

BOOKS, ARCHIVES, AND SCHOLARLY PROJECTS ON THE WEB

93. Book on the web

If the book was printed and then scanned, give the print publication information. Then give the name of the database or website in italics, the medium of publication (*Web*), and the date of access (day, month, and year).

> Prebish, Charles S., and Kenneth K. Tanaka. *The Faces of Buddhism in America*. Berkeley: U of California P, 2003. *eScholarship Editions*. Web. 2 May 2010.

94. Scholarly project or archive on the web

Give the name of the editor if available, the name of the scholarly project or archive in italics, and the publisher or sponsor followed by a comma. Then give the date (if unavailable, use *n.d.*), the medium of publication (*Web*), and the date of access (day, month, and year).

> McGann, Jerome J., ed. *The Rossetti Archive*. U of Virginia, n.d. Web. 30 Mar. 2010.

95. Document within a scholarly project or archive

Give the print information, then the title of the scholarly project or archive in italics, the medium of publication (*Web*), and the date of access (day, month, and year).

> "New York Quiet." *Franklin Repository* 5 Aug. 1863, 1. *Valley of the Shadow*. Web. 23 Feb. 2010.

96. Film or recording in an archive

If you download a film or recording from an archive, treat the works-cited entry as a digital file (see sample entry 88).

> Dickson, William Kennedy-Laurie, prod. *Buffalo Dance*. 1894. Lib. of Cong., Washington. MPEG file.

GOVERNMENT PUBLICATIONS ON THE WEB

97. Government publication

Government publications are issued in many formats. If you cannot locate the author of the document, give the name of the government and the agency that published it.

> Canada. Canada Revenue Agency. *2010-2011 Annual Report to Parliament*. Canada Revenue Agency, 2 Nov. 2011. Web. 31 Mar. 2012.

UNEDITED ONLINE SOURCES

98. Wiki entry

Wiki content is written collaboratively, thus no author is listed. Because the content on a wiki changes frequently, wikis are not considered reliable scholarly sources.

"Snowboard." *Wikipedia*. Wikimedia Foundation, 2010. Web. 30 Jan. 2010.

99. Email and text messaging

Give the name of the writer, the subject line, a description of the message, the date, and the medium of delivery (*Email, Text message*).

Ballmer, Steve. "A New Era of Business Productivity and Innovation." Message to Microsoft Executive Email. 30 Nov. 2006. Email.

100. Posting to a discussion list

Give the name of the writer, the subject line, the name of the list in italics, the publisher, the date of the posting, the medium (*Web*), and the date of access.

Dobrin, Sid. "Re: ecocomposition?" *Writing Program Administration*. Arizona State U, 19 Dec. 2008. Web. 5 Jan. 2009.

101. Course home page

Sparks, Julie. "English Composition 1B." Course home page. San Jose State U, Fall 2008. Web. 17 Sept. 2008.

102. Personal home page

List *Home page* without quotation marks in place of the title. If no date is listed. use *n.d.*

Graves, Roger. Home page. Department of English and Film Studies. U of Alberta, Edmonton, n.d. Web. 11 June 2011.

103. Blog entry

If there is no sponsor or publisher for the blog, use *N.p.*

Arrington, Michael. "Think Before You Voicemail." *TechCrunch*. N.p., 5 July 2008. Web. 10 Sept. 2010.

26i Visual Sources

104. Cartoon or comic strip

Give the author's name, the title of the cartoon or comic strip in quotation marks, and the description *Cartoon* or *Comic strip.*

Trudeau, G. B. "Doonesbury." Comic strip. *Washington Post* 21 Apr. 2008. C15. Print.

105. Advertisement

Begin with the name of the advertiser or product, then the word *Advertisement.*

Nike. Advertisement. ABC. 8 Oct. 2010. Television.

106. Map, graph, or chart

Specify *Map, Graph,* or *Chart* after the title.

Greenland. Map. Vancouver: International Travel Maps, 2004. Print.

107. Table reproduced in your text

This is how a table might appear in your text:

In *The Republic,* Plato explains how the three parts of the individual soul should be repeated in the structure of the ideal city-state (see Table 1).

Table 1
Plato's Politics

Soul	Reason	Courage	Appetites
State	Elite guardians	Soldiers	Masses

Source: Richard Osborne, *Philosophy for Beginners* (New York: Writers and Readers, 1992; print; 15).

This is how a table appears in your list of works cited:

Plato's Politics. Table. New York: Writers and Readers, 1992. 15. Print.

108. Painting, sculpture, or photograph

Give the artist's name if available, the title of the work in italics, its date of creation, the medium of composition, the name of the institution that houses the work and the city, or the name of the collection. In the text, mentioning the work and the artist is preferable to a parenthetical citation.

> Reid, Bill. *The Spirit of Haida Gwaii*. 1991. Bronze. Canadian Embassy, Washington, DC.

VISUAL SOURCES ON THE WEB

109. Video on the web

Video on the web often lacks a creator and a date. Begin the entry with a title if you cannot find a creator. Use *n.d.* if you cannot find a date.

> rcwgraves. *GramWow. YouTube.* YouTube, 27 Feb. 2009. Web. 10 Feb. 2012.

110. Work of art on the web

Include the artist, title of the work in italics, and the date. For works found on the web, omit the medium but include the location or museum, then add the name of the website, the medium (*Web*), and the date of access.

> Carr, Emily. *Totem Poles, Kitseukla*. 1912. Vancouver Art Gallery. Web. 15 Mar. 2012.

111. Map on the web

> "Lansing, Michigan." Map. *Google Maps*. Google, 2008. Web. 19 Nov. 2010.

112. Cartoon or comic strip on the web

> Tomorrow, Tom. "Modern World." Comic strip. *Huffington Post*. HuffingtonPost.com, 2 Jan. 2009. Web. 20 Jan. 2009.

26j Multimedia Sources

113. Work in more than one medium

Follow the format of the medium you primarily used and specify all the media you consulted.

> Shakespeare, William. *Hamlet*. Ed. Terri Bourus. New York: Longman, 2007. CD-ROM, print.

114. CD-ROM by a known author

When page numbers are not available, use the author's name in the text to avoid an awkward parenthetical citation.

> Hagen, Edward, and Phillip Walker. *Human Evolution: A Multimedia Guide to the Fossil Record*. New York: Norton, 2002. CD-ROM.

115. Multidisc CD-ROM

Follow the publication medium with either the total number of discs or the number of the specific disc you are using.

> Rey, H. A., and Margaret Rey. *The Complete Adventures of Curious George*. New York: Houghton, 2006. CD-ROM. 5 discs.

116. Musical composition

For a published musical score, follow the format for a book. If the publication is part of a series, list the series.

> Gershwin, George. *An American in Paris*. Secaucus: Warner Bros., 1987. Print. Gershwin 50th Anniversary Ed.

117. Sound recording

List the composer, performer, or group first, depending on which you wish to emphasize. Place a comma between the publisher and the date. Indicate the medium after the date.

> Barenaked Ladies. "If I Had a Million Dollars." *Gordon*. Sire Records, 1992. CD.

118. Podcast

Provide all relevant information, including the name of the host, the name of the program, the number of the episode if available, the name and publisher of the podcast if available, and original broadcast information if the podcast is a rebroadcast.

> Sussingham, Robin. "All Things Autumn." No. 2. *HighLifeUtah*. N.p., 20 Nov. 2006. Web. 28 Feb. 2010.

119. Film

Begin with the title in italics. List the director, the distributor, the date, and the medium. Other data, such as the names of the screenwriters and performers, is optional.

Wanted. Dir. Timur Bekmambetov. Perf. James McAvoy, Angelina Jolie, and Morgan Freeman. Universal, 2008. Film.

120. DVD

Follow the format for films.

Alegria. Dir. Nick Morris. Perf. Francesca Gagnon, Eve Monpetit, Ebon Grayman, Kristina Ivanova, and Cindy Whiteman. Cirque du Soleil, 2010. DVD.

121. Television or radio program

Provide the title of the episode or segment, followed by the title of the program and series (if any). After the titles, list any performers, narrators, directors, or others who might be pertinent. Then give the name of the network, call numbers and city for any local station, the broadcast date, and the medium of reception (*television* or *radio*).

"Wild Horses." *Heartland*. Perf. Amber Marshall, Graham Wardle, and Michelle Morgan. CBC. 11 Mar. 2012. Television.

122. Telephone interview

Minnelli, Liza. Telephone interview. 5 Mar. 2008.

123. Broadcast interview

Wells, Paul. Interview by Anna Maria Tremonti. *The Current*. CBC Radio One, Toronto. 27 Mar. 2012. Radio.

124. Musical, dramatic, dance, or artistic performance

The Lord of the Rings. By J. R. R. Tolkien. Adapted by Shaun McKenna and Matthew Warchus. Dir. Matthew Warchus. Perf. Brent Carver, James Loye, Michael Therriault, and Evan Buliung. Princess of Wales Theatre, Toronto. 24 Mar. 2006. Performance.

125. Speech, debate, mediated discussion, or public talk

Ignatieff, Michael. "Human Rights and the Rights of States: Are They on a Collision Course?" Hagey Lecture Series. U of Waterloo. 24 Jan. 2001. Address.

26k Informational Notes

The MLA style is designed to avoid the need for either footnotes or endnotes. Documentation should be handled using in-text citations and a list of works cited. However, two kinds of notes sometimes appear in MLA style. Notes may be placed at the bottom of the page or at the end of the paper.

Content notes supply additional information that would interrupt the flow of the text, yet may be important to provide the context of a source.

> Much speculation has blamed electronic media, especially television, for an alleged decline in literacy, following Newton N. Minow's famous 1961 description of television as a "vast wasteland."[1]

The note explains who Minow was and why the remark was newsworthy.

> 1. Minow, the newly appointed chairman of the Federal Communications Commission, told the assembled executives of the National Association of Broadcasters in May 1961 that "[w]hen television is bad, nothing is worse" (Adams). Minow's efforts to upgrade programming were met with cries of censorship from the television industry, and Minow resigned two years later.

You need to include any sources you use in notes in the list of works cited.

> Work Cited
>
> Adams, Val. "F.C.C. Head Bids TV Men Reform 'Vast Wasteland.'" *New York Times* 10 May 1961, late ed.: 11. Print.

Bibliographic notes give either evaluative comments about sources or additional references.

> "Fordism" is a summary term for the system of mass production consolidated by Henry Ford in the early decades of this century.[1]

The note gives the origin of the term "Fordism."

> 1. The term *Fordism* was first used by Italian political theorist Antonio Gramsci in his prison notebooks, written while he was jailed under Mussolini's fascist dictatorship.

> Work Cited
>
> Gramsci, Antonio. *Selections from the Prison Notebooks of Antonio Gramsci*. Ed. and trans. Quintin Hoare and Geoffrey Nowell Smith. New York: International, 1971. Print.

 Sample Research Paper with MLA Documentation

Chapters 19 through 25 discuss how to plan and write a research paper. The following research paper, written by Matt Loicano, makes a proposal argument. The paper is annotated to show specific features of MLA style and to show how the works-cited page is organized.

FORMATTING A RESEARCH PAPER IN MLA STYLE

MLA offers these general guidelines for formatting a research paper.

- **Use white, 8½-by-11-inch paper.** Don't use coloured or lined paper.
- **Double-space everything—the title, headings, body of the paper, quotations, and works-cited list.** Set the line spacing on your word processor for double spacing and leave it there.

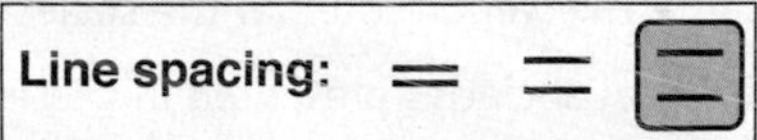

- **Put your last name and the page number at the top of every page, aligned with the right margin, ½ inch (1.25 cm) from the top of the page.** Your word processor has a header command that will automatically put a header with the page number on every page.
- **Specify 1-inch (2.5 cm) margins.** One-inch margins are the default setting for most word processors.
- **Do not justify (make even) the right margin.** Justifying the right margin throws off the spacing between words and makes your paper harder to read. Use the left-align setting instead.

- **Indent the first line of each paragraph ½ inch (5 spaces).** Set the paragraph indent command or the tab on the ruler of your word processor at ½ inch.
- **Use the same readable typeface throughout your paper.** Use a standard typeface such as Times New Roman, 12 point.
- **Use block format for quotations longer than four lines.** See page 323.
- **MLA does not require a title page.** Unless your instructor asks for a separate title page, put 1 inch from the top of the page your name, your instructor's name, the course, and the date on separate lines. Centre your title on the next line. Do not underline your title or put it inside quotation marks.

Include your last name and page number as page header, beginning with the first page, 1/2" from the top.*

Centre the title. Do not underline the title, put it inside quotation marks, or type it in all capital letters.

Loicano's thesis appears at the end of the first paragraph.

Specify 1" margins all around. Double-space everything.

1/2"

1"

Loicano 1

Matt Loicano

Professor Churchill

Comparative Literature 242

16 October 2011

Satiric Dystopia in *The Time Machine* and *We*

H. G. Wells's *The Time Machine* and Yevgeny Zamyatin's *We* are both widely considered to be classic works of dystopic science fiction. Both works extrapolate from the social and political climates in which they were written to paint a bleak, disturbing picture of the world rooted in the society of the times. The satirical societies presented in these works serve as warnings against continuing further down the same path. While *We* aims to draw attention to the problems of totalitarian communism in early 20th century Russia, *The Time Machine* points out flaws in the class-based capitalism of post-Industrial Revolution Europe. Both works aim to draw attention to the problems of the societies that inspired them, but the dystopic worlds used by the authors to illustrate these problems are very different due to the conflicting ideologies of the satirized societies.

1"

The two worlds explored in *We* and *The Time Machine* are both considered dystopias, despite their vast differences, because of the abstract and somewhat ambiguous definitions of what constitutes a utopia or dystopia. The etymology of the words *utopia* (*ouk:* "not" + *topos:* "place," alternatively *eu:* "good" +

1"

* Portions shown in this paper are adjusted to fit the space limitations of this book. Follow actual dimensions discussed in this book and your instructor's directions.

Loicano 2

topos: "place") and *dystopia* (*dus:* "bad, abnormal, diseased" + *topos:* "place") is itself fairly general (Churchill). Darko Suvin defines a utopia to be a "community where sociopolitical institutions, norms, and individual relationships are organized according to a more perfect principle than in the author's community," and he derives his definition of a dystopia by substituting a "less perfect principle" into his definition of utopia (49). Similarly, the main difference between dystopian literature and utopian literature according to Gregory Claeys is that "literary dystopia utilizes the narrative devices of literary utopia . . . but predicts that inherently subjective definition of what is 'bad,' or 'less perfect.'" As Claeys later notes, "One person's utopia [is] another's dystopia" (108). This subjective nature of dystopia allows the societies of both *We* and *The Time Machine* to be viewed as dystopic, even though the societies they satirize are based on the opposing principles of communism and capitalism.

Cite publications within the text by the name of the author (or authors).

In *The Time Machine*, H. G. Wells constructs a futuristic society projected from the society of post-Industrial Revolution Britain. The commercialization of the steam engine in 1781 spurred the Industrial Revolution, replacing the water wheel as the main source of power in factories by 1800 and allowing the factories to move into the more densely populated cities where workers were abundant (Liebedowski). The abundance of workers allowed factories to pay low wages by the hour while the

Indent each paragraph ½ inch.

Loicano 3

factory owners became rich (Liebedowski). By the end of the 19th century, this system of capitalism had created an enormous economic and social gap between the rich aristocracy and the poor workers, which formed the basis for the dystopic society of the Eloi and Morlocks in *The Time Machine* (Cook 100). When describing his theory of the origin of the Eloi and Morlocks, the Time Traveller himself states: "... proceeding from the problems of our own age, it seemed clear as daylight to me that the gradual widening of the present merely temporary and social difference between the Capitalist and the Labourer, was the key to the whole position" (Wells 24). Wells's experiences with capitalism heavily influenced his thoughts about the future of civilization, and hence the characteristics of his present-day world that he chose to satirize in the futuristic society of *The Time Machine*.

Sources not identified with an author are referenced in text by title.

The society of the Eloi and Morlocks contains many characteristics that satirize aspects of the society of Wells's time. The Time Traveller implies that the Morlocks' adaptation to living underground is the logical extension of the life of a factory worker, asking: "Even now, does not an East-end worker live in such artificial conditions as practically to be cut off from the natural surface of the earth?" (Wells 24). He further suggests that the working poor will be literally forced underground by the "exclusive tendency of richer people . . . [which] is already leading to the closing . . . of considerable portions of the surface of

Loicano 4

the land" (24). To make it clear that the resulting society is clearly dystopic and not an aristocrat's utopia, the Time Traveller mentions the extinction of farm animals and reveals the Morlocks' cannibalism of the aristocratic Eloi (14, 30). To be unequivocal about the need for social change, the Time Traveller describes the cannibalistic Eloi and Morlock society as the "logical conclusion [of] the industrial system of to-day" (24). By giving the futuristic society characteristics extrapolated from Wells's present day, and then introducing a universally detested concept such as cannibalism, Wells makes a scathingly critical statement about capitalism, the direction his society is headed, and the need for change.

Give page numbers for paraphrases as well as direct quotations.

Yevgeny Zamyatin also creates a satiric dystopia in *We* for the purpose of criticizing the society of his times. In 1917, with Russia heavily engaged in the First World War, bread riots in Petrograd (now St. Petersburg) escalated into socialist protests opposing the war and the monarchy (Pavlovic). Soldiers and workers rebelled, and the Russian Civil War began between the Bolshevik (majority) Red Army and the anti-Bolshevik White Army (Pavlovic). As the Bolshevik party consolidated power, dissenting views were increasingly suppressed. It was this progression toward an oppressive society that Yevgeny Zamyatin sought to avert.

Loicano 5

Unlike H. G. Wells's futuristic world that barely resembles the source society, Zamyatin makes the parallels very clear between the world of the One State in *We* and Soviet Russia: "While depicting a society of the far future, [Zamyatin] clearly takes as his starting point Lenin's Socialist Order . . . and project[s] a world where that order is now absolute" (Fern 107). The control of the One State extends to every aspect of citizens' lives, including aspects that Zamyatin's society would likely consider extremely intimate. The protagonist, D-503, prompts the reader to realize how easily privacy is taken for granted when he wonders about the state of the olden days: "Wasn't it absurd that the state (it dared to call itself a state!) could leave sexual life without any semblance of control?" (Zamyatin 13). Zamyatin is extrapolating from the oppressive Soviet regime past the point most people in his society would be comfortable with to reveal the impact of the oppressive Bolshevik regime on their lives and to dissuade people from supporting further oppression.

Zamyatin also criticizes the impact of the oppressive regime on the lives and freedoms of citizens in other ways. He uses the secret police of the One State, the Operational Section, several times to illustrate the dangers of state control. The protagonist, D-503, rationalizes the existence of the Operational Section thus:

> There were some fools who compared the Section to the ancient Inquisition, but that is as absurd as

Loicano 6

> equating a surgeon performing a tracheotomy with a highwayman; both may have the same knife in their hands, both do the same thing—cut a living man's throat—yet one is a benefactor, the other a criminal. (80)

Quotations of more than four lines should be indented one inch. Do not use quotation marks. Introduce block quotations rather than just dropping them into the text.

By using a faulty analogy to rationalize the existence of a secret police that tortures citizens to extract information using a "Gas Bell," Zamyatin refutes an important strategy of Soviet propaganda. He leads the reader to draw the conclusion that the secret police in an oppressive regime (like that of the Bolsheviks) should not exist and that change is needed in the author's present-day society.

Both *The Time Machine* and *We* satirize the societies of the era in which they were written by extrapolating from the then-current political and social climates to arrive at a disturbing dystopia. However, the futuristic dystopias that the authors create, as well as the societies they are criticizing, are based on opposing principles of capitalism and communism. While *The Time Machine* makes it clear that capitalism results to some degree in a "cannibalistic" stratified class system, *We* argues that the equality of communism enforced through totalitarian means is an equally dystopic system. As Fatima Vieira writes, "Since it is impossible for [man] to build an ideal society, then he must be committed to the construction of a better one" (17). In the end, both works succeed in suggesting that social change is necessary.

Loicano 7

Works Cited

Centre "Works Cited" on a new page.

Churchill, Belinda. "Alternate Society." Course Notes for Comparative Literature 242: Science Fiction. U of Alberta, Edmonton, 27 Sept. 2011. Print.

Claeys, Gregory. "The Origins of Dystopia: Wells, Huxley and Orwell." Introduction. *The Cambridge Companion to Utopian Literature*. Ed. Claeys. Cambridge: Cambridge UP, 2010. *Cambridge Collections Online*. Web. 16 Oct. 2011.

Cook, Paul. Afterword. *The Time Machine*. H. G. Wells. 1992. Web. 16 Oct. 2011.

Fern, Christopher. *Narrating Utopia: Ideology, Gender, Form in Utopian Literature*. Liverpool, Liverpool UP, 1999. Print.

Liebedowski, Lech. "Industrial Revolution." History 391: History of Technology [Course Notes]. U of Alberta, Edmonton. 11 Sept. 2011. Print.

Pavlovic, Srdja. "The Bolsheviks." History 295: History of 20th Century Warfare [Course Notes]. U of Alberta, Edmonton. 20 July 2011.

Suvin, Darko. *Metamorphoses of Science Fiction: On the Poetics and History of a Literary Genre*. New Haven: Yale UP, 1979. Print.

Vieira, Fátima. "The Concept of Utopia." *The Cambridge Companion to Utopian Literature*. Ed. Gregory Claeys. Cambridge: Cambridge UP, 2010. *Cambridge Collections Online*. Web. 18 Oct. 2011.

Wells, H. G. *The Time Machine*. 2011. PDF file.

Zamyatin, Evgeny. *We*. Trans. Mirra Ginsburg. New York: Avon, 1987.

Double-space all entries. Indent all but the first line in each entry by 1/2 inch.

Alphabetize entries by the last names of the authors or by the first important word in the title if no author is listed.

Italicize the titles of books and periodicals.

Go through your text and make sure that all the sources you have used are in the list of works cited.

FORMATTING THE WORKS CITED IN MLA STYLE

- **Begin the works-cited list on a new page.** Insert a page break with your word processor before you start the works-cited page.
- **Centre "Works Cited" on the first line at the top of the page.**
- **Double-space all entries.**
- **Alphabetize each entry by the last name of the author or, if no author is listed, by the first content word in the title (ignore *a, an, the*).**
- **Indent all but the first line in each entry ½ inch.**
- **Italicize the titles of books and periodicals.**
- **If an author has more than one entry, list the entries in alphabetical order by title. Use three hyphens in place of the author's name for the second and subsequent entries.**

  Murphy, Dervla. *Cameroon with Egbert*. Woodstock: Overlook, 1990. Print.

  ---. *Full Tilt: Ireland to India with a Bicycle*. London: Murray, 1965. Print.

- **Go through your paper to check that each source you have used is in the works-cited list.**

APA, CMS, CSE, and IEEE

27 APA Documentation 327

28 CMS Documentation 362

29 CSE Documentation 384

30 IEEE Documentation 392

You **can learn more and do more** with MyWritingLab and with the eText version of *The Brief Penguin Handbook*. For help with documenting your sources successfully in APA, CMS, and CSE style, click on "Resources," then select "Research." Look for the APA, CMS, and CSE Instruction and Multimedia resources within each topic, then complete the Exercises and click on the Gradebook to measure your progress.

27 APA Documentation

Social sciences disciplines—including government, linguistics, psychology, sociology, and education—frequently use the American Psychological Association (APA) documentation style. The APA style is similar to the MLA style in many ways. Both styles use parenthetical citations in the body of the text, with complete bibliographical citations in the list of references at the end. Both styles avoid using footnotes for references.

APA Documentation Map

Here are the steps in the process of documentation.

1 Collect the right information

For every source you need to have

- the name of the author or authors,
- the full title, and
- complete publication information.

For instructions go to the illustrated examples in Section 27b of the four major source types:

- **PERIODICAL SOURCES**
- **BOOKS AND NONPERIODICAL SOURCES**
- **ONLINE SOURCES**

For other kinds of sources, such as visual and multimedia, see the Index of References on pp. 332–333.

2 Cite sources in two places

Remember, this is a two-part process.

To create citations

a) in **the body of your paper**, go to 27a.
b) in a **list of references at the end of your paper**, go to 27b.

If you have questions that the examples in this chapter do not address, consult the *Publication Manual of the American Psychological Association*, sixth edition (2010).

3 Find the right model citations

You'll find **illustrated examples of sources** in Section 27b.

Once you match your source to one of those examples, you can move on to more specific examples:

- **PERIODICAL SOURCES,** go to 27c.
- **BOOKS AND NONPERIODICAL SOURCES,** go to 27d.
- **ONLINE SOURCES,** go to 27e.

A complete list of examples is found in the Index of References on pp. 332–333.

4 Format your paper

You will find a **sample research paper in APA style** and instructions on formatting the body of your paper and your References list in Section 27g.

A note about footnotes:

APA style does not use footnotes for documentation. Use in-text citations instead (see Section 27a).

27a In-text Citations in APA Style

APA style emphasizes the date of publication. When you cite an author's name in the body of your paper, always follow it with the date of publication. Notice too that APA style includes the abbreviation for page (p.) in front of the page number. A comma separates each element of the citation.

> Zukin (2004) observes that teens today begin to shop for themselves at age 13 or 14, "the same age when lower-class children, in the past, became apprentices or went to work in factories" (p. 50).

If the author's name is not mentioned in the sentence, the reference looks like this:

> One sociologist notes that teens today begin to shop for themselves at age 13 or 14, "the same age when lower-class children, in the past, became apprentices or went to work in factories" (Zukin, 2004, p. 50).

The corresponding entry in the references list would be

> Zukin, S. (2004). *Point of purchase: How shopping changed American culture.* New York, NY: Routledge.

Paraphrase, summary, or short quotation

In APA style a short quotation has fewer than 40 words.

> "The appeal of a shopping spree," one sociologist comments, "is not that you'll buy a lot of stuff; the appeal is that, among all the stuff you buy, you'll find what you truly desire" (Zukin, 2004, p. 112).

The author's name is provided in the parenthetical reference.

In this example, the author's name is provided inside the parentheses at the end of the sentence. Put the author's name in a signal phrase in your sentence when you want to give an affiliation or title to indicate the authority of your source.

"The appeal of a shopping spree," noted sociologist Sharon Zukin (2004) comments, "is not that you'll buy a lot of stuff; the appeal is that, among all the stuff you buy, you'll find what you truly desire" (p. 112).

Put the page number in parentheses after the quotation. Note that the period comes *after* the parentheses.

When the author of the quotation is clearly named in the sentence, add the date in parentheses after the author's name.

Quotations 40 words or longer

Orlean (2001) has attempted to explain the popularity of the painter Thomas Kinkade:

> People like to own things they think are valuable. . . . The high price of limited editions is part of their appeal; it implies that they are choice and exclusive, and that only a certain class of people will be able to afford them. (p. 128)

The sentence introducing the quotation names the author.

Note that the period appears before the parentheses in an indented "block" quote.

The date appears in parentheses immediately following the author's name.

Index of in-text citations

See also entries 48, 49, 50, 53, 62.

Sample in-text citations

1. **Author named in your text**

Astrobiologist Ranjit Patel (2006) argues that Enceladus, one of Saturn's moons, may have "extraterrestrial life" (p. 3).

2. **Author not named in your text**

According to Statistics Canada figures, women in 2003 were actually earning "slightly less—2%" than they had compared with men in 1995 (Grisson, 2006, p. 254).

3. **Work by a single author**

(Bell, 1973, p. 3)

4. **Work by two authors**

List both authors' last names, joined with an ampersand.

(Suzuki & Irabu, 2002, p. 404)

When you cite the authors' names in a sentence, use *and* in place of the ampersand.

Suzuki and Irabu (2002) report . . .

5. **Work by three to five authors**

The authors' last names follow the order of the title page.

(Francisco, Vaughn, & Romano, 2006, p. 7)

Subsequent references can use the first name and *et al.*

(Francisco et al., 2006, p. 17)

6. **Work by six or more authors**

Use the first author's last name and *et al.* for all in-text references.

(Swallit et al., 2007, p. 49)

7. **Work by a group or organization**

Identify the group in the text and place the page number in parentheses.

Statistics Canada (2012) notes that the paper and primary metals industries use more than seven times more water than the petroleum and coal industry (p. 8).

If you use the name of the group in an in-text citation, the first time you cite the source put its acronym (if there is one) in brackets.

(Statistics Canada [Statscan], 2012)

Use the acronym in subsequent in-text citations.

(Statscan, 2012)

8. Work by an unknown author

Use a shortened version of the title (or the full title if it is short) in place of the author's name. Capitalize all keywords in the title. If it is an article title, place it inside quotation marks.

("Greenpeace Guide to Greener Electronics," 2012, p. 2)

9. Two works by one author published in the same year

Assign the dates letters (*a*, *b*, etc.) according to their alphabetical arrangement in the references list.

The majority of books written about coauthorship focus on partners of the same sex (Laird, 2007a, p. 351).

10. Parts of an electronic source

If an online or other electronic source does not provide page numbers, use the paragraph number preceded by the abbreviation *para.*

(Robinson, 2007, para. 7)

11. Two or more sources within the same sentence

Place each citation directly after the statement it supports.

Some surveys report an increase in homelessness rates (Alford, 2004) while others chart a slight decrease (Rice, 2006a) . . .

If you need to cite two or more works within the same parentheses, list them in the order in which they appear in the references list.

(Alford, 2004; Rice, 2006a)

12. Work quoted in another source

Saunders and Kellman's study (as cited in Rice, 2006a)

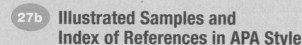

27b Illustrated Samples and Index of References in APA Style

Periodical Sources

Title of article

Practicing Engineers Talk about the Importance of Talk: A Report on the Role of Oral Communication in the Workplace

Authors' names

Ann L. Darling and Deanna P. Dannels

Abstract

In the last decade engineering education and industry have requested assistance from communication educators. Responding to increased attention on the changing expectations for practicing engineers and an attendant need for better communication skills, these teams of engineering and communication educators have been working to incorporate speaking and writing in engineering education. Despite a great deal of anecdotal evidence that communication is important to working engineers, relatively little data based information is available to help us understand better the specifics of how and why communication is important for these particular professionals. This paper reports the results of practicing engineers' descriptions of the importance of oral communication. These data suggest that engineering practice takes place in an intensely oral culture and while formal presentations are important to practicing engineers, daily work is characterized more by interpersonal and small group experiences. Communication skills such as translation, clarity, negotiation, and listening are vital. **Keywords:** communication in the professions, workplace teams, engineering education, oral presentations

Increasingly, oral communication is recognized as an essential element of the curriculum in technical disciplines (Beaufait, 1991; Bjorklund & Colbeck, 2001; Denton, 1998; Yu & Liaw, 1998). Disciplines such as biology, chemistry, engineering, and mathematics, with a long curricular tradition focused on technical knowledge, have begun to explore the role of oral performance as both a learning tool (e.g., use of cooperative learning groups) and outcome (i.e., students in these disciplines are expected to be proficient both technically and communicatively).

Engineering is one such discipline experiencing a shift toward incorporating oral communication instruction within a highly technical curriculum (Beaufait, 1991). The 1995 report from the National Board of Engineering Education includes recommendations for a redesign of the engineering curriculum toward a more professional focus with specific attention on instruction in communication. Additionally, the Accreditation Board for Engineering and Technology (ABET) has developed new standards for accreditation to evaluate departments and colleges of engineering around the country. Specifically, ABET assessment procedures are driven by 11 student outcome measures, one of which states that students should

Ann L. Darling (PhD, University of Washington) is Associate Professor and Chair of the Department of Communication at the University of Utah. *Deanna P. Dannels* (PhD, University of Utah) is Assistant Professor of Communication and Assistant Director of the Campus Writing and Speaking Program at North Carolina State University. The authors wish to thank the gracious and abundant contributions of the College of Engineering at the University of Utah, especially on the part of Professor Robert Roemer.

Publication information

Communication Education, Vol. 52, No. 1, January 2003, pp. 1–16

Darling, A. L., & Dannels, D. P. (2003). Practicing engineers talk about the importance of talk: A report on the role of oral communication in the workplace. *Communication Education, 52*, 11–16.

Elements of the citation

Author's Name

The author's last name comes first, followed by the author's initials.

Join two authors' names with a comma and an ampersand.

Date of Publication

Give the year the work was published in parentheses.

Newspapers and popular magazines are referenced by the day, month, and year of publication.

Title of Article

- Do not use quotation marks. If there is a book title in the article title, italicize it.
- Titles of articles in APA style follow standard sentence capitalization.

Publication Information

Name of journal

- Italicize the journal name.
- Put a comma after the journal name.

Volume, issue, and page numbers

- Italicize the volume number.
- If each issue of the journal begins on page 1, give the issue number in parentheses, followed by a comma.
- If the article has been assigned a DOI (Digital Object Identifier), list it after the page numbers but without a period at the end.

Find the right example as your model (you may need to refer to more than one model)

What type of article do you have?

A scholarly journal article or abstract?

- For an article in a journal with continuous pagination, go to page 340, #19.
- For an article in a journal paginated by issue, go to page 340, #20.
- For a weekly, biweekly, or monthly publication, go to page 340, #21–#22.
- For an abstract, go to pages 340–341, #23–#24.

A newspaper article, review, or letter to the editor?

- For a newspaper article, go to page 341, #25.
- For a review, go to page 341, #26.
- For a letter to the editor, go to page 241, #27.

A government document?

- Go to pages 344–345, #48–#49.

How many authors are listed?

- One, two, or more authors: go to page 339, #13–#15.
- Unknown author: go to page 340, #17.

Books and Nonperiodical Sources

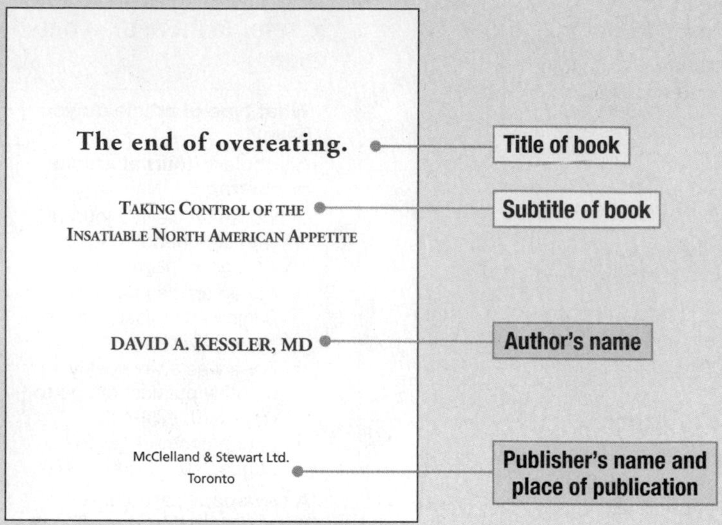
The end of overeating.

TAKING CONTROL OF THE
INSATIABLE NORTH AMERICAN APPETITE

DAVID A. KESSLER, MD

McClelland & Stewart Ltd.
Toronto

TITLE PAGE

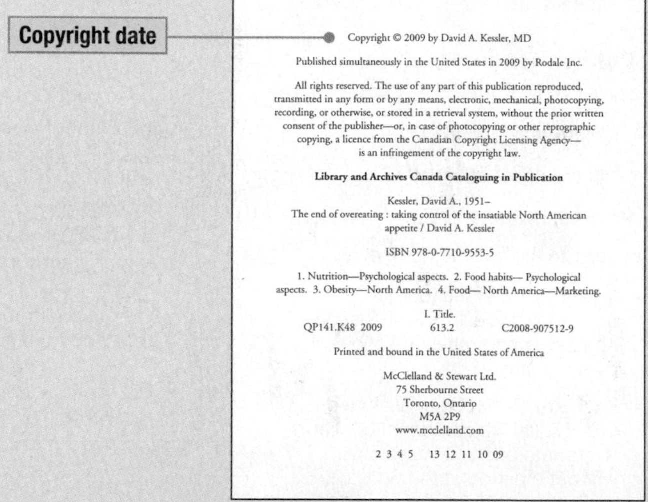

Copyright © 2009 by David A. Kessler, MD

Published simultaneously in the United States in 2009 by Rodale Inc.

All rights reserved. The use of any part of this publication reproduced, transmitted in any form or by any means, electronic, mechanical, photocopying, recording, or otherwise, or stored in a retrieval system, without the prior written consent of the publisher—or, in case of photocopying or other reprographic copying, a licence from the Canadian Copyright Licensing Agency—is an infringement of the copyright law.

Library and Archives Canada Cataloguing in Publication

Kessler, David A., 1951–
The end of overeating : taking control of the insatiable North American appetite / David A. Kessler

ISBN 978-0-7710-9553-5

1. Nutrition—Psychological aspects. 2. Food habits— Psychological aspects. 3. Obesity—North America. 4. Food— North America—Marketing.

I. Title.
QP141.K48 2009 613.2 C2008-907512-9

Printed and bound in the United States of America

McClelland & Stewart Ltd.
75 Sherbourne Street
Toronto, Ontario
M5A 2P9
www.mcclelland.com

2 3 4 5 13 12 11 10 09

COPYRIGHT PAGE

Kessler, D. A. (2009). *The end of overeating: Taking control of the insatiable North American appetite*. Toronto, ON: McClelland & Stewart.

Elements of the citation

Author's or Editor's Name

The author's last name comes first, followed by a comma and the author's initials.

If an editor, put the abbreviation *Ed.* in parentheses after the name: **Kavanagh, P. (Ed.).**

Year of Publication

- Give the year the work was copyrighted in parentheses.
- If no year of publication is given, write *n.d.* ("no date") in parentheses: **Smith, S. (n.d.).**
- If it is a multivolume edited work, published over a period of more than one year, put the span in parentheses: **Smith, S. (1999–2001).**

Book Title

- Italicize the title.
- Titles of books in APA style follow standard sentence capitalization: Capitalize only the first word, proper nouns, and the first word after a colon.

Publication Information

Place of publication

- List the city and province or state abbreviation.
- For publications outside of North America, spell out the city and country names (Paris, France).
- If more than one city is given on the title page, list only the first.

Publisher's name

Do not shorten or abbreviate words like *University* or *Press*. Omit words such as *Co.*, *Inc.*, and *Publishers*.

Find the right example as your model (you may need to refer to more than one model)

How many authors are listed?

- One, two, or more authors: go to pages 341–342, #28–#31.
- Unknown author: go to page 342, #33.
- Group or organization as the author: go to page 342, #34.

Do you have only a part of a book?

- For a chapter written by the same author as the book, go to page 343, #38.
- For a chapter in an edited collection, go to page 343, #30.
- For an article in a reference work, go to page 343, #41.

Do you have a printed document other than a book or article?

- For a technical report, go to page 344, #43.
- For published conference proceedings, go to page 344, #44.
- For a dissertation or thesis, go to page 344, #47.
- For a government document, go to page 344, #48.

Online Sources

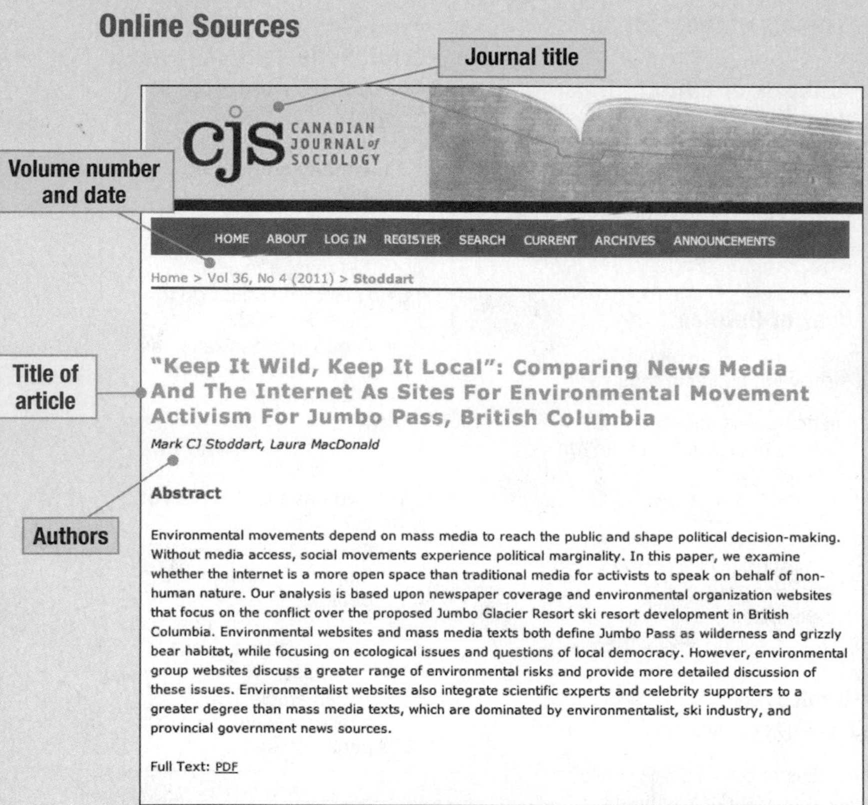

Stoddart, M. C. J., & MacDonald, L. (2011). "Keep it wild, keep it local": Comparing news media and the internet as sites for environmental movement activism for Jumbo Pass, British Columbia. *Canadian Journal of Sociology, 36,* 283–312. Retrieved from http://ejournals.library.ualberta.ca/index.php/CJS/index

TITLES AND URLS IN APA-STYLE REFERENCES

If you are citing a page or an article that has a title, treat the title as you would an article in a periodical.

Heiney, A. (2004). A gathering of space heroes. *NASA.org*. Retrieved from http://www.nasa.gov/missions

Otherwise, treat the name of the website itself as you would a book. No retrieval date is necessary if the content is not likely to be changed or updated. If no DOI is assigned, provide the home or entry page for the journal or report publisher.

Elements of the citation

Author's Name or Organization

- Authorship is sometimes hard to discern for online sources. if you do have an author or creator to cite, follow the rules for periodicals and books.
- If the only authority you find is a group or organization, list its name as the author.

Dates

Give the date the site was produced or last revised (sometimes the copyright date) after the author.

Title of Page or Article

Websites are often made up of many separate pages or articles. Each page or article on a website may or may not have a title.

URL

- Copy the address exactly as it appears in your browser window. You can even copy and paste the address into your text for greater accuracy.
- Break a URL at the end of a line *before* a mark of punctuation. Do not insert a hyphen.
- If the article has a DOI (Digital Object Identifier), give the DOI after the title. Do not list the URL.

Find the right example as your model (you may need to refer to more than one model)

What kind of publication do you have?

- For a publication in a database, go to page 345, #54
- For an article with a DOI assigned, go to page 347, #63
- For an article with no DOI assigned, go to page 347, #64
- For an article in a newspaper or magazine, go to page 347, #65–#66
- For a government publication, go to page 346, #62

Who is the author?

- For a known author, go to page 346, #57
- For a group or organization as the author, go to page 346, #58

Do you have a source that is posted by an individual?

- For a blog, go to page 347, #67
- For a post to a discussion list, go to page 347, #68
- For email or text messaging, go to page 348, #70

Index of References Entries

27c Periodical Sources in the APA-Style References List

JOURNAL AND MAGAZINE ARTICLES

13. Article by one author

Schindler, D. (2010). Tar sands need solid science. *Nature, 468,* 499–501.

14. Article by two authors

Stoddart, M. C. J., & MacDonald, L. (2011).

15. Article by three or more authors

List last names and initials for up to seven authors, with an ampersand between the last two names. For works with eight or more authors, list the first six names, then an ellipsis, then the last author's name.

Andis, S., Franks, D., Gee, G., Ng, K., Orr, V., Ray, B., . . . Tate, L.

16. Authors listed with the word *with*

Bettinger, M. (with Winthorp, E.).

17. Article by an unknown author

The green gene revolution [Editorial]. (2004, February). *Scientific American*, *291*, 8.

18. Article by a group or organization

Canadian Diabetes Association. (2005). *Living with diabetes.* Toronto, ON: Dorling Kindersley.

19. Article in a journal with continuous pagination

Include only the volume number and the year, not the issue number.

Engen, R., & Steen, S. (2000). The power to punish: Discretion and sentencing reform in the war on drugs. *American Journal of Sociology*, *105*, 1357–1395.

20. Article in a journal paginated by issue

If each issue of the journal begins on page 1, give the issue number in parentheses (not italicized) after the volume number.

Bunyan, T. (2010). Just over the horizon—the surveillance society and the state in the EU. *Race and Class*, *51*(3), 1–12.

MONTHLY, WEEKLY, AND BIWEEKLY PERIODICALS

APA DOES NOT ABBREVIATE ANY MONTH.

21. Weekly or biweekly periodicals

Hurtley, Stella. (2004, July 16). Limits from leaf litter. *Science*, *305*, 311–313.

22. Monthly publications

Barth, A. (2010, March). Brain science gets squishy. *Discover*, 11–12.

ABSTRACTS

23. Abstract from an original source

de Watteville, C. (1904). On flame spectra [Abstract]. *Proceedings of the Royal Society of London*, *74*, 84.

24. Abstract from a printed secondary source

Van Schaik, P. (1999). Involving users in the specification of functionality using scenarios and model-based evaluation. *Behaviour and Information Technology, 18*, 455–466. Abstract obtained from *Communication Abstracts*, 2000, *24*, 416.

NEWSPAPERS

25. Newspaper article

Olsen, E. (2010, June 22). A campaign for M&Ms with a salty center? Sweet. *The New York Times*, p. B6.

If an article has no author, list and alphabetize by the first significant word in the title of the article.

Sizing up a robo-scandal. (2012, March 6). *National Post*, p. A8.

REVIEWS AND LETTERS TO THE EDITOR

26. Review

Henig, R. N. (2010, June 27). The psychology of bliss [Review of the book *How Pleasure Works* by Paul Bloom]. *The New York Times*, p. BR6.

27. Letter to the editor or editorial

Wilkenson, S. E. (2001, December 21). When teaching doesn't count [Letter to the editor]. *The Chronicle of Higher Education*, p. B21.

27d Books and Nonperiodical Sources in the APA-Style References List

BOOKS

28. Book by one author

The author's last name comes first, followed by a comma and the first initial of the author's first name and middle initial, if any.

Gladwell, M. (2009). *What the dog saw*. New York, NY: Little, Brown.

If an editor, put the abbreviation *Ed.* in parentheses after the name.

Rasgon, N. L. (Ed.). (2006). *The effects of estrogen on brain function.* Baltimore, MD: Johns Hopkins University Press.

29. Two or more books by the same author

Arrange according to the date, with the earliest publication first, or alphabetically according to the names of additional authors.

Jules, R. (2003). *Internal memos and other classified documents.* London, England: Hutchinson.

Jules, R. (2004). *Derelict cabinet.* London, England: Corgi-Transworld.

30. Book by two authors

Schindler, D. W., & Vallentyne, J. R. (2008). *The algal bowl: Overfertilization of the world's freshwaters and estuaries.* Edmonton, AB: University of Alberta Press.

31. Book by three or more authors

List last names and initials for up to seven authors, with an ampersand between the last two names. For works with eight or more authors, list the first six names, then an ellipsis, then the last author's name.

Anders, K., Child, H., Davis, K., Logan, O., Orr, J., Ray, B., . . . Wood, G.

32. Authors listed with the word *with*

Bettinger, M. (with Winthorp, E.).

33. Book by an unknown author

Survey of developing nations. (2003). New York, NY: Justice for All Press.

34. Book by a group or organization

Centers for Disease Control and Prevention. (2003). *Men and heart disease: An atlas of racial and ethnic disparities in mortality.* Atlanta, GA: Author.

35. Translated book

Freud, S. (2010). *Three contributions to the theory of sex* (A. A. Brill, Trans.). Las Vegas, NV: IAP Publishing. (Original work published 1909)

36. Revised or later edition of a book

Weintraub, A. (2004). *Yoga for depression: A compassionate guide to relieve suffering through yoga* (2nd ed.). New York, NY: Broadway Books.

37. Multivolume book

Schwarzer, M., & Frensch, P. A. (2010). *Personality, human development and culture: International perspectives on psychological science* (Vol. 2). London, England: Psychology Press.

38. Chapter written by the same author as the book

Add the word *In* after the chapter title and before the book title. Include inclusive page numbers for the chapter inside parentheses.

Savage, T. (2004). Challenging mirror modeling in group therapy. In *Collaborative practice in psychology and therapy* (pp. 130–157). New York, NY: Haworth Clinical Practice Press.

39. Chapter in an edited collection

Boyaton, D. (2010). Behaviorism and its effect upon learning in schools. In G. Goodman (Ed.), *The educational psychology reader: The art and science of how people learn* (pp. 49–66). New York, NY: Peter Lang.

40. Chapter in a volume in a series

Jackson, E. (1998). Politics and gender. In F. Garrity (Series Ed.) & M. Halls (Vol. Ed.), *Political library: Vol. 4. Race, gender, and class* (2nd ed., pp. 101–151). New York, NY: Muse.

41. Article in a reference work

Viscosity. (2001). In *The Columbia encyclopedia* (6th ed.). New York, NY: Columbia University Press.

42. Selection reprinted from another source

Thompson, H. S. (1997). The scum also rises. In K. Kerrane & B. Yagoda (Eds.), *The art of fact* (pp. 302–315). New York, NY: Touchstone. (Reprinted from *The great shark hunt*, pp. 299–399, by H. S. Thompson, 1979, New York, NY: Simon & Schuster)

RESEARCH REPORTS, CONFERENCE PROCEEDINGS, AND DISSERTATIONS

43. Technical and research reports

Young, M. M., & Student Drug Use Surveys Working Group. (2011). *Cross-Canada report on student alcohol and drug use*. Ottawa, ON: Canadian Centre on Substance Abuse.

44. Published conference proceedings

Kresta, S. M., Nychka, J. A., & Graves, R. (2011, June). Writing well: Building traction and triumph into co-authorship. *Proceedings of the 2011 American Society for Engineering Education Annual Conference*, AC 2011-1164. Retrieved from http://www.asee.org

45. Unpublished paper presented at a symposium or meeting

Kelly, M. (2004, November). *Communication in virtual terms.* Paper presented at the annual meeting of the National Communication Association, Chicago, IL.

46. Poster session

Wilson, W. (2005, September). *Voting patterns among college students, 1992–2004.* Poster session presented at the annual meeting of the American Political Science Association, Washington, DC.

47. Dissertation or thesis

Tzilos, G. K. (2010). *A brief computer-based intervention for alcohol use during pregnancy* (Doctoral dissertation). Available from ProQuest Dissertations and Theses database. (UMI No. 3373111)

GOVERNMENT AND LEGAL DOCUMENTS

48. Government document

When the author and publisher are identical, use the word *Author* as the name of the publisher.

Health Canada. (2001). *Assessment report of the Canadian Food Inspection Agency activities related to the safety of aquaculture products* (Cat. H39-577/2001E). Ottawa, ON: Author.

In-text

(Health Canada, 2001)

49. ***Congressional Record*** **(Senate resolution)**

S. Res. 103, 107th Cong., 147 Cong. Rec. 5844 (2001) (enacted).

In-text

(S. Res. 103, 2001)

RELIGIOUS TEXTS, PAMPHLETS, INTERVIEWS, AND LETTERS

50. Religious or classical texts

Reference entries are not required for major classical works or the Bible, but in the first in-text citation, identify the edition used.

John 3:16 (Modern Phrased Version)

(Qur'an 5:3–4)

51. Bulletins or pamphlets

SecuriCan General Insurance. (2005). *Health insurance for your pet* [Brochure]. Winnipeg, MB: Author.

52. Published interview

Frum, L. (2006, January 30). Peter Bergen talks to Linda Frum. *Maclean's,* 119(5), 10–11.

53. Unpublished letter

Personal communications are not listed in the references list; they are cited in text only.

(D. Brent personal communication, March 6, 2012)

27e Online Sources in the APA-Style References List

LIBRARY DATABASES AND ENCYCLOPEDIAS

54. Document from a database

APA no longer requires listing the names of well-known databases. Include the name of the database only for hard-to-find books and other items.

Holloway, J. D. (2004). Protecting practitioners' autonomy. *Monitor on Psychology, 35*(1), 30.

55. Electronic copy of an abstract retrieved from a database

Putsis, W. P., & Bayus, B. L. (2001). An empirical analysis of firms' product line decisions. *Journal of Marketing Research, 37*(8), 110–118. Abstract retrieved from PsychINFO database.

56. Online encyclopedia

Swing. (2002). In *Britannica Online*. Retrieved from http://www.britannica.com

ONLINE PUBLICATIONS

57. Online publication by a known author

Hyland, T. (2012, March 6). Writing in the changing post-secondary environment [Web log message]. Retrieved from http://www.inkshed.ca/blog/newsletter/january-2012/writing-changing-environment

58. Online publication by a group or organization

Girls Incorporated. (2003). *Girls' bill of rights*. Retrieved from http://www.girlsinc.org/gc/page.php?id=9

59. Informally published or self-archived work

Bjork, O. (2004, May 5). *MOO bots*. Retrieved from http://www.cwrl.utexas.edu/professional/whitepapers/2004/040512-1.pdf

60. Online publication with no known author or group affiliation

Begin the reference with the title of the document.

Halloween costumes from my warped mind. (n.d.). Retrieved from http://home.att.net/~jgola/hallow01.htm

61. Online publication with no copyright or revision date

If no copyright or revision date is given, use *(n.d.)*, as shown in entry 60.

62. Online government publication

Canadian International Development Agency. (2011). *Development for results 2009–2010*. Retrieved from http://www.acdi-cida.gc.ca

In-text

(Canadian International Development Agency [CIDA], 2011)

ONLINE PERIODICALS

Because URLs frequently change, many scholarly publishers have begun to use a Digital Object Identifier (DOI), a unique alphanumeric string that is permanent. If a DOI is available, use the DOI instead of the URL.

63. Online article with DOI assigned

You may need to click on a button such as "Article" or "PubMed" to find the DOI. There is no need to list the database, or the URL if the DOI is listed.

Hall, P. V., & Khan, A. J. (2008). Differences in high-tech immigrant earnings and wages across Canadian cities. *Canadian Geographer, 52*, 271–290. doi:10.1111/j.1541-0064.2008.00213.x

64. Online article with no DOI assigned

Brown, B. (2004). The order of service: The practical management of customer interaction. *Sociological Research Online, 9*(4). Retrieved from http://www.socresonline.org.uk/9/4/brown.html

65. Article in an online newspaper

Frard, M. (2001, November 16). A colossal wreck. *Austin Chronicle.* Retrieved from http://www.austinchronicle.com

66. Article in an online magazine

Resnikoff, N. (2010, June 22). Media ignores Gulf tragedy: Focuses on campaign narrative. *Salon*. Retrieved from http://www.salon.com

UNEDITED ONLINE SOURCES

67. Blog entry

Spinuzzi, C. (2010, January 7). In the pipeline [Web log message]. Retrieved from http://spinuzzi.blogspot.com/search?updated-max=2010-01-25T12%3A35%3A00-06%3A00

68. Message posted to a newsgroup, online forum, or discussion group

Tjelmeland, A. (2010, January 26). Zacate Creek [Electronic mailing list message]. Retrieved from http://server1.birdingonthe.net/mailinglists/TEXS.html#1264558433

69. Wiki

Mount Everest [Wikipedia entry]. (n.d.). Retrieved November 12, 2010, from http://en.wikipedia.org/wiki/Mt._Everest

70. Email

Email sent from one individual to another should be cited as a personal communication. Personal communication is cited in the text but not included in the reference list.

(D. Jenkins, personal communication, July 28, 2012)

 Visual and Multimedia Sources in the APA-Style References List

MULTIMEDIA

71. Television program

Ball, A. (Writer), & Winant, S. (Director). (2008). The first taste [Television series episode]. In A. Ball (Producer), *True Blood*. New York, NY: HBO.

72. Film, video, or DVD

Stroller, N. (Writer and Director). (2010). *Get him to the Greek* [Motion picture]. United States: Universal Studios.

73. Musical recording

Waits, T. (1980). Ruby's arms. On *Heartattack and Vine* [CD]. New York, NY: Elektra Entertainment.

74. Audio recording

King, M. L., Jr. (Speaker). (1968). *In search of freedom* (Cassette Recording No. SR61170). Los Angeles, CA: Mercury Records.

75. Graphic, audio, or video files

Aretha Franklin: A life of soul. (2004, January 24). *NPR Online*. Retrieved from http://www.npr.org/features/feature.php?wfId=1472614

Sample Research Paper with APA Documentation

Major kinds of papers written in APA style include the following.

Reports of research

Reports of experimental research follow a specific organization in APA style:

- **The abstract** gives a brief summary of the report.
- **The introduction** identifies the problem, reviews previous research, and states the hypothesis that was tested. Because the introduction is identified by its initial position in the report, it does not have to be labelled "introduction."
- **The method section** describes how the experiment was conducted and how the participants were selected.
- **The results section** reports the findings of the study. This section often includes tables and figures that provide statistical results and tests of statistical significance. Tests of statistical significance are critical for experimental research because they give the probability that the results could have occurred by chance.
- **The discussion section** interprets the findings and often refers to previous research.

Case studies

Case studies report material about an individual or a group that illustrates some problem or issue of interest to the field. See pages 106–109.

Reviews of literature

Reviews of literature summarize what has been published on a particular subject and often evaluate that material to suggest directions for future research.

Thesis-driven arguments

Thesis-driven arguments are similar to reviews of research, but they take a particular position on a theoretical or a real-life issue. The APA paper that follows by Danielle Mitchell is a thesis-driven proposal argument that advocates a particular course of action.

FORMATTING A RESEARCH PAPER IN APA STYLE

APA offers these general guidelines for formatting a research paper.

- **Use white, 8½-by-11-inch paper.** Don't use coloured or lined paper.
- **Double-space everything—the title page, abstract, body of the paper, quotations, and list of references.** Set the line spacing on your word processor for double spacing and leave it there.
- **Include a running head aligned with the left margin on every page.** The running head is an abbreviated title set in all caps with a maximum of 50 characters. Include a page number for every page aligned with the right margin.
- **Specify 1-inch (2.5 cm) margins.** One-inch margins are the default setting for most computers.
- **Do not justify (make even) the right margin.** Justifying the right margin throws off the spacing between words and makes your paper harder to read. Use the left-align setting instead.
- **Indent the first line of each paragraph ½ inch (1.25 cm).** Set the paragraph indent command or the tab on the ruler at ½ inch.
- **Use block format for quotations longer than 40 words.**
- **Create an abstract.** The abstract appears on a separate page after the title page. Insert and centre "Abstract" at the top. Do not indent the first line of the abstract. The abstract should be a brief (120 words or under) summary of the paper.
- **Create a title page.** Follow the format below for your title page. It should have
  1. a running head beginning with the words *Running head:* followed by a short title in ALL CAPS at the top left and a page number at the top right,
  2. a descriptive title that is centred in the top half of the page with all words capitalized except *a, an, the*, prepositions, and conjunctions under four letters,
  3. your name centred on a separate line,
  4. your school centred on a separate line.

:lude a running ad, consisting a short rsion of your e in ALL CAPS d the page mber. This ader should about 1/2" m the top of page. Set the argins of your per to 1".*

Running head: HOW THE MEDIA DEPICT NURSING 1

Centre your title in the top half of the page. The title should clearly describe the content of the paper and should be no longer than 12 words. If the title runs to 2 lines, double-space it.

How the Media Depict Nursing Impacts Stereotypes

and Nursing Practice

Danielle Mitchell

University of Alberta

On the line below the title, include your name, also centred. On the next line below, include the name of your school. Double-space between these lines.

* Portions shown in this paper are adjusted to fit the space limitations of this book. Follow the actual dimensions discussed in this book and your instructor's directions.

Continue the running head.

HOW THE MEDIA DEPICT NURSING 2

The abstr[...] appears o[...] separate [...] with the t[...] *Abstract* centred at the top.

Do not indent the first line of the abstract.

Abstract

The misperceptions of nursing in popular media include nurses as unprofessional and as intellectually incapable of being independent and critical thinkers, which, in turn, affects nursing practice. Since the 1960s, nurses have been seen in many roles that depict them as simple-minded, drug addicted, and sexual props for physicians. This diminished view of nurses in the media does have an effect on society's view of nursing as a profession. To close the gap between nurses' depiction in the media and what nurses actually do will require effort from associations such as the Canadian Nurses Association (CNA) and the College & Association of Registered Nurses of Alberta (CARNA) as well as from nurses themselves. The regulatory bodies can launch campaigns, indicating the significance of nurses and what their jobs truly entail. By taking a proactive role, negative stereotypes can be minimized, solving problems induced by media bias.

The abstract should be a brief (120 words or fewer) summary of your paper's argument.

How the Media Depict Nursing Impacts
Stereotypes and Nursing Practice

Centre your title at the beginning of the body of your paper. If it runs to 2 lines, double-space it.

The term *media* is defined as the "main means of mass communication" ("Media," n.d.). In today's society, the media play a large part in everyday life. From the drive to work to sitting at a restaurant, it is hard to avoid topics that are in the media. Nursing is no exception. Nursing has been portrayed in the media in many different ways, but rarely is there a portrayal that depicts a nurse's true role. This is rather disconcerting due to all the progress and effort made by many strong, intelligent nurses such as Florence Nightingale, Mary Agnes Snively, and Jean I. Gunn (among others) to advance the image of nursing as intellectual and professional (Potter & Perry, 2010). The misrepresented roles of nurses in popular media do have an effect on society's perception of nurses. For nursing to be able to be considered a professional position in today's culture, the static and inaccurate image of nursing must be drastically rebranded. The misperceptions of nursing in the media include nurses as unprofessional and intellectually incapable of being independent and critical thinkers, which, in turn, affects nursing practice. Nurses must get actively involved to correct this image, which is seen in movies and on television.

If you include the author's name in the text, include the publication year in parentheses immediately after it. If necessary, include the page number in parentheses with the abbreviation *p.* following the citation.

In a parenthetical citation, use *&* instead of *and* when listing more than one author.

Negative Stereotypes in Popular Media.

Nurses are constantly being cast in roles that do not resemble reality in the slightest. The Canadian Nurses Association (2011b) states that nursing requires an individual to constantly uphold and develop professionalism within him- or herself as well as with others. The media portray nurses as the opposite of professional. Since the 1960s, nurses have often been seen in roles that are sexually exploitative, wearing scantily clad outfits and being a sexual prop for men—especially male physicians (Cabaniss, 2011, p. 114). This depiction detracts from the expectation that nurses are professionals. The portrayal of nurses as "sexual mascots" (Kalisch & Kalisch, 1982, p. 267) must come to a halt for nurses to be able to establish respect as professionals.

In the popular drama series *Private Practice*, one of the main characters, Dell, gets into an accident and needs to have brain surgery (The Truth About Nursing, 2010b). Not only is Dell a nurse who has recently been accepted into medical school (which suggests that nursing is not enough), one of the doctors states that she would get "one of their most attractive nurses" to shave his head. This depiction sends the message that nurses, again, are only there to look pretty. Although this portrayal of a nurse is rather offensive, one of the most outrageous scenes involving nurses comes from an episode of the hit drama *Grey's Anatomy*. In the episode a plastic surgeon, Dr. Sloane, is talking to a resident about their fellow colleagues (who are doctors) who are going to attend a baby shower (The Truth About Nursing, 2010a). The resident buys generic cupcakes from a store for the occasion, and Dr. Sloan reacts by saying that it is not "a baby shower for some nurse who couldn't keep her knees together" and that their colleagues deserve "better than off-brand crap" (The Truth About Nursing, 2010a). The fact that the doctor blatantly said what scriptwriters have been subtly hinting at for years (that nurses are promiscuous) portrays a whole other level of unprofessionalism to the public. This example shows no respect toward nurses; the scriptwriters are making it almost impossible for the nurses on the show to have a professional image by demeaning them.

Some say that nurses are progressively being depicted as professional individuals (Stanley, 2008, p. 94) in popular media. However, the examples given show that even in the most recent years, their profession has been tarnished by demeaning sexual overtones, and that a lot of improvement is still to be made for the nursing profession to actually be portrayed as professional in popular media.

The media also tend to depict nurses as simple-minded, with a motherly overtone. There have been ads that represent nurses as "guardian angels" (Gordon & Nelson, 2005, p. 66), which creates a disconnect between the nursing profession and intelligence.

Kindness, compassion, and lovingness are all great qualities for nurses to have, but they should not be their only qualities. The "virtue script" (Gordon & Nelson, 2005, p. 63) that the media group nurses into encompasses all of these qualities but does not involve any knowledge-based characteristics. This makes nurses appear unable to make decisions by themselves or do anything that requires critical thinking.

Nurses are also used to create a realistic setting for the show to take place in (Kalisch & Kalisch, 1982). A good example of nurses as props is evident in their portrayal as doctor's assistant. In *Grey's Anatomy*, doctors bark out orders, and the nurses simply reply with "Right away, doctor" (The Truth About Nursing, 2010a). This reaction creates the impression that nurses cannot think for themselves and can only succeed when taking orders from those superior to them. Other portrayals of nurses, dating back to the 1960s, have shown nurses doing tasks that require minimal judgment and essentially no skill (Kalisch & Kalisch, 1982, p. 266).

These portrayals send the message that nurses are only there to do menial tasks. They devalue a nurse's true role, which the Canadian Nurses Association (2011a) says involves complex, critical healthcare-related tasks. Nurses are also involved in a continuing competency program, which ensures they engage in constant learning and evolution, demonstrating their great intellectual and critical thinking abilities (Davis, 2011).

This is not to say that good portrayals of nurses have been absent over the years. A show such as *Nurse Jackie*, which was rated the most realistic portrayal of nurses (The Truth About Nursing, 2011), has advanced the image of nursing and portrayed it as a more intelligent, critical thinking profession. Nurse Jackie is seen as a strong, independent nurse, who has great clinical skills and strongly advocates for her patients (The Truth About Nursing, 2009). This show depicts nurses as intellectually capable, which is positive; however, Nurse Jackie is also a character who forges signatures and is addicted to drugs. Some may say that Nurse Jackie is a step in the right direction, but no matter how much the show portrays her as intelligent, the fact that she is a drug addict completely diminishes the image of a strong, independent, intelligent nurse.

Implications for Nursing Practice and Active Solutions

This diminished portrayal of nurses in the media does have an effect on society's view of nursing as a profession. It risks patient trust and confidence in nursing care (Cabaniss, 2011, p. 114), and nursing clinical practice and research may be underfunded due to the misconception that nurses do not play a vital role. The depiction of nurses in the media also discourages individuals from choosing nursing as a profession. A study done by Dundee University showed that high-achieving primary school children were less likely to choose nursing as a career based on media stereotypes of nurses (Summers, 2010).

Spear (2010) summarizes it well by saying that although shows such as *Nurse Jackie, HawthoRNe, and Mercy* often portray their main characters, who are nurses, in a good light, there are still many inaccuracies in the media regarding nursing. To close the gap between the depiction of nurses in the media and what nurses actually do will require effort from associations such as CNA and CARNA, as well as from nurses themselves. The regulatory bodies can launch information campaigns to show the significance of nurses and what their jobs truly entail. Nurses have to stop reinforcing their own stereotypes in saying they are "just nurses" (Cabaniss, 2011, p. 117). They must also work with the media to ensure accurate portrayals of nurses and the nursing profession (Stanley, 2008, p. 94). By taking this proactive role, negative stereotypes can be minimized, solving problems induced by media bias.

The Nursing Image

Nursing stereotypes in the media are ever-present and need to be addressed. The media portrayal of nurses as unprofessional, sexual props needs to be abolished for nurses to become a respected, professional occupation in the eyes of the public. As well, the depiction of nurses as unintelligent needs to be addressed; it indicates to the

HOW THE MEDIA DEPICT NURSING 9

public that nurses do not hold a vital role in healthcare. Knowledge-based practices must become evident in popular media for this stereotype to be dissolved. Nursing has been facing these stereotypes for decades. Images project demeaning characteristics and reduce public confidence in nurses (Kalisch & Kalisch, 1982, p. 264). Nurses, along with their associations, must become more involved to rebuild the media's image of nursing. The media are a strong and powerful source of information. Society must be careful not to stereotype nurses based on how the media portray them: seemingly harmless ideas can turn into a completely inaccurate image.

HOW THE MEDIA DEPICT NURSING 10

References

Centre *References* at the top.

Cabaniss, R. (2011). Educating nurses to impact change in nursing's image. *Teaching and Learning in Nursing, 6*, 112–118. doi: 10.1016/j.teln.2011.01.003

Canadian Nurses Association. (2011a). *Registered nurses and baccalaureate education*. Retrieved from http://www.cna-nurses.ca/cna/nursing/education/baccalaureate/default_e.aspx

Canadian Nurses Association. (2011b). *Standards and best practices*. Ottawa, ON: Author. Retrieved from http://www.cna-nurses.ca/CNA/practice/standards/default_e.aspx

Alphabetize entries by last name of the first author.

Indent all but the first line of each entry.

HOW THE MEDIA DEPICT NURSING 11

Double-space all entries.

Davis, P. (2011). *Understanding your regulatory college and professional association*. Edmonton, AB: College Association of Registered Nurses of Alberta. Retrieved from https://vista4.srv.ualberta.ca/webct/urw/1c5122011.tp0/cobaltMainFrame .dowebct

Gordon, S., & Nelson, S. (2005). An end to angels. *American Journal of Nursing, 105*(5), 62–69.

Kalisch, P. A., & Kalisch, B. J. (1982). Nurses on prime-time television. *American Journal of Nursing, 82*, 264–270. Retrieved from http://www.jstor.org/stable/3463069

Media. [n.d]. In *Oxford Dictionaries Online*. Retrieved from http://oxforddictionaries.com/definition/media?rskey=p7YaEJ&result=2

Potter, P. A., Perry, A. G., Ross-Kerr, J. C., & Wood, M. J. (2010). *Canadian fundamentals of nursing*. Toronto: Moseby/Elsevier.

Spear, H. J. (2010). TV nurses: Promoting a positive image of nursing? *Journal of Christian Nursing, 27*, pp. 218–221.

Stanley, D. J. (2008). Celluloid angels: A research study of nurses in feature films 1900–2007. *Journal of Advanced Nursing, 64*(1), 84–95. doi: 10.1111/j.1365-2648.2008.04793.x

Summers, S. (2010, September 9). The image of nursing: Does nursing's media image matter? *Nursing Times*. Retrieved from http://www.nursingtimes.net/nursing-practice/clinical-specialisms/educators/the-image-of-nursing-does-nursings-media-image-matter/5019099.article

The Truth About Nursing. (2009). *Nurse Jackie:* The henchman of god. *The Truth About Nursing.* Retrieved from http://www.truthaboutnursing.org/news/2009/jun/08_jackie.html

The Truth About Nursing. (2010a). *Grey's Anatomy:* Right away doctor. *The Truth About Nursing.* Retrieved from http://www.truthaboutnursing.org/news/2010/nov/greys.html

The Truth About Nursing. (2010b) *Private Practice:* I got in. *The Truth About Nursing.* Retrieved from http://www.truthaboutnursing.org/news/2010/aug/2009-10_pp.html

The Truth About Nursing. (2011). Reviews of television series featuring nurses. *The Truth About Nursing.* Retrieved from http://www.truthaboutnursing.org/media/tv

Go through your text and make sure that everything you have cited, except for personal communication, is in the list of references.

FORMATTING THE REFERENCES IN APA STYLE

- **Begin the references on a new page.** Insert a page break with your word processor before you start the references page.
- **Centre "References" on the first line at the top of the page.**
- **Double-space all entries.**
- **Alphabetize each entry by the last name of the author or, if no author is listed, by the first content word in the title (ignore *a, an, the*).**
- **Indent all but the first line in each entry ½ inch (1.25 cm).**
- **Italicize the titles of books and periodicals.**
- **Go through your paper to check that each source you have used (except personal communication) is in the list of references.**

28 CMS Documentation

QUICK*TAKE*

- Use in-text citations in CMS style (see below)
- Create citations for books and nonperiodical sources (see p. 365)
- Create citations for periodical sources (see p. 372)
- Create citations for online, electronic, and multimedia sources (see p. 376)
- Format a paper in CMS style (see p. 381)

Writers who publish in business, social sciences, fine arts, and humanities outside the discipline of English often use *The Chicago Manual of Style* (CMS) method of documentation. CMS guidelines allow writers a clear way of using footnotes and endnotes (rather than MLA and APA in-text citations) for citing the sources of quotations, summaries, and paraphrases. If you have questions after consulting this chapter, you can refer to *The Chicago Manual of Style*, sixteenth edition (Chicago: University of Chicago Press, 2010), or visit the website (www.chicagomanualofstyle.org).

28a In-text Citations in CMS Style

In-text citations

CMS describes two systems of documentation, one similar to APA and the other a style that uses footnotes or endnotes, which is the focus of this chapter. In the footnote style CMS uses a superscript number directly after any quotation, paraphrase, or summary. Notes are numbered consecutively throughout the essay, article, or chapter. This superscript number corresponds to either a footnote, which appears at the bottom of the page, or an endnote, which appears at the end of the text.

> In *Canadian Women: A History*, Prentice and colleagues note ironically that the Upper Canada seduction law of 1837 aimed to protect the interests of fathers rather than masters, and that it "ignored" the rights of the young women involved.[1]

Note

> 1. Alison Prentice et al., *Canadian Women: A History* (Toronto: Harcourt Brace Jovanovich, 1988), 93.

Bibliography

Prentice, Alison, Paula Bourne, Gail Cuthbert Brandt, Beth Light, Wendy Mitchinson, and Naomi Black. *Canadian Women: A History*. Toronto: Harcourt Brace Jovanovich, 1988.

Footnote and endnote placement

Footnotes appear at the bottom of the page on which each citation appears. Begin your footnote four lines from the last line of text on the page. Double-space footnotes and endnotes.

Endnotes are compiled at the end of the text on a separate page entitled *Notes*. Centre the title at the top of the page and list your endnotes in the order they appear within the text. The entire endnote section should be double-spaced—both within and between each entry. Even with endnotes it's still possible to include explanatory footnotes, which are indicated by asterisks or other punctuation marks.

CMS bibliography

Because footnotes and endnotes in CMS format contain complete citation information, a separate list of references is often optional. This list of references can be called the *Bibliography*, or if it has only works referenced in your text, *Works Cited, Literature Cited*, or *References*.

THE CHICAGO MANUAL OF STYLE AND PUBLISHING

The *Chicago Manual of Style* is the favourite of the publishing industry because it is far more comprehensive than either the *MLA Handbook* or the *Publication Manual of the American Psychological Association*. The sixteenth edition has been updated to include instruction on how to create and edit electronic publications, including websites and e-books. Because many businesses and organizations now produce electronic publications, a basic knowledge of the electronic publishing process could be a valuable item on your resumé.

The *Chicago Manual* also gives advice on copyright law, such as how a work is granted copyright, what may constitute copyright violation, and what is fair use.

In addition, writers and publishers turn to the *Chicago Manual* for the fine points of writing. For example, there are two kinds of dashes: a longer dash called an *em dash* (discussed in Chapter 45) and a shorter dash called an *en dash*. If you want to know when to use an en dash, the *Chicago Manual* is the place to look.

Index of CMS Documentation

Books and Nonperiodical Sources in CMS Style

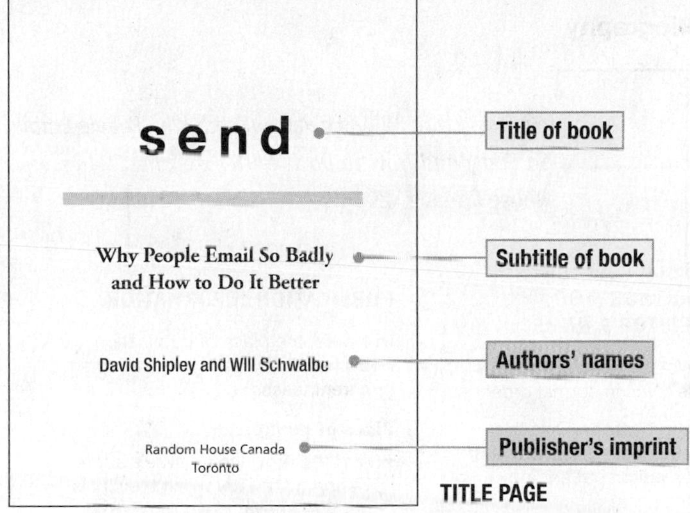
send

Why People Email So Badly
and How to Do It Better

David Shipley and Will Schwalbe

Random House Canada
Toronto

TITLE PAGE

 Published in the United States by Vintage Books, a division of Random House, Inc., New York, and in Canada by Random House of Canada Limited, Toronto. Originally published in hardcover in the United States as *Send: The Essential Guide to Email* by Alfred A. Knopf, a division of Random House, Inc., New York, in 2007, and subsequently in a revised hardcover edition by Alfred A. Knopf, a division of Random House, Inc., New York, in 2008.

The Library of Congress has cataloged the Knopf edition as follows:
Shipley, David, 1963–
Send : why people email so badly and how to do it better /
by David Shipley and Will Schwalbe.—Rev. ed.
p. cm.
Includes bibliographical references and index.
1. Electronic mail messages. 2. Business communication.
3. Communication in management. 4. Interpersonal
communication. I. Schwalbe, Will. II. Title.
HD30.37.S5 2008
658'.054692—dc22
2008010346

Vintage ISBN: 978-0-307-27599-8

10 9 8 7 6 5 4 3 2

Copyright date

DETAIL OF COPYRIGHT PAGE

Note

1. David Shipley and Will Schwalbe, *Send: Why People Email So Badly and How to Do It Better* (Toronto: Random House Canada, 2008), 206.

Bibliography

Shipley, David, and Will Schwalbe. *Send: Why People Email So Badly and How to Do It Better.* Toronto: Random House Canada, 2008

AUTHOR'S OR EDITOR'S NAME

Note: The author's name is given in normal order.

Bibliography: Give the author's last name first. If an editor, put *ed*. after the name.

BOOK TITLE

Use the exact title, as it appears on the title page (not the cover).

Italicize the title.

Capitalize all nouns, verbs, adjectives, adverbs, and pronouns, and the first word of the title and subtitle.

PUBLICATION INFORMATION

In a note, the place of publication, publisher, and year of publication are in parentheses.

Place of publication

- Add the province or state's abbreviation or country when the city is not well known (*Brandon, MB*) or ambiguous (London, ON, or London, UK).
- If more than one city is given on the title page, use the first.

Publisher's name

- Omit an initial *The* and abbreviations such as *Co., Publishing Co., Inc., Ltd.,* or *S.A*.
- For works published prior to 1900, the place and date are sufficient.

Year of publication

- If no year of publication is given, write *n.d.* ("no date") in place of the date.
- If it is a multivolume edited work published over a period of more than one year, put the span of time as the year.

Sample citations for books and nonperiodical sources

BOOKS

1. Book by one author

In a note, the author's name is given in normal order.

1. Ezra Levant, *Ethical Oil: The Case for Canada's Oil Sands* (Toronto: McClelland & Stewart, 2010), 81.

In subsequent references, cite the author's last name and a shortened version of the title:

2. Levant, *Ethical Oil*, 81.

If the reference is to the same work as the preceding note, you can use the abbreviation *Ibid.*:

3. Ibid., 83.

In the bibliography, give the author's name in reverse order.

Levant, Ezra. *Ethical Oil: The Case for Canada's Oil Sands.* Toronto: McClelland & Stewart, 2010.

For edited books, put *ed.* after the name.

Chen, Kuan-Hsing, ed. *Trajectories: Inter-Asia Cultural Studies.* London, UK: Routledge, 1998.

2. Book by multiple authors

For books with two or three authors, in a note, put all authors' names in normal order. For subsequent references, give only the authors' last names:

4. Taylor Hauser and June Kashpaw, *January Blues* (Foster City, CA: IDG Books, 2003), 32.

In the bibliography, give second and third names in normal order.

Hauser, Taylor, and June Kashpaw. *January Blues.* Foster City, CA: IDG Books, 2003.

When there are more than three authors, in a note, give the name of the first author listed, followed by *et al.* List all the authors in the bibliography.

3. Book by an unknown author

Begin both the note and the bibliography entries with the title.

Note

6. *Remarks upon the Religion, Trade, Government, Police, Customs, Manners, and Maladys of the City of Corke* (Cork, 1737), 4.

Bibliography

Remarks upon the Religion, Trade, Government, Police, Customs, Manners, and Maladys of the City of Corke. Cork, 1737.

4. Book by a group or organization

Treat the group or organization as the author of the work.

Note

7. World Health Organization, *Advancing Safe Motherhood through Human Rights* (Geneva, Switzerland: World Health Organization, 2001), 18.

Bibliography

World Health Organization. *Advancing Safe Motherhood through Human Rights*. Geneva, Switzerland: World Health Organization, 2001.

PARTS OF BOOKS

5. A single chapter by the same author as the book

Note

1. Ann Ardis, "*The Lost Girl, Tarr,* and the Moment of Modernism," in *Modernism and Cultural Conflict, 1880–1922* (New York: Cambridge University Press, 2002), 78–113.

Bibliography

Ardis, Ann. "*The Lost Girl, Tarr,* and the Moment of Modernism." In *Modernism and Cultural Conflict, 1880–1922*, 78–113. New York: Cambridge University Press, 2002.

6. A selection in an anthology or a chapter in an edited collection

Note

2. Mikael Adolphson, "Benkei's Ancestors: Monastic Warriors in Heian Japan," in *Currents in Medieval Japanese History: Essays in Honor of Jeffrey P. Mass*, ed. Gordon Berger, Andrew Goble, Lorraine Harrington, and G. Cameron Hurst III (Los Angeles: Figueroa Press, 2009), 87–128.

Bibliography

Adolphson, Mikael. "Benkei's Ancestors: Monastic Warriors in Heian Japan." In *Currents in Medieval Japanese History: Essays in Honor of Jeffrey P. Mass*, edited by Gordon Berger, Andrew Goble, Lorraine Harrington, & G. Cameron Hurst III, 87–128. Los Angeles: Figueroa Press, 2009.

7. Article in a reference work

Publication information is usually omitted from citations of well-known reference volumes. The edition is listed instead. The abbreviation *s.v.* (*sub verbo* or "under the word") replaces an entry's page number.

Note

4. *Encyclopaedia Britannica*, 2009 ed., s.v. "mercantilism."

8. Introduction, foreword, preface, or afterword

When citing an introduction, foreword, preface, or afterword written by someone other than the book's main author, the other writer's name comes first, and the main author's name follows the title of the book.

Note

5. Edward Larkin, introduction to *Common Sense*, by Thomas Paine (New York: Broadview, 2004).

Bibliography

Larkin, Edward. Introduction to *Common Sense*, by Thomas Paine, 1–16. New York: Broadview, 2004.

REVISED EDITIONS, VOLUMES, AND SERIES

9. A revised or later edition of a book

Note

1. Fred S. Kleiner, *Gardner's Art through the Ages: A Global History*, 13th ed. (Boston: Wadsworth, 2010), 85.

Bibliography

Kleiner, Fred S. *Gardner's Art through the Ages: A Global History* 13th ed. Boston: Wadsworth, 2010.

10. Work in more than one volume

Note

1. Oscar Wilde, *The Complete Works of Oscar Wilde*, vol. 3 (New York: Dragon Press, 1998), 1024.

Bibliography

Wilde, Oscar. *The Complete Works of Oscar Wilde*. Vol. 3. New York: Dragon Press, 1998.

EDITIONS AND TRANSLATIONS

11. Book with an editor

Note

1. Thomas Hardy, *Jude the Obscure*, ed. Norman Page (New York: Norton, 1999), 35.

Bibliography

Hardy, Thomas. *Jude the Obscure*. Edited by Norman Page. New York: Norton, 1999.

12. Book with a translator

Follow the style shown in entry 11, but substitute "trans." for "ed." in the note and "Translated" for "Edited" in the bibliographic entry.

GOVERNMENT DOCUMENTS

13. Government document

Note

5. Health Canada Food Safety Assessment Program, *Assessment Report of the Canadian Food Inspection Agency Activities Related to the Safety of Aquaculture Products* (Ottawa: Minister of Public Works and Government Services Canada, 2001), 24.

Bibliography

Health Canada Food Safety Assessment Program. *Assessment Report of the Canadian Food Inspection Agency Activities Related to the Safety of Aquaculture Products.* Ottawa: Minister of Public Works and Government Services Canada, 2001.

14. Congressional Record

For legal documents including the *Congressional Record*, CMS now follows the recommendations in *The Bluebook: A Uniform System of Citations* issued by the Harvard Law Review. The *Congressional Record* is issued in biweekly and permanent volumes. If possible, cite the permanent volumes.

Note

6. 156 Cong. Rec. 11,265 (2010).

RELIGIOUS TEXTS

15. Religious texts

Citations from religious texts appear in the notes but not in the bibliography. Give the version in parentheses in the first citation only.

Note

4. John 3:16 (King James Version).

LETTERS

16. Published letter

Note

5. Oscar Wilde to Robert Ross, 25 November 1897, in *The Complete Letters of Oscar Wilde*, ed. Merlin Holland and Rupert Hart-Davis (New York: Holt, 2000), 992.

Bibliography

Wilde, Oscar. *The Complete Letters of Oscar Wilde*. Edited by Merlin Holland and Rupert Hart-Davis. New York: Holt, 2000.

17. Personal letter to author

Personal communications are not usually listed in the bibliography because they are not accessible to the public.

Note

7. Ann Williams, letter to author, May 8, 2007.

DISSERTATIONS AND CONFERENCE PROCEEDINGS

18. Unpublished dissertation

Note

7. James Elsworth Kidd, "The Vision of Uncertainty: Elizabethan Windows and the Problem of Sight" (PhD diss., Southern Illinois University, 1998), 236.

Bibliography

Kidd, James Elsworth. "The Vision of Uncertainty: Elizabethan Windows and the Problem of Sight." PhD diss., Southern Illinois University, 1998.

19. Published proceedings of a conference

Note

8. Joyce Marie Jackson, "Barrelhouse Singers and Sanctified Preachers," in *Saints and Sinners: Religion, Blues, and (D)evil in African-American Music and Literature: Proceedings of the Conference held at the Université de Liège* (Liège, Belgium: Société Liègeoise de Musicologie, 1996), 14–28.

Bibliography

Jackson, Joyce Marie. "Barrelhouse Singers and Sanctified Preachers." In *Saints and Sinners: Religion, Blues, and (D)evil in African-American Music and Literature: Proceedings of the Conference held at the Université de Liège*, 14–28. Liège, Belgium: Société Liègeoise de Musicologie, 1996.

28c Periodical Sources in CMS Style

Note

1. Marie Vander Kloet, "A Trip to the Co-op: The Production, Consumption and Salvation of Canadian Wilderness," *International Journal of Canadian Studies* 39–40 (2009): 231–51.

Bibliography

Vander Kloet, Marie. "A Trip to the Co-op: The Production, Consumption and Salvation of Canadian Wilderness." *International Journal of Canadian Studies* 39–40 (2009): 231–51.

AUTHOR'S OR EDITOR'S NAME

Note: The author's name is given in normal order.

Bibliography: Give the author's last name first.

TITLE OF ARTICLE

- Put the title in quotation marks. If there is a title of a book within the title, italicize it.
- Capitalize nouns, verbs, adjectives, adverbs, and pronouns, and the first word of the title and subtitle.

PUBLICATION INFORMATION

Name of journal

- Italicize the name of the journal.
- Journal titles are normally not abbreviated in the arts and humanities unless the title of the journal is an abbreviation (*PMLA, ELH*).

Volume, issue, and page numbers

- Place the volume number after the journal title without intervening punctuation.
- For journals that are paginated from issue to issue within a volume, you do not have to list the issue number.
- When a journal uses only issue numbers, not volumes, put a comma after the journal title. The abbreviation *no*. precedes the issue number.

Date

- The year of publication, sometimes preceded by the exact day, month, or year, is given in parentheses after the volume number, or issue number, if provided.

Sample citations for periodical sources

JOURNAL ARTICLES

20. Article by one author

Note

1. Sumit Guha, "Speaking Historically: The Changing Voices of Historical Narration in Western India, 1400–1900," *American Historical Review* 109 (2004): 1084–98.

In subsequent references, cite the author's last name and a shortened version of the title:

2. Guha, "Speaking Historically," 1085.

If the reference is to the same work as the reference before it, you can use the abbreviation *Ibid.*:

3. Ibid., 1087.

Bibliography

Guha, Sumit. "Speaking Historically: The Changing Voices of Historical Narration in Western India, 1400–1900." *American Historical Review* 109 (2004): 1084–98.

21. Article by two or three authors

Note

3. Pamela R. Matthews and Mary Ann O'Farrell, "Introduction: Whose Body?" *South Central Review* 18, nos. 3–4 (Fall–Winter 2001): 1–5.

All authors' names are printed in normal order. For subsequent references, give both authors' last names.

4. Matthews and O'Farrell, "Introduction: Whose Body?" 4.

Bibliography

Matthews, Pamela R., and Mary Ann O'Farrell. "Introduction: Whose Body?" *South Central Review* 18, nos. 3–4 (Fall–Winter 2001): 1–5.

22. Article by more than three authors

Note

Give the name of the first listed author, followed by *et al.*

5. Michael J. Thompson et al., "The Internal Rotation of the Sun," *Annual Review of Astronomy and Astrophysics* 41 (2003): 602.

Bibliography

List all the authors (inverting only the first author's name).

Thompson, Michael J., Jorgen Christensen-Dalsgaard, Mark S. Miesch, and Juri Toomre. "The Internal Rotation of the Sun." *Annual Review of Astronomy and Astrophysics* 41 (2003): 599–643.

23. Article by an unknown author

Note

6. "Japan's Global Claim to Asia," *American Historical Review* 109 (2004): 1196–98.

Bibliography

"Japan's Global Claim to Asia." *American Historical Review* 109 (2004): 1196–98.

DIFFERENT TYPES OF PAGINATION

24. Journals paginated by volume

Note

4. Susan Welsh, "Resistance Theory and Illegitimate Reproduction," *College Composition and Communication* 52 (2001): 553–73.

Bibliography

Welsh, Susan. "Resistance Theory and Illegitimate Reproduction." *College Composition and Communication* 52 (2001): 553–73.

25. Journals paginated by issue

For journals paginated separately by issue, list the issue number after the volume number.

Note

5. Tzvetan Todorov, "The New World Disorder," *South Central Review* 19, no. 2 (2002): 28–32.

Bibliography

Todorov, Tzvetan. "The New World Disorder." *South Central Review* 19, no. 2 (2002): 28–32.

POPULAR MAGAZINES

26. Weekly and biweekly magazines

For a weekly or biweekly popular magazine, give both the day and month of publication as listed on the issue.

Note

5. Michael Petrou, "Retribution the Canadian Way," *Maclean's*, March 19, 2012, 20.

Bibliography

Petrou, Michael. "Retribution the Canadian Way." *Maclean's*, March 19, 2012, 20.

27. Regular features and departments

Do not put titles of regular features or departments of a magazine in quotation marks.

Note

3. Taste, *Maclean's*, March 19, 2012, 65.

REVIEWS AND EDITORIALS

28. A review

Provide the title, if given, and name the work reviewed. If there is no title, just name the work reviewed.

Note

1. Mark Medley, review of *The Purchase*, by Linda Spalding, *National Post*, October 13, 2012, WP9.

Bibliography

Medley, Mark. Review of *The Purchase*, by Linda Spalding. *National Post*, October 13, 2012, WP9.

29. A letter to the editor or an editorial

Add *letter to the editor* or *editorial* after the name of the author (if there is one). If there is no author, start with the descriptor.

Note

2. Zbigniew Filek, letter to the editor, *National Post*, March 18, 2012, A17.

Bibliography

Filek, Zbigniew. Letter to the editor. *National Post*, March 18, 2012, A17.

NEWSPAPERS

30. Newspaper article

Note

1. Andrew Coyne, "Canada at the Crossroads of Trade," *National Post*, March 18, 2012, sec. A.

- The month, day, and year are essential in citations of materials from daily newspapers. Cite them in this order: Month–Day–Year (November 3, 2012).
- For an item in a large city newspaper that has several editions a day, give the edition after the date.
- If the newspaper is published in sections, include the name, number, or letter of the section after the date or the edition (sec. C).
- Page numbers are usually omitted. If you put them in, your instructor might ask you to use *p.* and *col.* (column) to avoid ambiguity.

28d Online Sources in CMS Style

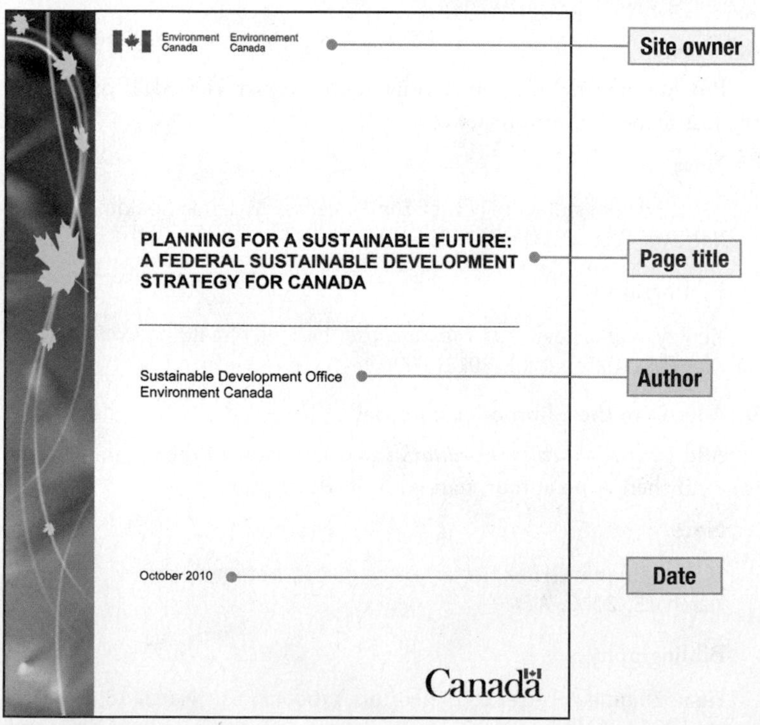

ONLINE PUBLICATIONS

31. Document or page from a website

To cite original content from within a website, include as many descriptive elements as you can: author of the page, title of the page, title and owner of the website, and the URL. Include the date accessed only if (1) the online content has no date of publication or revision or (2) your instructor asks you to do so. If you cannot locate an individual author, the owner of the site can stand in for the author.

Note

11. Sustainable Development Office Environment Canada, Planning for a sustainable future: A federal sustainable development strategy for Canada. Ottawa: Environment Canada, 2010. http://ec.gc.ca/dd-sd/F93CD795-0035-4DAF-86D1 53099BD303F9 /FSDS_v4_FN.pdf.

Bibliography

Sustainable Development Office Environment Canada. Planning for a sustainable future: A federal sustainable development strategy for Canada. Ottawa: Environment Canada, 2010. http://ec.gc .ca/dd-sd/F93CD795-0035-4DAF-86D1-53099BD303F9 /FSDS_v4_EN.pdf.

32. Online book

Note

12. Angelina Grimké, *Appeal to the Christian Women of the South* (New York: New York Anti-slavery Society, 1836), accessed November 2, 2010, http://history.furman.edu/~benson/docs /grimke2.htm.

Bibliography

Grimké, Angelina. *Appeal to the Christian Women of the South*. New York: New York Anti-slavery Society, 1836. Accessed November 2, 2010. http://history.furman.edu/~benson/docs /grimke2.htm.

33. Online article

Note

13. Peter V. Hall and Amir J. Khan, "Differences in Hi-Tech Immigrant Earnings and Wages across Canadian Cities," *Canadian Geographer* 52 (2008): 271–90, doi:10.1111/j.1541-0064.2008.00213.x.

Bibliography

Hall, Peter V., and Amir J. Khan. "Differences in Hi-Tech Immigrant Earnings and Wages across Canadian Cities." *Canadian Geographer* 52 (2008): 271–90. doi:10.1111/j.1541-0064.2008.00213.x.

CITING ONLINE SOURCES IN CMS STYLE

CMS advocates a style for citing online and electronic sources that is adapted from its style for citing print sources. Titles of complete works are italicized. Quotation marks and other punctuation in citations for online sources should be used in the same manner as for print sources.

Access dates: List the date of access (if needed) before the URL or DOI.

Revision dates: Use revision dates for frequently updated works, such as wikis; in other cases, avoid them in favour of specifying the last modified or accessed dates.

DOIs and URLs: If the book or article has a Document Object Identifier (DOI) assigned, list it and not the URL. Otherwise, list the URL. If a URL has to be broken at the end of a line, the line break should be made before a slash (/) or other mark of punctuation. CMS does not advocate the use of angle brackets (<>) to enclose URLs.

For details not covered in this section, consult *The Chicago Manual of Style*, sixteenth edition, sections 14d–14m.

OTHER ELECTRONIC SOURCES

34. Posting to a discussion list or group

To cite material from archived internet forums, discussion groups, or blogs, include the name of the post author, the name of the list or site, the date of the posting, and the URL. Limit your citation to notes or in-text citations.

Note

16. Janyce McGregor, "Not Up for Debate: The Throne Speech," *Inside Politics* (blog), *CBC News*, June 3, 2011, http://www.cbc.ca/news/politics/inside-politics-blog/2011/06/throne-speech-debate-dont-hold-your-breath.html.

35. Email

Because personal emails are not available to the public, they are not usually listed in the bibliography.

Note

11. Erik Lynn Williams, "Social Anxiety Disorder," email message to author, August 12, 2007.

28e Multimedia Sources in CMS Style

36. Musical recording

Note

8. The Tragically Hip, "Ahead by a Century," *Trouble at the Henhouse,* MCA Music Entertainment MCAD 81011, 1996, compact disc.

Bibliography

The Tragically Hip. "Ahead by a Century." *Trouble at the Henhouse.* MCA Music Entertainment MCAD 81011, 1996, compact disc.

37. Film or video

Note

9. *Invictus*, directed by Clint Eastwood (2009; Hollywood, CA: Warner Home Video, 2009), DVD.

Bibliography

Invictus. Directed by Clint Eastwood. Released 2009. Hollywood, CA: Warner Home Video, 2009. DVD.

38. Speech, debate, mediated discussion, or public talk

Note

16. Katherine Tiede, "Using Storyboarding to Engineer Genre" (paper presented at the Conference on College Composition and Communication, Chicago, IL, March 2006).

Bibliography

Tiede, Katherine. "Using Storyboarding to Engineer Genre." Paper presented at the Conference on College Composition and Communication, Chicago, IL, March 2006.

39. Interview

Note

15. Belinda Stronach, "The Dave McGraw Interview: Belinda Stronach, Redux," by Dave McGraw, *The Hammer*, May 19, 2005, http://www.thehammer.ca/content/view.php?news=2005-05-19-belinda-stronach-interview-redux.

Bibliography

Stronach, Belinda. "The Dave McGraw Interview: Belinda Stronach, Redux." By Dave McGraw. *The Hammer*, May 19, 2005, http://www.thehammer.ca/content/view.php?news=2005-05-19-belinda-stronach-interview-redux.

40. Illustrations, figures, and tables

When citing figures from sources, use the abbreviation *fig*. However, spell out the word when citing tables, graphs, maps, or plates. The page number on which the figure appears precedes any figure number.

Note

16. Christian Unger, *America's Inner-City Crisis* (New York: Childress, 2003), 134, fig. 3.4.

Sample Pages with CMS Documentation*

1

Elizabeth Moore

British History and Literature 102

April 24, 2006

Love and Marriage in the Works and Lives of Elizabeth Cary and Lady Mary Wroth

The work of Elizabeth Cary, titled Lady Falkland, and Lady Mary Wroth looks with a critical eye at the coupling of love and marriage. For early modern women, reality often composed itself in the form of marriage and love of something unrelated to one's husband. Forced to eke out a place in their prescribed roles as wife and mother for their own intellectual expression, Cary and Wroth wrote stories about women who found themselves caught between their own powerful desires and the men who controlled their lives. Their writing is important today not only as literature but as an invaluable record of the thoughts and self-expression of women in a time when their lives were not their own. The protagonists of Cary's and Wroth's work explore the meaning of love and marriage, both topics complex and often dissatisfying in the context of their time. Like their fictional characters, Cary and Wroth navigated the rocky terrain of the heart and the mind. Their biographies both inform and contradict their writing.

* Portions shown in this paper are adjusted to fit the space limitations of this book. Follow the actual dimensions discussed in this book and your instructor's directions.

2

The dialogue between their realities and their fiction considers what it meant to a be a woman in the early modern period.

Elizabeth Cary and Mary Wroth were born Elizabeth Tanfield and Mary Sidney, respectively. They were both eminently well educated in childhood. Tanfield, born in 1585, had taught herself "French, Spanish, Italian, Latin, Hebrew and 'Transylvanian'" by the age of 4 and successfully argued for the acquittal of a woman accused of witchcraft at 10.[1] Sidney, born in 1587, was the niece of noted Renaissance poet and literary patron Mary Herbert, countess of Pembroke, for whom she was named. She spent part of her childhood in extended visits with her aunt. She was active in the court of King James I and VI and performed in several masques.[2] Both Sidney and Tanfield were brought up in academically fertile environments. . . .

3

Notes

1. Nancy Cotton Pearse, "Elizabeth Cary, Renaissance Playwright," *Texas Studies in Literature and Language* 18 (1977): 601–8.

2. Josephine Roberts, "The Biographical Problem of *Pamphilia to Amphilanthus*," *Tulsa Studies in Women's Literature* 1, no. 1 (1982): 43–53, http://www.jstor.org/stable/464091.

4

Bibliography

Pearse, Nancy Cotton. "Elizabeth Cary, Renaissance Playwright." *Texas Studies in Literature and Language* 18 (1977): 601–8.

Roberts, Josephine. "The Biographical Problem of *Pamphilia* to *Amphilanthus*." *Tulsa Studies in Women's Literature* 1, no. 1 (1982): 43–53. http://www.jstor.org/stable/464091.

29 CSE Documentation

QUICK*TAKE*

- Use in-text references in CSE style (see p. 385)
- Create references for books and nonperiodical sources (see p. 386)
- Create references for periodical sources (see p. 388)
- Create references for online sources (see p. 389)
- Format a paper in CSE style (see p. 390)

Within the disciplines of the natural and applied sciences, citation styles are highly specialized. Many disciplines follow the guidelines of particular journals or style manuals within their individual fields. Consult your instructor to determine which documentation style he or she prefers. Widely followed by writers in the sciences is the comprehensive guide published by the Council of Science Editors: *Scientific Style and Format: The CSE Manual for Authors, Editors, and Publishers*, seventh edition (2006).

The CSE outlines three documentation options, including a name-year system similar to APA's and a citation-sequence system with numbered references.

The preferred documentation system in CSE places references in the body of the text marked by a superscript number preceded by a space and placed inside punctuation. For example,

> Cold fingers and toes are common circulatory problems found in most heavy cigarette smokers [1].

This number corresponds to a numbered entry on the alphabetized CSE source list, titled *References*.

The CSE References page lists all sources cited in the paper. To create a CSE References page, follow these guidelines:

1. Title your page "References," and centre this title at the top of the page.
2. Double-space between citations and single-space within citations.
3. List and number citations in alphabetical order by author. Begin each citation with its citation number, followed by a period, flush left.
4. Authors are listed by last name, followed by initials. Capitalize only first words and proper nouns in cited titles. Titles are not italicized or underlined, and articles are not placed in quotations. Names of journals should be abbreviated where possible.
5. Cite publication year, and volume or page numbers if applicable.

29a In-text References in CSE Style

CSE documentation of sources does not require the names of authors in the text but only a number that refers to the References list at the end.

> In 1997, the Gallup poll reported that 55% of adults in the United States think second-hand smoke is "very harmful," compared to only 36% in 1994 [1].

The superscript [1] refers to the first entry on the References list, where readers will find a complete citation for this source.

What if you need more than one citation in a passage?

If the numbers are consecutive, separate with a hyphen or an en dash. If non-consecutive, use a comma without a space.

> The previous work [1,3,5–8,11]

 Books and Nonperiodical Sources in CSE-Style References

1. Nance JJ. What goes up: the global assault on our atmosphere. New York: W. Morrow; 1991. 324 p.

AUTHOR'S OR EDITOR'S NAME

The author's last name comes first, followed by the initials of the author's first name and middle name (if provided). If an editor, put the word *editor* after the name.

BOOK TITLE

- Do not italicize or underline titles.
- Capitalize only the first word and proper nouns.

PUBLICATION INFORMATION

Year of publication

- The year comes after the other publication information. It follows a semicolon.
- If it is a multivolume edited work, published over a period of more than one year, give the span of years.

Page numbers

- When citing an entire book, give the total number of pages: *324 p.*
- When citing part of a book, give the page range for the selection: *p. 60–90.*

Sample references

BOOKS

1. Book by a single author/editor

2. Lay DC. Linear algebra and its applications. Boston: Pearson; 2006. 492 p.

2. Book by two or more authors/editors

3. O'Day DH, Horgen PA, editors. Sexual interactions in eukaryotic microbes. New York: Academic Press; 1981. 407 p.

3. Book by a group or organization

4. Biological Survey of Canada. Insects of the Yukon. Ottawa: BSC; 1997. 1034 p.

4. Two or more books by the same author

Number the references alphabetically by author's last name, and maintain that numbering for in-text citations. For two or more books by the same author, alphabetize by the first major word in the title.

5. Gould SJ. The structure of evolutionary theory. Cambridge: Harvard University Press; 2002. 1433 p.

8. Gould SJ. Wonderful life: the Burgess Shale and the nature of history. New York: Norton; 1989. 347 p.

PARTS OF BOOKS

5. A single chapter written by the same author as the book

6. Ogle M. All the modern conveniences: American household plumbing, 1840–1890. Baltimore: Johns Hopkins University Press; 2000. Convenience embodied; p. 60–92.

6. A selection in an anthology or a chapter in an edited collection

7. Kraft K, Baines DM. Computer classrooms and third grade development. In: Green MD, editor. Computers and early development. New York: Academic Press; 1997. p. 168–79.

REPORTS

7. Technical and research reports

9. Austin A, Baldwin R, editors. Faculty collaboration: enhancing the quality of scholarship and teaching. Washington, DC: George Washington University; 1991. ASCHE-ERIC Higher Education Report 7.

29c Periodical Sources in CSE-Style References

1. Bohannon J. Climate change: IPCC report lays out options for taming greenhouse gases. Science. 2007;316(5826):812–814.

AUTHOR'S NAME

The author's last name comes first, followed by the initials of the author's first name and middle name (if provided).

TITLE OF ARTICLE

- Do not italicize or underline titles.
- Capitalize only the first word and proper nouns.

PUBLICATION INFORMATION

Name of journal

- Do not abbreviate single-word titles. Abbreviate multiple-word titles according to the National Information Standards Organization (NISO) list of serials.
- Capitalize all words in a journal title, including abbreviated words (see example 9 below).

Date of publication, volume, and issue numbers

- Include the issue number inside parentheses if it is present in the document. Leave no spaces between these items.

Page numbers

- After the volume or issue number of the periodical, use a colon and include the page range for the article. Leave no spaces between these items.

JOURNAL ARTICLES

8. Article by one author

1. Nielsen TV, Gosselin LA. Can a scavenger benefit from environmental stress? Role of salinity stress and abundance of preferred food items in controlling population abundance of the snail *Lirabuccinum dirum*. J Exp Mar Biol Ecol. 2011;410:80–86.

9. Article by two or more authors/editors

2. Almeda R, Messmer KM, Sampedro N, Gosselin LA. Feeding rates and abundance of marine invertebrate planktonic larvae under harmful algal bloom conditions off Vancouver Island. Harmful Algae. 2011;10:194–206.

10. Article by a group or organization

4. PrioNet Canada. Network partnerships: collaborations catalyze crucial vaccine. PrioNet Canada Annual Report 2010-2011;10.

11. Article with no identifiable author

Alphabetize the article by title.

12. Journals paginated by issue

Use the month or season of publication (and day, if given) for journals that have no volume or issue number.

8. Solar-Tuttle R. The invincible ones. Harv AIDS Rev. 2000 Spring-Summer:19–20.

Interviews

13. Insert a parenthetical reference in the text—"(interview)"— to cite an interview with a person if the interview has not been published. Do not include an entry in the References for any unpublished material, including an unpublished interview.

29d Online Sources in CSE-Style References

13. Online journal articles

2. Schunck CH, Shin Y, Schirotzek A, Zwierlein MW, Ketterle A. Pairing without superfluidity: the ground state of an imbalanced fermi mixture. Science [Internet]. 2007 [cited 2007 June 15]; 316(5826):867–870. Available from: http://www.sciencemag.org/cgi/content/full/3165826/867/DC1

14. Scientific databases on the internet

3. Comprehensive Large Array data Stewardship System [Internet]. 2007. Release 4.2. Silver Spring (MD): National Environmental Satellite, Data, and Information Service (US). [updated 2007 May 2; cited 2007 May 14]. Available from: http://www.class.noaa.gov/saa/products/welcome

29e Sample Pages with CSE Documentation

1

Thuydung Do

BIO 206L Fall 2007

November 13, 2007

The Preference of Home Soil over Foreign Soil in *Pogonomyrmex barbatus*

Abstract

Tests were conducted to see whether or not harvester ants of the species *Pogonomyrmex barbatus* can actually distinguish home soil from foreign soil. These ants were exposed to different types of soils and the time they spent on each soil was recorded. The Wilcoxon Signed Rank test was performed to analyze the collected data. It was observed that *Pogonomyrmex barbatus* does show preference for home soil over foreign soil.

Introduction

Pieces of food are sometimes seen surrounded by hundreds of ants a while after they were dropped on the table or the ground. There are also trails of ants that line up in an orderly fashion leading from the food to the nests. How do these ants know to follow one another in a line instead of scattering all over? The main method is through releasing pheromones [1]. The pheromones allow the ants to trail after one another, but where will they go? What makes these different ant mounds distinct from one another? Based on research done by Wagner and her group,

2

soil biota and soil chemistry of each nest can set themselves apart[2]. Can the harvester ants detect these differences in the soils at all or are all soils the same to them? In this experiment, the null hypothesis that harvester ants *Pogonomyrmex barbatus* cannot distinguish home soil from foreign soil and neutral soil was tested in an attempt to find the answer to this question.

. . .

3

References

1. Holldobler B, Morgan ED, Oldham NJ, Liebig J. Recruitment pheromone in the harvester ant genus *Pogonomyrmex*. J Insect Phys. 2001;47(4-5): 369–374.
2. Wagner D, Brown M, Gordon D. Harvester ant nests, soil biota, and soil chemistry. Oecologia. 1997;112: 232–236.

30 IEEE Documentation

QUICK*TAKE*

- Use citation numbers for in-text references in IEEE style (see p. 392)
- Create references for periodical sources (see p. 394)
- Create references for books (see p. 396)
- Create references for reports (see p. 396)
- Create references for online sources (see p. 397)

The Institute of Electrical and Electronic Engineers, Inc. (IEEE) publishes the *IEEE Editorial Style Manual* to provide editorial guidelines for IEEE transactions, journals, and letters. For additional information on how to format citations and references using IEEE documentation, see www.ieee.org/documents/stylemanual.pdf.

30a The Elements of IEEE Documentation

IEEE documentation style uses citation numbers in the body of the document to identify sources of information and a list of references at the end of the document that provides complete and detailed information for all the sources cited.

Citations

IEEE documentation style encloses citation numbers in the text of the paper in square brackets, for example, [1]. All additional bibliographical information about the citation appears in the list of references at the end of the document. Place citation numbers directly after the reference. Punctuate outside the square bracket, and use commas to separate multiple references (for example, [2, 17, 7]).

Citation-name substitution

IEEE style suggests substituting reference list numbers for the name of the author(s) where appropriate. For example, if you want to attribute a finding to a research group, substitute the number of the reference for the list of authors' names. In contrast, if you want to attribute something like a theory to the person who developed it, use the author's name.

List of references

Your list of references should include all the sources that you used in writing the document.

Title, aligned flush left

References

[1] M. M. Lay, *Technical Communication*. Chicago: Irwin, 1995, p. 237.

Indent all entries 2 or 3 spaces to the right of citation number

Arrange list by order of citation, not by alphabetical order

[2] V. Wilczynski and S. M. Douglas, "Integrating design across the curriculum: A report from the trenches," *Journal of Engineering Education*, vol. 84, no. 3, pp. 235–240, July 1995.

Double-space within and between entries

30b Periodical Sources in IEEE-Style References

APPLIED THEORY

SUMMARY (Summary)
- Explores the claim that current internationalization and localization efforts presume particular cultural rather than structural or architectural reconsideration
- Maps cultural dimensions to different elements of information architecture

Information Architecture: Intercultural Human Factors

(Article title)

MATTHEW MCCOOL (Author's name)

INTRODUCTION

During the past nine years I have developed a variety of online products for domestic and international audiences, ranging from the simple to the complex, for both public and private sectors. During this time the most difficult projects I worked on were not how to modify Java APIs or customize complex applications, but rather making basic information available to international and intercultural audiences. Although I teamed with reputable localization personnel from Germany, Japan, France, and Spain to make our online documentation accessible for these respective audiences, the result was generally disappointing. In nearly every case something seemed to go wrong, a conclusion based on the excessive number of call center questions from our international customers.

We arrived at this realization when comparing not only previous product support calls from these same customers but also in comparing these calls with those from our domestic audience. From our perspective, nothing was considerably different. We accounted for time, currency, and color. The translations were rhetorical and not literal, ensuring linguistic transference from English to the target language. And these customers were also very important, comprising the bulk of total revenue, a fact that justified the enormous time and expense of our localization efforts. Everything else was the same—the same content, the same information superstructure, the same chunking and navigation.

We were mystified as to how our international deliverables, especially for Japan, were failing so much more than the domestic equivalent. In the end the problem was never solved, the companies I worked for endured turbulent times, and I moved on to other equally interesting projects. It was several years later when I learned about cultural dimensions, and so I began to wonder whether the absence of these core values in our design may have caused our troubles.

Traditionally, the process of making online information accessible to different cultures amounted to basic adaptations of time, currency, and color (Hoft 1995). Translation, although never a direct transmission from one language to the next (Kaplan 1966; Connor 1996), incorporated few if any rhetorical considerations. Despite earnest efforts to design for a rather different audience, albeit internationalization or localization, numerous cultural adaptations failed to be considered.

Excellent research has been conducted about both information architecture and intercultural communication, but until recently, they rarely found cause for convergence. For example, in the May 2000 *Technical communication* special section on information design, none of the articles specifically address the coalescence of superstructures, chunking, and navigation for the online environment. Similarly, although excellent articles have been published regarding online media and cultural values (for example, Fukuoka and colleagues 1999; Arnold 2000; Qiuye 2000), touching on core cultural dimensions, none have addressed their convergence with and effect on information architecture.

(Text of article)

While authors in these two areas have focused on specific or exclusive problems, they have never been meaningfully considered or studied together. If internationalization and localization processes are to be useful and effective, overlaying cultural dimensions on information structures may prove to be the final variable toward effective online localization.

The process of overlaying cultural dimensions on information architecture is a new approach toward internationalization and localization. Much good and useful work has been done with regard to culture and online information, but rarely have these explorations incorporated the deeper currents of culture. This fact is unfortunate because core cultural values, those dimensions which influence how we perceive and ascribe meaning to the world (Kaplan 1966; Victor 1992; Connor 1996; Hofstede 1997; Trompenaars 1998), are possibly the most important factors

Manuscript received 27 February 2005; revised 3 December 2005; accepted 5 December 2005.

(Journal title)

[30] M. McCool, "Information architecture: Intercultural human factors," *Technical Communication*, vol. 53, no. 2, pp. 167–183, May 2006.

AUTHOR'S NAME

Use author's initials, then surname, followed by a comma.

TITLE OF ARTICLE

Put the title in quotation marks.

Capitalize first word of title and subtitle and all proper nouns.

PUBLICATION INFORMATION

Name of journal

Italicize the name of the journal.

Abbreviate journal titles, as appropriate.

Volume, issue, and page numbers

Abbreviate the words "volume" and "number," as shown, separated by a comma.

Include page numbers, formatted as shown.

Include the abbreviated month and the year of the journal issue.

Date

Date is included with month at the end of the citation.

1. Article by one author

[1] S. Shimizu, "Wide-angle foveation for all-purpose use," *IEEE/ASME Transactions on Mechatronics*, vol. 13, no. 5, pp. 587–597, Oct. 2008.

2. Article by two or more authors

[2] P. Gochenour and C. Radcliff, "TWiki: Introduction to a structured wiki," *Intercom*, vol. 54, no. 8, pp. 20–24, Sept./Oct. 2007.

3. Article by a group or organization

[3] Centre for Science in the Public Interest, "Behind the label," *Nutrition Action Healthletter*, vol. 34, no. 7, p. 11, Sept. 2007.

30c Books in IEEE-Style References

4. Book by a single author/editor

[5] D.A. Norman, *Emotional Design: Why We Love (or Hate) Everyday Things*. New York: Basic Books, 2004.

5. Book by two or more authors/editors

[1] A. Prentice, P. Bourne, G.C. Brandt, E. Light, W. Mitchinson, and N. Black, *Canadian Women: A History*. Toronto: Harcourt Brace Jovanovich, 1988.

6. Book by a group or organization

[3] World Health Organization, *Advancing Safe Motherhood Through Human Rights*. Geneva, Switzerland: World Health Organization, 2001.

30d Reports in IEEE-Style References

7. Report by a single author

[4] C. Rudin-Brown, "Strategies for reducing drive distraction from in-vehicle telematics devices: Report on industry and public consultations." Road Safety and Motor Vehicle Regulation Directorate, Ottawa, ON, Rep. TP 14409 E, 2005.

8. Report by an organization

[3] Health Canada Food Safety Assessment Program, Assessment reports of the Canadian Food Inspection Agency activities related to the safety of aquaculture products. Ministry of Public Works and Government Services, Ottawa, ON, Cat. H39-577/2001E, 2001.

30e Online Sources in IEEE-Style References

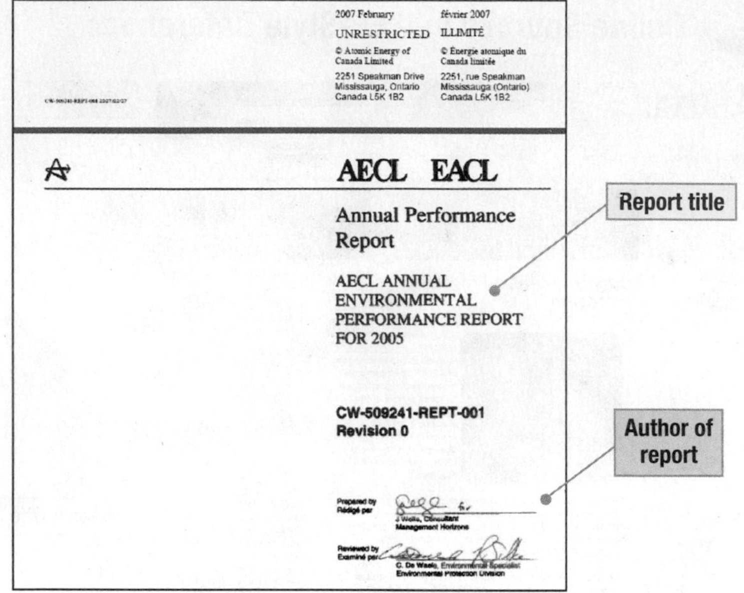

2007 February | février 2007

UNRESTRICTED | ILLIMITÉ

© Atomic Energy of Canada Limited | © Énergie atomique du Canada limitée

2251 Speakman Drive, Mississauga, Ontario, Canada L5K 1B2 | 2251, rue Speakman, Mississauga (Ontario), Canada L5K 1B2

AECL EACL

Annual Performance Report

AECL ANNUAL ENVIRONMENTAL PERFORMANCE REPORT FOR 2005

CW-509241-REPT-001
Revision 0

Prepared by / Rédigé par: J Wells, Consultant, Management Horizons

Reviewed by / Examiné par: C. De Waele, Environmental Specialist, Environmental Protection Division

9. Documents from a website

Online Report

[7] J. Wells. (2007, February). AECL annual environmental performance report for 2005. Atomic Energy of Canada Ltd. Mississauga, ON. [PDF Online]. Available: http://www.aecl.ca/Assets/Publications/Reports/CW-509241-REPT-001.pdf

Online Article

[3] P. Agre. (1998, Mar.). The Internet and public discourse. *First Monday* [Online]. *3* (3). Available: http://www.firstmonday.dk/issues/issue3_3/agre

Online Book

[4] A. Grimké. (1836). *Appeal to Christian women of the South*. [Online]. Available: http://history.furman.edu/~benson/docs/grimke2.htm

Email

[2] C. Skolnick. (1998, Aug. 13). The relation between professional writing and professional development. [Online]. Available email: Inkshed listserv at http://www.stthomasu.ca/inkshed/profwrit.htm

PART

7 Effective Style and Language

You **can learn more and do more** with MyWritingLab and with the eText version of *The Brief Penguin Handbook*. Find resources in MyWritingLab to help you successfully complete your assignment.

31 Write with Power 399

32 Write Concisely 406

33 Write with Emphasis 412

34 Find the Right Words 420

35 Write to Be Inclusive 427

31 Write with Power

QUICKTAKE

- **How do you make your writing active?** (see p. 400)
  Passive: The snowboard was invented by Sherman Poppen.
  Active: Sherman Poppen invented the snowboard.
- **What are agents, and how do you use them in your writing?** (see p. 402)
  No agent: It was made as a plaything for his daughter
  With agent: Poppen made the first snowboard as a plaything for his daughter.
- **How do you vary your sentences?** (see p. 404)
  Choppy and repetitive: It was called the *Snurfer*. The name was a combination of snow and surfer. It was a skateboard without wheels. It was manufactured as a toy the next year.
  Variety: Poppen named his snowboard the *Snurfer*, which was a combination of snow and surfer. Essentially a skateboard without wheels, the Snurfer was manufactured as a toy the next year.

Keeping a few principles in mind can make your writing a pleasure to read instead of a boring slog.

In visuals
You imagine actions when subjects are captured in motion.

In writing
Your readers expect actions to be expressed in verbs: *fly, rip, freeride, jump, lay down, charge.*

In visuals
Viewers interpret the most prominent person or thing as the subject—what the visual is about.

In writing
Readers interpret the first person or thing they meet in a sentence as what the sentence is about (the snowboarder, the snowboard). They expect that person or thing to perform the action expressed in the verb.

31a Pay Attention to Verbs

A teacher may once have told you that verbs are "action words." Where are the action words in the following paragraph?

> Red hair flying, professional snowboarder and skateboarder Shaun White is a two-time Olympic gold medalist with a record score of 48.4 at the 2010 Winter Olympics. White was a skier before he was five, but became a snowboarder at age six, and by age seven he was a professional, receiving corporate sponsorships. At age nine, White became friends with professional skateboarder Tony Hawk, who was White's mentor in becoming a professional skateboarder. White is known for accomplishing several "firsts" in snowboarding, including being the first to land back-to-back double corks and to master a trick called a Cab 7 Melon Grab. He is also the holder of the record for the highest score in the men's halfpipe at the Winter Olympics.

No action words here! The paragraph describes a series of actions, yet most of the verbs are *was* and *is*. These sentences typify writing that uses *be* verbs (*is, are, was, were*) when better alternatives are available. Think about what the actions are and choose powerful verbs that express those actions.

> Red hair flying, professional snowboarder and skateboarder Shaun White **scored** a 48.4 during the 2010 Winter Olympics and **won** his second gold medal. White **skied** before he was five, but **switched** to snowboarding at age six, and by age seven **received** corporate sponsorships. At age nine, White **befriended** professional skateboarder Tony Hawk, who **mentored** White and **helped** him become a professional skateboarder. White **has accomplished** several "firsts" in snowboarding, including landing back-to-back double corks and mastering a trick called a Cab 7 Melon Grab. He also **holds** the record for the highest score in the men's halfpipe at the Winter Olympics.

STAYING ON TRACK

Express actions as verbs

Many sentences contain words that express action, but those words are nouns instead of verbs. Often the nouns can be changed into verbs. For example:

> The arson unit ~~conducted an investigation of~~ **investigated** the mysterious fire.

> The committee ~~had a debate over~~ **debated** how best to spend the surplus funds.

Notice that changing nouns into verbs also eliminates unnecessary words.

31b Stay Active

When you were a very young child, you learned an important lesson about language. Perhaps you can remember the day you broke the cookie jar. Did you tell Mom, "I knocked over the jar"? Probably not. Instead, you might have said, "The jar got broken." This short sentence accomplishes an amazing sleight of hand. Who broke the jar and how the jar was broken remain mysterious. Apparently, it just broke.

Got is often used for *was* in informal speech. In written language, the sentence would read, "The jar was broken," which is an example of the passive voice. Passives can be as useful for adults as for children to conceal who is responsible for an action:

> The laptop containing our customers' personal information **was misplaced.**

Who misplaced the laptop? Who knows?

Sentences with transitive verbs (labelled *TV* below; these are verbs that need an object; see Section 39c) can be written in the **active** or **passive** voice. In the active voice the subject of the sentence is the actor. In the passive voice the subject is being acted upon.

Active [SUBJ] **Leonardo da Vinci** [TV] **painted** *Mona Lisa* between 1503 and 1506.

Passive [SUBJ] ***Mona Lisa*** [TV] **was painted** by Leonardo da Vinci between 1503 and 1506.

STAYING ON TRACK

Prefer the active voice

To write with power, consider different ways of saying the same thing. The extra effort will bring noticeable results.

Passive A request on your part for special consideration based on your experience working in the profession **will be reviewed** by the admissions committee.

Active If you ask for special consideration because you have worked in the profession, the admissions committee **will review** your request.

The passive is created with a form of *be* and the past participle of the main verb. In a passive-voice sentence, you can either name the actor in a *by* phrase following the verb or omit the actor altogether.

Passive *Mona Lisa* was painted between 1503 and 1506.

31c Find Agents

The *agent* is the person or thing that does the action. The most powerful writing usually highlights the agent in a sentence.

Focus on people

Read the following sentence aloud.

> Mayoral approval of the recommended zoning change for a strip mall on Walnut Street will negatively impact the traffic and noise levels of the Walnut Street residential environment.

It sounds dead, doesn't it? Think about the meaning of the sentence for a minute. It involves people—the mayor and the people who live on Walnut Street. Putting those people in the sentence makes it come alive.

With people

> If the **mayor** approves the recommended zoning change to allow a strip mall on Walnut Street, **people who live on the street** will have to endure much more noise and traffic.

Identify characters

If people are not your subject, then keep the focus on other types of characters.

Without characters

> The ceremony for Remembrance Day had to be postponed because of inclement weather.

With characters

> A severe ice storm forced the city to postpone the Remembrance Day ceremony.

Focus on your agents

Even when you are not writing about people, keep the focus on your agents. Read this short section from a report written by an engineer who was asked to recommend which of two types of valves an oil company should purchase for one of its refineries.

> Although the two systems function similarly, Farval valves have two distinct advantages. First, Farval grease valves include a pin indicator that shows whether the valve is working. Alemite valves must be checked by taking them apart. Second, Farval valves have metal seals, while Alemite valves have rubber grommet seals. If an Alemite valve fails, the pressure will force grease past the rubber grommet seals, creating a grease puddle on the floor. By contrast, Farval's metal seals contain the grease if the valve fails.

This engineer not only provides a definite recommendation supported by reasons but also makes her report easy to read by keeping the focus on the two types of valves she is comparing.

STAYING ON TRACK

Include people

Including people makes your writing more emphatic. Most readers relate better to people than to abstractions. Putting people in your writing also introduces active verbs because people do things.

Without people

> The use of a MIDI keyboard for playing the song will facilitate capturing it in digital form on our laptop for the subsequent purpose of uploading it to our website.

With people

> By playing the song on a MIDI keyboard, we can record the digitized sound on our laptop and then upload it to our website.

31d Vary Your Sentences

Read the following passage.

> On the first day Garth, Jim, and I paddled 22 kilometres down Johnstone Strait. The strait is off the northeast coast of Vancouver Island. The morning was moist and deceptively calm. We stopped to watch a few commercial fishing boats net salmon on the way. Then we set up camp on a rocky beach. We headed down the strait about eight more kilometres to Robson Bight. It is a famous scratching place for orcas. The Bight is a small bay. We paddled out into the strait so we could see the entire Bight. There were no orcas inside. By this time we were getting tired. We were hungry. The clouds assumed a wintry dark thickness. The wind was kicking up against us. Our heads were down going into the cold spray.

The subject matter is interesting, but the writing isn't. The paragraph is a series of short sentences, one after the other, that have a thumpety-thump, thumpety-thump rhythm. When you have too many short sentences one after the other, try combining a few of them. For example, the second and third sentences can be merged into the first sentence (see the paragraphs marked "Revised" on page 405).

The choppiness of the last five sentences destroys the effect of impending danger. These sentences can easily be combined (see the revised paragraphs).

This next passage suffers from a different problem. The sentences are not short, but too many are linked by *and*.

> Ahead of us we heard what sounded like a series of distant shotgun blasts, and when it happened again, we could see the fins of a pod of orcas, and we stopped paddling. The orcas were feeding on the salmon, and they were surfacing at six- to eight-second intervals, and they were coming straight at us. They swam in twos and threes, and there were at least 12 of them. There was a mix of the long fins of the bulls and the shorter, more rounded fins of the cows, and the noise of their exhaling was becoming louder and louder.

The paragraph builds to a climax but, as in the previous passage, the effect is lost. The use of too many *and*s becomes monotonous. The passage becomes more intense when the paddlers first see the orcas swimming toward them. The sentence should reflect this intensity, speeding up the pace as the paddlers' hearts start racing. Several of the *and*s can be eliminated and short sentences joined (see the revision below). The result of combining some (but not all) short sentences and revising other statements joined by *and* is a paragraph with sentences that raise interest and control the pace.

Revised

> On the first day Garth, Jim, and I paddled 22 kilometres down Johnstone Strait **off the northeast coast of Vancouver Island on a moist and deceptively calm morning.** We stopped to watch a few commercial fishing boats net salmon before we set up camp on a rocky beach and headed down the strait about eight more kilometres to Robson Bight, a small bay known as a famous scratching place for orcas. We paddled out into the strait so we could see the entire Bight, but there were no orcas inside. **By this time we were tired and hungry, the clouds had assumed a wintry dark thickness, and the wind was kicking up against us—our heads dropped going into the cold spray.**
>
> Ahead of us we heard what sounded like a series of distant shotgun blasts, and when it happened again, we could see the fins of a pod of orcas. We stopped paddling. **The orcas were feeding on the salmon, surfacing at six- to eight-second intervals, coming straight at us, swimming in twos and threes, at least twelve of them, a mix of the long fins of the bulls and the shorter, more rounded fins of the cows, the noise of their exhaling becoming louder and louder.**

Another kind of sentence monotony sets in when sentences are consistently long and complex. The solution to this problem is to simplify some of them and eliminate excess words (see Chapter 32).

31e Give Your Writing Personality

Nobody likes listening to the voice of a robot. Good writing—no matter what the genre—has two unfailing qualities: a human personality that bursts through the page or the screen and a warmth that suggests the writer genuinely wishes to engage readers.

> From age 11 to age 16 I lived a spartan life without the usual adolescent uncertainty. I wanted to be the best swimmer in the world, and there was nothing else.
>
> —Diana Nyad

> You don't choose your family. They are God's gift to you, as you are to them.
>
> —Desmond Tutu

Sentences like these convince your readers that you are genuinely interested in reaching out to them.

32 Write Concisely

QUICK*TAKE*

- **How do you eliminate unnecessary words?** (see p. 407)
  Wordy: I was 14 years of age when my friends and I happened upon the totally abandoned house in the exact middle of the woods.
  Less wordy: I was 14 when my friends and I happened upon the abandoned house in the middle of the woods.
- **How do you reduce wordy phrases?** (see p. 408)
  Wordy: At that point in time I was of the opinion that I alone amongst all the people in my family of origin recognized the hypocrisy of a bourgeois, middle-class existence.
  Less wordy: At that time, I believed that in my family I alone recognized the hypocrisy of middle-class life.
- **How do you simplify tangled sentences?** (see p. 409)
  Wordy: There were no words exchanged by us as we surveyed the unsettling array of stuff left behind by the house's former occupants.
  Less wordy: Nobody said a word as we surveyed the unsettling array of stuff that the house's former occupants had left behind.

■ Clutter creeps into our lives every day.

Clutter also creeps into our writing in the form of unnecessary words, inflated constructions, and excessive jargon.

> **In regards to** the website, the content is **pretty** successful **in consideration of** the topic. The site is **fairly** good **writing-wise** and is **very** unique in telling you how to adjust the rear derailleur one step at a time.

The words in **red** are clutter. Get rid of the clutter. You can say the same thing with half the words and gain more impact as a result.

> The well-written website on bicycle repair provides step-by-step instructions on adjusting your rear derailleur.

 32a Eliminate Unnecessary Words

Empty words resemble the foods that add calories without nutrition. Put your writing on a diet.

Redundancy

Some words act as modifiers, but when you look closely at them, they repeat the meaning of the word they pretend to modify. Have you heard expressions such as *red in colour*, *small in size*, *round in shape*, *several in number*, *past history*, *attractive in appearance*, *visible to the eye*, or *honest truth*? Imagine *red* not referring to colour or *round* not referring to shape.

Legalese

Legal language often attempts to remove ambiguity through repetition and redundancy. For example, think about what a flight attendant says when your plane arrives.

> Please remain seated, with your seatbelt fastened, until the airplane has come to a full and complete stop; when you deplane from the airplane, be sure to take with you all your personal belongings.

Is there a difference between a *full* stop and a *complete* stop? Can you *deplane* from anything but an airplane? Would you have any *non-personal* belongings?

Some speech situations like the flight attendant's instructions may require redundancy to ensure that listeners understand, but in writing, say it once.

COMMON ERRORS

Empty intensifiers

Intensifiers modify verbs, adjectives, and other adverbs, and they are often overused. One of the most overused intensifiers is *very*.

> The new copper roof was **very bright** on a sunny day.

A new copper roof reflects almost all light. *Very bright* isn't an accurate description. Another adjective would be more accurate:

> The new copper roof was **blinding** on a sunny day.

Very and *totally* are but two of a list of empty intensifiers that can usually be eliminated with no loss of meaning. Other empty intensifiers include *absolutely*, *awfully*, *definitely*, *incredibly*, *particularly*, and *really*.

Remember: When you use *very*, *totally*, or another intensifier before an adjective or adverb, always ask yourself whether you could use a more accurate adjective or adverb to better express the same thought.

32b Reduce Wordy Phrases

We acquire bad writing and speaking habits because we read and hear so much wordy language. Many inexperienced writers use phrases such as "It is my opinion that" or "I think that" to begin sentences. These phrases are deadly to read. If you find them in your prose, cut them. Unless a writer is citing a source, we assume that the ideas are the writer's. (See "When to use *I*" on page 421.)

Coaches are among the worst in using many words for what could be said in a few:

> After much deliberation about Brown's future in hockey with regard to possible permanent injuries, I came to the conclusion that it would be in his best interest not to continue his pursuit of playing hockey again.

The coach might have said simply,

> Because Brown risks permanent injury if he plays hockey again, I decided to release him from the team.

STAYING ON TRACK

Replace wordy phrases

Certain stock phrases plague writing in the workplace, in the media, and in academia. Many wordy phrases can be replaced by one or two words with no loss in meaning.

Wordy **Within the time period of no more than** the past decade, email has replaced handwritten and printed personal letters.

Concise **In** the past decade email has replaced handwritten and printed personal letters.

Wordy	Concise
at this point in time	now
at that point in time	then
due to the fact that	because
for the purpose of	for
have the ability to	can
in spite of the fact that	although
in the event that	if
in the modern world of today	today
in the neighbourhood of	about
it is possible that there might be	possibly
make an attempt	try
met with her approval	she approved
The great writer by the name of Margaret Atwood	Margaret Atwood

32c Simplify Tangled Sentences

Long sentences can be graceful and forceful. Such sentences, however, often require several revisions before they achieve elegance. Too often long sentences reflect wandering thoughts that the writer did not bother to go back and sort out. Two of the most important strategies for untangling long sentences are described in Chapter 31: using active verbs (Section 31a) and naming your agents (Section 31c). Here are some other strategies.

Revise expletives

Expletives are empty words that can occupy the subject position in a sentence. The most frequently used expletives are *there is*, *there are*, and *it is*.

Wordy **There is** another banking option that gives you free chequing.

To simplify the sentence, find the agent and make it the subject.

Revised Another **banking option** gives you free chequing.

Wordy **There were** several important issues raised by the candidates in the debate.

Revised The **candidates** raised several important issues in the debate.

A few kinds of sentences—for example, *It is raining*—do require you to use an expletive. In most cases, however, expletives add unnecessary words, and sentences usually read better without them.

Use positive constructions

Sentences become wordy and hard to read when they include two or more negatives, such as the words *no*, *not*, and *nor* and the prefixes *un-* and *mis-*. For example,

Difficult A **not un**common complaint among employers of new university and college graduates is that they **cannot** communicate effectively in writing.

Revised Employers frequently complain that new university and college graduates cannot write effectively.

Even simpler Employers value the rare university or college graduate who can write well.

Phrasing sentences positively usually makes them more economical. Moreover, it makes your style more forceful and direct.

STAYING ON TRACK

Focus on the main clause

The main clause should express the main idea of the sentence. When you find a tangled, hard-to-read sentence, try revising it by finding the main clause and putting it at the front, letting the details follow.

STAYING ON TRACK *(Continued)*

Tangled

> **When you approach the ice cream parlour area of the building, you see that** the back and side walls of the ice cream parlour area are covered with Bertram High School memorabilia, such as clothing like varsity jackets, cheerleader uniforms, and football jerseys, and other stuff like newspaper clippings and photographs.

Untangled

> **The back and side walls of the ice cream parlour are covered with Bertram High School memorabilia:** varsity jackets, cheerleader uniforms, football jerseys, newspaper clippings, and photographs.

Simplify sentence structure

Long sentences can be hard to read, not because they are long but because they are convoluted and hide the relationships among ideas. Consider the following sentence:

> When the cessation of eight years of hostility in the Iran–Iraq War occurred in 1988, it was not the result of one side defeating the other but the exhaustion of both after losing thousands of people and much of their military capability.

This sentence is hard to read. To rewrite sentences such as this one, find the main ideas, then determine the relationships among them.

After examining the sentence, you decide there are two key ideas:

1. Iran and Iraq stopped fighting in 1988 after eight years.
2. Both sides were exhausted from losing people and equipment.

Next ask what the relationship is between the two ideas. When you identify the key ideas, the relationship is often obvious; in this case (2) is the cause of (1). Thus the word you want to connect the two ideas is *because.*

> Iran and Iraq stopped fighting after eight years of an indecisive war **because** both sides had lost thousands of people and most of their equipment.

The revised sentence is both clearer and more concise, reducing the number of words from 43 to 25.

33 Write with Emphasis

QUICK*TAKE*

- **How do you manage emphasis in your sentences?** (see below)
  Main idea unclear: Pluto was once classified as a planet. Now it is classified as a dwarf planet. It does not meet the IAU's official definition of a planet.
  Main idea made clear: Pluto's classification changed from planet to dwarf planet **because** it does not meet the IAU's official definition of a planet.
- **What is parallelism, and how do you use it correctly?** (see p. 416)
  Not parallel: To be a planet, a celestial body must **be in orbit** around the Sun, **mass must be sufficient** to assume a nearly round shape, and **enough gravitational force to have** no other comparably sized objects in its orbit must be shown.
  Parallel: To be a planet, a celestial body must **orbit around the Sun, have sufficient mass** to assume a nearly round shape, and **exert enough gravitational force** to have no other comparably sized objects in its orbit.

33a Manage Emphasis in Sentences

Put your main ideas in main clauses

Emphasize your most important information by placing it in main clauses, with your less important information in **subordinate clauses** (for a description of main and subordinate clauses, see Section 38c).

In the following paragraph all the sentences are main clauses.

> More Canadians are taking herbal remedies. They think natural herbs must be safe. The remedies can cause bad reactions. They can blunt the effectiveness of prescription drugs. They can also interact with other health products.

This paragraph is grammatically correct, but it does not help the reader understand which pieces of information the author wants to emphasize. Combining the simple sentences into main and subordinate clauses and phrases can improve the paragraph. First, identify the main ideas:

> More Canadians are taking herbal remedies. They think natural herbs are safe.

These ideas can be combined into one sentence:

> More Canadians are taking herbal remedies because they think they are safe.

Now think about the relationship of the three remaining sentences to the main ideas. Those sentences explain the contrasting view; thus, the relationship is *but*.

> More Canadians are taking herbal remedies because they think natural herbs are safe, **but** herbal remedies can cause bad reactions when they blunt prescription drugs or interact with other health products.

Put key ideas at the beginning and end of sentences

Read these sentences aloud.

1 This experiment tests a variety of antimicrobial agents on a range of microorganisms to collect information about **antibiotic resistance**.

2 This experiment collects information on **antibiotic resistance** by testing a variety of antimicrobial agents on a range of microorganisms.

3 **Antibiotic resistance** is a growing problem, so experiments are important in providing insight into the effects of microbial agents on a range of microorganisms.

Most readers put the primary emphasis on the words at the beginning and end of sentences. Sentence 1 emphasizes the link between the experiment and antibiotic resistance. Sentence 2 highlights the method used to gain information on this resistance. Sentence 3 emphasizes what antibiotic resistance is—the (negative) effect of microbial agents on microorganisms. Usually at the front of a sentence is what is known: the topic. At the end is the new information about the topic. Subordinate information is in the middle. If a paragraph is about antibiotic resistance we would not expect the writer to choose sentence 2 over 1 or 3. In sentence 2 antibiotic resistance is buried in the middle.

Photographs and writing gain energy when they emphasize key ideas.

In visuals

Photographers create emphasis by composing the image to direct the attention of the viewer. Putting people and objects in the foreground and making them stand out against the background gives them emphasis.

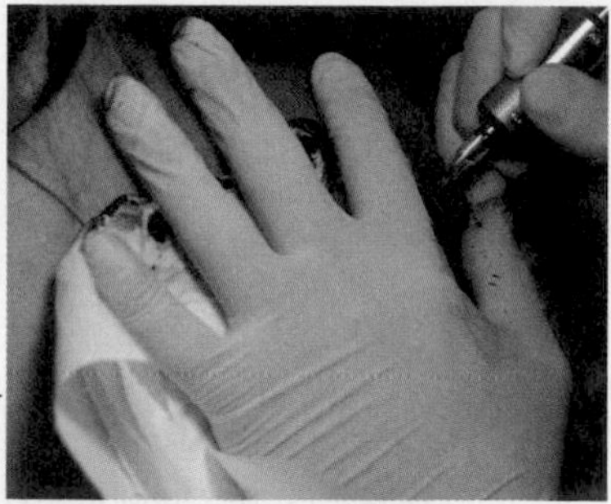

In writing

You have many tools for creating emphasis. Writers can design a page to gain emphasis by using headings, white space, type size, colour, and boldfacing. Just as important, learning the craft of structuring sentences will empower you to give your writing emphasis.

33b Forge Links Across Sentences

When your writing maintains a focus of attention across sentences, the reader can distinguish the important ideas and how they relate to one another. To achieve this coherence, control which ideas occupy the positions of greatest emphasis. The words and ideas you repeat from sentence to sentence act as links.

Link sentences from front to front

In front-to-front linkage, the subject of the sentence remains the focus from one sentence to the next. In the following sequence, sentences 1 through 6 are about three antibiotics: tetracycline, erythromycin, and cycloheximide. The subject of each sentence refers to the first sentence with the pronoun *it*.

1 **Tetracycline**, **erythromycin**, and **cycloheximide** all act by inhibiting protein synthesis within the bacterial cell.

2 **Tetracycline** acts by binding to the 30S subunit of the bacterial ribosome, distorting **it** so that the tRNA does not line up with the codon on the mRNA.

3 **Erythromycin** acts on the 50S subunit of the bacterial ribosome, inhibiting translation and consequently protein synthesis.

4 **It** inhibits growth for most organisms but actually kills some gram-positive species.

5 **Cycloheximide** also inhibits protein synthesis, but **it** acts on the 60S subunit of the eukaryotic ribosome, and because of this, **it** is very toxic to people.

6 These antibiotics that act by inhibiting protein synthesis can affect a much broader range of organisms than the cell-wall–attacking antibiotics.

Each sentence adds more information about the repeated topic, antibiotics.

Link sentences from back to front

In back-to-front linkage, the new information at the end of the sentence is used as the topic of the next sentence. Back-to-front linkage allows new material to be introduced and commented on.

1 One antibiotic that works by inhibiting protein synthesis within the bacterial cell is **erythromycin**.

2 **Erythromycin** acts on the 50S subunit of the bacterial ribosome, inhibiting translation and consequently **protein synthesis**.

3 While it inhibits **protein synthesis** and therefore growth for most organisms, it actually kills some gram-positive species.

Back-to-front linkage is useful when ideas need to be advanced quickly, as when you are telling stories. Rarely, however, will you use either front-to-front linkage or back-to-front linkage for long. You will mix them, using front-to-front linkage to add more information and back-to-front linkage to move the topic along.

STAYING ON TRACK

Check links across sentences

Where in the following paragraph is your attention disrupted?

> In February 1888, Vincent van Gogh left cloudy Paris for Arles in the sunny south of France. Later that year he persuaded fellow painter Paul Gauguin to join him. Gauguin, who had travelled in the tropics, did not find Arles colourful and exotic. Critics hail this period as the most productive in van Gogh's brilliant but short career.

The last sentence connects distantly with what has come before by mentioning art and van Gogh, but it jars you when you read it because new information, "critics," comes where we expect to find known information. Adding a clause provides a bridge between the old and new information.

> In February 1888, Vincent van Gogh left cloudy Paris for Arles in the sunny south of France. Later that year he persuaded fellow painter Paul Gauguin to join him. Gauguin, who had travelled in the tropics, did not find Arles colourful and exotic. **Although van Gogh and Gauguin argued and soon parted company,** critics hail this period as the most productive in van Gogh's brilliant but short career.

33c Use Parallel Structure with Parallel Ideas

What if Nellie McClung had said, "Don't bother taking back your point, apologizing, or explaining, but get the work finished and ignore their howling"? Would we remember those words today? Many of us do remember the words she did write: "Never retract, never apologize, never explain—get the thing done and let them howl." Writers who use parallel structure often create memorable sentences:

> Let us be French, let us be English, but most importantly let us be Canadian.
>
> —John A. Macdonald

> Behind every successful man is a surprised woman.
>
> —Maryon Pearson

> Man can now fly in the air like a bird, swim under the ocean like a fish, he can burrow into the ground like a mole. Now if only he could walk the earth like a man, this would be paradise.
>
> —Tommy Douglas

Using parallel structure can also help your readers understand your ideas more easily.

Use parallelism with *and, or, nor, but*

When you join elements at the same level with coordinating conjunctions, including *and*, *or*, *nor*, *yet*, *so*, *but*, and *for*, use parallel grammatical structure.

Awkward

> In today's global economy, **the method of production and where factories are located** have become relatively unimportant in comparison with **the creation of new concepts and marketing those concepts.**

Parallel

> In today's global economy, **how goods are made and where they are produced** have become relatively unimportant in comparison with **creating new concepts and marketing those concepts.**

COMMON ERRORS

Faulty parallel structure

When writers neglect to use parallel structure, the result can be jarring. Reading your writing aloud will help you catch problems in **parallelism**. Read this sentence aloud.

> At our club meeting we identified problems in **finding** new members, **publicizing** our activities, and **maintenance** of our website.

The end of the sentence does not sound right because the parallel structure is broken. We expect to find another verb + *ing* following *finding* and *publicizing*. Instead, we run into *maintenance*, a noun. The problem is easy to fix: Change the noun to the *-ing* verb form.

> At our club meeting we identified problems in finding new members, publicizing our activities, and **maintaining** our website.

Remember: Use parallel structure for parallel ideas.

Use parallelism with *either/or, not only/but*

Make identical in structure the parts of sentences linked by correlative conjunctions: *either . . . or, neither . . . nor, not only . . . but also, whether . . . or.*

Awkward

> Purchasing the undeveloped land **not only** gives us a new park **but also** is something that our children will benefit from in the future.

Parallel

> Purchasing the undeveloped land **will not only** give our city a new park **but also** leave our children a lasting inheritance.

The more structural elements you match, the stronger the effect the parallelism will achieve.

Correct

> Either we find a way to recruit new members or we settle for the current number of sailboats.

Improved

> Either we find a way to recruit new members or we drop the plan to increase our fleet.

The first sentence is correct but still clunky. The parallelism is limited to *we find/we settle.* The second sentence delivers more punch by extending the parallelism: *we find a way to recruit new members/we drop the plan to increase our fleet.* Matching structural elements exactly—verb for verb, article for article, adjective for adjective, object for object—provides the strongest parallelism.

33d Use Parallel Structure with Lists

Lists are frequently used in visual aids for oral presentations and in announcements, brochures, instructions, and other kinds of writing. The effectiveness of a bulleted list is lost, however, when the items are not in parallel form. In a list of action items, such as a list of goals, beginning each item with a verb emphasizes the action. See the example on the next page.

Sailing Club Goals

- Increase the membership by 50% this year
- Compete in all local regattas
- Offer introductory and advanced classes
- Purchase eight new Flying Juniors
- Organize a spring banquet
- Publicize all major events

33e Use Parallel Structure in Paragraphs

Use parallelism to create rhythm

Parallel structure does not have to be used in rigid, mechanical ways. Repeating elements of structure can build a rhythm that gives your prose a distinctive voice.

> Our links to the past, our bonds with the present, our path to a civilized tomorrow are all maintained by libraries.
>
> —Adrienne Clarkson

Use parallel structure to pair ideas

Parallel structure is also useful for pairing ideas. The closer the similarity in structure, the more emphasis you will achieve.

> Being a grown-up means assuming responsibility for yourself, for your children, and—here's the big curve—for your parents. In other words, you do get to stay up later, but you want to go to sleep sooner.
>
> —Wendy Wasserstein, from *Bachelor Girls*

■ Parallel structure in images also creates emphasis. Notice how the snowboarder and skier have a similar posture and trajectory.

34 Find the Right Words

QUICK*TAKE*

- **How do you choose the right level of formality?** (see below)
  Informal: The reporter was all up in Senator Grimes's face about the scandal.
  Formal, post-secondary writing: The reporter confronted Senator Grimes about the scandal.
- **How do you choose the right words?** (see p. 422)
  Imprecise and incorrect: The senator said he had received bad **council** from someone.
  More precise and correct: Senator Grimes admitted accepting bad **counsel** from his financial adviser.
- **What is figurative language, and how can you use it in your writing?** (see p. 425)
  Literal: Senator Grimes was very nervous under the scrutiny of the press.
  Figurative: Senator Grimes melted under the scrutiny of the press.

34a Be Aware of Levels of Formality

Colloquialisms

Colloquialisms are words or expressions that are used informally, often in conversation but less often in writing.

> I'm not happy with my marks, but that's **the way the cookie crumbles.**
>
> I've **had it up to here** with all of Tom's complaining.
>
> Liz is always **running off at the mouth** about something.

Aside from carrying meanings that aren't always obvious to your reader, colloquialisms usually indicate a lack of seriousness that runs counter to what you'll be trying to accomplish in most academic and professional writing. Colloquialisms can suggest a flippant attitude, carelessness, or even thoughtlessness.

Writing in higher education does not mean, however, that you should try to use big words when small ones will do as well, or that you should use ten words instead of two.

Slang

The most conspicuous kind of language to be avoided in most writing in higher education is slang. The next time a friend talks to you, listen closely to the words he or she uses. Chances are you will notice several words that you probably would not use in a college or university writing assignment. Slang words are created by and for a particular group—even if that group is just you and your friend.

Joey's new **ride** is totally **pimped** out.

The party was **bumpin'** with all my **peeps**.

Aside from being a fun way to play with language, slang asserts a sense of belonging to a group. But because slang excludes those who are not members of the group, it is best avoided in post-secondary writing.

STAYING ON TRACK

When to use *I*

You may have been taught to avoid the first person *(I, we)* in academic and professional writing. Some instructors feel that first-person references reflect a self-indulgence that is inappropriate outside of autobiography. Sentences beginning with *I* refer to the author and make him or her the subject. In a sentence such as *I think Montreal's party scene is better in every way than Vancouver's*, the reader's attention is divided between the party scenes and the person evaluating the party scenes.

Another reason some instructors prohibit use of the first person is the tendency of writers to overuse it. Some writers feel that nothing can be invalidated as long as each potentially arguable assertion starts with *I think* or *I feel*. *I* becomes a shield that the writer uses to escape the work of building an argument.

Occasionally, the use of *I* is redundant. In the following sentence, the nature of the assertion clearly indicates that it's the writer's opinion:

Redundant *I* I think the Canadian Pacific Railway was the greatest engineering achievement of nineteenth-century Canada.

Here you can safely drop *I think* without changing the sentence's meaning. Sometimes, however, you will want to indicate plainly that an assertion is tentative. *I* is critical to the meaning of this sentence:

Tentative *I* I thought that the dim, distant light was a planet.

If you're unsure whether or not first-person references are permissible, ask your instructor.

34b Be Aware of Denotation and Connotation

Words have both literal meanings, called *denotations*, and associated meanings, called *connotations*. The contrast is evident in words that mean roughly the same thing but have different connotations. For example, some people are set in their opinions, a quality that can be described positively as *persistent*, *firm*, and *steadfast* or negatively as *stubborn*, *bull-headed*, and *close-minded*.

In post-secondary and professional writing, writers are expected not to rely on the connotations of words to make important points. For example, the statement *It's only common sense to fund education adequately* carries high positive connotations but is not precise enough for post-secondary writing. Most people believe in common sense, and most people want good education systems. What is common sense for one person, however, is not common sense for another; how *adequate* is defined varies greatly. You have the obligation in post-secondary writing to support any judgment with evidence.

34c Use Specific Language

Be precise

Effective writing conveys information clearly and precisely. Words such as *situation*, *sort*, *thing*, *aspect*, and *kind* often signal undeveloped or even lazy thinking.

Vague The violence aspect determines how video games are rated.

Better The level of violence determines how video games are rated.

When citing numbers or quantities, be as exact as possible. A precise number, if known, is always better than slippery words such as *several* or *many*, which some writers use to cloak the fact that they don't know the quantity in question. If you know an approximate quantity, indicate the quantity but qualify it: *about 25* tells readers much more than *many*.

Use a dictionary

There is no greater tool for writers than the dictionary. When you write, always have a dictionary handy—either a book or an online version—and get into the habit of using it. As well as checking your spelling, you can find additional meanings of a word that perhaps you had not considered, and you can find the etymology—the origins of a word. In many cases knowing the etymology of a word can help you use the word to better effect. For example, if you want to argue that universities as institutions have succeeded because

STAYING ON TRACK

Find the exact word

When you use words like *things,* always ask if there is a more specific word.

Vague Members of the kayaking club also enjoy **things** such as mountain biking, caving, and climbing.

Specific Members of the kayaking club also enjoy **outdoor activities** such as mountain biking, caving, and climbing.

Animals, birds, insects, fish, trees, flowers, clouds, and rocks all have names. If you don't know the names of what you are writing about, look them up.

Vague A big flock of **black birds** came to roost on the **big tree** beside our apartment.

Specific Over 300 **boat-tailed grackles** descended on the four-storey **red oak** beside our apartment to roost for the night.

they bring people together in contexts that prepare them for their lives after post-secondary education, you might point out the etymology of *university. University* can be traced back to the late Latin word *universitas,* which means "society or guild," thus emphasizing the idea of a community of learning.

COMMON ERRORS

Words often confused

Words with different meanings that are pronounced in the same way are called *homonyms.* Be particularly careful that you select the correct one. These pairs can cause confusion.

bare—unadorned
bear—(1) an animal; (2) to carry

capital—(1) government seat; (2) material wealth; (3) uppercase letter
capitol—a building housing a government seat

cite—(1) to make mention of; (2) to quote as an example
sight—something seen
site—place, location

(Continued on next page)

COMMON ERRORS *(Continued)*

coarse—rough
course—plotted-out path or matter

council—a deliberative body
counsel—(1) advice; (2) lawyer; (3) to advise

complement—to go with, as in *That tie complements that suit.*
compliment—to flatter

fair—(1) just; (2) carnival
fare—(1) ticket price; (2) to get along

hear—to listen to
here—location

passed—went by
past—time before the present

patience—the state of calmly waiting
patients—people receiving medical care

peace—serenity
piece—a part of

plain—(1) simple; (2) level land
plane—(1) short for *airplane*; (2) level surface; (3) carpenter's tool

principal—(1) head of an organization; (2) a sum of money
principle—a basic law or guideline

wear—(1) to don clothes; (2) to erode
where—location

weather—climatic condition
whether—if

Other words do not sound exactly alike, only similar. The words in the following pairs are frequently confused:

accept—to receive
except (as preposition)—excluding

advice—a suggestion
advise—to suggest

affect—to act upon or to have an effect on something or somebody
effect—a change caused by an action

allude—to make reference to
elude—to evade

allusion—an indirect reference
illusion—a false impression

COMMON ERRORS *(Continued)*

conscience—moral compass
conscious—aware

continually—(1) consistently; (2) regularly
continuously—without stopping

desert—(1) geographical feature; (2) to abandon
dessert—sweet snack

elicit—to bring out
illicit—unlawful

loose—not tight
lose—(1) to misplace; (2) to fail to win a game

personal—(1) individual; (2) private
personnel—staff

presence—opposite of absence
presents—(1) gifts; (2) introduces

respectfully—demonstrating respect
respectively—in the given order

Remember: Use a dictionary to check that you are using the right word.

34d Use Effective Figurative Language

Figurative language—figures of speech that help readers get a more vivid sense of an object or idea—is what you use when literal descriptions seem insufficient.

Literal The prosecutor presented a much stronger legal case than did the defence attorney.

Figurative The prosecutor took the defence lawyer apart like a dollar watch.

The two most common figures of speech are the simile and the metaphor. A *simile* usually begins with *as* or *like*, and makes an explicit comparison.

In the past, talking about someone's children was **like** talking about the weather.

Metaphor is from a Greek term that means "carry over," which describes what happens when you encounter a metaphor: You carry over the meaning from one word to another. Metaphors make a comparison without using *like* or *as*.

She reached the **pinnacle** of her profession.

[highest point ⟶ best]

Two other forms of figurative language are *synecdoche*, in which the part is used to represent the whole (a hood ornament that represents a car) and *metonymy*, in which something related stands in for the thing itself (*legislature* for the provincial government; *brass* for military officers).

If not used imaginatively, figurative language merely dresses up a literal description in fancy clothes without adding to the reader's understanding of the object or idea. The purpose of figurative language is to convey information vividly to help the reader grasp your meaning.

You'll want to avoid *clichés*, which are relics of figurative language, phrases used so often that they have become tired and stripped of meaning. Among countless others, the following expressions have hardened into clichés.

better late than never
blind as a bat
easier said than done
hard as a rock
ladder of success
nutty as a fruitcake
out like a light
playing with fire
pride and joy
thin as a rail
water under the bridge
wise as an owl

STAYING ON TRACK

Think fresh

You might find yourself resorting to clichés when you're low on inspiration or energy. Read your drafts aloud to yourself to identify clichés, listening for the phrases that you've used or heard before. Make a note of them and either change the clichés to literal description or, better still, create fresh new phrases to convey what you were trying to say with the cliché.

Cliché

When we entered the old café with the screen door banging behind us, we knew **we stood out like a sore thumb.**

Specific

When we entered the old café with the screen door banging behind us, we knew **we stood out like a hybrid Prius in a parking lot full of pickup trucks.**

35 Write to Be Inclusive

QUICK*TAKE*

- **How do you avoid stereotypical assumptions?** (see below)
  Stereotype: Like all Italian men, the author was fiercely loyal to his mother.
  Stereotype avoided: The author was fiercely loyal to his mother.
- **How can you be inclusive about gender?** (see p. 428)
  Not inclusive: Who will be manning the information booth this year?
  More inclusive: Who will be staffing the information booth this year?
- **How can you be inclusive about race, ethnicity, and other differences?** (see p. 430)
  Not inclusive: He was raised in the usual large Irish Catholic family.
  More inclusive: He was raised in a large family.

Although the conventions of inclusiveness change continually, three guidelines for inclusive language toward all groups remain constant.

- Do not point out people's differences unless those differences are relevant to your argument.
- Call people whatever they prefer to be called.
- When given a choice of terms, choose the more accurate one.

35a Be Aware of Stereotypes

Reject stereotypes

A *stereotype* makes an assumption about a group of people by applying a characteristic to all of them based on the knowledge of only a few of them. The idea that Asian women are submissive, for instance, is a stereotype; it tries to apply one personality trait to many individuals whose only shared characteristics are their gender and ethnicity. Such a stereotype is just as ridiculous as a belief that all residents of P.E.I. are potato farmers.

Of course you want to avoid obviously harmful (not to mention inaccurate) stereotypes such as *people on welfare are lazy*, *gay men are effeminate*, or *NASCAR fans are rednecks*. More subtle stereotypes, however, may be harder to identify and eliminate from your writing. If you want to offer an engineer as an example, will you make the engineer a man? If you want your reader to envision a child living in subsidized housing, will you describe the child as an immigrant? Instead of using these examples that perpetuate stereotypes, try to choose cases that go against them.

Watch for assumptions about what's "normal"

Assumptions about what's "normal" or "regular" can create bias. Calling one person or group "normal" implies that others are abnormal.

Problematic norm

Gloria Nuñez isn't like the regular sprinters at the Greater Toronto Meet; while other runners gingerly settle their feet into the blocks, Nuñez plants her prosthetic foot in the block and waits for the starting gun.

Better

Gloria Nuñez is one sprinter at the Greater Toronto Meet who might surprise you; while other runners gingerly settle their feet into the blocks, Nuñez plants her prosthetic foot in the block and waits for the starting gun.

 Be Inclusive About Gender

Gender is a term that refers to the social designations of men, women, and their sexual orientations.

Avoid exclusive nouns and pronouns

Don't use masculine nouns and pronouns to refer to both men and women. *He, his, him, man,* and *mankind* are outmoded and inaccurate terms for both genders.

- Don't say *boy* when you mean *child.*
- Use *men and women* or *people* instead of *man.*
- Use *humanity* or *humankind* in place of *mankind.*

Eliminating *he, his,* and *him* when referring to both men and women is more complicated. Many readers consider *he/she* to be an awkward alternative. Try one of the following approaches instead.

- Make the noun and its corresponding pronoun plural. The pronoun will change from *he, him,* or *his* to *they, them,* or *theirs.*

Biased masculine pronouns

An undercover agent won't reveal **his** identity, even to other agents, if **he** thinks it will jeopardize the case.

Better

Undercover agents won't reveal **their** identities, even to other agents, if **they** think it will jeopardize the case.

- Replace the pronoun with another word.

Biased masculine pronoun

Anyone who wants to rent scuba gear must have **his** certification.

Better

Anyone who wants to rent scuba gear must have **diver** certification.

Use gender-neutral names for professions

Professional titles that indicate gender—*chairman, waitress*—falsely imply that the gender of the person doing the job changes the essence of the job being done. Terms such as *woman doctor* and *male nurse* imply that a woman working as a doctor and a man working as a nurse are abnormal. Instead, write simply *doctor* and *nurse*.

Biased, gender-specific	Better, gender-neutral
chairman	chair, chairperson
clergyman	member of the clergy
congressman	Member of Congress
fireman	firefighter
foreman	supervisor
hostess	host
mailman	mail carrier
manpower	personnel, staff
policeman	police officer
salesman	salesperson
stewardess	flight attendant
waitress	server
weatherman	meteorologist
workmen	workers

Eliminate bias when writing about sexual orientation

Sexual orientation refers to a person's identification as bisexual, heterosexual, homosexual, or transsexual. *Heterosexual* and *homosexual* carry a somewhat clinical connotation. Referring to people who are homosexual as *gays* can lead to confusion: It sometimes connotes men and women, sometimes just men. Instead, use *gay men* and *lesbians*. Again, the principle is to use terms that individuals in specific groups prefer.

 35c Be Inclusive About Race and Ethnicity

Use the terms for racial and ethnic groups that the groups use for themselves. For example, use *native peoples* or *Aboriginals* to refer to members of

Canada's First Nations, and *Inuit* to refer to native peoples of the far north. If you are writing about specific people, use the name of the specific American or Canadian First Nations group (Cree, Hopi, Mi'kmaq, Ute).

If you are still in doubt, err on the side of specificity. For instance, while *Latino(a)*, *Hispanic*, and *Chicano(a)* are all frequently accepted terms for many people, a term that identifies a specific country (*Mexican* or *Puerto Rican*) would be more accurate. *Asian* is currently preferred over *Oriental*; however, terms such as *Vietnamese* and *Japanese* are even more specific. Also, *English* and *British* are different. The people who live in England are English, but people from elsewhere in Great Britain—Scotland, Wales, Northern Ireland—will be quick to tell you that they are not English. Call people from Wales *Welsh* and those from Scotland *Scots*.

 Be Inclusive About Other Differences

Writing about people with disabilities

The *Publication Manual of the American Psychological Association* (sixth ed.) offers some good advice: "use people-first language to describe groups of people with disabilities" (76). Write *people who are deaf* instead of *the deaf* and *a student who is quadriplegic* instead of *a quadriplegic student*. Discuss *a man who has depression*, not *a depressive*, and *a woman who uses a wheelchair*, not *a wheelchair-bound woman*.

Writing about people of different ages

Avoid bias by choosing accurate terms to describe age. If possible, use the person's age rather than an adjective, like *elderly* or *older*, which might offend. *Eighty-two-year-old Adele Schumacher* is better than *elderly Adele Schumacher* or *Adele Schumacher, an older resident*.

Writing about people of different financial statuses

When writing about financial status, be careful not to make assumptions (*People who live in trailer parks are uneducated*) or value judgments (*Dishwashing is a less respectable job than managing a restaurant*). While *upper class* and *middle class* are acceptable terms, *lower class* implies a bias. Instead use *working class*.

Writing about people of different religions

Avoid making assumptions about someone's beliefs or practices based on religious affiliation. Even though the Vatican opposes capital punishment, many Roman Catholics support it. Likewise, not all Jewish men wear yarmulkes. The tremendous variation within religions and among individual practitioners makes generalizations questionable.

35e Recognize International Varieties of English

English today comes in various shapes and forms. Many applied linguists now speak of "World Englishes" in the plural, to highlight the diversity of the English language as it is used worldwide. English has long been established as the dominant language in Australia, New Zealand, the United Kingdom, and the United States. English is one of the official languages in Canada, along with French. The Englishes used in various countries share many characteristics, but there are also differences in sentence structures, vocabulary, spelling, and punctuation. For example,

Canadian English	What **mark** did you get on the midterm?
U.S. English	What **grade** did you get on the midterm?
Canadian English	We have analyzed the problem with **labour** relations.
U.S. English	We have analyzed the problem with **labor** relations.

Newer varieties of English have emerged outside of traditionally English-speaking countries. Many former British and U.S. colonies—Hong Kong, India, Malaysia, Nigeria, Papua New Guinea, the Philippines, Singapore, and others—continue to use a local variety of English for both public and private communication. Englishes used in many of these countries are based primarily on the British variety, but they also include many features that reflect the local context.

Indian English	**Open** the air conditioner.
Canadian English	**Turn on** the air conditioner.
Indian English	They're **late** always.
Canadian English	They're always **late**.
Philippine English	You don't **only know**.
Canadian English	You just don't **realize**.
Philippine English	I **had seen** her yesterday.
Canadian English	I **saw** her yesterday.
Singaporean English	I was **arrowed** to lead the discussion.
Canadian English	I was **selected** to lead the discussion.
Singaporean English	I am not sure **what is it**.
Canadian English	I am not sure **what it is**.

Remember that what is correct differs from one variation of English to another.

PART 8

Understanding Grammar

You **can learn more and do more** with MyWritingLab and with the eText version of *The Brief Penguin Handbook*. Find resources in MyWritingLab to help you use grammar successfully.

8 Understanding Grammar

36 Grammar Basics 433

37 Fragments, Run-ons, and Comma Splices 444

38 Subject-Verb Agreement 452

39 Verbs 458

40 Pronouns 467

41 Modifiers 477

36 Grammar Basics

QUICK*TAKE*

- **What are the parts of a sentence?** (see below)
  Subject: Hippopotamuses (noun)
  Predicate: kill (main verb) more humans (direct object) than any other African mammal (prepositional phrase).
- **What are phrases and clauses, and how can you tell the difference?** (see p. 439)
  Clause: Hippos will open their mouths wide
  Phrase: to warn other creatures to stay away.
- **What are the types of sentences?** (see p. 443)
  Simple: Hippos are vegetarian.
  Compound: Hippos are vegetarian, but they will attack other animals.
  Complex: Hippos attack other animals when they feel threatened.
  Compound-complex: Hippos may look fat and slow when they are on land, but a fully grown hippo can easily outrun a person.

36a Sentence Basics

Sentences are the basic units in writing. Many people think of a sentence as a group of words that begins with a capital letter and ends with a period, but that definition includes grammatically incomplete sentences called **fragments** (see Section 37a).

Subjects and predicates

Regular sentences must have a **subject** and a **predicate** that includes a main verb. Typically the subject announces what the sentence is about, and the predicate says something about that subject or conveys the action of the subject.

Subject	Predicate
I	want a new monitor.
Those who adapt to change	survive.
By 1910, 26 million Americans	were going to the movies at nickelodeon theatres every week.

The exception to this rule is a class of sentences called **imperatives**, in which the subject is usually implied. In these sentences, we know that the subject is *you* without stating it.

Measure the precipitation.

Help me carry in the groceries.

Sentence patterns

Sentences can be classified into four major patterns according to function.

- **Declaratives.** Declarative sentences make statements.

  Professor Paul Manger claims that the bottlenose dolphin is "dumber than a goldfish."

- **Interrogatives.** Interrogatives are usually referred to as questions.

  Is there any truth to this truism?

- **Imperatives.** Imperatives request or demand some action.

  Stop complaining.

- **Exclamations.** Exclamations are used to express strong emotion.

  What an incredible performance you gave!

Sentences can be classified as either *positive* or *negative*. A sentence can be made negative by inserting a negative word, usually *not* or a contracted form of *not* (*can't, isn't*).

Positive The research shows a relationship between brain size and intelligence.

Negative The research does **not** show a relationship between brain size and intelligence.

Sentences with transitive verbs (see Section 39c) can be considered as **active** or **passive** (see Section 31b). Sentences can be made passive by changing the word order.

Active In 1935 a Liberal victory entitled William Lyon Mackenzie King to an unprecedented third term as prime minister.

Passive In 1935 William Lyon Mackenzie King **was entitled** by a Liberal victory to an unprecedented third term as prime minister.

36b Word Classes

Like players in a team sport who are assigned to different positions, words are classified into **parts of speech.** The different positions on a team have different functions. The forwards in soccer and hockey do most of the scoring; goalies are responsible for preventing scoring. The parts of speech also serve different functions in sentences. And just as individuals can play more than one position on a team, so too can individual words belong to more than one part of speech. *Try* is a noun in *The third try was successful,* but a verb in *I would not try it.*

Nouns

A **noun** is the name of a person, place, thing, concept, or action. Names of particular persons, places, organizations, companies, titles, religions, languages, nationalities, ethnicities, months, and days are called **proper nouns** and are almost always capitalized (see Section 50a). More general nouns are called **common nouns** and are seldom capitalized unless they begin a sentence. Most common nouns can be made plural, and most are preceded by articles (*a, an, the*). Nouns have several functions. They can be possessive (indicating ownership: *cat's, Ivan's*), collective (referring to a group: *family, jury*), concrete (referring to people, places, and things: *girl, truck*), and abstract (referring to qualities and states of mind: *humour, belief*).

Multilingual writers can find out more about the rules governing count and non-count nouns in Section 53b.

Pronouns

Pronouns are a subclass of nouns and are generally used as substitutes for nouns. Pronouns themselves are divided into several subclasses.

- **Personal pronouns:** *I, you, he, she, it, we, they, me, him, her, us, them*

  He adapts to changing circumstances so that **he** can survive.

- **Possessive pronouns:** *my, mine, his, hers, its, our, ours, your, yours, their, theirs*

  His family was lost, so he joined **hers**.

- **Demonstrative pronouns:** *this, that, these, those*

  Those are the mittens I want.

- **Indefinite pronouns:** *all, any, anyone, anybody, anything, both, each, either, everyone, everything, many, neither, no one, none, nothing, one, some, someone, somebody, something*

  Everyone was relieved that the driver's injuries were minor.

- **Relative pronouns:** *that, which, what, who, whom, whose, whatever, whoever, whomever, whichever*

  The house, **which** hung off a steep ridge, had a stunning view of the bay.

- **Interrogative pronouns:** *who, which, what, where*

  What feedback mechanisms regulate the earth's temperature?

- **Reflexive pronouns:** *myself, ourselves, yourself, yourselves, himself, herself, itself, themselves*

  Hock Seng reinvents **himself** as Anderson's assistant.

- **Reciprocal pronouns:** *each other, one another*

  The brothers didn't like **each other**.

See Chapter 40 for more on pronouns.

Verbs

Verbs indicate actions, states of mind, occurrences, and states of being. Verbs are divided into two primary categories: *main verbs* and *auxiliaries*. A main verb must be present in the predicate. The main verb may be the only word in the predicate.

She **slept**.

Biological organisms **evolve**.

Auxiliaries (often called *helping verbs*) include forms of *be, have,* and *do*. A subset of auxiliaries are **modals**: *can, could, may, might, must, shall, should, will, would.*

Evolutionary theory **does not** explain the origins of life.

Many scientists argue that DNA similarities among humans **may have been due** to *Homo sapiens'* recent evolution.

See Chapter 38 and Chapter 39 for more on verbs.

Verbals

Verbals are forms of verbs that function as nouns, adjectives, and adverbs. The three kinds of verbals are infinitives, participles, and gerunds.

- **Infinitives:** An infinitive is the base or *to* form of the verb. Infinitives can be used in place of nouns, adjectives, or adverbs.

  NOUN
  To fly has been a centuries-old dream of people around the world.

  ADJECTIVE
  Scientists often use rhetoric **to gain** public support.

- **Participles:** Participles are either present (*flying*) or past (*defeated*). They always function as adjectives.

  The **flying** insects are annoying.

  The **accepted** theory of the origin of life is evolution.

- **Gerunds:** Gerunds have the same form as present participles, but they always function as nouns.

  Flying was all that she wanted to do in life.

Adjectives

Adjectives modify nouns and pronouns. Some adjectives are used frequently: *good, bad, small, tall, handsome, green, short.* Many others are recognizable by their suffixes: *-able* (*dependable*), *-al* (*cultural*), *-ful* (*hopeful*), *-ic* (*frenetic*), *-ive* (*decisive*), *-ish* (*foolish*), *-less* (*hopeless*), *-ous* (*erroneous*).

> The **forgetful** manager was always backed up by her **dependable** assistant.

Adjectives often follow **linking verbs.**

> That drumbeat is **relentless.**

Numbers are considered adjectives.

> Only **10** team members showed up for practice.

See Chapter 41 for more about adjectives and adverbs.

Adverbs

Adverbs modify verbs, other adverbs, adjectives, and entire clauses. The usual suffix for adverbs is *-ly*. Many adverbs do not have suffixes (*then, here*) and others have the same form as adjectives (*fast, hard, long, well*).

> Tramo found **little** relationship between brain size and intelligence. [modifies the verb *found*]

> Tramo found **very** little relationship. [modifies the adverb *little*]

Wickett found a **much** stronger correlation between brain size and IQ. [modifies the adjective *stronger*]

Frankly, I could not care less. [modifies the clause *I could not care less*]

Conjunctive adverbs often modify entire clauses and sentences. Like coordinating conjunctions, they indicate the relationship between two clauses or two sentences. Commonly used conjunctive adverbs include *also, consequently, furthermore, hence, however, indeed, instead, likewise, moreover, nevertheless, otherwise, similarly, therefore, thus.*

Wickett showed a correlation between head size and intelligence; **however**, she found a much stronger correlation between brain size and intelligence.

Prepositions

Prepositions indicate the relationship of nouns or pronouns to other parts of a sentence. Prepositions come before nouns and pronouns, and in this sense prepositions are "prepositioned." The noun(s) or pronoun(s) that follow are called the objects of prepositions.

She took the job **of** [PREP] **speech writer** [OBJ] **for** [PREP] **the prime minister** [OBJ].

Here are some common prepositions.

about	behind	from	than
above	below	in	through
across	beside	inside	to
after	between	of	toward
against	but	off	under
among	by	on	until
around	despite	out	up
as	down	over	upon
at	during	past	with
before	for	since	without

Some prepositions are compounds.

according to	due to	in front of	next to
as well as	except for	in spite of	out of
because of	in addition to	instead of	with regard to

Conjunctions

Conjunctions indicate the relationship between words or groups of words. The two classes of conjunctions are **coordinate,** indicating units of equal status, and **subordinate,** indicating that one unit is more important than the other.

- **Coordinating conjunctions:** The seven coordinating conjunctions are *and, but, or, yet, for, so,* and *nor.*

  The media often recycle this trivial **and** ridiculous image of nurses.

  Real-life nurses regularly make life-saving decisions, **yet** on television they only answer the phone.

- **Subordinating conjunctions:** Subordinating conjunctions introduce subordinate clauses. Common subordinating conjunctions are *after, although, as, because, before, if, since, that, unless, until, when, where, while.*

  If the public holds inaccurate images of nursing, the public will misunderstand a nurse's job.

Articles

There are two classes of **articles:**

- **Definite article:** *the*
- **Indefinite article:** *a, an*

Multilingual writers can find more on articles in Section 53d.

Interjections

Interjections are words such as *oops, ouch, ugh,* and *ah.* They are usually punctuated separately, and they do not relate grammatically to other words.

36c Clauses

Clauses are the grammatical structures that underlie sentences. Each clause has a subject and a predicate, but not all clauses are sentences. The variety of clauses is nearly infinite because phrases and other clauses can be embedded within them in a multitude of ways. Nevertheless, a few basic patterns are central to English clause structure.

Subject-verb-object

On the predicate side of a clause, you always find a main verb and often a direct object that is affected by the action of the verb.

S V DO
Nurses find **their voices.**

This basic pattern, called **subject-verb-object** or *S-V-O*, is one of the most common in English. Verbs that take objects (*kick, revise*) are called **transitive verbs.** Some transitive verbs can take two objects: a **direct object** that completes the sentence and an **indirect object,** usually a person, indirectly affected by the action.

S V IO DO
Nurses give **patients** good care.

Clauses without objects

Not all clauses have objects.

S V
Maria slept.

S V
The engine runs rough. [*Rough* is an adverb, not an object.]

S V
The staff cannot work on weekends. [*On weekends* is a prepositional phrase.]

This clause pattern is **subject-verb** or *S-V*. Verbs that do not require objects are called **intransitive verbs.** Many verbs can be both transitive and intransitive.

Intransitive Mario runs fast.

Transitive Mario runs the company.

For more on the verbs *lay/lie,* and *raise/rise,* see Section 39c.

Linking-verb clauses

A third major pattern links the subject to a noun or an adjective that follows the verb and restates or describes the subject. The most commonly used verbs for this pattern are forms of *be.*

Michaëlle Jean was **governor general** of Canada from 2005 to 2010.

The chemicals essential for life are **in meteor fragments.**

Fossils show that **the earth** is **older** than 10 000 years.

What follows the verb is the subject **complement,** either a noun or noun phrase (*governor general, in meteor fragments*) or a predicate adjective describing the subject (*older*).

Other **linking verbs** besides *be* are *appear, become, feel, look, remain,* and *seem*. These linking verbs often refer to people's perceptions or senses.

Creationists **feel** certain that spontaneous generation is impossible.

Main versus subordinate clauses

All the examples of clauses we have looked at up to now can stand by themselves as sentences. These clauses are called **main** or **independent clauses.** Other clauses have the necessary ingredients to count as clauses—a subject and a main verb—yet they are incomplete as sentences.

Where you choose to live

While those who fail to adapt

As fast as my legs could pedal

These clauses are examples of **subordinate** or **dependent clauses.** They do not stand by themselves but must be attached to another clause:

Those who adapt to change survive, **while those who fail to adapt do not**.

Subordinate clauses as modifiers

- **Adjective clauses:** Adjective clauses modify nouns and pronouns. They are also called *relative clauses* and usually begin with a relative pronoun.

  The existence **of the caves that make up this karst system** is evident in Maligne Canyon at several points.

  The site **where the river partially disappears** indicates that an underground cave system exists.

- **Adverb clauses:** Adverb clauses function as adverbs, modifying verbs, other adverbs, adjectives, and entire clauses. They begin with a subordinating conjunction such as *after, although, as, because, before, if, since, that, unless, until, when, where, while.*

Modifies verb	Researchers **found** the location and path of the water flowing through a karst system **after they studied caves located below ground**.
Modifies phrase	One of the first experiments for large-scale water tracing **was done in 1878** **when sodium fluorescein and potassium chloride were used as tracers**.

Modifies adjective	A karst system can be **extensive** due to the dissolving power of surface or underground waters.
Modifies clause	While much water flows into Medicine Lake from the rivers, **very little flows out.**

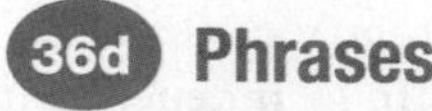

36d Phrases

Phrases are groups of words that modify or develop parts of a sentence. Some phrases can be confused with clauses, but phrases lack either a subject or a main verb.

Prepositional phrases

Prepositional phrases consist of a preposition and its object, including modifiers of the object. They can modify nouns, verbs, or adjectives.

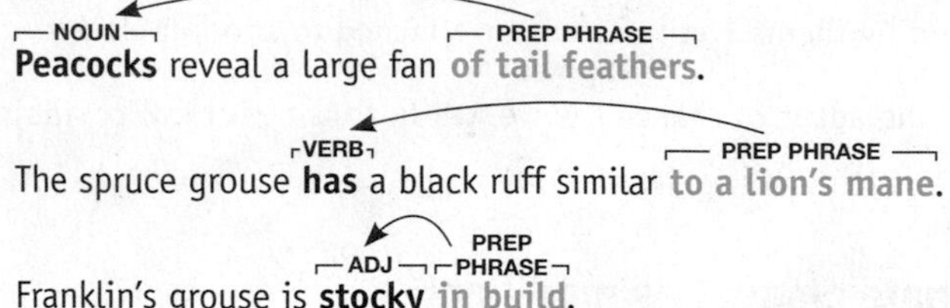

NOUN
PREP PHRASE
Peacocks reveal a large fan of tail feathers.
VERB
PREP PHRASE
The spruce grouse has a black ruff similar to a lion's mane.
ADJ
PREP PHRASE
Franklin's grouse is stocky in build.

Verbal phrases

Each of the three kinds of verbals—infinitives, participles, and gerunds—can be used to create phrases.

- **Infinitive phrases:** Infinitive phrases can function as nouns, adverbs, and adjectives. As nouns they can be subjects, objects, or complements.

  SUBJECT

  To find a spruce grouse is a stroke of good luck.

- **Participial phrases:** Participial phrases are formed with either present participles (*flying*) or past participles (*defeated*); they function as adjectives.

  The spruce grouse populating the coniferous forests of the Rockies eat only conifer needles in the winter.

- **Gerund phrases:** Gerund phrases formed from the present participle (*-ing*) function as nouns.

  SUBJECT

  Fanning tail feathers is a popular move in the spruce grouse mating dance.

Appositives

Appositive phrases modify nouns and are often set off by a pair of commas. They usually follow the noun they modify. They are quite useful as identifying tags for nouns.

> The spruce grouse ruff, **adapted to impress females**, does not serve as camouflage to conceal it from predators.

Absolutes

Absolute phrases are nearly clauses because they include a noun or pronoun and a verb; however, the verb is a participle ending in *-ing* or *-ed* and not a main verb. Absolute phrases can appear anywhere in a sentence and are set off by commas.

> Pine trees have numerous and shallow roots, **outcompeting other plants for water and nutrients**.

36e Sentence Types

Simple sentences

A simple sentence consists of one main clause and no subordinate clauses. Simple sentences can be quite short.

> SUBJ VERB
> Pine **cones contain** seeds.

Simple sentences can become quite long if phrases are added.

> MAIN CLAUSE
> **Pine cones contain seeds**, requiring heat from forest fires and chemicals from smoke to germinate.

Compound sentences

Compound sentences have two or more main clauses and no subordinate clauses. The main clauses are connected in one of three ways: (1) by a semicolon, (2) by a comma and a coordinating conjunction (*and, but, or, for, so, nor, yet*), or (3) by punctuation and a conjunctive adverb (*furthermore, however, indeed, nevertheless, therefore*).

> MAIN CLAUSE | MAIN CLAUSE
> Ann Talbot was a prominent nurse character, **but** she served no purpose beyond being Dr. Hudson's personal assistant.

> MAIN CLAUSE
> The *Windup Girl* seems a classic extrapolative work of dystopic science fiction; **however**, on closer inspection, this subversive novel contains strong messages about embracing change.
> MAIN CLAUSE

Complex sentences

Complex sentences have one main clause and one or more subordinate clauses.

> MAIN CLAUSE
> Abandoning genetic engineering won't prevent all disease and famine,
> SUBORDINATE CLAUSE
> **since** genetic engineering doesn't cause all disease and famine.

Compound-complex sentences

Compound-complex sentences have at least two main clauses and at least one subordinate clause.

> MAIN CLAUSE — SUBORDINATE CLAUSE
> Montana's National Park had 150 glaciers **when** the park was established in 1910, **but** today only 27 glaciers remain.
> MAIN CLAUSE

37 Fragments, Run-ons, and Comma Splices

QUICK*TAKE*

- **How do you find and fix fragments?** (see below)
  Error: Early travelling salesmen once literally drummed up business. **Beating drums and ringing bells.**
  Correct: Early travelling salesmen once literally drummed up business by beating drums and ringing bells.
- **What are run-on or "fused" sentences?** (see p. 448)
  Error: The first deadbeats were "debt beaters" they left their debts behind.
  Correct: The first deadbeats were "debt beaters." They left their debts behind.
- **What are comma splices, and how do you avoid them?** (see p. 450)
  Error: Dressed to the nines doesn't refer to the 1–10 scale, it's slang for "dressed to thine eyes."
  Correct: Dressed to the nines doesn't refer to the 1–10 scale. It's slang for "dressed to thine eyes."

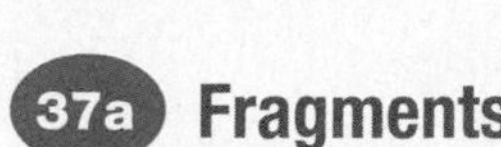

37a Fragments

Fragments in speech and writing

Fragments are incomplete sentences. They are punctuated to look like sentences, but they lack a key element—often a subject or a verb—or else they are a subordinate clause or phrase. In spoken language we usually pay little attention to fragments.

Missing subject; missing verb	**Although debate that this is the earth's climate cycle due to orbital shifts.**
Missing subject	Some scientists claim that the retreat of glaciers is a cycle linked to the earth's warming. **And not caused by humanity.**
Missing verb	**You too?**
Subordinate clause	**If you think so.**

In writing, however, fragments usually interrupt the reader. Consider another example of a full sentence followed by a fragment:

> The university's enrolment rose unexpectedly during the fall semester. **Because the percentage of students who accepted offers of admission was much higher than previous years and fewer students than usual dropped out or transferred.**

Such fragments compel a reader to stop and reread. When a sentence starts with *because*, we expect to find a main clause later. But here, the *because* clause refers back to the previous sentence. The writer no doubt knew that the fragment gave reasons why enrolment rose, but a reader must stop to determine the connection.

In formal writing you should avoid fragments. Readers expect words punctuated as a sentence to be a complete sentence. They expect writers to complete their thoughts rather than force readers to guess the missing element.

COMMON ERRORS

Recognizing fragments

If you can spot fragments, you can fix them. Grammar checkers can find some of them, but they miss many fragments and identify other sentences wrongly as fragments. Ask these questions when you are checking for sentence fragments:

(Continued on next page)

COMMON ERRORS *(Continued)*

- **Does the sentence have a subject?** Except for commands, sentences need subjects:

  These changes in the environment are not new. **But have been occurring since the last Ice Age.**

- **Does the sentence have a complete verb?** Sentences require complete verbs. Verbs that end in *-ing* must have an auxiliary verb to be complete.

  Raoul keeps changing majors. **He trying to figure out what he really wants to do after college.**

- **If the sentence begins with a subordinate clause, is there a main clause in the same sentence?** A good test to determine if a subordinate clause is a fragment is to say "I think that" before a possible fragment.

  Even though Vancouver is cloudy much of the year, no Canadian city is more beautiful when the sun shines. **Which is one reason people continue to move there.**

Remember: 1. A sentence must have a subject and a complete verb.
2. A subordinate clause cannot stand alone as a sentence.

Watch for these fragments

1. Pay close attention to sentences that begin with transitional words, coordinating conjunctions, and subordinating conjunctions.

Among the most common fragments are those that begin with a transitional word (*also, therefore, however, consequently*), a coordinating conjunction (*and, but, or*), or a word indicating a subordinate clause (*although, because, if, since*). Prepositional or verbal phrase fragments are also common.

Transitional words and phrases such as *also, however*, and *therefore* mark movement from one idea to another, such as introducing another example, a change in direction, or a conclusion. Writers often produce fragments when trying to separate these shifts with a period.

> Naomi found ways to avoid working during her shift~~. T~~, *t*herefore making more work for the rest of the employees.

Compound predicates are linked by a coordinating conjunction such as *and, but,* or *or*. Because compound predicates share the same subject, the solution for a coordinating conjunction fragment is to incorporate it into the sentence with the subject.

> Heroin use among urban professionals is on the rise in the United States~~. A~~ and also in Europe, after several decades during which cocaine was the preferred drug among this group.

2. Look for subordinate clause fragments. Subordinate clauses resemble sentences because they contain subjects and verbs. But subordinate clauses cannot stand alone as sentences because their meaning is dependent on another clause. Subordinate clauses begin with words such as *although, after, before, despite, if, though, unless, whether, while, when, who,* and *that.* Subordinate clause fragments often follow the sentence to which they actually belong. You can fix the subordinate clause fragment by incorporating it into the preceding sentence.

> The movie *Gladiator* is fiction, but it is based on extensive research with much of the plot inspired by actual people and historical events~~. W~~, which explains why it seems more realistic than earlier movies about Rome such as *Spartacus*.

Or you can fix the subordinate clause fragment by turning it into a sentence.

> The movie *Gladiator* is fiction, but it is based on extensive research with much of the plot inspired by actual people and historical events. This attention to historical detail, if not historical accuracy, explains why *Gladiator* seems more realistic than earlier movies about Rome such as *Spartacus*.

3. Look for phrase fragments. Phrases also cannot stand alone as sentences because they lack either a subject, a verb, or both. There are many kinds of phrase fragments. Prepositional phrase fragments are easy to spot and fix.

> As Sohela looked over the notes for her autobiography, she mused about how much her life had changed~~. I~~, in ways she could not have predicted.

> Andrew accepted the university's award for outstanding dissertation~~. W~~, with great dignity and humility.

Appositive phrases, which rename or describe a noun, are often fragments.

> For his advanced history course, Professor Hibbard assigned J. J. Scarisbrick's *Henry VIII*~~. A~~, an older text that historians still regard as essential when studying sixteenth-century English history and politics.

Verbal phrase fragments are sometimes difficult to spot because verbals look like verbs. But remember: They function as adjectives, nouns, or adverbs.

> On their last trip to Halifax, Greta went to the Maritime Museum, but Roger didn't go. ~~Roger~~, having visited that museum twice already.

4. Watch for list fragments. Do not isolate a list from the sentence that introduces it. Words or phrases such as *for example, for instance, namely,* and *such as* often introduce lists or examples. Make sure these lists are attached to a sentence with a subject and verb.

> Several Ben and Jerry's ice cream flavours are puns. ~~S~~, such as Cherry Garcia, Phish Food, and The Full VerMonty.

37b Run-on Sentences

Run-on sentences are the opposite of sentence fragments. While fragments are incomplete sentences, run-ons jam together two or more sentences, failing to separate them with appropriate punctuation. And while fragments are sometimes acceptable, especially in informal writing, run-on sentences are never acceptable.

Fixing run-on sentences

Take three steps to fix run-on sentences: (1) identify the problem, (2) determine where the run-on sentence needs to be divided, and (3) choose the punctuation that best indicates the relationship between the main clauses.

1. Identify the problem. When you read your writing aloud, run-on sentences will often trip you up, just as they confuse readers. You can also search for subject and verb pairs to check for run-ons. If you find two main clauses with no punctuation separating them, you have a run-on sentence.

> **Internet businesses** [SUBJ] **are** not **bound** [VERB] to specific locations or old ways of running a business **they** [S] **are** [V] more flexible in allowing employees to telecommute and to determine the hours they work.

2. Determine where the run-on sentence needs to be divided.

> Internet businesses are not bound to specific locations or old ways of running a business | they are more flexible in allowing employees to telecommute and to determine the hours they work.

COMMON ERRORS

Recognizing run-on sentences

When you read the following sentence, you realize something is wrong.

> **Animations of polar bears frantically searching for an iceberg strong enough to bear their weight instill a sense of urgency that forces us to act quickly we must rush into action before polar bears go extinct.**

The problem is that the two main clauses are not separated by punctuation. The reader must look carefully to determine where one main clause stops and the next one begins.

> Animations of polar bears frantically searching for an iceberg strong enough to bear their weight instill a sense of urgency that forces us to act quickly | we must rush into action before polar bears go extinct.

A period should be placed after *quickly,* and the next sentence should begin with a capital letter:

> Animations of polar bears frantically searching for an iceberg strong enough to bear their weight instill a sense of urgency that forces us to act quickly. We must rush into action before polar bears go extinct.

Run-on sentences are major errors.

Remember: Two main clauses must be separated by correct punctuation.

3. Determine the relationship between the main clauses. You will revise a run-on more effectively if you determine the relationship between the main clauses and understand the effect or point you are trying to make. There are several punctuation strategies for fixing run-ons.

- **Insert a period.** This is the simplest way to fix a run-on sentence.

  Internet businesses are not bound to specific locations or old ways of running a business. They are more flexible in allowing employees to telecommute and to determine the hours they work.

However, if you want to indicate the relationship between the two main clauses more clearly, you may want to choose one of these strategies:

- **Insert a semicolon (and possibly a transitional word indicating the relationship between the two main clauses).**

  Internet businesses are not bound to specific locations or old ways of running a business; therefore, they are more flexible in allowing employees to telecommute and to determine the hours they work.

- **Insert a comma and a coordinating conjunction (*and, but, or, nor, for, so, yet*).**

  Internet businesses are not bound to specific locations or old ways of running a business, so they are more flexible in allowing employees to telecommute and to determine the hours they work.

- **Make one of the clauses subordinate.**

  Because internet businesses are not bound to specific locations or old ways of running a business, they are more flexible in allowing employees to telecommute and to determine the hours they work.

 37c Comma Splices

Comma splices are a kind of run-on sentence. They do include a punctuation mark—a comma—but it is not a strong enough punctuation mark to separate two main clauses. Comma splices often do not cause the same problems for readers as run-ons. The following sentence can be read aloud with no problem.

> Most of us were taking the same classes, if someone had a question, we would all help out.

On the page such sentences may cause confusion because commas are used to distinguish between elements within sentences, not to mark the boundary between sentences. Most readers see comma splices as errors, which is why you should avoid them.

Fixing comma splices

You have several options for fixing comma splices. Select the one that best fits where the sentence is located and the effect you are trying to achieve.

1. Change the comma to a period. Most comma splices can be fixed by changing the comma to a period.

> Forest fires are going to occur in extreme amounts if the temperature rises by only one degree ~~Celsius, everyone~~ Celsius. Everyone better do their best to stop global temperatures from rising.

2. Change the comma to a semicolon. A semicolon indicates a close connection between the two main clauses.

> Forest fires are going to occur in extreme amounts if the temperature rises by only one degree ~~Celsius,~~ *Celsius;* everyone better do their best to stop global temperatures from rising.

COMMON ERRORS

Recognizing comma splices

When you edit your writing, look carefully at sentences that contain commas. Does the sentence contain two main clauses? If so, are the main clauses joined by a comma and a coordinating conjunction (*and, but, for, or, not, so, yet*)?

Incorrect The **concept** of "nature" **depends** on the concept of human "culture," the **problem is** that "culture" is itself shaped by "nature."
[Two main clauses joined by only a comma]

Correct Even though the concept of "nature" depends on the concept of human "culture," "culture" is itself shaped by "nature."
[Subordinate clause plus a main clause]

Correct The concept of "nature" depends on the concept of human "culture," but "culture" is itself shaped by "nature."
[Two main clauses joined by a comma and a coordinating conjunction]

Treating the word *however* as a coordinating conjunction produces some of the most common comma splice errors. *However* does not function grammatically in the same way as the coordinating conjunctions *and, but, or, nor, yet, so*, and *for* (see Section 36b).

Incorrect Commercials that depict women as sex objects to sell products are obviously demeaning to women, however the always-present man, off-screen, who represents the viewers' gaze is equally demeaning to men.

Correct Commercials that depict women as sex objects to sell products are obviously demeaning to women; however, the always-present man, off-screen, who represents the viewers' gaze is equally demeaning to men.
[Two main clauses joined by a semicolon]

Remember: Do not use a comma as a period.

3. Insert a coordinating conjunction. Other comma splices can be repaired by inserting a coordinating conjunction (*and, but, or, nor, so, yet, for*) to indicate the relationship of the two main clauses. The coordinating conjunction must be preceded by a comma.

> Digital technologies have intensified a global culture that affects us daily in large and small ways, **yet** their impact remains poorly understood.

4. Make one of the main clauses a subordinate clause. If a comma splice includes one main clause that is subordinate to the other, rewrite the sentence using a subordinating conjunction.

> *Because community*
> ~~Community~~ is the vision of a great society trimmed down to the size of a small town, it is a powerful metaphor for real-estate developers who sell a mini-utopia along with a house or a condo.

5. Make one of the main clauses a phrase. You can also rewrite one of the main clauses as a phrase.

> Community—**the vision of a great society trimmed down to the size of a small town**—is a powerful metaphor for real-estate developers who sell a mini-utopia along with a house or a condo.

38 Subject-Verb Agreement

QUICK*TAKE*

- **How do you know if a subject is singular or plural?** (see below)
  Singular: **Neither curling nor diving** is considered an extreme sport.
  Plural: Ernest Hemingway is believed to have said that **bullfighting, motor racing, and mountaineering** are the only real sports.
- **How do you choose the right verb for indefinite pronouns and collective nouns?** (see p. 455)
  Indefinite pronouns: **Some** say that this statement implies that a sport must involve peril. (plural)
  Collective nouns: This **generation** seems to like sports that involve peril. (singular)
- **What do you do with subjects that describe amounts, numbers, and pairs?** (see p. 457)
  Treat as singular: **Two decades** was all the time extreme sports needed to become mainstream.
  Treat as plural: **Baggy pants** are the choice of many extreme athletes.

38a Agreement in the Present Tense

When your verb is in the present tense, agreement in number is straightforward: The subject takes the base form of the verb in all but the third person singular. For example, the verb *walk* in the present tense agrees in number with most subjects in its base form:

First person singular	I walk
Second person singular	You walk
First person plural	We walk
Second person plural	You walk
Third person plural	They walk

Third person singular subjects are the exception to this rule. When your subject is in the third person singular (*he, it, Fido, Lucy, Mr. Jones*) you need to add an *s* or *es* to the base form of the verb.

Third person singular (add *s*)	He walks. It walks. Fido walks.
Third person singular (add *es*)	Lucy goes. Mr. Jones goes.

38b Singular and Plural Subjects

Sometimes it will be difficult to determine whether your subject is singular or plural, especially when subjects joined by *and* refer to the same thing or idea (*toast and jam, peace and quiet*) or when subjects are linked by *either . . . or* or *neither . . . nor*. Follow these rules when you have trouble determining whether to use a singular or a plural verb form.

Subjects joined by *and*

When two subjects are joined by *and*, treat them as a compound (plural) subject.

> **Etta and Maija** are leaving for Winnipeg in the morning.

Some compound subjects are treated as singular. These kinds of compounds generally work together as a single noun. Although they appear to be compound and therefore plural, these subjects take the singular form of the verb:

> **Rock and roll** thrives in the twenty-first century.

Also, when two nouns linked by *and* are modified by *every* or *each*, these two nouns are likewise treated as one singular subject:

Every hill and valley is aglow with light.

An exception to this rule arises when the word *each* follows a compound subject. In these cases, usage varies depending on the number of the direct object.

The provincial and the federal court systems each have their own judges and prosecutors.

The owl and the pussycat each has a personal claim to fame.

Subjects joined by *or*, *either . . . or*, or *neither . . . nor*

When a subject is joined by *or, either . . . or,* or *neither . . . nor*, make sure the verb agrees with the subject closest to the verb.

SING / PLURAL / PL
Is it **the sky or the mountains** that are blue?

PLURAL / SING / SING
Is it **the mountains or the sky** that surrounds us?

PLURAL / SING / SING
Neither the visitors nor the zookeeper knows how to relock the gate.

SING / PLURAL / PL
Either a pack of coyotes or several dogs were howling last night.

Subjects along with another noun

Verbs agree with the subject of a sentence, even when a subject is linked to another noun with a phrase such as *as well as, along with*, or *alongside.* These modifying phrases are usually set off from the main subject with commas.

IGNORE THIS PHRASE
Chicken, alongside various steamed vegetables, is my favourite meal.

IGNORE THIS PHRASE
Besides David Bowie, **the Beatles** are my favourite band of all time.

Multilingual writers can find more on singular and plural subjects in Section 53c.

COMMON ERRORS

Subjects separated from verbs

The most common agreement errors occur when words come between the subject and the verb. These intervening words do not affect subject-verb agreement. To ensure that you use the correct verb form, identify the subject and the verb. Ignore any phrases that come between them.

IGNORE THIS PHRASE

Incorrect **Students** who live in residence **doesn't** have to cook or clean.

Correct **Students** who live in residence **don't** have to cook or clean.

Students is plural and *do* is plural; subject and verb agree.

Incorrect **The whale shark,** the largest of all sharks, **feed** on plankton.

Correct **The whale shark**, the largest of all sharks, **feeds** on plankton.

The plural noun *sharks* that appears between the subject *the whale shark* and the verb *feeds* does not change the number of the subject. The subject is singular and the verb is singular. Subject and verb agree.

Remember: When you check for subject-verb agreement, identify the subject and the verb. Ignore any words that come between them.

38c Indefinite Pronouns as Subjects

The choice of a singular or a plural pronoun is determined by the **antecedent**—the noun that a pronoun refers to. For instance, the sentence *My friend likes soup* might be followed by another sentence, *She makes a new kind daily*. The pronoun must be singular because *she* refers to the singular noun *friend*.

Indefinite pronouns, such as *some, few, all, someone, everyone,* and *each,* often do not refer to identifiable subjects; hence they have no antecedents. Most indefinite pronouns are singular and agree with the singular forms of verbs. Some, such as *both* and *many*, are always plural and agree with the plural forms of verbs. Other indefinite pronouns are variable and can agree with either singular or plural verb forms, depending on the context of the sentence.

COMMON ERRORS

Agreement errors using *each*

The indefinite pronoun *each* is a frequent source of subject-verb agreement errors. If a pronoun is singular, its verb must be singular. This rule holds true even when the subject is modified by a phrase that includes a plural noun.

A common stumbling block to this rule is the pronoun *each*. *Each* is always treated as a singular pronoun in post-secondary writing. When *each* stands alone, the choice is easy to make:

Incorrect **Each are** an outstanding student.
Correct **Each is** an outstanding student.

But when *each* is modified by a phrase that includes a plural noun, the choice of a singular verb form becomes less obvious:

Incorrect **Each** of the girls **are** fit.
Correct **Each** of the girls **is** fit.

Incorrect **Each** of our dogs **get** a present.
Correct **Each** of our dogs **gets** a present.

Remember: *Each* is always singular.

38d Collective Nouns as Subjects

Collective nouns refer to groups (*administration, audience, class, committee, crew, crowd, faculty, family, fleet, gang, government, group, herd, jury, mob, public, team*). When members of a group are considered as a unit, use singular verbs and singular pronouns.

The **audience was** patient with the novice performer.

The **fleet leaves** port on June 29, and **it** will not return until next year.

When members of a group are considered as individuals, use plural verbs and plural pronouns.

The **faculty have their** differing opinions on how to address the problems caused by reduced provincial support.

Base form

The base form of a verb is the one you find listed in the dictionary. This form indicates an action or condition in the present.

> I **like** Montreal in June.
>
> We **talk** often on weekends.

Third person singular

The base form of the verb changes when used with third person singular subjects. Third person singular subjects include *he, she, it,* and the nouns they replace, as well as other pronouns, including *someone, anybody,* and *everything.* (See Section 38c.) Present tense verbs in the third person singular end with an *s* or an *es.*

> Ms. Nessan **speaks** in riddles.
>
> He **watches** too much television.

Past tense

The past tense describes an action or condition that occurred in the past. For most verbs, the past tense is formed by adding *d* or *ed* to the base form of the verb.

> I **called** at nine, but no one **answered**.
>
> She **inhaled** the night air.

Many verbs, however, have irregular past tense forms. (See Section 39b.)

COMMON ERRORS

Missing verb endings

Verb endings are not always pronounced in speech, especially in some dialects of English. It's also easy to omit these endings when you are writing quickly. Spell-checkers will not mark these errors, so you have to find them while proofreading.

Incorrect Jeremy **feel** as if he's catching a cold.
Correct Jeremy **feels** as if he's catching a cold.

Incorrect Sheila **hope** she would get the day off.
Correct Sheila **hoped** she would get the day off.

Remember: Check verbs carefully for missing *s* or *es* endings in the present tense and missing *d* or *ed* endings in the past tense.

Past participle

The past participle is used with *have* to form verbs in the perfect tense, and with *be* to form verbs in the passive voice (see Section 31b) and to form adjectives derived from verbs.

Past perfect	They **had** gone to the grocery store prematurely.
Passive	The book **was** written 30 years before it **was** published.
Adjective	In the 1960s, **teased** hair was all the rage.

Present participle

The present participle functions in one of three ways. Used with an auxiliary verb, it can describe a continuing action. The present participle can also function as a noun, known as a **gerund,** or as an adjective. The present participle is formed by adding *ing* to the base form of a verb.

Present participle	Wild elks **are** competing for limited food resources.
Gerund	Sailing around the Cape of Good Hope is rumoured to bring good luck.
Adjective	We looked for shells in the ebbing tide.

39b Irregular Verbs

A verb is *regular* when its past and past participle forms are created by adding *ed* or *d* to the base form. If this rule does not apply, the verb is considered an **irregular verb.** Here are common irregular verbs and their basic conjugations.

Common irregular verbs

Base form	Past tense	Past participle
arise	arose	arisen
be (is, am, are)	was, were	been
bear	bore	borne or born
beat	beat	beaten
become	became	become
begin	began	begun
bend	bent	bent
break	broke	broken

Common irregular verbs *(Continued)*

bring	brought	brought
buy	bought	bought
choose	chose	chosen
cling	clung	clung
come	came	come
cost	cost	cost
creep	crept	crept
deal	dealt	dealt
dig	dug	dug
dive	dived or dove	dived
do	did	done
draw	drew	drawn
drink	drank	drunk
drive	drove	driven
eat	ate	eaten
fall	fell	fallen
feed	fed	fed
feel	felt	felt
fight	fought	fought
fling	flung	flung
fly	flew	flown
forbid	forbade	forbidden
forget	forgot	forgotten or forgot
forgive	forgave	forgiven
freeze	froze	frozen
get	got	got or gotten
give	gave	given
go	went	gone
grow	grew	grown
hang	hung	hung
have	had	had
know	knew	known
lay	laid	laid
lend	lent	lent
lie	lay	lain
make	made	made
read	read	read
run	ran	run
say	said	said

(Continued on next page)

Common irregular verbs *(Continued)*

see	saw	seen
send	sent	sent
shine	shone	shone
show	showed	shown or showed
sit	sat	sat
sleep	slept	slept
speak	spoke	spoken
spring	sprang or sprung	sprung
swim	swam	swum
take	took	taken
teach	taught	taught
tell	told	told
think	thought	thought
understand	understood	understood
wear	wore	worn
write	wrote	written

COMMON ERRORS

Past tense forms of irregular verbs

The past tense and past participle forms of irregular verbs are often confused. The most frequent error is using a past tense form instead of the past participle with *had.*

Incorrect She had never **rode** (PAST TENSE) a horse before.

Correct She had never **ridden** (PAST PARTICIPLE) a horse before.

Incorrect He had **saw** (PAST TENSE) many white pelicans in Saskatoon.

Correct He had **seen** (PAST PARTICIPLE) many white pelicans in Saskatoon.

Remember: Change any past tense verbs preceded by *had* to past participles.

39c Transitive and Intransitive Verbs

Lay/lie and *raise/rise*

Do you know whether you raise or rise from bed in the morning? Do your house keys lay or lie on the kitchen table? *Raise/rise* and *lay/lie* are transitive and intransitive verbs that writers frequently confuse. Transitive verbs take direct objects, nouns that receive the action of the verb. Intransitive verbs act in sentences that lack direct objects.

The following charts list the trickiest pairs of transitive and intransitive verbs and the correct forms for each verb tense. Pay special attention to *lay* and *lie*, which are irregular.

	lay (put something down)	**lie (recline)**
Present	lay, lays	lie, lies
Present participle	laying	lying
Past	laid	lay
Past participle	laid	lain

Transitive Once you complete your test, please **lay** your pencil (direct object, the thing being laid down) on the desk.

Intransitive The *Titanic* **lies** upright in two pieces at a depth of 4000 metres.

	raise (elevate something)	**rise (get up)**
Present	raise, raises	rise, rises
Present participle	raising	rising
Past	raised	rose
Past participle	raised	risen

Transitive We **raise** our glasses (direct object, the things being raised) to toast Uncle Han.

Intransitive The sun **rises** over the bay.

39d Shifts in Tense

Appropriate shifts in verb tense

Changes in verb tense are sometimes necessary to indicate a shift in time.

Present to past I never **shop** (PRESENT TENSE) online anymore because I **heard** (PAST TENSE) that hackers **have stolen** (PRESENT PERFECT TENSE) thousands of credit card numbers used in internet transactions.

Past to future Because Oda **won** (PAST TENSE) the lottery, she **will quit** (FUTURE TENSE) her job at the hospital as soon as her supervisor **finds** (PRESENT TENSE) a qualified replacement.

Inappropriate shifts in verb tense

Be careful to avoid confusing your reader with unnecessary shifts in verb tense. Once you reach the proofreading stage of your writing, dedicate one careful reading of your text to finding inappropriate tense changes.

Incorrect While Brazil **looks** (PRESENT TENSE) to ecotourism to fund rainforest preservation, other South American nations **relied** (PAST TENSE) on foreign aid and conservation efforts.

The shift from present tense (*looks*) to past tense (*relied*) is confusing. The sentence attempts to compare Brazil with other South American countries, but the shift in tenses muddles the comparison. Correct the mistake by putting both verbs in the present tense.

Correct While Brazil **looks** (PRESENT TENSE) to ecotourism to fund rainforest preservation, other South American nations **rely** (PRESENT TENSE) on foreign aid and conservation efforts.

COMMON ERRORS

Unnecessary tense shift

Notice the tense shift in the following example.

Incorrect In May of 2000 the "I Love You" virus PAST TENSE **crippled** the computer systems of major North American companies and PAST TENSE **irritated** millions of private computer users. As the virus PRESENT TENSE **generates** millions of emails and PRESENT TENSE **erases** millions of computer files, companies such as Ford and Time Warner PRESENT TENSE **are** forced to shut down their clogged email systems.

The second sentence shifts unnecessarily to the present tense, confusing the reader. Did the "I Love You" virus have its heyday several years ago, or is it still wreaking havoc now? Changing the verbs in the second sentence to the past tense eliminates the confusion.

Correct In May of 2000 the "I Love You" virus PAST TENSE **crippled** the computer systems of major North American companies and PAST TENSE **irritated** millions of private computer users. As the virus PAST TENSE **generated** millions of emails and PAST TENSE **erased** millions of computer files, companies such as Ford and Time Warner PAST TENSE **were** forced to shut down their clogged email systems.

Remember: Shift verb tense only when you are referring to different time periods.

39e Shifts in Mood

Indicative, imperative, and subjunctive verbs

Verbs can be categorized into three moods—indicative, imperative, and subjunctive—defined by the functions they serve.

Indicative verbs state facts, opinions, and questions.

Fact	The human genome project **seeks** to map out human DNA.
Opinion	The scientific advances spurred by the human genome project, including cloning and designer genes, **will allow** normal people to play God.
Question	How long **does** it **take** to map out the entire human genome?

Imperative verbs make commands, give advice, and make requests.

Command	**Research** the technology being used to carry out the human genome project.
Advice	**Try** to join a high-profile research project such as the human genome project if you want to make a name for yourself in the scientific community.
Request	**Could** you please **explain** the role you played in the human genome project?

Subjunctive verbs express wishes, unlikely or untrue situations, hypothetical situations, requests with *that* clauses, and suggestions.

Wish	We **wish** that unlocking the secrets of our DNA **were** a surefire way to cure genetic diseases.
Unlikely or untrue situation	If the genome project **were** as simple as the news media made it out to be, scientists could complete it over a long weekend.
Hypothetical situation	If the genome project **were** to lose government funding, the scientists working on it would not be able to afford the equipment they need to complete it.

The subjunctive in past and present tenses

Subjunctive verbs are usually the trickiest to handle. In the present tense subjunctive clauses call for the base form of the verb (*be, have, see, jump*).

> It is essential that children **be** immunized before they enter kindergarten.

In the past tense they call for the standard past tense of the verb (*had, saw, jumped*), with one exception. In counterfactual sentences the *to be* verb always becomes *were*, even for subjects that take *was* under normal circumstances.

Indicative	I **was** surprised at some of the choices she made.
Subjunctive	If I **were** in her position, I'd do things differently.
Indicative	The young athletes found that gaining muscle **was** not easy.
Subjunctive	If being muscular **were** easy, everyone would look like Arnold Schwarzenegger.

40 Pronouns

QUICKTAKE

- **How do you choose the correct pronoun case?** (see below)
  Incorrect: She and **me** gave a better presentation than **him**.
  Correct: **She and I** gave a better presentation than **he** did.
- **How do you identify and correct errors in pronoun agreement?** (see p. 472)
  Incorrect: **Everybody** in the class had a chance to give **their** opinions.
  Correct: **All students** had a chance to give **their** opinions.
- **How do you identify and correct vague pronoun references?** (see p. 475)
  Vague: Tom thought he could run a marathon after he finished a 10K race. **This** was a mistake. [*This what?*]
  Better: Tom thought he could run a marathon after he finished a 10K race. **This overconfidence** was a mistake.

 40a Pronoun Case

Pronoun case refers to the forms **pronouns** take to indicate their function in a sentence. Pronouns that function as the subjects of sentences are in the **subjective case.** Pronouns that function as direct or indirect objects are in the **objective case.** Pronouns that indicate ownership are in the **possessive case.**

Subjective pronouns	Objective pronouns	Possessive pronouns
I	me	my, mine
we	us	our, ours
you	you	your, yours
he	him	his
she	her	her, hers
it	it	its
they	them	their, theirs
who	whom	whose

People who use English regularly usually make these distinctions among pronouns without thinking about them.

> S O P S O O S O
> I let him use my laptop, but he lent it to her, and I haven't seen it since.

Nonetheless, choosing the correct pronoun case can sometimes be difficult.

Pronouns in compound phrases

Picking the right pronoun can sometimes be confusing when the pronoun appears in a compound phrase.

> If we work together, you and **me** can get the job done quickly.
>
> If we work together, you and **I** can get the job done quickly.

Which is correct—*me* or *I*? Removing the other pronoun usually makes the choice clear.

> **Incorrect** **Me** can get the job done quickly.
>
> **Correct** **I** can get the job done quickly.

Similarly, when compound pronouns appear as objects of prepositions, sometimes the correct choice isn't obvious until you remove the other pronoun.

> When you finish your comments, give them to Isidora or **I**.
>
> When you finish your comments, give them to Isidora or **me**.

Again, the choice is easy when the pronoun stands alone.

Incorrect Give them to **I**.

Correct Give them to **me**.

We and *us* before nouns

Another pair of pronouns that can cause difficulty is *we* and *us* before nouns.

Us friends must stick together.

We friends must stick together.

Which is correct—*us* or *we*? Removing the noun indicates the correct choice.

Incorrect **Us** must stick together.

Correct **We** must stick together.

Who versus *whom*

Choosing between *who* and *whom* is often difficult, even for experienced writers. When you answer the phone, which do you say?

1. To **whom** do you wish to speak?
2. **Who** do you want to talk to?

Probably you chose 2. *To whom do you wish to speak?* may sound stuffy, but technically it is correct. The reason it sounds stuffy is that the distinction between *who* and *whom* is disappearing from spoken language. *Who* is more often used in spoken language, even when *whom* is correct.

COMMON ERRORS

Who or *whom*

In writing, the distinction between *who* and *whom* is still often observed. *Who* and *whom* follow the same rules as other pronouns: *Who* is the subject pronoun; *whom* is the object pronoun. If you are dealing with an object, *whom* is the correct choice.

Incorrect **Who** did you send the letter to?
Who did you give the present to?

Correct To **whom** did you send the letter?
Whom did you give the present to?

(Continued on next page)

COMMON ERRORS *(Continued)*

Who is always the right choice for a subject pronoun.

Correct	**Who** gave you the present?
	Who brought the cookies?

If you are uncertain of which one to use, try substituting *she* and *her* or *he* and *him*.

Incorrect	You sent the letter to **she [who]**?
Correct	You sent the letter to **her [whom]**?
Incorrect	**Him [Whom]** gave you the present?
Correct	**He [Who]** gave you the present?

Remember: ***Who*** **= subject**
Whom **= object**

Whoever versus *whomever*

With the same rule in mind, you can distinguish between *whoever* and *whomever*. Which is correct?

Her warmth touched **whoever** she met.

Her warmth touched **whomever** she met.

In this sentence the pronoun functions as a direct object: Her warmth touched everyone she met, not someone who touched her. Thus *whomever* is the correct choice.

Pronouns in comparisons

When you write a sentence using a comparison that includes *than* or *as* followed by a pronoun, usually you will have to think about which pronoun is correct. Which of the following is correct?

Vimala is a faster swimmer than **him.**

Vimala is a faster swimmer than **he.**

The test that will give you the correct answer is to add the verb that finishes the sentence—in this case, *is.*

Incorrect	Vimala is a faster swimmer than **him is.**
Correct	Vimala is a faster swimmer than **he is.**

Adding the verb makes the correct choice evident.

In some cases the choice of pronoun changes the meaning. Consider these examples:

> She likes ice cream more than **me**. [A bowl of ice cream is better than hanging out with me.]
>
> She likes ice cream more than **I**. [I would rather have frozen yogourt.]

In such cases it is better to complete the comparison:

> She likes ice cream more than **I do**.

Possessive pronouns

Possessive pronouns are confusing at times because possessive nouns are formed with apostrophes, but possessive pronouns do not require apostrophes. Pronouns that use apostrophes are always *contractions.*

It's	=	It is
Who's	=	Who is
They're	=	They are

The test for whether to use an apostrophe is to determine whether the pronoun is possessive or a contraction. The most confusing pair is *its* and *it's*.

Incorrect	**Its** a sure thing she will be elected. [Contraction]
Correct	**It's** a sure thing she will be elected. [**It is** a sure thing.]
Incorrect	The dog lost **it's** collar. [Possessive]
Correct	The dog lost **its** collar.

Whose versus *who's* follows the same pattern.

Incorrect	**Who's** bicycle has the flat tire? [Possessive]
Correct	**Whose** bicycle has the flat tire?
Incorrect	**Whose** on first? [Contraction]
Correct	**Who's** on first? [**Who is** on first?]

Possessive pronouns before *-ing* verbs

Pronouns that modify an *-ing* verb (called a *gerund*) or an *-ing* verb phrase (*gerund phrase*) should appear in the possessive.

Incorrect	The odds of **you** making the team are excellent.
Correct	The odds of **your** making the team are excellent.

40b Pronoun Agreement

Because pronouns usually replace or refer to other nouns, they must match those nouns in number and gender. The noun that the pronoun replaces is called its **antecedent.** If pronoun and antecedent match, they are in **agreement.** When a pronoun is close to the antecedent, usually there is no problem.

> Maria forgot **her** coat.
>
> The band members collected **their** uniforms.

When pronouns and the nouns they replace are separated by several words, sometimes the agreement in number is lost.

> When World Wrestling Entertainment (WWE) used wrestlers (PLURAL) to represent nations, there was no problem identifying the villains. He (SING) was the enemy if he (SING) came from Russia. But after the Cold War, wrestlers (PLURAL) can switch from good guys to bad guys. We don't immediately know how he (SING) has been scripted—good or bad.

Careful writers make sure that pronouns match their antecedents.

Collective nouns

Collective nouns (such as *audience, class, committee, crowd, family, herd, jury, team*) can be singular or plural depending on whether the emphasis is on the group or the particular individuals.

Correct The **committee** was unanimous in its decision.

Correct The **committee** put their opinions ahead of the goals of the unit.

Often a plural antecedent is added if the sense of the collective noun is plural.

Correct The individual committee **members** put their opinions ahead of the goals of the unit.

COMMON ERRORS

Indefinite pronouns

Indefinite pronouns (such as *anybody*, *anything*, *each*, *either*, *everybody*, *everything*, *neither*, *none*, *somebody*, *something*) refer to unspecified people or things. Most take singular pronouns.

Incorrect **Everybody** can choose **their** roommates.
Correct **Everybody** can choose **his or her** roommate.
Correct alternative **All students** can choose **their** roommates.

A few indefinite pronouns (*all*, *any*, *either*, *more*, *most*, *neither*, *none*, *some*) can take either singular or plural pronouns.

Correct **Some** of the shipment was damaged when **it** became overheated.
Correct **All** thought **they** should have a good seat at the concert.

A few are always plural (*few*, *many*, *several*).

Correct **Several** want refunds.

Remember: Words that begin with *any, some,* and *every* are usually singular.

COMMON ERRORS

Pronoun agreement with compound antecedents

Antecedents joined by *and* take plural pronouns.

Correct **Moncef and Driss** practised **their** music.

Exception: When compound antecedents are preceded by *each* or *every*, use a singular pronoun.

Correct **Every male cardinal and warbler** arrives before the female to define **its** territory.

(Continued on next page)

COMMON ERRORS *(Continued)*

When compound antecedents are connected by *or* or *nor*, the pronoun agrees with the antecedent closer to it.

Incorrect **Either the Ross twins or Angela** should bring **their** CDs.

Correct **Either the Ross twins or Angela** should bring **her** CDs.

Better **Either Angela or the Ross twins** should bring **their** CDs.

When you put the plural *twins* last, the correct choice becomes the plural pronoun *their*.

Remember:

1. **Use plural pronouns for antecedents joined by *and*.**
2. **Use singular pronouns for antecedents preceded by *each* or *every*.**
3. **Use a pronoun that agrees with the nearest antecedent when compound antecedents are joined by *or* or *nor*.**

40c Problems with Pronouns and Gender

English does not have a neutral singular pronoun for a group of mixed genders or a person of unknown gender. Referring to a group of mixed genders using male pronouns is unacceptable to many people. Unless the school in the following example is all male, many readers would object to the use of *his*.

Sexist **Each student** must select **his** courses using the online registration system.

Some writers attempt to avoid sexist usage by substituting a plural pronoun. This strategy, however, produces a grammatically incorrect sentence that also risks putting off some readers.

Incorrect **Each student** must select **their** courses using the online registration system.

One strategy is to use *his or her* instead of *his*.

Correct **Each student** must select **his or her** courses using the online registration system.

Often you can avoid using *his or her* by changing the noun to the plural form.

Better **All students** must select **their** courses using the online registration system.

In some cases, using *his or her* may be necessary. Use this construction sparingly.

COMMON ERRORS

Problems created by the pronoun *one* used as a subject

Some writers use *one* as a subject in an attempt to sound more formal. At best this strategy produces writing that sounds stilted, and at worst it produces annoying errors.

Sexist **One** can use **his** brain instead of a calculator to do simple addition.

Incorrect **One** can use **their** brain instead of a calculator to do simple addition. [Agreement error: *Their* does not agree with *one*.]

Incorrect When **one** runs a 10K race for the first time, **you** often start out too fast. [Pronoun shift error: *One* changes to *you*.]

Correct **One** can use **his or her** brain instead of a calculator to do simple addition.

Correct **One** can use **one's** brain instead of a calculator to do simple addition.

You're better off avoiding using *one* as the subject of sentences.

Better **Use your brain** instead of a calculator for simple addition.

Remember: Avoid using the pronoun *one* as a subject.

40d Vague Reference

Pronouns can sometimes refer to more than one noun, thus confusing readers.

> The **coach** rushed past the injured **player** to yell at the **referee. She** was hit in the face by a stray elbow.

You have to guess which person *she* refers to—the coach, the player, or the referee. Sometimes you cannot even guess the antecedent of a pronoun.

> The new subdivision destroyed the last remaining habitat for wildlife within the city limits. **They** have ruined our city with their unchecked greed.

Whom does *they* refer to? The mayor and city council? the developers? the people who live in the subdivision? or all of the above?

Pronouns should never leave the reader guessing about antecedents. If different nouns can be confused as the antecedent, then the ambiguity should be clarified.

Vague Mafalda's pet boa constrictor crawled across Tonya's foot. **She** was mortified.

Better When Mafalda's pet boa constrictor crawled across Tonya's foot, **Mafalda** was mortified.

If the antecedent is missing, then it should be supplied.

Vague Mafalda wasn't thinking when she brought her boa constrictor into the crowded writing centre. **They** got up and left the room in the middle of consultations.

Better Mafalda wasn't thinking when she brought her boa constrictor into the crowded writing centre. **A few students** got up and left the room in the middle of consultations.

COMMON ERRORS

Vague use of *this*

Always use a noun immediately after *this*, *that*, *these*, *those*, and *some*.

Vague Enrique asked Meg to remove the viruses on his computer. **This** was a bad idea.

Was it a bad idea for Enrique to ask Meg because she was insulted? because she didn't know how? because removing viruses would destroy some of Enrique's files?

Better Enrique asked Meg to remove the viruses on his computer. **This imposition** on Meg's time made her resentful.

Remember: Ask yourself "*this* what?" and add the noun that *this* refers to.

41 Modifiers

QUICK*TAKE*

- **How do you use comparatives and superlatives correctly?** (see below)
  Incorrect: The 1849 Great Fire of Toronto destroyed the city core and was the **most large** fire in the city's history.
  Correct: The 1849 Great Fire of Toronto destroyed the city core and was the **largest** fire in the city's history.
- **How do you identify and correct dangling modifiers?** (see p. 487)
  Incorrect: **After decreeing that all new buildings had to be made of stone or brick**, the new building code did not save the city from burning again in 1904.
  Correct: **After decreeing that all new buildings had to be made of stone or brick, Toronto's leaders found that the new** building code did not save the city from burning again in 1904.

41a Choose the Correct Modifier

Modifiers come in two varieties: **adjectives** and **adverbs.** The same words can function as adjectives or adverbs, depending on what they modify.

Adjectives modify

nouns—*iced* tea, *power* forward
pronouns—He is *brash.*

Adverbs modify

verbs—*barely* reach, drive *carefully*
adjectives—*truly* brave activist, *shockingly* red lipstick
other adverbs—*not* soon forget, *very* well
clauses—*Honestly,* I find ballet boring.

Adjectives answer the questions *Which one? How many?* and *What kind?* Adverbs answer the questions *How often? To what extent? When? Where? How?* and *Why?*

Use the correct forms of comparatives and superlatives

As kids, we used comparative and superlative modifiers to argue that Superman was *stronger* than Batman and recess was the *coolest* part of the day.

Comparatives and superlatives are formed differently; all you need to know to determine which to use is the number of items you are comparing.

Comparative modifiers weigh one thing against another. They either end in *er* or are preceded by *more.*

Road bikes are **faster** on pavement than mountain bikes.

The **more courageous** juggler tossed flaming torches.

Superlative modifiers compare three or more items. They either end in *est* or are preceded by *most.*

April is the **hottest** month in New Delhi.

Wounded animals are the **most ferocious**.

When should you add a suffix instead of *more* or *most*? The following guidelines work in most cases:

Adjectives

- For adjectives of one or two syllables, add *er* or *est.*

  redder, heaviest

- For adjectives of three or more syllables, use *more* or *most.*

  more viable, most powerful

Adverbs

- For adverbs of one syllable, use *er* or *est.*

  nearer, slowest

- For adverbs with two or more syllables, use *more* or *most.*

  more convincingly, most humbly

Some frequently used comparatives and superlatives are irregular. The following list can help you become familiar with them:

Adjective	**Comparative**	**Superlative**
good	better	best
bad	worse	worst
little (amount)	less	least
many, much	more	most
Adverb	**Comparative**	**Superlative**
well	better	best
badly	worse	worst

Do not use both a suffix (*er* or *est*) and *more* or *most.*

Incorrect	The service at Siam Palace is **more slower** than the service at the Lotus Garden.
Correct	The service at Siam Palace is **slower** than the service at the Lotus Garden.

Be sure to name the elements being compared if they are not clear from the context.

Unclear comparative	Mice are **cuter.**
Clear	Mice are **cuter than rats.**
Unclear superlative	Nutria are the **creepiest.**
Clear	Nutria are the **creepiest rodents.**

Absolute modifiers cannot be comparative or superlative

Absolute modifiers are words that represent an unvarying condition and thus aren't subject to the degrees that comparative and superlative constructions convey. How many times have you heard something called *very unique* or *totally unique*? *Unique* means "one of a kind." There's nothing else like it. Thus something cannot be *very unique* or *totally unique*. It is either unique or it isn't. The United States Constitution makes a classic absolute modifier blunder when it begins, "We the People of the United States, in Order to form a more perfect Union. . . ." What is a *more perfect Union*? What's more perfect than perfect itself? The construction is nonsensical.

Absolute modifiers should not be modified by comparatives (*more* + modifier or modifier + *er*) or superlatives (*most* + modifier or modifier + *est*). Note the following list of common absolute modifiers:

absolute	impossible	unanimous
adequate	infinite	unavoidable
complete	main	uniform
entire	minor	unique
false	perfect	universal
fatal	principal	whole
final	stationary	
ideal	sufficient	

Double negatives

In English, as in mathematics, two negatives equal a positive. Avoid using two negative words in one sentence, or you'll end up saying the opposite of what you mean. The following are negative words that you should avoid doubling up:

barely	nobody	nothing
hardly	none	scarcely
neither	no one	

Incorrect, double negative **Barely no one** noticed that the pop star lip-synched during the whole performance.

Correct, single negative **Barely anyone** noticed that the pop star lip-synched during the whole performance.

Incorrect, double negative When the pastor asked if anyone had objections to the marriage, **nobody** said **nothing**.

Correct, single negative When the pastor asked if anyone had objections to the marriage, **nobody** said **anything**.

COMMON ERRORS

Irregular adjectives and adverbs

Switch on a baseball interview and you will likely hear numerous modifier mistakes.

> Manager: We didn't play **bad** tonight. Bautista hit the ball **real good**, and I was glad to see Morrow pitch **farther** into the game than he did in his last start. His fastball was on, and he walked **less** hitters.

While this manager has his sports clichés down pat, he makes errors with five of the trickiest modifier pairs. In three cases he uses an adjective where an adverb would be correct.

Adjectives	**Adverbs**
bad	badly
good	well
real	really

[*Bad*, an adjective modifying the noun *call*.] The umpire made a **bad** call at the plate.

[*Badly*, an adverb modifying the verb *play*.] We didn't play **badly**.

COMMON ERRORS *(Continued)*

[*Good*, an adjective modifying the noun *catch.*] Arencibia made a **good** catch.

[*Well*, an adverb modifying the verb *hit.*] Bautista hit the ball **well.**

Exception: *Well* acts as an adjective when it describes someone's health: Injured players must stay on the disabled list until they feel **well** enough to play every day.

[*Real*, an adjective modifying the noun *wood.*] While university players hit with aluminum bats, the professionals still use **real** wood.

[*Really*, an adverb modifying the adverb *well.*] Bautista hit the ball **really well.**

The coach also confused the comparative adjectives *less* and *fewer*, and the comparative adverbs *farther* and *further*.

Adjectives

less—a smaller, uncountable amount
fewer—a smaller number of things

Less Baseball stadiums with pricey luxury suites cater **less** to families and more to business people with expense accounts.

Fewer He walked **fewer** hitters.

Adverbs

farther—a greater distance
further—to a greater extent, a longer time, or a greater number

Farther Some players argue that today's baseballs go **farther** than baseballs made just a few years ago.

Further The commissioner of baseball curtly denied that today's baseballs are juiced, refusing to discuss the matter **further**.

Remember: ***Bad, good, real, less*** **(for uncountables), and** ***fewer*** **(for countables) are adjectives.** ***Badly, well, really, farther*** **(for distance), and** ***further*** **(for extent, time, or number) are adverbs.** ***Well*** **is an adjective when it describes health.**

41b Place Adjectives Carefully

As a general rule, the closer you place a modifier to the word it modifies, the less chance there is of confusing your reader. This section and the next elaborate on this maxim, giving you the details you need to put it into practice. Most native speakers have an ear for many of the guidelines presented here, with the notable exception of the placement of limiting modifiers, which is explained in Section 41c.

Place adjective phrases and clauses carefully

Adjective clauses frequently begin with *when*, *where*, or a relative pronoun such as *that*, *which*, *who*, *whom*, or *whose*. An adjective clause usually follows the noun or pronoun it modifies.

Adjective clause modifying *salon*: The **salon** where I get my hair styled is raising its prices.

Adjective clause modifying *stylist*: I need to find a **stylist** who charges less.

Adjective phrases and clauses can also come before the person or thing they modify.

Adjective phrase modifying *girl*: Proud of her accomplishment, the little **girl** showed her trophy to her grandmother.

Adjective phrases or clauses can be confusing if they are separated from the word they modify.

Confusing Watching from the ground below, the kettle of broadwing hawks circled high above the observers.

Is the kettle of hawks watching from the ground below? You can fix the problem by putting the modified subject immediately after the modifier or by placing the modifier next to the modified subject.

Better The kettle of broadwing hawks circled high above the **observers**, who were watching from the ground below.

Better Watching from the ground below, the **observers** saw a kettle of broadwing hawks circle high above them.

See dangling modifiers in Section 41e.

Place one-word adjectives before the modified word(s)

One-word adjectives almost always precede the word or words they modify.

Pass the hot sauce, please.

When one-word adjectives are not next to the word or words being modified, they can create misunderstandings.

Unclear Before his owner withdrew him from competition, the **fiercest** rodeo's bull injured three riders.

Readers may think *fiercest* modifies *rodeo's* instead of *bull*. Placing the adjective before *bull* will clarify the meaning.

Better Before his owner withdrew him from competition, the rodeo's **fiercest** bull injured three riders.

Exception: Predicate adjectives follow linking verbs

Predicate adjectives are the most common exception to the norm of single-word adjectives preceding words they modify. Predicate adjectives follow linking verbs such as *is*, *are*, *was*, *were*, *seem*, *feel*, *smell*, *taste*, and *look*. Don't be fooled into thinking they are adverbs. If the word following a linking verb modifies the subject, use a predicate adjective. If it modifies an action verb, use an adverb. Can you identify the word being modified in the following sentence?

I feel **odd**.

Odd modifies the subject *I*, not the verb *feel*. Thus, *odd* is a predicate adjective that implies the speaker feels ill. If it were an adverb, the sentence would read *I feel oddly*. The adverb *oddly* modifying *feel* would imply the speaker senses things in unconventional ways. Try the next one:

The bruise looked **bad**.

Since *bad* modifies *bruise*, *bad* is a predicate adjective implying a serious injury. *Looked* is the linking verb that connects the two. If we made the modifier an adverb, the sentence would read *The bruise looked badly*, conjuring the creepy notion that the bruise had eyes but couldn't see well. You can avoid such bizarre constructions if you know when to use predicate adjectives with linking verbs.

Put subjective adjectives before objective adjectives

When you have a series of adjectives expressing both opinion and more objective description, put the subjective adjectives before the objective ones. For example, in

the sultry cabaret singer

sultry is subjective and *cabaret* is objective.

Put determiners before other adjectives

Determiners are a group of adjectives that include possessive nouns (such as *woman's* prerogative and *Pedro's* violin), possessive pronouns (such as *my*, *your*, and *his*), demonstrative pronouns (such as *this*, *that*, *these*, *those*), and indefinite pronouns (such as *all*, *both*, *each*, *either*, *few*, and *many*). When you are using a series of adjectives, put the determiners first.

our finest hour

Tara's favourite old blue jeans

those crazy kids

When you are using a numerical determiner with another determiner, put the numerical determiner first.

both **those** tattoos

all **these** people

Multilingual writers can find more on the placement of modifiers in Section 55c.

41c Place Adverbs Carefully

For the most part, the guidelines for adverb placement are not as complex as the guidelines for adjective placement.

Place adverbs before or after the words they modify

Single-word **adverbs** and adverbial clauses and phrases can usually sit comfortably either before or after the words they modify.

Dimitri quietly **walked** down the hall.

Dimitri **walked** quietly down the hall.

Conjunctive adverbs—*also, however, instead, likewise, then, therefore, thus*, and others—are adverbs that show how ideas relate to one another. They prepare a reader for contrasts, exceptions, additions, conclusions, and other shifts in an argument. Conjunctive adverbs can usually fit well into more than one place in the sentence. In the following example, *however* could fit in three different places.

Between two main clauses

Professional football players earn exorbitant salaries; however, they pay for their wealth with lifetimes of chronic pain and debilitating injuries.

Within second main clause

Professional football players earn exorbitant salaries; they pay for their wealth, **however**, with lifetimes of chronic pain and debilitating injuries.

At end of second main clause

Professional football players earn exorbitant salaries; they pay for their wealth with lifetimes of chronic pain and debilitating injuries, **however**.

Subordinating conjunctions—words such as *after*, *although*, *because*, *if*, *since*, *than*, *that*, *though*, *when*, and *where*—often begin **adverb clauses**. Notice that we can place adverb clauses with subordinating conjunctions either before or after the word(s) being modified:

After someone in the audience yelled, he **forgot** the lyrics.

He **forgot** the lyrics **after someone in the audience yelled**.

While you have some leeway with adverb placement, follow the advice in Section 41d: Avoid distracting interruptions between the subject and the verb, the verb and the object, or within the verb phrase. A long adverbial clause is usually best placed at the beginning or end of a sentence.

COMMON ERRORS

Placement of limiting modifiers

Words such as *almost*, *even*, *hardly*, *just*, *merely*, *nearly*, *not*, *only*, and *simply* are called limiting modifiers. Although people often play fast and loose with their placement in everyday speech, limiting modifiers should always go immediately before the word or words they modify in your writing. Many writers have difficulty with the placement of *only*. Like other limiting modifiers, *only* should be placed immediately before the word it modifies.

Incorrect The gross domestic product **only** gives one indicator of economic growth.

Correct The gross domestic product gives **only** one indicator of economic growth.

Remember: Place limiting modifiers immediately before the word(s) they modify.

41d Revise Disruptive Modifiers

The fundamental way readers make sense of sentences is to identify the subject, verb, and object. Modifiers can sink a sentence if they interfere with the reader's ability to connect the three. Usually, single-word modifiers do not significantly disrupt a sentence. However, avoid placing modifying clauses and phrases between a subject and a verb, between a verb and an object, and within a verb phrase.

Disruptive The forest fire, **no longer held in check by the exhausted firefighters**, jumped the firebreak. [Separates the subject from the verb]

Better **No longer held in check by the exhausted firefighters**, the forest fire jumped the firebreak. [Puts the modifier before the subject]

Disruptive The fire's heat seemed to melt, **at a temperature hot enough to liquefy metal**, the saplings in its path. [Separates the verb from the object]

Better **At a temperature hot enough to liquefy metal**, the fire's heat seemed to melt the saplings in its path. [Puts the modifier before the subject]

WRITING SMART

Split infinitives

An infinitive is *to* plus the base form of a verb. A **split infinitive** occurs when an adverb separates *to* from the base verb form.

Infinitive = *To* + Base verb form

Examples: **to feel, to speak, to borrow**

Split infinitive = *To* + Modifier + Base verb form

Examples: **to strongly feel, to barely speak, to liberally borrow**

The most famous split infinitive in recent history occurs in the opening credits of *Star Trek* episodes: "to boldly go where no one has gone before." The alternative without the split infinitive is "to go boldly where no one has gone before." The *Star Trek* writers were no doubt

WRITING SMART *(Continued)*

aware that they were splitting an infinitive, but they chose *to boldly go* because they wanted the emphasis on *boldly*, not *go*.

Nevertheless, many split infinitives are considered awkward for good reason.

Awkward You have to get away from the city lights **to better see** the stars in the night sky.

Better You have to get away from the city lights **to see** the stars in the night sky **better**.

Awkward **To, as planned, stay** in Venice, we need to reserve a hotel room now.

Better **To stay** in Venice **as planned**, we need to reserve a hotel room now.

When a sentence would sound strange without the adverb's splitting the infinitive, you can either retain the split or, better yet, revise the sentence to avoid the problem altogether.

Acceptable When found by the search party, the survivors were able **to barely whisper** their names.

Alternative When found by the search party, the survivors **could barely whisper** their names.

 Revise Dangling Modifiers

Some modifiers are ambiguous because they could apply to more than one word or clause. **Dangling modifiers** are ambiguous for the opposite reason; they don't have a word to modify. In such cases the modifier is usually an introductory clause or phrase. What is being modified should immediately follow the phrase, but in the following sentence it is absent.

> **After bowling a perfect game**, Surfside Lanes hung Marco's photo on the wall.

Neither the subject of the sentence, *Surfside Lanes*, nor the direct object, *Marco's photo*, is capable of bowling a perfect game. Since a missing noun or pronoun causes a dangling modifier, simply rearranging the sentence will not resolve the problem. You can eliminate a dangling modifier in two ways:

1. Insert the noun or pronoun being modified immediately after the introductory modifying phrase.

   After bowling a perfect game, Marco was honoured by having his photo hung on the wall at Surfside Lanes.

2. Rewrite the introductory phrase as an introductory clause to include the noun or the pronoun.

   After Marco bowled a perfect game, Surfside Lanes hung his photo on the wall.

PART

9 Understanding Punctuation and Mechanics

You **can learn more and do more** with MyWritingLab and with the eText version of *The Brief Penguin Handbook*. Find resources in MyWritingLab to help you use punctuation successfully.

9 Understanding Punctuation and Mechanics

42 Commas

QUICKTAKE

- **What parts of a sentence should be set off with commas?** (see below)
  Incorrect: Although bears have a better sense of smell than bloodhounds there are reasons why the military cannot fly them into dangerous areas, and have them sniff out enemy combatants.
  Correct: Although bears have a better sense of smell than bloodhounds, there are reasons why the military cannot fly them into dangerous areas and have them sniff out enemy combatants.
- **When do you use commas with long modifiers?** (see p. 494)
  Restrictive: Anyone who thinks bears could be trained to carry out a military mission hasn't really thought the idea through.
  Nonrestrictive: The Pentagon, which recently added a virtual suggestion box to its website, has been receiving some unusual ideas.
- **How do you use commas with quotations?** (see p. 500)
  Incorrect: "Bears are the best sniffers", wrote someone.
  Correct: "Bears are the best sniffers," wrote someone.

42a Commas with Introductory Elements

Introductory elements usually need to be set off by commas. Introductory words or phrases signal a shift in ideas or a particular arrangement of ideas; they help direct the reader's attention to the writer's most important points.

Common introductory elements

Conjunctive adverbs	Introductory phrases
however	of course
therefore	above all
nonetheless	for example
also	in other words
otherwise	as a result
finally	on the other hand
instead	in conclusion
thus	in addition

When a conjunctive adverb or introductory phrase begins a sentence, the comma follows.

> **Therefore,** the suspect could not have been at the scene of the crime.
>
> **Above all,** remember to let water drip from the faucets if the temperature drops below freezing.

When a conjunctive adverb comes in the middle of a sentence, set it off with commas preceding and following.

> If you really want to prevent your pipes from freezing, **however,** you should insulate them before the winter comes.

Conjunctive adverbs and phrases that do not require commas

Occasionally the conjunctive adverb or phrase blends into a sentence so smoothly that a pause would sound awkward.

Awkward	Of course, we'll come.
Better	Of course we'll come.
Awkward	Even if you take every precaution, the pipes in your home may freeze, **nevertheless**.
Better	Even if you take every precaution, the pipes in your home may freeze **nevertheless**.

Sometimes the presence or absence of a comma can affect the meaning. For example:

> Of course, we'll come. [Be reassured that we will come.]
>
> Of course we'll come. [There is no doubt we will come.]

COMMON ERRORS

Commas with long introductory modifiers

Long subordinate clauses or phrases that begin sentences should be followed by a comma. The following sentence needs a comma:

Incorrect Because cellphones now have organizers and email stand-alone personal digital assistants have become another technology of the past.

When you read this sentence, you likely had to go back to sort it out. The words *organizers and email stand-alone personal digital assistants* tend to run together. When the comma is added, the sentence is easier to

COMMON ERRORS *(Continued)*

understand because the reader knows where the subordinate clause ends and where the main clause begins.

Correct Because cellphones now have organizers and email**,** stand-alone personal digital assistants have become another technology of the past.

How long is a long introductory modifier? Short introductory adverbial phrases and clauses of five words or fewer can get by without the comma if the omission does not mislead the reader. Using the comma is still correct after short introductory adverbial phrases and clauses:

Correct In the long run stocks have always done better than bonds.

Correct In the long run**,** stocks have always done better than bonds.

Remember: Put commas after long introductory modifiers.

42b Commas with Compound Clauses

Two main clauses joined by a coordinating conjunction (*and, or, so, yet, but, nor, for*) form a compound sentence (see Section 36e). Writers sometimes get confused about when to insert a comma before a coordinating conjunction.

Use a comma to separate main clauses

Main clauses carry enough grammatical weight to be punctuated as sentences. When two main clauses are joined by a coordinating conjunction, place a comma before the coordinating conjunction in order to distinguish them.

> Sandy borrowed two boxes full of CDs on Tuesday**, and** she returned them on Friday.

Very short main clauses joined by a coordinating conjunction do not need commas.

> She called **and** she called, but no one answered.

Do not use a comma to separate two verbs with the same subject

Incorrect Sandy borrowed two boxes full of CDs on Tuesday, **and** returned them on Friday.

Sandy is the subject of both *borrowed* and *returned*. This sentence has only one main clause; it should not be punctuated as a compound sentence.

Correct Sandy borrowed two boxes full of CDs on Tuesday **and** returned them on Friday.

Exceptions to this rule occur when there is a lapse of time or after *said*.

He did not study, and failed.

"That's fine," he said, and went on reading.

COMMON ERRORS

Commas in compound sentences

The easiest way to distinguish between compound sentences and sentences with phrases that follow the main clause is to isolate the part that comes after the conjunction. If the part that follows the conjunction can stand on its own as a complete sentence, insert a comma. If it cannot, omit the comma.

Main clause plus phrases
Mario thinks he lost his passport while riding the bus or by absentmindedly leaving it on the counter when he checked into the hostel.

Look at what comes after the coordinating conjunction *or*:

by absentmindedly leaving it on the counter when he checked into the hostel

This group of words is not a main clause and cannot stand on its own as a complete sentence. Do not set it off with a comma.

Main clauses joined with a conjunction
On Saturday Mario went to the Canadian consulate to get a new passport, but the officer told him that replacement passports could not be issued on weekends.

COMMON ERRORS (Continued)

Read the clause after the coordinating conjunction *but*:

> the officer told him that replacement passports could not be issued on weekends

This group of words can stand on its own as a complete sentence. Thus, it is a main clause; place a comma before *but*.

Remember:

1. **Place a comma before the coordinating conjunction (*and, but, for, or, nor, so, yet*) if there are two main clauses.**
2. **Do not use a comma before the coordinating conjunction if there is only one main clause.**

Do not use a comma to separate a main clause from a restrictive clause or phrase

When clauses and phrases that follow the main clause are essential to the meaning of a sentence, they should not be set off with a comma.

Incorrect Sandy plans to borrow Felicia's record collection, while Felicia is on vacation.

Correct Sandy plans to borrow Felicia's record collection while Felicia is on vacation.

Incorrect Sandy plans to borrow Felicia's records while Felicia is on vacation, in order to convert them to CDs.

Correct Sandy plans to borrow Felicia's records while Felicia is on vacation in order to convert them to CDs.

COMMON ERRORS

Do not use a comma to set off a *because* clause that follows a main clause

Writers frequently place unnecessary commas before *because* and similar subordinate conjunctions that follow a main clause. *Because* is not a coordinating conjunction; thus it should not be set off by a comma unless the comma improves readability.

(Continued on next page)

COMMON ERRORS *(Continued)*

Incorrect I struggled to complete my term papers last year, because I didn't know how to type.

Correct I struggled to complete my term papers last year because I didn't know how to type.

But do use a comma after an introductory *because* clause.

Incorrect Because Danny left his red jersey at home Coach Russell benched him.

Correct Because Danny left his red jersey at home, Coach Russell benched him.

Remember: Use a comma after a *because* clause that begins a sentence. Do not use a comma to set off a *because* clause that follows a main clause.

42c Commas with Non-restrictive Modifiers

Imagine that you are sending a friend a group photo that includes your aunt. Which sentence is correct?

In the back row the woman wearing the pink hat is my aunt.

In the back row the woman, wearing the pink hat, is my aunt.

Both sentences can be correct depending on what is in the photo. If there are three women standing in the back row and only one is wearing a pink hat, this piece of information is necessary for identifying your aunt. In this case the sentence without commas is correct because it identifies your aunt as the woman wearing the pink hat. Such necessary modifiers are **restrictive** and do not require commas.

If only one woman is standing in the back row, *wearing the pink hat* is extra information and not necessary to identify your aunt. The modifier in this case is **non-restrictive** and is set off by commas.

Distinguish restrictive and non-restrictive modifiers

You can distinguish restrictive and non-restrictive modifiers by deleting the modifier and then deciding whether the remaining sentence is

changed. For example, delete the modifier *still stained by its bloody Tiananmen Square crackdown* from the following sentence:

> Some members of the Olympic Site Selection Committee wanted to prevent China, **still stained by its bloody Tiananmen Square crackdown**, from hosting the 2008 games.

The result leaves the meaning of the main clause unchanged.

> Some members of the Olympic Site Selection Committee wanted to prevent China from hosting the 2008 games.

The modifier is non-restrictive and should be set off by commas.

In contrast, deleting *who left work early* does change the meaning of this sentence:

> The employees **who left work early** avoided driving home in the blizzard.

Without the modifier the sentence reads,

> The employees avoided driving home in the blizzard.

Now it sounds as if all the employees avoided driving home in the blizzard instead of just the ones who left early. The modifier is clearly restrictive and does not require commas.

Recognize types and placement of non-restrictive modifiers

Non-restrictive modifiers are used frequently to add details. You can add several kinds of non-restrictive modifiers to a short, simple sentence (see Sections 36c and 36d).

> The student ran across campus,
>
> which left him panting when he got to class. [adjective clause]
> his backpack swaying back and forth. [absolute phrase]
> weaving his way down the crowded sidewalks. [participial phrase]

Non-restrictive modifiers can be placed at the beginning of sentences.

> When he realized his watch had stopped, [adverb clause]
> With his thoughts on the intramural championship later that afternoon, [prepositional phrase]
> Rushing to get to class, [participial phrase]
>
> the student ran across campus.

They also can be placed in the middle of sentences.

The student,

who had woken up only 15 minutes before class, [adjective clause]
my old roommate, [appositive]
wearing a ripped black trenchcoat, [participial phrase]
with one arm in a cast and the other clutching a stack of books, [prepositional phrase]

ran across campus.

Pay special attention to appositives

Clauses and phrases can be restrictive or non-restrictive, depending on the context. Often the difference is obvious, but some modifiers require close consideration, especially appositives. An **appositive** is a noun or noun phrase that identifies or adds information to the noun preceding it.

Consider the following pair.

1 The world's most popular music players iPods changed the way people purchase and listen to music.

2 The world's most popular music players, iPods, changed the way people purchase and listen to music.

Which is correct? The appositive *iPods* is not essential to the meaning of the sentence and offers additional information. Sentence 2 is correct.

Here's another pair.

1 The disgruntled slave Marie-Joseph Angélique was executed for starting a devastating fire in Montreal on April 10, 1734.

2 The disgruntled slave, Marie-Joseph Angélique, was executed for starting a devastating fire in Montreal on April 10, 1734.

The name *Marie-Joseph Angélique* is essential to identifying which of the slaves kept in Montreal in the early eighteenth century is under discussion. Thus, it is a restrictive appositive and should not be set off with commas. Sentence 1 is correct.

Use commas around non-restrictive clauses within a *that* clause

Restrictive clauses beginning with *that* sometimes have a non-restrictive clause embedded within them.

Incorrect I want you to know that **despite all the arguments we have had over the past few months** I still value your advice.

Correct I want you to know that, **despite all the arguments we have had over the past few months,** I still value your advice.

Use commas to mark off parenthetical expressions

A *parenthetical expression* provides information or commentary that is usually not essential to the sentence's meaning.

Incorrect My mother much to my surprise didn't say anything when she saw my pierced nose.

Correct My mother, much to my surprise, didn't say anything when she saw my pierced nose.

Some parenthetical expressions are essential to the point of the sentence, especially ones that make contrasts, but they too are set off by commas.

Incorrect The candidate's conversational skills not her resumé landed her the job.

Correct The candidate's conversational skills, not her resumé, landed her the job.

However, do not use a comma when the parenthetical expression is one word and its function is not obviously parenthetical.

Incorrect The first-year writing course is, fundamentally, an introduction to writing arguments.

Correct The first-year writing course is fundamentally an introduction to writing arguments.

Use commas to mark off absolute phrases

An *absolute phrase* contains at least one noun or pronoun and at least one participle (see Section 36d). **Absolutes** can modify a noun or a whole sentence.

Incorrect Her project completed Marianne decided to splurge on a beach vacation.

Correct Her project completed, Marianne decided to splurge on a beach vacation.

Incorrect Their recess privileges taken away the boys sat slumped in the classroom's uncomfortable chairs.

Correct Their recess privileges taken away, the boys sat slumped in the classroom's uncomfortable chairs.

COMMON ERRORS

Commas with *that* and *which* clauses

Writers often confuse when to use commas to set off modifying phrases beginning with *that* and *which*. *That* clauses follow a hard and fast rule: They are used only as restrictive modifiers.

A *that* clause is a restrictive modifier: Omit commas

Two other women were wearing the same dress **that Sherice bought specifically to wear to the awards banquet**.

Which clauses are usually used as non-restrictive modifiers. While *which* clauses can also function as restrictive modifiers, careful writers observe the difference and change *which* to *that* if the clause is restrictive.

A *which* clause is a non-restrictive modifier: Use commas

Jina had to leave her cat with her parents this term because her new apartment**, which is much closer to the campus,** prohibits pets of any kind.

When a *which* clause acts as a restrictive modifier, change *which* to *that*

Incorrect The uncertainty **which** surrounded the selection of the new coach was created by the sudden and unexpected resignation of her predecessor.

Correct The uncertainty **that** surrounded the selection of the new coach was created by the sudden and unexpected resignation of her predecessor.

Remember:

1. ***That* clauses are restrictive modifiers and do not take commas.**
2. ***Which* clauses can be either restrictive or non-restrictive, but careful writers use them as non-restrictive modifiers and set them off with commas.**

 42d Commas with Items in a Series

In a series of three or more items, place a comma after each item but the last one. The comma between the last two items goes before the coordinating conjunction (*and, or, nor, but, so, for, yet*).

> Health officials in Burlington, Hamilton, and Oakville have all reported new cases of the West Nile virus.

WRITING SMART

Commas between the last two items in a series

Whether you should insert a comma between the last two items in a series depends on what kind of writing you're doing. In newspapers and magazines, the comma is typically omitted; however, academic, business, and professional writing includes a comma before the last series item. Omitting the comma sometimes causes confusion.

Journalistic convention	I thank my parents, Robert Pirsig and Harley-Davidson for my outlook on life.
Academic convention	I thank my parents, Robert Pirsig, and Harley-Davidson for my outlook on life.

 42e Commas with Coordinate Adjectives

Coordinate adjectives are two or more adjectives that independently modify the same noun. Coordinate adjectives that are not linked by *and* must be separated by a comma.

> Since the NASDAQ bubble burst in 2000 and 2001, the internet technology companies that remain are no longer the **fresh-faced, giddy** kids of Wall Street.

Distinguish coordinate adjectives

You can recognize coordinate adjectives by reversing their order; if their meaning remains the same, the adjectives are coordinate and must be linked by *and* or separated by a comma. When the order of the adjectives changes in the following example, the description of *lifestyles* retains the same meaning:

> Because border collies are bred to herd sheep, their energetic temperaments may not suit city dwellers' more **sedentary, staid** lifestyles.
>
> Because border collies are bred to herd sheep, their energetic temperaments may not suit city dwellers' more **staid, sedentary** lifestyles.

Do not use commas to link cumulative adjectives

Commas are not used between cumulative adjectives. Cumulative adjectives are two or more adjectives that work together to modify a noun: *deep blue sea, inexpensive mountain bike*. If reversing their order changes the description of the noun (or violates the order of English, such as *mountain inexpensive bike*), the adjectives are cumulative and should not be separated by a comma.

The following example doesn't require a comma in the cumulative adjective series *massive Corinthian.*

> Visitors to Rome's Pantheon pass between the **massive Corinthian** columns flanking the front door.

We know they are cumulative because reversing their order to read *Corinthian massive* would alter the way they modify *columns*—in this case, so much so that they no longer make sense.

 42f Commas with Quotations

Properly punctuating quotations with commas can be tricky unless you know a few rules about when and where to use commas.

When to use commas with quotations

Commas set off phrases that attribute quotations to a speaker or a writer, such as *he argues, they said,* and *she writes.*

> "When you come to a fork in the road," said Yogi Berra, "take it!"

If the attribution follows a quotation that is a complete sentence, replace the period that would normally come at the end of the quotation with a comma.

> **Incorrect** "I believe in good omens. I don't believe in the bad ones." notes Silken Laumann.
>
> **Correct** "I believe in good omens. I don't believe in the bad ones," notes Silken Laumann.

When an attribution is placed in the middle of a quotation, put the comma preceding the attribution within the quotation mark just before the phrase.

Incorrect "You have not seen Canada", argued Pierre Elliott Trudeau, "until you have seen the north."

Correct "You have not seen Canada," argued Pierre Elliott Trudeau, "until you have seen the north."

When not to use commas with quotations

Do not replace a question mark or exclamation point with a comma.

Incorrect "Bart, stop pestering Satan," said Marge Simpson.

Correct "Bart, stop pestering Satan!" said Marge Simpson.

Not all phrases that mention the author's name are attributions. When quoting a term or using a quotation within a subordinate clause, do not set off the quotation with commas.

"Stonewall" Jackson gained his nickname at the First Battle of Bull Run when General Barnard Bee shouted to his men that "Jackson is standing like a stone wall."

Even a quotation that is a complete sentence can be used in a subordinate clause. Such quotations should not be set off with commas. Pay special attention to quotations preceded by *that, which,* and *because*; these words are the most common indicators of a subordinate clause.

About immigration in Canada, Peter Stoffer has noted that if "[y]ou look at the history—the aboriginal people welcomed the first settlers here with open arms, fed us and took care of us . . . today, we welcome people from all nations to come in and share."

42g Commas with Dates, Numbers, Titles, and Addresses

Some of the easiest comma rules to remember are those we use every day in dates, numbers, personal titles, place names, direct address, and brief interjections.

Commas with dates

Use commas to separate the day of the week from the month and to set off a year from the rest of the sentence.

March 25, 1942

Monday, November 18, 2002

On July 27, 2012, the opening ceremony of the World Scout Jamboree was televised.

Do not use a comma when the month immediately precedes the year.

12 June 1988

April 2008

Commas with numbers

Commas are not used with numbers in the international system of units (i.e., metric). Leave spaces to mark off thousands, millions, billions, and so on.

16 500 000

However, do not use spaces or commas in street addresses or page numbers.

page 1542

7602 Yonge Street

Commas with personal titles

When a title follows a person's name, set the title off with commas.

Frederick Banting, MD

Jackie Hart, Vice President for Operations, reported that her company's earnings were far ahead of projections.

Commas with place names

Place a comma between street addresses, city names, province names, and countries.

Fredericton, New Brunswick

Lima, Peru

The prime minister lives at 24 Sussex Drive, Ottawa, Ontario.

Commas in direct address

When addressing someone directly, set off that person's name in commas.

I was happy to get your letter yesterday, Jamie.

Yes, Virginia, there is a Santa Claus.

Commas with brief interjections

Use commas to set off brief interjections such as *yes* and *no*, as well as short questions that fall at the ends of sentences.

The director said that, no, the understudy would not have to stand in for the lead tonight.

Have another piece of pie, won't you?

42h Commas to Avoid Confusion

Certain sentences can confuse readers if you do not indicate where they should pause within the sentence. Use a comma to guide the reader through these usually compact constructions.

Unclear With supplies low prices of gasoline and fuel oil will increase.

This sentence could be read as meaning *With supplies, low prices will increase.*

Clear With supplies low, prices of gasoline and fuel oil will increase.

42i Unnecessary Commas

Do not place a comma between a subject and a predicate

Incorrect Not all Canadian children of immigrant parents, speak their parents' native language.

Correct Not all Canadian children of immigrant parents speak their parents' native language.

However, you do use commas to set off modifying phrases that separate subjects from verbs.

Incorrect Steven Pinker author of *The Language Instinct* argues that the ability to speak and understand language is an evolutionary adaptive trait.

Correct Steven Pinker, author of *The Language Instinct*, argues that the ability to speak and understand language is an evolutionary adaptive trait.

Do not use a comma with a coordinating conjunction unless it joins two main clauses

Incorrect Susana thought finishing her first novel was hard, but soon learned that getting a publisher to buy it was much harder.

Correct Susana thought finishing her first novel was hard but soon learned that getting a publisher to buy it was much harder.

Correct Susana thought finishing her first novel was hard, but **she** soon learned that getting a publisher to buy it was much harder.

Do not use a comma after a subordinating conjunction such as *although, despite,* or *while*

Incorrect Although, soccer is gaining popularity in Canada, it will never be as popular as hockey.

Correct Although soccer is gaining popularity in Canada, it will never be as popular as hockey.

Do not use a comma before *than*

Some writers mistakenly use a comma with *than* to try to heighten the contrast in a comparison.

Incorrect Any teacher will tell you that acquiring critical thinking skills is more important, than simply memorizing information.

Correct Any teacher will tell you that acquiring critical thinking skills is more important than simply memorizing information.

Do not use a comma before a list

A common mistake is to place a comma after *such as* or *like* before introducing a list.

Incorrect Many hourly workers, such as, waiters, dishwashers, and cashiers, do not receive health benefits from their employers.

Correct Many hourly workers, such as waiters, dishwashers, and cashiers, do not receive health benefits from their employers.

43 Semicolons and Colons

QUICKTAKE

- **How do you use semicolons to link related ideas?** (see below)
  Incorrect: The first reports of an elephant arriving in the United States are from 1796**;** which may have been an elephant named Old Bet.
  Correct: The first reports of an elephant arriving in the United States are from 1796**;** they may have been referring to an elephant named Old Bet.
- **Where do you use colons?** (see p. 507 and p. 509)
  In a sentence: There is one elephant behaviour that keepers look out for as a warning of possible aggression**:** rocking.
  With lists: Elephants need a few things to keep them healthy and happy**:** fresh food, plenty of water, room to roam, and the companionship of other elephants.

43a Semicolons with Closely Related Main Clauses

Why use semicolons? Sometimes we want to join two main clauses to form a complete sentence in order to indicate their close relationship. We can connect them with a comma and a coordinating conjunction such as *or*, *but*, or *and*. However, using those constructions too often can make your writing cumbersome. Instead you can omit the comma and coordinating conjunction and insert a semicolon between the two clauses.

Semicolons can join only clauses that are grammatically equal. In other words, they join main clauses only to other main clauses, not to phrases or subordinate clauses. Look at the following examples:

Incorrect [MAIN CLAUSE: Gloria's new weightlifting program will help her recover from knee surgery]**;** [PARTICIPIAL PHRASE: doing a series of squats and presses with a physical therapist].

Incorrect [MAIN CLAUSE: Gloria's new weightlifting program will help her regain strength in her knee]**;** [SUBORDINATE CLAUSE: which required surgery after she injured it skiing].

Correct Gloria's new weightlifting program will help her recover from knee surgery; a physical therapist leads her through a series of squats and presses.

(MAIN CLAUSE: Gloria's new weightlifting program will help her recover from knee surgery) (MAIN CLAUSE: a physical therapist leads her through a series of squats and presses)

COMMON ERRORS

Main clauses connected with transitional words and phrases

Closely related main clauses sometimes use a conjunctive adverb (such as *however, therefore, moreover, furthermore, thus, meanwhile, nonetheless, otherwise*; see the list in Section 42a) or a transition (*in fact, for example, that is, for instance, in addition, in other words, on the other hand, even so*) to indicate the relationship between them. When the second clause begins with a conjunctive adverb or a transition, a semicolon is needed to join the two clauses. This sentence pattern is frequently used; therefore, it pays to learn how to punctuate it correctly.

Incorrect (comma splice) The police and city officials want to crack down on drug use at raves, however, their efforts have been unsuccessful so far.

Correct The police and city officials want to crack down on drug use at raves; however, their efforts have been unsuccessful so far.

The semicolon separates the second main clause from the first. Note that a comma is also needed to separate *however* from the rest of the second clause.

Incorrect (comma splice) The poster design left much to be desired, for example, the title was printed in garish red, orange, and green.

Correct The poster design left much to be desired; for example, the title was printed in garish red, orange, and green.

Note that in addition to the semicolon, a comma separates *for example* from the rest of the second clause.

Remember: Main clauses that use a conjunctive adverb or a transitional phrase require a semicolon to join the clauses.

Do not use a semicolon to introduce quotations

Use a comma or a colon instead of a semicolon when introducing a quotation.

Incorrect Pauline Johnson's poem "Canadian Born" opens with these lines**;** "We first saw light in Canada, the land beloved of God / We are the pulse of Canada, its marrow and its blood."

Correct Pauline Johnson's poem "Canadian Born" opens with these lines**:** "We first saw light in Canada, the land beloved of God / We are the pulse of Canada, its marrow and its blood."

Do not use a semicolon to introduce lists

Incorrect William Shakespeare wrote four romance plays at the end of his career**;** *The Tempest*, *The Winter's Tale*, *Cymbeline*, and *Pericles*.

Correct William Shakespeare wrote four romance plays at the end of his career**:** *The Tempest*, *The Winter's Tale*, *Cymbeline*, and *Pericles*.

43b Semicolons Together with Commas

When an item in a series already includes a comma, adding more commas to separate it from the other items will only confuse the reader. Use semicolons instead of commas between items in a series that have internal punctuation.

Confusing The church's design competition drew entries from as far away as Gothenburg**,** Sweden**,** Caracas**,** Venezuela**,** and Athens**,** Greece.

Clearer The church's design competition drew entries from as far away as Gothenburg, Sweden**;** Caracas, Venezuela**;** and Athens, Greece.

43c Colons in Sentences

Like semicolons, colons can join two closely related main clauses (complete sentences). Colons indicate that what follows will explain or expand on what comes before the colon. Use a colon in cases where the second main clause interprets or sums up the first.

> Because most victims of bird flu catch the virus from animals, it is not likely to cause a pandemic in its present form**:** the influenza virus would have to mutate so that it could be easily transmitted from person to person for a pandemic to be possible.

You may choose to capitalize the first word of the main clause following the colon or to leave it lowercase. Either is correct as long as you are consistent throughout your text.

Colons linking main clauses with appositives

A colon calls attention to an appositive, a noun, or a noun phrase that renames the noun preceding it. If you're not certain whether a colon would be appropriate, put *namely* in its place. If *namely* makes sense when you read the main clause followed by the appositive, you probably need to insert a colon instead of a comma. Remember, the clause that precedes the colon must be a complete sentence.

> I know the perfect person for the job, **namely** me.

The sentence makes sense with *namely* placed before the appositive. Thus, a colon is appropriate.

> I know the perfect person for the job**:** me.

Never capitalize a word following a colon unless the word starts a complete sentence or is normally capitalized (see Chapter 50).

Colons joining main clauses with quotations

Use a colon to link a main clause and a quotation that interprets or sums up the clause. Be careful not to use a colon to link a phrase with a quotation.

> **Incorrect: noun phrase–colon–quotation**
>
> Jacques Cartier's first encounter with the land that would be Canada**:** "I am rather inclined," he confessed, "to believe that this is the land God gave to Cain."

> **Correct: main clause–colon–quotation**
>
> Jacques Cartier's first encounter with the land that would be Canada was not promising**:** "I am rather inclined," he confessed, "to believe that this is the land God gave to Cain."

Also, a colon is often used after a main clause to introduce an indented block quotation (see Section 24d).

WRITING SMART

Punctuation following quotations

Writing often requires quoting someone else's words. Use the correct sequence of punctuation marks when sharing a quotation with readers.

Place semicolons and colons outside quotation marks

Commas and periods that come after a quotation sit inside the quotation marks. The rule is different, however, for semicolons and colons: They sit outside the quotation marks. Because commas and periods always appear inside the quotation marks, semicolons and colons may seem incorrectly placed if you don't know that they follow a different rule.

Put commas and periods inside quotation marks
"The length of a film," said Alfred Hitchcock, "should be directly related to the endurance of the human bladder."

Put semicolons outside quotation marks
June Callwood wrote, "The beaver, which has come to represent Canada as the eagle does the United States and the lion Britain, is a flat-tailed, slow-witted, toothy rodent known to bite off its own testicles or to stand under its own falling trees"; her point underscores the irony in our choice of national symbol.

Put colons outside quotation marks
"I believe, absolutely, that if you do not break out in that sweat of fear when you write, then you have not gone far enough": Dorothy Allison reassures would-be writers that they can begin on guts alone.

Remember: Little dogs (commas, periods) sleep in the house. Big dogs (semicolons, colons) sleep outside.

For more on using quotation marks correctly, see Chapter 47.

43d Colons with Lists

Use a colon to join a main clause to a list. The main clauses in these cases sometimes include the phrases *the following* or *as follows*. Remember that a colon cannot join a phrase or an incomplete clause to a list.

Incorrect: noun phrase–colon–list

Three posters decorating Juan's apartment**:** an Our Lady Peace concert poster, a view of Grouse Mountain, and a Diego Rivera mural.

Correct: main clause–colon–list

Juan bought three posters to decorate his apartment**:** an Our Lady Peace concert poster, a view of Grouse Mountain, and a Diego Rivera mural.

Incorrect: incomplete clause–colon–list

Volunteers aid biologists in**:** erosion control, trail maintenance, tree planting, and cleanup.

Correct: main clause without a colon

Volunteers aid biologists in erosion control, trail maintenance, tree planting, and cleanup.

COMMON ERRORS

Colons misused with lists

Some writers think that any time they introduce a list, they should insert a colon. Colons are used correctly only when a complete sentence precedes the colon.

Incorrect Jessica's entire wardrobe for her trip to Cancun included**:** two swimsuits, one pair of shorts, two T-shirts, a party dress, and a pair of sandals.

Correct Jessica's entire wardrobe for her trip to Cancun included two swimsuits, one pair of shorts, two T-shirts, a party dress, and a pair of sandals.

Correct Jessica jotted down what she would need for her trip**:** two swimsuits, one pair of shorts, two T-shirts, a party dress, and a pair of sandals.

Remember: A colon should be placed only after a clause that can stand by itself as a sentence.

44 Hyphens

QUICK*TAKE*

- **When do you hyphenate compound modifiers?** (see below)
  Incorrect: His apartment was on the second-storey.
  Correct: He had a second-storey apartment.
- **Which compound nouns are hyphenated?** (see p. 512)
  Incorrect: self awareness, nation state
  Correct: self-awareness, nation-state
- **How can hyphens help with clarity?** (see p. 514)
  Less clear: He tried to recreate the atmosphere of Yorkville during the 1960s.
  Clearer: He tried to re-create the atmosphere of Yorkville during the 1960s.

Hyphens (-) are frequently confused with dashes (—), which are similar but longer. Dashes are used to separate phrases. Hyphens are used to join words.

 Hyphens with Compound Modifiers

When to hyphenate

Hyphenate a compound modifier that precedes a noun.

When a compound modifier precedes a noun, you should usually hyphenate the modifier. A compound modifier consists of words that join together as a unit to modify a noun. Since the first word modifies the second, compound modifiers will not make sense if the word order is reversed.

Hyphenate a phrase when it is used as a modifier that precedes a noun.

middle-class values	self-fulfilling prophecy
best-before date	soft-hearted friend
well-known musician	ill-mannered child
out-of-body experience	step-by-step instructions
all-you-can-eat buffet	all-or-nothing payoff
devil-may-care attitude	over-the-counter drug

Hyphenate the prefixes *pro-*, *anti-*, *post-*, *pre-*, *neo-*, and *mid-* before proper nouns.

pro-Catholic sentiment
neo-Nazi racism
pre-Columbian art
mid-Atlantic states
anti-NAFTA protests
post-Freudian theory

Hyphenate a compound modifier with a number when it precedes a noun.

eighteenth-century drama
tenth-grade class
one-way street
47-minute swim

When not to hyphenate

Do not hyphenate a compound modifier that follows a noun.

Avoid using hyphens in compound modifiers when they come after the noun.

The instructor's approach is student centred.

Among country music fans George Strait is well known.

Do not hyphenate compound modifiers when the first word is *very* or ends in *ly*.

newly recorded data
freshly painted bench
very cold day
very jolly baby

Do not hyphenate chemical terms.

calcium chloride base
hydrochloric acid solution

Do not hyphenate foreign terms used as adjectives.

a priori decision
post hoc fallacy

44b Hyphens with Compound Nouns

A compound noun is made up of two or more words that work together to form one noun. You cannot change the order of words in a compound noun or remove a word without altering the noun's meaning. No universal rule guides the use of hyphens with compound nouns; the best way to determine whether a compound noun is hyphenated is to check the dictionary.

Some hyphenated compound nouns

T-shirt	one-bagger	time-out
sister-in-law	heart-to-heart	great-grandfather
play-by-play	speed-reading	run-through

Some compound nouns that are not hyphenated

picture window	oneself	time zone
hedgehog	heartland	baby boom
open house	speed of light	playbook

While there's no set rule for all cases of compound nouns, some prefixes and suffixes that commonly require hyphens are *ex-*, *all-*, *self-*, and *-elect.*

All-American	president-elect
self-conscious	ex-employee

COMMON ERRORS

Hyphens with numbers

Whole numbers between twenty-one and ninety-nine are hyphenated when they are written as words.

Incorrect twentysix
Correct twenty-six

Incorrect sixteen-hundred
Correct sixteen hundred

Incorrect fiftytwo
Correct fifty-two

Also, hyphens connect the numerators and denominators in most fractions.

The glass is one-half full.

A few fractions used as nouns, especially fractions of time, distance, and area, do not take hyphens.

A half century passed before the mistake was uncovered.

Remember: Numbers between twenty-one and ninety-nine and most fractions are hyphenated when written as words.

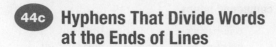

44c Hyphens That Divide Words at the Ends of Lines

A hyphen can show that a word is completed on the next line. Hyphens divide words only between syllables.

> The Jackson family waited out the tor-
> nado in their storm cellar.

Unless you have a special reason for dividing words at the ends of lines, you should avoid doing it. One special situation might be the need to fit as much text as possible on each line of the narrow columns in a newsletter format. Another might be the need to fit text inside the cells of a table.

WRITING SMART

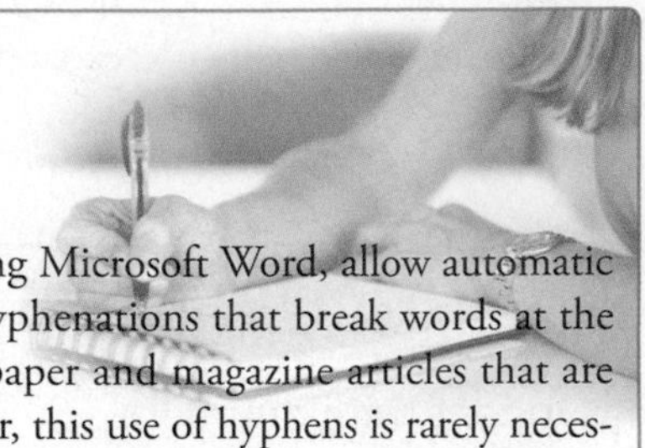

Automatic hyphenation

Word processing programs, including Microsoft Word, allow automatic hyphenation of your document. Hyphenations that break words at the ends of lines are common in newspaper and magazine articles that are printed in narrow columns. However, this use of hyphens is rarely necessary in academic papers. Unless you are creating a brochure or other document with narrow columns, leave the automatic hyphenation turned off.

44d Hyphens for Clarity

Certain words, often ones with the prefixes *anti-*, *re-*, and *pre-*, can be confusing without hyphens. Adding hyphens to such words will show the reader where to pause to pronounce them correctly.

> The courts are in much need of **repair**.

> The doubles final will **re-pair** the sister team of Venus and Serena Williams.

> **Reform** in court procedure is necessary to bring cases quickly to trial.

> The thunderclouds **re-formed** after the hard rain, threatening another deluge.

45 Dashes and Parentheses

QUICK*TAKE*

- **When do you use dashes and parentheses rather than commas to set off information?** (see below)
  Regular emphasis: Marie set her pie, a lemon meringue, on the table.
  More emphasis: Mother scowled (after telling Marie in advance that she hated meringue).
  Greatest emphasis: Mother—who had planned this party for months—was about to lose her temper.
- **How do you type a dash?** (see p. 520)
  Incorrect: We can get home unless - heaven forbid! - I lose my credit card.
  Correct: We can get home unless—heaven forbid!—I lose my credit card.

 45a Dashes and Parentheses Versus Commas

Like commas, parentheses and dashes enclose material that adds, explains, or digresses. However, the three punctuation marks are not interchangeable. The mark you choose depends on how much emphasis you want to place on the material. Dashes indicate the most emphasis. Parentheses offer somewhat less, and commas offer less still.

Commas indicate a moderate level of emphasis

Bill covered the new tattoo on his bicep, a pouncing tiger, because he thought it might upset our mother.

Parentheses lend a greater level of emphasis

I'm afraid to go bungee jumping (though my brother tells me it's less frightening than a roller coaster).

Dashes indicate the highest level of emphasis and, sometimes, surprise and drama

Christina felt as though she had been punched in the gut; she could hardly believe the stranger at her door was really who he claimed to be—the brother she hadn't seen in 20 years.

45b Dashes and Parentheses to Set Off Information

Dashes and parentheses call attention to groups of words. In effect, they tell the reader that a group of words is not part of the main clause and should be given extra attention. Compare the following sentences:

> When Shanele's old college roommate, Traci, picked her up at the airport in a new car, a Porsche Boxster S convertible, she knew that Traci's finances had changed for the better.

> When Shanele's old college roommate, Traci, picked her up at the airport in a new car (a Porsche Boxster S convertible), she knew that Traci's finances had changed for the better.

> When Shanele's old college roommate, Traci, picked her up at the airport in a new car—a Porsche Boxster S convertible—she knew that Traci's finances had changed for the better.

The Porsche Boxster S convertible is weighted differently in these three sentences because of punctuation. In the first, it is the name of the car. But in the third, it's as if an exclamation point were added—a Porsche Boxster S convertible!

The lesson here is simple enough. If you want to make an element stand out, especially in the middle of a sentence, use parentheses or dashes instead of commas.

Dashes with final elements

A dash is often used to set off an element at the end of a sentence that offers significant comments about the main clause. This construction is a favourite of newscasters, who typically pause for a long moment where the dash would be inserted in writing.

> The *Titanic* sank just before midnight on April 14, 1912, at a cost of over 1500 lives—a tragedy that could have been prevented easily by reducing speed in dangerous waters, providing adequate lifeboat space, and maintaining a full-time radio watch.

Dashes can also anticipate a shift in tone at the end of a sentence.

> A full-sized SUV can take you wherever you want to go in style—if your idea of style is a gas-guzzling tank.

Parentheses with additional information

Parentheses are more often used for identifying information, afterthoughts or asides, examples, and clarifications. You can place full sentences, fragments, or brief terms within parentheses.

Some argue that ethanol (the pet solution of politicians for achieving energy independence) requires more energy to produce and ship than it produces.

COMMON ERRORS

Do not use dashes as periods

Do not use dashes to separate two main clauses (clauses that can stand as complete sentences). Use dashes to separate main clauses from subordinate clauses and phrases when you want to emphasize the subordinate clause or phrase.

Incorrect: main clause–dash–main clause

I was one of the few women in my computer science classes—most of the students majoring in computer science at that time were men.

Correct: main clause–dash–phrase

I was one of the few women in computer science—a field then dominated by men.

Remember: Dashes are not periods and should not be used as periods.

45c Other Punctuation with Parentheses

Parentheses with numbers or letters that order items in a series

Parentheses around letters or numbers that order a series within a sentence make the list easier to read.

Angela Creider's recipe for becoming a great novelist is to (1) set aside an hour during the morning to write, (2) read what you've written out loud, (3) revise your prose, and (4) repeat every morning for the next 30 years.

Parentheses with abbreviations

Abbreviations made from the first letters of words are often used in place of the unwieldy names of institutions, departments, organizations, or terms. In order to show the reader what the abbreviation stands for, the first time it appears in a text the writer must state the complete name, followed by the abbreviation in parentheses.

> The University of California, Santa Cruz (UCSC) supports its mascot, the banana slug, with pride and a sense of humour. And although it sounds strange to outsiders, UCSC students are even referred to as "the banana slugs."

Parentheses with in-text citations

The various documentation styles require that information quoted, paraphrased, or summarized from an outside source be indicated with a research citation. In several of the styles, including MLA (see Chapter 26) and APA (see Chapter 27), the citation is enclosed in parentheses.

> E. B. White's advice on writing style is to use your natural voice (Strunk and White 70).

COMMON ERRORS

Using periods, commas, colons, and semicolons with parentheses

When an entire sentence is enclosed in parentheses, place the period before the closing parenthesis.

Incorrect Our fear of sharks, heightened by movies such as *Jaws,* is vastly out of proportion with the minor threat sharks actually pose. (Dying from a dog attack, in fact, is much more likely than dying from a shark attack).

Correct Our fear of sharks, heightened by movies such as *Jaws,* is vastly out of proportion with the minor threat sharks actually pose. (Dying from a dog attack, in fact, is much more likely than dying from a shark attack.)

When the material in parentheses is part of the sentence and the parentheses fall at the end of the sentence, place the period outside the closing parenthesis.

Incorrect Reports of sharks attacking people are rare (much rarer than dog attacks.)

Correct Reports of sharks attacking people are rare (much rarer than dog attacks).

COMMON ERRORS *(Continued)*

Place commas, colons, and semicolons after the closing parenthesis.

Incorrect Although newspaper editors generally prize concise letters to the editor, (the shorter the better) they will occasionally print longer letters that are unusually eloquent.

Correct Although newspaper editors generally prize concise letters to the editor (the shorter the better), they will occasionally print longer letters that are unusually eloquent.

Remember: When an entire sentence is enclosed in parentheses, place the period inside the closing parenthesis; otherwise, put the punctuation outside the closing parenthesis.

45d Other Punctuation with Dashes

Dashes with a series of items

Dashes can set off a series. They are especially appropriate when the series comes in the middle of a sentence or when the series simply elaborates on what comes before it without changing the essential meaning of the sentence. Normally commas enclose non-essential clauses; however, placing commas around items separated by commas would confuse readers about where the list begins and ends.

> Rookie Luke Scott became the first player in major league baseball history to hit for the reverse cycle—a home run, a triple, a double, and a single in that order—in last night's game against the Diamondbacks.

Dashes with interrupted speech

Dashes also indicate that a speaker has broken off in the middle of a statement.

> "Why did everybody get so quiet all of a—" Silvia stopped in her tracks when she noticed that the customer had a pistol pointed at the clerk.

COMMON ERRORS

The art of typing a dash

Although dashes and hyphens look similar, they are actually different marks. The distinction is small but important because dashes and hyphens serve different purposes. A dash is a line twice as long as a hyphen. Most word processors will create a dash automatically when you type two hyphens together. Or you can type a special character to make a dash. Your manual will tell you which keys to press to make a dash.

Do not leave a space between a dash or a hyphen and the words that come before and after them. Likewise, if you are using two hyphens to indicate a dash, do not leave a space between the hyphens.

Incorrect A well - timed effort at conserving water may prevent long - term damage to drought - stricken farms -- if it's not already too late.

Correct A well-timed effort at conserving water may prevent long-term damage to drought-stricken farms—if it's not already too late.

Remember: Do not put spaces before or after hyphens and dashes.

46 Apostrophes

QUICK*TAKE*

- **How do you use apostrophes to show possession?** (see below)
  Jimmy's collar, alumni's donations, states' rights, passersby's glance, Jim and Victoria's office, Sanjay's and Cho's performances *BUT* Aristophanes's plays, Moses's death
- **How do you use apostrophes to show omitted letters and numbers?** (see p. 522)
  No omissions: Do not tease me for liking 1970s rock and roll.
  Omissions: Don't tease me for liking '70s rock'n'roll.
- **Do you use apostrophes to make nouns plural?** (**NO**, see p. 523)
  Incorrect: Her three goal's registered her first hat trick.
  Correct: Her three goals registered her first hat trick.

46a Possessives

Nouns and indefinite pronouns (e.g., *everyone, anyone*) that indicate possession or ownership are in the *possessive case*. The possessive case is marked by attaching an apostrophe and an *s* or an apostrophe only to the end of a word.

Singular nouns and indefinite pronouns

For singular nouns and indefinite pronouns, add an apostrophe plus *s*: *'s*. Even singular nouns that end in *s* usually follow this principle.

Iris**'s** coat

everyone**'s** favourite

a woman**'s** choice

today**'s** news

the team**'s** equipment

There are a few exceptions to adding *'s* for singular nouns:

- **Awkward pronunciations:** *Herodotus' travels, Jesus' sermons*
- **Official names of certain places, institutions, companies:** *Zellers, Loblaws, Staples, Shoppers Drug Mart, KidsAbility Centre for Child Development*. Note, however, that many companies do include the apostrophe: *Denny***'s** *Restaurant, McDonald***'s**, *Wendy***'s** *Old Fashioned Hamburgers*.

Plural nouns

For plural nouns that do not end in *s*, add an apostrophe plus *s*: *'s*.

women**'s** rights

media**'s** responsibility

children**'s** section

For plural nouns that end in *s*, add only an apostrophe at the end.

dancer**s'** costumes

lawyer**s'** briefs

the Trudeau**s'** legacy

Compound nouns

For compound nouns, add an apostrophe plus *s* to the last word: *'s*.

my mother-in-law**'s** house

the premier of Nova Scotia**'s** speech

Two or more nouns

For joint possession, add an apostrophe plus *s* to the final noun: *'s*.

> mother and dad**'s** yard
>
> Lakes, Trails, and Travel**'s** spring sale

When people possess or own things separately, add an apostrophe plus *s* to each noun: *'s*.

> Roberto**'s** and Edward**'s** views are totally opposed.
>
> Dominique**'s**, Sally**'s**, and Vinatha**'s** cars all need new tires.

COMMON ERRORS

Possessive forms of personal pronouns never take the apostrophe

Incorrect *her's, it's, our's, your's, their's*

The bird sang in **it's** cage.

Correct *hers, its, ours, yours, theirs*

The bird sang in **its** cage.

Remember: It's = It is

46b Contractions and Omitted Letters

In speech we often leave out sounds and syllables of familiar words. In writing these omissions are noted with apostrophes.

Contractions

Contractions combine two words into one, using the apostrophe to mark what is left out.

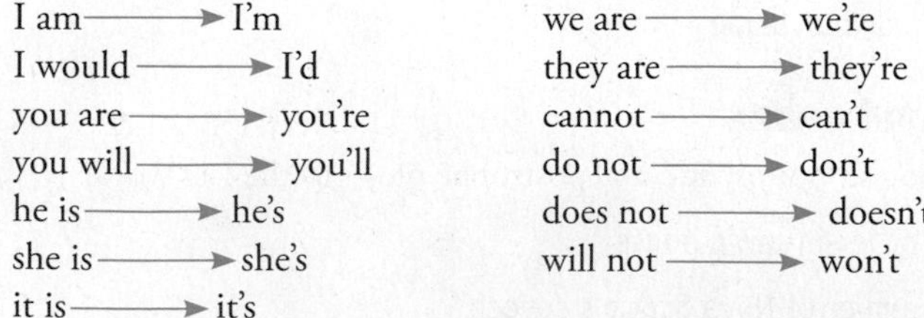

I am → I'm
I would → I'd
you are → you're
you will → you'll
he is → he's
she is → she's
it is → it's
we are → we're
they are → they're
cannot → can't
do not → don't
does not → doesn't
will not → won't

Omissions

Using apostrophes to signal omitted letters is a way of approximating speech in writing. They can make your writing look informal and slangy, but overuse can become annoying in a hurry.

rock and roll → rock'n'roll
the 1960s → the '60s
neighbourhood → 'hood

46c Plurals of Letters, Symbols, and Words Referred to as Words

When to use apostrophes to make plurals

The trend is away from using apostrophes to form plurals of letters, symbols, and words referred to as words. In a few cases adding the apostrophe and *s* is still used, as in this old saying.

Mind your p's and q's.

Words used as words are italicized and their plural is formed by adding an *s* not in italics, not an apostrophe and *s*.

Take a few of the ***and*s** out of your writing.

Words in quotation marks, however, typically use an apostrophe and *s*.

She had too many "probably's" in her letter for me to be confident that the remodelling will be finished on schedule.

WRITING SMART

Apostrophes are not used with the plurals of numbers and acronyms

The style manuals of the Modern Language Association (MLA) and the American Psychological Association (APA) do not use apostrophes for indicating plurals of numbers and acronyms. They add only *s*.

1890**s**	four CEO**s**	several DVD**s**
eight**s**	these URL**s**	the images are all JPEG**s**

When not to use apostrophes to make plurals

Do not use an apostrophe to make family names plural.

Incorrect You've heard of keeping up with the Jones's.

Correct You've heard of keeping up with the Joneses.

COMMON ERRORS

Do not use an apostrophe to make a noun plural

Incorrect The two government's agreed to meet.
Correct The two governments agreed to meet.

Incorrect The video game console's of the past were one-dimensional.
Correct The video game consoles of the past were one-dimensional.

Remember: Add only *s* = plural
Add apostrophe plus *s* = possessive

47 Quotation Marks

QUICK*TAKE*

- **How do you incorporate words from sources?** (see below)
  Direct quotation: Warren Zevon's final piece of advice was to "enjoy every sandwich."
  Paraphrase: Warren Zevon's final piece of advice was to enjoy it all, even the small things.
- **How do you use periods and commas with quotation marks?** (see p. 529)
  Incorrect: Groucho Marx once said, "I was married by a judge; I should have had a jury".
  Correct: Groucho Marx once said, "I was married by a judge; I should have had a jury."
  Correct: Groucho Marx once said, "I was married by a judge; I should have had a jury" (Kanfer 45).
- **How do you use colons and semicolons with quotation marks?** (see p. 529)
  Incorrect: As Flannery O'Connor wrote in 1955, "The truth does not change according to our ability to stomach it;" many today would do well to heed these words.
  Correct: As Flannery O'Connor wrote in 1955, "The truth does not change according to our ability to stomach it"; many today would do well to heed these words.

47a Direct Quotations

Use quotation marks to enclose direct quotations

Enclose direct quotations—someone else's words repeated verbatim—in quotation marks.

> Anne Lamott advises writers to look at everything with compassion, even something as seemingly inconsequential as a chipmunk: "I don't want to sound too Cosmica Rama here, but in those moments, you see that you and the chipmunk are alike, are part of a whole" (98).

Even brief direct quotations, such as the repetition of someone else's original term or turn of phrase, require quotation marks.

> Though she fears appearing overly "Cosmica Rama," Anne Lamott argues that with compassion, writers' observations can be spiritually transcendent (98).

Do not use quotation marks with indirect quotations

Do not enclose an indirect quotation—a paraphrase of someone else's words—in quotation marks. However, do remember that you need to cite your source not only when you quote directly but also when you paraphrase or borrow ideas.

> Anne Lamott encourages writers to become compassionate observers who ultimately see themselves as equals to everything else, even something as seemingly inconsequential as a chipmunk (98).

Do not use quotation marks with block quotations

When a quotation is long enough to be set off as a block quotation, do not use quotation marks. MLA style defines long quotations as more than four lines of prose or three lines of poetry. APA style defines a long quotation as one of more than 40 words. In the following example, notice that the long quotation is indented and quotation marks are omitted. Also notice that the parenthetical citation for a long quotation comes after the period.

> Complaints about maintenance in the dorms have been on the rise ever since the physical plant reorganized its crews into teams in August. One student's experience is typical:
>
> > When our ceiling started dripping, my roommate and I went to our resident director right away to file an emergency maintenance request. Apparently the physical plant felt that "emergency" meant they could get around to it in a week or two. By the fourth day without any word from a maintenance person, the ceiling tiles began to fall and puddles began to pool on our carpet. (Trillo)
>
> The physical plant could have avoided expensive ceiling tile and carpet repairs if it had responded to the student's request promptly.

Set off quotations in dialogue

Dialogue is traditionally enclosed within quotation marks. Begin a new paragraph with each change of speaker.

> Before Jim and Lester walk 50 metres on a faint animal trail, they hear the brush rattle in front of them and the unmistakable snorting of a rhino. Jim crouches and looks through the brush. Lester watches Jim, wondering why he isn't retreating, then scrambles up a nearby tree. "Come on back," he yells to Jim, who is now out of sight.
>
> After a few minutes Jim reappears. "I got right next to it but I never did get a good look. I was so close I could even smell it."
>
> "The other one is still out there in the grass. And I heard a third one behind us toward the river."
>
> "We better get out of here before it gets dark. Are you going to spend the night in the tree?"
>
> "I'm thinking about it."

47b Titles of Short Works

While the titles of longer works such as books, magazines, and newspapers are italicized, titles of shorter works should be set off with quotation marks. Use quotation marks with the following kinds of titles:

Short stories	"Boys and Girls," by Alice Munro
Magazine articles	"Born Again in Syria," by Michael Petrou
Newspaper articles	"Stamp Auction Revives Canada's Postal Scandal," by Randy Boswell
Short poems	"We Real Cool," by Gwendolyn Brooks
Essays	"Self-Reliance," by Ralph Waldo Emerson
Songs	"Sk8er Boi," by Avril Lavigne
Speeches, lectures, and sermons	"Zero to Web Page in Sixty Minutes," by Jean Lavre
Chapters	"Cigs," *Souvenir of Canada*, by Douglas Coupland
Short films	"Bed Head," by Robert Rodriguez
Episodes of television shows	"Treehouse of Horror," an episode of *The Simpsons*
Episodes of radio shows	"Building a Bladder," an episode of *Quirks and Quarks*

The exception. Don't put the title of your own paper in quotation marks. If the title of another short work appears within the title of your paper, retain the quotation marks around the short work. The title of a paper about Alice Munro, for instance, might read as follows:

> Gender Rules in Alice Munro's "Boys and Girls"

47c Other Uses of Quotation Marks

Quotation marks to indicate the novel use of a word

Quotation marks around a term can indicate that the writer is using the term in a novel way, often with skepticism, irony, or sarcasm. The quotation marks indicate that the writer is questioning the term's conventional definition. Notice the way quotation marks indicate skepticism about the conventional definition of *savages* in the following passage.

> In the early days of England's empire building, it wasn't unusual to hear English anthropologists say that conquered native people were savages. Yet if we measure civilization by peacefulness and compassion for fellow humans, those "savages" were really much more civilized than the British.

Quotation marks to indicate that a word is being used as a word

Italics are usually used to indicate that a word is being used as a word, rather than standing for its conventional meaning. However, quotation marks are correct in these cases as well.

> Beginning writers sometimes confuse "their," "they're," and "there."

47d Misuses of Quotation Marks

Do not use quotation marks for emphasis

It's becoming more and more common to see quotation marks used to emphasize a word or phrase. Resist the temptation in your own writing; it's an incorrect usage. In fact, because quotation marks indicate that a writer is using a term with skepticism or irony, adding quotation marks for emphasis will highlight unintended connotations of the term.

> **Incorrect** "fresh" seafood

By using quotation marks here, the writer seems to call into question whether the seafood is really fresh.

Correct fresh seafood

Incorrect Enjoy our "live" music every Saturday night.

Again, the quotation marks unintentionally indicate that the writer is skeptical that the music is live.

Correct Enjoy our live music every Saturday night.

You have better ways of creating emphasis using your word processing program: **boldfacing**, underlining, *italicizing*, and **using colour**.

Do not use quotation marks around indirect quotations or paraphrases

Incorrect The airport security guard announced that "all bags will be searched and then apologized for the inconvenience to the passengers."

Correct The airport security guard announced, "All bags will be searched. I apologize for the inconvenience." [direct quotation]

Correct The airport security guard announced that all bags would be searched and then apologized for the inconvenience to the passengers. [indirect quotation]

Avoid using quotation marks to acknowledge the use of a cliché

You may have seen other writers enclose clichés in quotation marks. Avoid doing this; in fact, avoid using clichés at all. Clichés are worn-out phrases; fresh words engage readers more.

Incorrect To avoid "letting the cat out of the bag" about forthcoming products, most large companies employ security experts trained in preventing commercial espionage.

Correct but stale To avoid letting the cat out of the bag about forthcoming products, most large companies employ security experts trained in preventing commercial espionage.

Correct and effective To prevent their savvy competitors from peeking at forthcoming products, most large companies employ security experts trained in preventing commercial espionage.

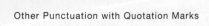

 Other Punctuation with Quotation Marks

The rules for placing punctuation with quotation marks fall into three general categories.

Periods and commas with quotation marks

Place periods and commas inside closing quotation marks.

Incorrect "The smartest people", Dr. Geisler pointed out, "tell themselves the most convincing rationalizations".

Correct "The smartest people," Dr. Geisler pointed out, "tell themselves the most convincing rationalizations."

Exceptions occur when a parenthetical citation follows a short quotation. In MLA and APA documentation styles, the period follows the closing parenthesis.

Incorrect "The smartest people," Dr. Geisler pointed out, "tell themselves the most convincing rationalizations." (52)

Correct "The smartest people," Dr. Geisler pointed out, "tell themselves the most convincing rationalizations" (52).

Colons and semicolons with quotation marks

Place colons and semicolons outside closing quotation marks.

Incorrect "From Stettin in the Baltic to Trieste in the Adriatic, an iron curtain has descended across the Continent;" Churchill's statement rang through Cold War politics for the next 50 years.

Correct "From Stettin in the Baltic to Trieste in the Adriatic, an iron curtain has descended across the Continent"; Churchill's statement rang through Cold War politics for the next 50 years.

Exclamation points, question marks, and dashes with quotation marks

When an exclamation point, question mark, or dash belongs to the original quotation, place it inside the closing quotation mark. When it applies to the entire sentence, place it outside the closing quotation mark.

In the original quotation

"Are we there yet?" came the whine from the back seat.

Applied to the entire sentence

Did the driver in the front seat respond, "Not even close"?

COMMON ERRORS

Quotations within quotations

Single quotation marks are used to indicate a quotation within a quotation. In the following example single quotation marks clarify who is speaking. The rules for placing punctuation with single quotation marks are the same as the rules for placing punctuation with double quotation marks.

Incorrect When he showed the report to Paul Probius, Michener reported that Probius "took vigorous exception to the sentence "He wanted to close down the university," insisting that we add the clarifying phrase "as it then existed"" (Michener 145).

Correct When he showed the report to Paul Probius, Michener reported that Probius "took vigorous exception to the sentence 'He wanted to close down the university,' insisting that we add the clarifying phrase 'as it then existed'" (Michener 145).

Remember: Single quotation marks are used for quotations within quotations.

48 Other Punctuation Marks

QUICK*TAKE*

- **When do you use question marks?** (see p. 533)
  Incorrect: A group of artists and computer hackers wondered if there was a way to draw with the eyes? [a period should be used here]
  Correct: A group of artists and computer hackers wondered, "Is there a way to draw with the eyes?"
- **When do you use brackets?** (see p. 534)
  Incorrect: Describing the Battle of Tarawa, World War II photographer Norman Hatch said "they (the Japanese) were just mown down."
  Correct: Describing the Battle of Tarawa, World War II photographer Norman Hatch said "they [the Japanese] were just mown down."
- **When do you use ellipses?** (see p. 575)
  Full quotation: Author Seth Grahame-Smith explains how he equates slaveholders with vampires in *Abraham Lincoln: Vampire Hunter*: "Both creatures, basically slaveholders and vampires, steal lives—take the blood of others—to enrich themselves."
  Shortened quotation: Author Seth Grahame-Smith explains how he equates slaveholders with vampires in *Abraham Lincoln: Vampire Hunter*: "Both creatures . . . steal lives . . . to enrich themselves."

48a Periods

Periods at the ends of sentences

Place a period at the end of a complete sentence if it is not a direct question or an exclamatory statement. As the term suggests, a direct question asks a question outright. Indirect questions, on the other hand, report the asking of a question.

Direct question Hunters who participate in the annual seal hunt wonder, "Why do animal rights activists value the welfare of baby seals over the welfare of my children?"

Indirect question Hunters who participate in the annual seal hunt wonder why animal activists value the welfare of baby seals over the welfare of the hunters' children.

Periods with quotation marks and parentheses

When a quotation falls at the end of a sentence, place the period inside the closing quotation marks.

> Although he devoted decades to a wide range of artistic and political projects, Allen Ginsberg is best known as the author of the poem "Howl."

When a parenthetical phrase falls at the end of a sentence, place the period outside the closing parenthesis.

> Mrs. Chen, a grandmother in Kenora, is training for her first 10K race (a fundraiser for the local food bank).

When parentheses enclose a whole sentence, place the period inside the closing parenthesis.

> Computer science researchers have been able to identify people in anonymous databases, including Netflix's, by collecting information on services such as Facebook, Flickr, and Twitter. (Even more unsettling to privacy advocates, researchers have been able to predict individual social security numbers by using publicly available information.)

Periods with abbreviations

Many abbreviations require periods; however, there are few set rules. Use the dictionary to check how to punctuate abbreviations on a case-by-case basis.

Sir John A. Macdonald	Mr.	misc.	Wed.
a.m.	p.m.	a.s.a.p.	etc.

The rules for punctuating two types of abbreviations do remain consistent: Postal abbreviations for provinces and states and most abbreviations for organizations do not require periods.

ON for Ontario	CMHA for Canadian Mental Health Association
CA for California	JTF-2 for Joint Task Force 2

When an abbreviation with a period falls at the end of a sentence, do not add a second period to conclude the sentence.

Incorrect Her flight arrives at 6:22 p.m..

Correct Her flight arrives at 6:22 p.m.

Periods in citations of poetry and plays

Use a period to separate the components of the following kinds of literary citations.

A poem divided into sections such as books or cantos

book.lines *The Inferno* 27.79–84

A prose play

act.scene *Beyond Therapy* 1.4

A verse play

act.scene.lines *Twelfth Night* 3.4.194–98

Periods as decimal points

Decimal points are periods that separate integers from tenths, hundredths, and so on.

99.98% pure silver	37.6° Celsius
on sale for $399.97	2.6-litre engine

Since large numbers with long strings of zeros can be difficult to read accurately, writers sometimes shorten them by using decimal points. Notice how the decimal points make the second sentence easier to read than the first.

A letter to the editor pointed out that while the Canadian government had contributed **US$1 600 000 000** toward building the U.S. Joint Strike Fighter, Canadian companies had received only **$1 300 000 000** in contracts, leaving Canadian taxpayers to make up the shortfall.

A letter to the editor pointed out that while the Canadian government had contributed **US$1.6 billion** toward building the U.S. Joint Strike Fighter, Canadian companies had received only **$1.3 billion** in contracts, leaving Canadian taxpayers to make up the shortfall.

48b Question Marks

Question marks with direct questions

Place a question mark at the end of a direct question. A direct question is one that the questioner puts to someone outright. In contrast, an indirect question merely reports the asking of a question. Question marks give readers a cue to read the end of the sentence with rising inflection. Read the following sentences aloud. Hear how your inflection rises in the second sentence to convey the direct question.

Indirect question

Desirée asked whether Dan rode his motorcycle without a helmet.

Direct question

Desirée asked, "Does Dan ride his motorcycle without a helmet?"

Question marks with quotations

When a quotation falls at the end of a direct question, place the question mark outside the closing quotation mark.

Did Brian Mulroney really say, "My father dreamed of a better life for his family. I dream of a better life for my country"?

Place the question mark inside the closing quotation mark when only the quoted material is a direct question.

Slowly scientists are beginning to answer the question, "Is cancer a genetic disease?"

When quoting a direct question in the middle of a sentence, place a question mark inside the closing quotation mark and place a period at the end of the sentence.

Market researchers estimate that asking Burger World's customers "Do you want fries with that?" was responsible for a 15% boost in its french fries sales.

Question marks to indicate uncertainty about dates or numbers

Place a question mark in parentheses after a date or number whose accuracy is in question. If the questionable item is already in parentheses, as in the example below, simply add the question mark.

After his escape from slavery, Frederick Douglass (1817?–95) went on to become a great orator and statesman.

48c Exclamation Points

Exclamation points to convey strong emotion

Exclamation points conclude sentences and, like question marks, tell the reader how a sentence should sound. They indicate strong emotion. As with any display of strong emotion, occasional doses can be invigorating, but too many exclamation points quickly become grating. Instead of relying on exclamation points to convey heightened emotion, use strong words and careful phrasing. Use exclamation points sparingly in formal writing; they are rarely appropriate in academic and professional prose.

Exclamation points with emphatic interjections

Exclamation points can convey a sense of urgency with brief interjections. Interjections can be incorporated into sentences or stand on their own.

> Run! They're about to close the doors to the jetway.

Use commas to set off interjections that are not emphatic.

> One study has found that, yes, humans can contract a strain of mad cow disease.

Exclamation points with quotation marks

In quotations, exclamation points follow the same rules as question marks. If a quotation falls at the end of an exclamatory statement, place the exclamation point outside the closing quotation mark.

> The singer forgot the words to "O Canada"!

When quoting an exclamatory statement at the end of a sentence that is not itself exclamatory, place the exclamation point inside the closing quotation mark.

> Jerry thought his car would be washed away in the flood, but Anna jumped into action, declaring, "Not if I can help it!"

When the quotation of an exclamatory statement does not fall at the end of a sentence, place the exclamation point inside the closing quotation mark and place a period at the end of the sentence.

> Someone yelled "Loser!" when the candidate walked on stage.

 48d Brackets

While brackets (sometimes called *square brackets*) look quite similar to parentheses, the two perform different functions. Brackets have a narrow set of uses.

Brackets to provide clarification within quotation marks

Quoted material sometimes requires clarification because it is removed from its context. Adding clarifying material in brackets can allow you to make the quotation clear while still accurately repeating the exact words of your source. In the following example the writer quotes a sentence with the pronoun *they,* which refers to a noun in a previous, unquoted sentence. The material in brackets clarifies to whom the pronoun refers.

> A quick comparison shows that "In the last three years, they [Pauline Johnson Senior Public School students] collected three times as many donations for the local homeless shelter as their peers at Brebeuf."

Brackets within parentheses

Since parentheses within parentheses might confuse readers, use brackets to enclose parenthetical information within a parenthetical phrase.

> My mother drove off (taking her purse [which contained one set of house keys] and her jacket [which contained the other]), leaving me a virtual prisoner, unable to lock the doors and thereby leave the house.

48e Ellipses

Ellipses let a reader know that a portion of a passage is missing. You can use ellipses to keep quotations concise and direct readers' attention to what is important to the point you are making. An ellipsis is a string of three periods with spaces separating the periods. MLA style formerly required square brackets around the three periods. Your instructor may prefer that you use brackets surrounding ellipses when you delete words from quotations.

Ellipses to indicate an omission from a prose quotation

When you quote only a phrase or short clause from a sentence, you usually do not need to use ellipses.

> Mao Zedong first used "let a hundred flowers blossom" in a Beijing speech in 1957.

Except at the beginning of a quotation, indicate omitted words with an ellipsis. Type a space between each ellipsis dot and between the ellipses and the words preceding and following them.

WRITING SMART

Using quotations that contain errors

In scholarly writing you should copy quotations exactly as they appear in your source, but you must also produce a paper free of grammatical and mechanical errors. So how should you handle a source that contains an error? One way is to rephrase the quotation in your own words, crediting your source for the idea. However, if the quotation is so eloquent or effective that you decide to include it despite the error, use *[sic]* (an abbreviation of the Latin *sicut*, meaning *thus*) to indicate that the original source is responsible for the mistake.

Spelling error in original source (*to* instead of *too*)

"One taste tester reported that the Carb Charge energy bar was to dry; she said it had the consistency of sawdust" (Cisco 22).

Rephrased

One of the participants in the taste test likened the Carb Charge energy bar to sawdust because it had so little moisture (Cisco 22).

Quote using [*sic*]

"One taste tester reported that the Carb Charge energy bar was to [*sic*] dry; she said it had the consistency of sawdust" (Cisco 22).

The original source

"The female praying mantis, so named for the way it holds its front legs together as if in prayer, tears off her male partner's head during mating. Remarkably, the headless male will continue the act of mating. This brutal dance is a stark example of the innate evolutionary drive to pass genes on to offspring; the male praying mantis seems to live and die only for this moment."

An ellipsis indicates omitted words

"The female praying mantis . . . tears off her male partner's head during mating."

Note: Retain any punctuation mark falling before the omitted passage if it clarifies the sentence. In this case the comma before the omitted passage would not make the sentence any clearer, so it was not retained.

Ellipses to indicate the omission of a whole line or lines of poetry

Using more than three periods is appropriate in just one instance: to signal the omission of a full line or lines of poetry in the middle of a poetry quotation. In such instances, use an entire line of spaced periods.

Original

My Shakespeare, rise; I will not lodge thee by
Chaucer or Spenser, or bid Beaumont lie
A little further, to make thee a room;
Thou art a monument, without a tomb,
And art alive still, while thy book doth live,
And we have wits to read, and praise to give.

—Ben Jonson, "To the Memory of My Beloved,
the Author, Mr. William Shakespeare" (1623)

Omitted lines of poetry

My Shakespeare, rise;
. . . .
Thou art a monument, without a tomb,
And art alive still, while thy book doth live,
And we have wits to read, and praise to give.

Ellipses to indicate a pause or an interrupted sentence

Ellipses can provide a visual cue that a speaker is taking a long pause or that a speaker has been interrupted.

"And the winner is . . . David Goldstein."

"That ball is going, going, . . . gone!"

"Be careful that you don't spill . . ."

48f Slashes

Slashes to indicate alternative words

Slashes between two words indicate that a choice between them is to be made. When using slashes for this purpose, do not put a space between the slash and words.

Incorrect Maya was such an energetic baby that her exhausted parents wished she had come with an on / off switch.

Correct Maya was such an energetic baby that her exhausted parents wished she had come with an on/off switch.

The following are common instances of the slash used to indicate alternative words:

actor/director	on/off	player/coach
and/or	pass/fail	win/lose
either/or		

Slashes to indicate line breaks in short quotations of verse

Line breaks—where the lines of a poem end—are artistic choices that affect how we understand a poem. Thus it is important to reproduce them accurately when quoting poetry. The task is not difficult in MLA style when the quotation is four or more lines long: Simply indent the quoted lines 10 spaces and mimic the line breaks of the original verse. When you quote three or fewer lines of poetry, however, and must integrate the quotation into the paragraph rather than setting it off in a block, use slashes to indicate line breaks. Type a space on either side of the slash.

> The concluding lines of T. S. Eliot's "Animula" offer a surprising revision of a common prayer. He writes, "Pray for Floret, by the boarhound slain between the yew trees / Pray for us now and at the hour of our birth." Replacing "death," the final word in the prayer, with "birth" at the end of this dark poem connotes an uneasy sense that we find ourselves adrift in a new and unfamiliar world.

Slashes with fractions

Place a slash between the numerator and the denominator in a fraction. Do not put spaces around the slash.

Incorrect 3 / 4

Correct 3/4

Slashes with dates

In informal writing, slashes divide the month, day, and year in a date. A longer format is appropriate for formal academic and professional writing. Omit the slashes, spell out the month, and place a comma after the day.

Informal	Javy, save **1/14/13** on your calendar; I reserved two tickets for the talent show.
Formal	It was a pleasure to meet you during my December 14 interview for Universal Oil's marketing internship. As we discussed, I will not be available for full-time employment until my graduation on **May 12, 2013**. However, I am hopeful that we can work out the part-time arrangement you suggested until that date.

WRITING SMART

Should you use *he/she* or *s/he*?

Using *he* as an indefinite pronoun (a pronoun that refers to a person in general rather than to a specific individual) can seem sexist because it omits women. Some writers use *he/she* or the even shorter *s/he* instead. These solutions are unacceptable to many readers, who consider them ugly. Likewise, many readers consider *he or she* annoying. The best solution is to avoid the *he/she* and *he or she* constructions altogether.

Sexist	Despite popular lore, a hiker bitten by a snake should never suck out the poison. Instead, **he** should tie a tourniquet above the wound to prevent the poison from circulating to vital organs.
inclusive but cumbersome	Despite popular lore, a hiker bitten by a snake should never suck out the poison. Instead, **s/he** should tie a tourniquet above the wound to prevent the poison from circulating to vital organs.
Inclusive but cumbersome	Despite popular lore, a hiker bitten by a snake should never suck out the poison. Instead, **he or she** should tie a tourniquet above the wound to prevent the poison from circulating to vital organs.
Better	Despite popular lore, a hiker bitten by a snake should never suck out the poison. Instead, tying a tourniquet above the wound will prevent the poison from circulating to vital organs.

Chapter 35 offers more tips for avoiding sexist language and awkward indefinite pronouns.

49 Write with Accurate Spelling

QUICK*TAKE*

- **Do spell-checkers catch every spelling mistake?** (see below)
  Incorrect: **Mini** people believe **their** able **two** think **four** themselves, but a few experiments **half** shown that this is often **knot** the case.
  Correct: **Many** people believe **they're** able **to** think **for** themselves, but a few experiments **have** shown that this is often **not** the case.

49a Know the Limitations of Spell-Checkers

Spell-checkers do help you become a better speller. But spell-checkers are quite limited and miss many errors. If you type *ferry tail* for *fairy tale,* your spell-checker will not catch the error.

WRITING SMART

Electronic dictionaries

A number of reputable dictionaries now maintain searchable electronic versions on CD or the internet. If you don't own a dictionary, these websites offer a convenient, inexpensive alternative.

General dictionaries

Dictionary.com	http://dictionary.reference.com
Merriam-Webster Dictionary	www.merriam-webster.com
Oxford English Dictionary	Most research libraries offer access to an online version free to people with borrowing privileges.

How do you look up a word if you have no idea how it is spelled?

Use Google as a quick way to check if you have the right spelling. If your guess is incorrect, Google will suggest the correct spelling. Also, you can find definitions by using the "define:" operator in Google; for example, "define: crepuscular."

49b Distinguish Homonyms

Homonyms are pairs (*your, you're*) and trios (*their, there, they're*) of words that sound alike but have different spellings and meanings. They are tricky words to spell because we don't learn to distinguish them in spoken language, and spell-checkers don't flag incorrectly used homonyms as errors because, according to the spell-checkers' databases, the words are not misspelled. It's easy to type *there* for *their* or *web sight* for *website* and not catch the error when you proofread.

COMMON ERRORS

Commonly misspelled words

Is *accommodate* spelled with one *m* or two? Is *harass* spelled with one *r* or two? You'll find a list of words commonly misspelled at MyWritingLab.com.

Remember: Always check a dictionary when you are unsure of how a word is spelled.

50 Capitalization and Italics

QUICK*TAKE*

- **Which words do you capitalize?** (see below)
  Incorrect: Some canadians are surprised to learn that most south africans are protestants, and while no sect has the majority, there are more pentacostals than any other denomination.
  Correct: Some Canadians are surprised to learn that most South Africans are Protestants, and while no sect has the majority, there are more Pentacostals than any other denomination.
- **Which words do you italicize?** (see p. 545)
  Incorrect: An English major doesn't "have" to read Herman Melville's novel **"Moby-Dick"** or read any of his short stories, such as ***Bartleby, the Scrivener***, but it couldn't hurt.
  Correct: An English major doesn't have to read Herman Melville's novel *Moby-Dick* or read any of his short stories, such as "Bartleby, the Scrivener," but it couldn't hurt.

50a Capital Letters

Capitalize the initial letters of proper nouns and proper adjectives

Capitalize the initial letters of proper nouns (nouns that name particular people, places, and things), including the following:

Names	Pierre Elliott Trudeau	David Johnston
Titles preceding names	Sir Frederick Banting	Queen Elizabeth the Second
Place names	Bay of Fundy	Northwest Territories
Institution names	Ministry of Labour	St. Francis Xavier University
Organization names	World Health Organization	Canadian Cancer Society
Company names	Canadian Tire	JoJo's Café and Bakery
Religions	Protestant	Islam
Languages	Chinese	Swahili
Months	November	March
Days of the week	Monday	Friday
Nationalities	Italian	Puerto Rican
Holidays	Passover	Thanksgiving
Departments	Chemistry Department	Department of English
Historical eras	Enlightenment	Middle Ages
Regions	the Atlantic	Southwestern Ontario
Course names	Eastern Religions	Microbiology
Job title when used with a proper noun		President Benjamin Ladner

Capitalize the initial letters of proper adjectives (adjectives based on the names of people, places, and things).

Afro-Caribbean bookstore	Avogadro's number	Irish music

Avoid unnecessary capitalization

Do not capitalize the names of seasons, academic disciplines (unless they are languages), or job titles used without a proper noun.

Seasons	fall, winter, spring, summer
Academic disciplines (except languages)	chemistry, computer science, psychology, English, French, Japanese
Job titles used without a proper noun	The vice president is on maternity leave.

Capitalize titles of publications

In MLA and CMS styles, when capitalizing titles, capitalize the initial letters of all first and last words and all other words except articles, prepositions, and coordinating conjunctions. Capitalize the initial letter of the first word in the subtitle following a colon.

James and the Giant Peach

The Penelopiad

The Writing on the Wall: An Anthology of Graffiti Art

WRITING SMART

Capitalization in email

some people never press the shift key when typing email. while there are no rules for informal email, long stretches of text with no capitalization are tiresome to read, even in email sent between close friends.

SIMILARLY, SOME PEOPLE TYPE EMAIL IN ALL CAPS, WHICH LIKEWISE IS ANNOYING TO READ OVER LONG STRETCHES. ALSO, SOME PEOPLE FEEL READING ALL CAPS IS LIKE BEING SHOUTED AT.

Capitalization conventions are familiar to readers and thus help make messages easy to read. Using both uppercase and lowercase letters, even in the most informal writing, is a friendly act.

COMMON ERRORS

Capitalizing with colons, parentheses, and quotations

Capitalizing with colons

Except when a colon follows a heading, do not capitalize the first letter after a colon unless the colon links two main clauses (which can stand as complete sentences). If the material following the colon is a quotation, a formal statement, or consists of more than one sentence, capitalize the first letter. In other cases capitalization is optional.

Incorrect We are all being integrated into a global economy that never sleeps: **A**n economy determining our personal lives and our relationships with others.

Correct We are all being integrated into a global economy that never sleeps: **W**e can work, shop, bank, and be entertained 24 hours a day.

Capitalizing with parentheses

Capitalize the first word of material enclosed in parentheses if the words stand on their own as a complete sentence.

> Beginning with Rachel Carson's *Silent Spring* in 1962, we stopped worrying so much about what nature was doing to us and began to worry about what we were doing to nature. (**S**cience and technology, which had been viewed as the solution to problems, suddenly became viewed as their cause.)

If the material enclosed in parentheses is part of a larger sentence, do not capitalize the first letter enclosed in the parentheses.

> Beginning with Rachel Carson's *Silent Spring* (**f**irst published in 1962), we stopped worrying so much about what nature was doing to us and began to worry about what we were doing to nature.

Capitalizing with quotations

If the quotation of part of a sentence is smoothly integrated into a sentence, do not capitalize the first word. Smoothly integrated quotations do not require a comma to separate the sentence from the rest of the quotation.

> It's no wonder the *Gazette* wrote that Armand's poutine was "**t**he best in Montreal, bar none"; he spends whole days in his kitchen experimenting over bubbling pots.

COMMON ERRORS *(Continued)*

But if the sentence contains an attribution and the quotation can stand as a complete sentence, capitalize the first word. In such sentences a comma should separate the attribution from the quotation.

> According to Andrée of the *Gazette,* "The poutine Armand fusses over for hours in his kitchen is the best in Montreal, bar none."

Remember: For elements following colons or within parentheses or quotation marks, capitalize the first letter only if the group of words can stand as a complete sentence.

50b Italics

The titles of entire works (books, magazines, newspapers, films) are italicized in print. The titles of parts of entire works are placed within quotation marks. When italicizing is difficult because you are using a typewriter or writing by hand, underline the titles of entire works instead.

Books	*Souvenir of Canada*
Magazines	*Rolling Stone*
Journals	*Canadian Journal of Physics*
Newspapers	*Whitehorse Star*
Feature-length films	*Barbarians*
Long poems	*The Divine Comedy*
Plays, operas, and ballets	*The Lord of the Rings*
Television shows	*Heartland*
Radio shows and audio recordings	*As It Happens*
Paintings, sculptures, and other visual works of art	*Starry Night*
Pamphlets and bulletins	*Lactose Intolerance or Milk Allergy?*

Also italicize the names of ships and aircraft.

Spirit of St. Louis | *Challenger*
Titanic | *Pequod*

The exceptions. Do not italicize the names of religious texts.

The text for our Comparative Religions course, *Sacred Texts from Around the World,* contains excerpts from the Bible, the Qur'an, the Talmud, the Upanishads, and the Bhagavad Gita.

WRITING SMART

Italicizing for emphasis

Italicizing a word can show the reader where to place the emphasis, but not all readers find italics appropriate. Use them sparingly. If you often find yourself italicizing words to indicate stresses, try to find stronger words that will do the same work.

Not Effective

"You don't *have* to let me win at chess *just because I'm younger,* Lynne."

"I'm not trying to let you win. *I'm just a bad chess player."*

Effective

"You don't have to let me win at chess just because I'm younger, Lynne."

"I'm *not* trying to let you win. I'm just a bad chess player."

51 Abbreviations, Acronyms, and Numbers

QUICK*TAKE*

- **How do you use abbreviations?** (see below)
  Incorrect: Although he demands to be called "Dr. Hastings," Robert's **Dr. of Phil.** degree is strictly honorary.
  Correct: Although he demands to be called "Doctor Hastings," Robert's **PhD** is strictly honorary.
- **When do you spell out numbers?** (see p. 550)
  Incorrect: There are about **20 000 000 000** chickens in the world, which is about **3** chickens for every person.
  Correct: There are about **20 billion** chickens in the world, which is about **three** chickens for every person.

51a Abbreviations

Abbreviations are shortened forms of words. Because abbreviations vary widely, you will need to look in the dictionary to determine how to abbreviate words on a case-by-case basis. Nonetheless, there are a few patterns that abbreviations follow.

Abbreviate titles before and degrees after full names

Ms. Rita MacNeil	**Dr.** Suzanne Smith	David Suzuki, **PhD**
Prof. Vijay Aggarwal	San-qi Li, **MD**	Marissa Limon, **LLD**

Write out the professional title when it is used with only a last name.

Professor Chin	**Doctor** Rodriguez	**Reverend** Ames

Conventions for using abbreviations with years and times

BCE (before the common era) and CE (common era) are now preferred for indicating years, replacing BC (before Christ) and AD (*anno Domini* ["the year of our Lord"]). Note that all are now used without periods.

479 **BCE** (or BC)

1610 **CE** (or AD, but AD is placed before the number)

The preferred written conventions for times are a.m. (*ante meridiem*) and p.m. (*post meridiem*).

9:03 **a.m.**

3:30 **p.m.**

An alternative is the 24-hour clock:

The morning meal is served from **0600** to **0815**; the evening meal is served from **1730** to **1945**.

COMMON ERRORS

Making abbreviations and acronyms plural

Plurals of abbreviations and acronyms are formed by adding *s*, not *'s*.

Technology is changing so rapidly these days that **PCs** become obsolete husks of circuits and plastic in only a few years.

Use an *'s* only to show possession.

The **CEO's** sole criterion for selecting VPs was that they play golf well.

Remember: When making abbreviations and acronyms plural, add *s*, not *'s*.

Conventions for using abbreviations in post-secondary writing

Most abbreviations are inappropriate in formal writing except when the reader would be more familiar with the abbreviation than with the words it represents. When your reader is unlikely to be familiar with an abbreviation, spell out the term, followed by the abbreviation in parentheses, the first time you use it in a paper. The reader will then understand what the abbreviation refers to, and you may use the abbreviation in subsequent sentences.

> The **World Health Organization (WHO)** has warned that a mutation of the H5N1 from birds to humans could spark a worldwide flu pandemic. The **WHO** has been monitoring outbreaks of the virus in countries around the world.

WRITING SMART

Latin abbreviations

Some writers sprinkle Latin abbreviations throughout their writing, apparently thinking that they are a mark of learning. Frequently these abbreviations are used inappropriately. If you use Latin abbreviations, make sure you know what they stand for.

cf.	(*confer*) compare
e.g.	(*exempli gratia*) for example
et al.	(*et alia*) and others
etc.	(*et cetera*) and so forth
i.e.	(*id est*) that is
N.B.	(*nota bene*) note well
viz.	(*videlicet*) namely

In particular, avoid using *etc.* to fill out a list of items. Use of *etc.* announces that you haven't taken the time to finish a thought.

Lazy The contents of his grocery cart described his eating habits: a big bag of chips, hot sauce, frozen pizza, **etc.**

Better The contents of his grocery cart described his eating habits: a big bag of chips, a large jar of hot sauce, two frozen pizzas, a 12-pack of cola, three Mars bars, and a package of Twinkies.

51b Acronyms

Acronyms are abbreviations formed by capitalizing the first letter in each word. Unlike other abbreviations, acronyms are pronounced as words.

> **AIDS** for Acquired Immunodeficiency Syndrome
> **NASA** for National Air and Space Administration
> **NATO** for North Atlantic Treaty Organization

A subset of acronyms is initial-letter abbreviations that have become so common that we know the organization or thing by its initials.

> **RCMP** for Royal Canadian Mounted Police
> **HIV** for human immunodeficiency virus
> **rpm** for revolutions per minute
> **YMCA** for Young Men's Christian Association

Familiar acronyms and initial-letter abbreviations such as CBC, CIBC, CIA, FBI, IQ, and UN are rarely spelled out.

Unfamiliar acronyms and abbreviations should always be spelled out. Acronyms and abbreviations frequent in particular fields should be spelled out on first use. For example, MMPI (Minnesota Multiphasic Personality Inventory) is a familiar abbreviation in psychology but is unfamiliar to those outside that discipline. Even when acronyms are generally familiar, few readers will object to your giving the terms from which an acronym derives on the first use.

> The **Canadian Association of Retired Persons (CARP)** is Canada's largest advocacy group for people over 50. Having begun in 1984 with 10 friends sitting around a kitchen table, **CARP** now has more than 400 000 members.

COMMON ERRORS

Punctuation of abbreviations and acronyms

The trend now is away from using periods with many abbreviations. In formal writing you can still use periods, with certain exceptions.

Do not use periods with

1. **Acronyms and initial-letter abbreviations:** CPP, MPP, NAFTA, NFL, OPEC
2. **Two-letter mailing abbrevations:** BC (British Columbia), MB (Manitoba), NL (Newfoundland and Labrador), YT (Yukon)

(Continued on next page)

COMMON ERRORS *(Continued)*

3. **Compass points:** NE (northeast), SW (southwest)
4. **Technical abbreviations:** kph (kilometres per hour), SS (sum of squares), SD (standard deviation)

Remember: Do not use periods with postal abbreviations for provinces, compass points, technical abbreviations, and established organizations.

51c Numbers

In formal writing, spell out any number that can be expressed in one or two words, as well as any number, regardless of length, at the beginning of a sentence. Also, hyphenate two-word numbers from twenty-one to ninety-nine.

> My office is **twenty-three** blocks from my apartment—too far to walk but a perfect bike-riding distance.

When a sentence begins with a number that requires more than two words, revise it if possible.

Correct but awkward

> **Fifteen thousand six hundred** runners left the Hopkinton starting line at noon in the Boston Marathon.

Better

> At the start of the Boston Marathon, **15 600** runners left Hopkinton at noon.

The exceptions. In scientific reports and some business writing that requires the frequent use of numbers, using numerals more often is appropriate. Most styles do not write out in words a year, a date, an address, a page number, the time of day, decimals, sums of money, phone numbers, rates of speed, or the scene and act of a play. Use numerals instead.

> In **2001** only **33**% of respondents said they were satisfied with the City Council's proposals to help the homeless.

> The **17** trials were conducted at temperatures **12–14°C** with results ranging from **2.43** to **2.89** mg/dl.

When one number modifies another number, write one out and express the other in numeral form.

> Only after Meryl had run in **12 ten**-kilometre races did she finally win first place in her age group.

PART

10 If English Is Not Your First Language

You **can learn more and do more** with MyWritingLab and with the eText version of *The Brief Penguin Handbook*. Find resources in MyWritingLab to help you complete your assignment successfully if English is not your first language.

10 If English Is Not Your First Language

52 Write in a Second Language 551

53 Nouns, Articles, and Prepositions 556

54 Verbs 562

55 English Sentence Structure 568

Credits

Text Credits

p. 20: Student sample courtesy Kris Sifeldeen

pp. 27–28: Sample introduction "Material reprinted with the express permission of: Edmonton Journal, a division of Postmedia Network Inc."

pp. 54–57: Sample rhetorical analysis courtesy Katie Lee

pp. 70–76: Sample paper Trent Gray

pp. 102–106: Sample observation report courtesy Katie Lee

p. 125: "Ruins of a Great House" by Derek Walcott

pp. 131–136: Sample literary analysis. "Walcott, Extended Metaphors, and Ruins of a Great House" © 2009 Eric Graves

pp. 143–149: Sample analysis, "The Woman in the Window" © Justin Kamal

pp. 351–361: Sample research paper "How the Media Depict Nursing" by Danielle Mitchell

pp. 381–383: Samples pages "Love and Marriage in the Works and Lives of Elizabeth Cary" and Lady Mary Wrothby C.A. Chambers

Photo Credits

p. 4: Copyright 2012 Consumers Union of U.S., Inc. Yonkers, NY 10703-1057, a nonprofit organization. Reprinted with permission from Consumer Reports® or educational purposes only. www.ConsumerReports.org.

p. 5t: Daniel Beltrá/Greenpeace

p. 5b:Youth Canada URL: http://www.youth.gc.ca/eng/home.shtml Human Resources and Skills

Development Canada, 2012. Reproduced by permission of the Minister of Public Works and Government Services Canada, 2012.

p. 12:Golden Pixels LLC /Shutterstock

p. 28: Lucas, John / The Edmonton Journal

p. 46t: Pearson Canada

p. 46c: Charles Maxwell/Underwater Video Services

p. 51t: (c) Archives of Manitoba, Events 173/3 (N9905)

p. 51b: (c) Archives of Manitoba, Winnipeg - Theatres - Walker Theatre 9(N13272)

p. 58: CARE Canada

p. 69: © Copyright 2006 SASI Group (University of Sheffield) and Mark Newman (University of Michigan)

p. 102: Courtesy Katie Lee

p. 138t: Film Studies: UC Berkeley Library

p. 138b: Permission provided by Denis Lacroix and Nicole S La Pointe

p. 141: Courtesy Film Studies Association of Canada website

p. 163, 194: CASLL / Inkshed; site designed by Tania Smith; moderator Margaret Procter.

p. 164: Spread the Net Homepage, www.spreadthenet.org

p. 162: www.milebymile.com

p. 178b: Joe Sallmen

p. 182b: milesgilmour /Fotolia

p. 214: The screenshot and its contents are reproduced with permission of ProQuest LLC. Further reproduction is prohibited without permission.

p. 215: University of Toronto Libraries

p. 218: ©EBSCO Publishing, Inc. All rights reserved.

p. 225: NASA

p. 229t: Dreamstime

p. 229b: University of Alberta

p. 241: Source: Vaccine safety: What about reports that vaccines are linked to chronic diseases or problems such as sudden infant death syndrome (SIDS)? http://www.phac-aspc.gc.ca/im/vs-sv/vs-faq13-eng.php Public Health Agency of Canada Reproduced with the permission of the Minister of Public Works and Government Services Canada, 2012

p. 243: Permission by House of Anansi Press

p. 248: © Richard G. Bingham II / Alamy

p. 257: Robbin Hollan

p. 271: Energy Resources Conservation Board/Alberta Geological Society

p. 336: Permission courtesy Department os Sociology, University of Alberta

p. 376: © Her Majesty The Queen in Right of Canada, Environment Canada, 2001. Reproduced with the permission of the Minister of Public Works and Government Services Canada.

p. 398: Used with permission of Atomic Energy of Canada Limited. All Rights Reserved.

p. 399: Samot /Shutterstock

p. 400l: © Ronald Karpilo / Alamy

p. 400r: Copyright: AISPIX by Image Source /Shutterstock

p. 414tl: Banana Republic images /Shutterstock

p. 414tr: jbor /Shutterstock

p. 419: iStock

Index

A

B

D

J

K

L

N

Q

R

S

T

STAYING ON TRACK GUIDE

"Staying on Track" boxes throughout this handbook focus on common writing problems and give students concrete guidance on how to avoid them. You can quickly locate advice on any of these common problems by using the list below.

REVISION GUIDE

Commonly used editing and proofreading symbols are listed here, along with references to the relevant chapters and sections of this handbook. See Chapter 4 for general advice on rewriting, editing, and proofreading.

Words, Sentences, and Paragraphs

abbr	Abbreviation problem: 51a
adj	Adjective problem: 41a-b
adv	Adverb problem: 41a, 41c
agr	Agreement problem, either subject-verb or pronoun-antecedent: 38, 40b
apos	Apostrophe missing or misused: 46
art	Article is missing or misused: 53d
cap	Capitalization is needed: 50a
case	Case of a pronoun is incorrect: 40a
coh	Coherence lacking in a paragraph: 3c
cs	Comma splice occurs: 37c
dm	Dangling modifier appears: 41e
frag	Fragment instead of complete sentence: 37a
ital	Italics missing or misused: 50b
lc	Lower case needed: 50a
mm	Misplaced modifier: 41d, 41e
num	Number problem: 51c
p	Punctuation problem: 42-48
pass	Passive voice misused: 31b
pl	Plural form misused or needed: 53c
pron	Pronoun problem: 40
ref	Reference of a pronoun unclear: 40d
run-on	Run-on sentence problem: 37b
sexist	Sexist language: 35b
sp	Spelling needs to be checked: 49
sub	Subordination is faulty: 33a
trans	Transition needed, use transitional terms: 3c
vb	Verb problem: 39
w	Wordy: 32
ww	Wrong word: 34
¶	Paragraph break needed: 3
no ¶	No paragraph break needed: 3
//	Parallelism needs to be checked: 33c-e

Punctuation and Mechanics

^,^	Comma needed: 42
˅'˅	Apostrophe needed: 46
˅"˅ ˅"˅	Quotation marks needed: 47
⊙	Period needed: 48a
?	Question mark needed: 48b
!	Exclamation point needed: 48c
—	Dash needed: 45
. . .	Ellipses needed: 48e
( )	Parentheses needed: 45
[ ]	Brackets needed: 48e
#	Add a space
⁀	Close up a space
~e~	Delete this
^	Insert something
∼	Transpose (switch the order)

Detailed Contents

PART 1 Planning, Drafting, and Revising

PART 2 Writing for Different Purposes

PART 3 Writing in the Disciplines

PART 4 Designing and Presenting

52 Write in a Second Language

QUICKTAKE

- **How do you use English idioms?** (see p. 553)
  Incorrect: Did he **kick the calendar**? [literal translation of Polish *kopnąć w kalendarz* with the same idiomatic meaning as "kick the bucket" in English]
  Correct: Did he **kick the bucket**?

 Understand the Demands of Writing in a Second Language

Many multilingual writers find that the main challenges of writing in a second language are more than just grammar and vocabulary. While grammar and vocabulary are important, sometimes too much focus on the details of writing can take your attention away from other issues that affect your ability to communicate effectively. If English is not your first language, you may have noticed some differences between writing in English and in your native language. Some of the differences are relatively easy to identify, such as the direction of writing (left to right instead of right to left or top to bottom), the uses of punctuation (€2,500.00 instead of €2.500,00), and conventions of capitalization and spelling. Other differences are more subtle and complex, such as the citation of sources, the uses of persuasive appeals, and the level of directness expected in a given situation.

Talk with other writers

When you write in an unfamiliar situation, it may be helpful to find a few examples of the type of writing you are trying to produce. If you are writing a letter of application to send with a resumé, for example, ask your friends to share similar letters of application with you and look for the various ways they present themselves in writing in that situation. Ask them to read their letters out loud and to explain the decisions they made as they wrote and revised their letters.

Know what is expected in post-secondary writing

Understanding what is expected in post-secondary writing is as important as understanding English language conventions. Students at colleges and universities are expected to meet the expectations listed on the next page.

You will find detailed information on these expectations in other parts of this book.

WRITING SMART

A guide to expectations for writing in college and university

Address the specific demands of the assignment.	See Section 2a for general assignment analysis. See Section 19a for analyzing research assignments.
Use the appropriate format and sources for particular disciplines.	See Part 3.
Pay close attention to document design.	See Chapter 15 for print design. See Chapter 18 for presentation design.
Follow specific formatting rules.	See Chapters 14 and 26 for MLA style. See Chapters 14 and 27 for APA style.
Document the sources of all ideas not originally yours.	See Chapter 23.
Choose words carefully, and connect ideas clearly.	See Part 7.
Use accepted grammatical forms.	See Part 8. See Chapters 53, 54, and 55 for specific explanations of English grammar and mechanics for second-language speakers.
Spell and punctuate correctly.	See Part 9.
Use your instructor's and peers' comments to revise and improve your writing.	See Chapter 4.

 52b Use Your Native Language as a Resource

As you continue to develop your ability to write in English, you will find that many of the strategies you developed in your native language are useful in English as well. The ability to think critically, for example, is important in any language, although what it means to be *critical* may differ from one context to another. Imagery, metaphors, and expressions adapted from your native language may make your writing culturally richer and more interesting to read.

You can also use your native language to develop your texts. Many people, when they cannot find an appropriate word in English, write down a word, a phrase, or even a sentence in their native language and consult a dictionary or a handbook later; it helps to avoid interrupting the flow of thought in the process of writing. Incorporating key terms from your native language is also a possible strategy. Here, for example, a term from Japanese adds flavour and perspective to a sentence: "Some political leaders need to have *wakimae*—a realistic idea of one's own place in the world."

52c Use Dictionaries

You can use regular English dictionaries for definitions, but most English dictionaries designed for native English speakers do not include all of the information that many non-native English speakers find useful. For example, you may know the word *audience* but not whether and when *audience* can function as a count noun. Learner's dictionaries, such as the *Collins Cobuild Advanced Learner's English Dictionary*, include information about count/non-count nouns and transitive/intransitive verbs (see Chapters 53 and 54). Many of them also provide sample sentences to help you understand how a word is used.

Some non-native English speakers also find a bilingual dictionary useful. Bilingual dictionaries are especially useful when you want to check your understanding of an English word or when you want to find equivalent words for culture-specific concepts and technical terms. Some bilingual dictionaries also provide sample sentences. When sample sentences are not provided, check the usage in another dictionary or search for the word or phrase on the web.

 52d Understand English Idioms

Some English *idioms* function like proverbs, familiar expressions that offer wisdom. In North America, for example, if someone has to "eat crow," he or she has been forced to admit being wrong about something. When people "walk a fine line," they are being careful not to irritate or anger people on different sides of an argument. Simpler examples of idiomatic usage—word order, word choice, and combinations that follow no obvious or set rules—are common even in the plainest English.

The way certain prepositions are paired with certain words is often idiomatic. It might be possible to use a preposition other than the one usually used, but the preferred combination is accepted as correct because it sounds "right" to long-time English speakers. Any other preposition sounds "wrong," even if it makes sense.

"Incorrect" idiom	Here is the answer *of* your question.
Accepted idiom	Here is the answer *to* your question.

Note that the second sentence is no more logical than the first. But to first-language English speakers, that first sentence sounds imprecise and strange. In a paper written for college or university, an instructor would likely mark such a sentence as having "poor word choice." See Section 53e for more information on English preposition usage.

Placement order for modifiers is often idiomatic in English—or at least the rules are arbitrary enough that it may make more sense to memorize certain patterns than to try to place modifiers entirely by logic. Say you want to modify the noun "dogs" with three adjectives:

brown
three
small

In English, all these adjectives will be placed before the noun they are modifying. But in what order should they go? The possibilities are as follows:

Small three brown dogs
Three brown small dogs
Small brown three dogs
Three small brown dogs
Brown small three dogs
Brown three small dogs

Only two of these options may sound at all correct to first-language English speakers: "Three brown small dogs" and "Three small brown dogs." To put the adjective for number anywhere but first sounds unnatural to native speakers. The other two adjectives, describing size and colour, also have a natural "order" to the ears of native speakers. Thus "three small brown dogs" sounds more natural than "three brown small dogs."

Placing the modifier for colour ahead of that for size seems peculiar—in fact, doing so might make a native English speaker wonder if there is some special reason to emphasize the out-of-place modifier. Perhaps you are trying to distinguish between several groups of three small dogs, and need to stress that the brown ones (not the grey or black or spotted ones) were the ones you meant. There is no real reason to place size before colour, but if you don't, readers will assume you *did* have a reason for not following the customary order. Placing modifiers in the order that native speakers expect to hear is important to avoid miscommunication.

Verb phrases in English are also governed by complex rules that most native speakers learn "by ear" rather than from books. These *phrasal verbs* can be particularly tricky for second-language speakers because languages other than English handle such forms quite differently. Yet verb phrases must be used correctly if you wish to avoid confusing readers. English phrasal verbs allow writers to give very specific information about the action taking place, and English speakers expect to receive that information in a consistent way. See Section 54h for information on using phrasal verbs in English.

Though idioms may be frustrating, you can take comfort in the fact that many first-language English speakers struggle with them, especially when using prepositions. Because idioms are not governed by a single set of rules, you can learn idioms only one example at a time. Thus, the more you speak, read, and hear English, the better your grasp of idioms, especially preposition usage, will become.

WRITING SMART

Use the web to check English idioms

Many combinations of English words don't follow hard and fast rules but simply sound right to native speakers of English. If you are unsure whether you should write "disgusted with" or "disgusted for," use Google or another search engine to find out how they are used.

Put the words inside quotation marks in the search box. You'll get many hits for both "disgusted with" and "disgusted for," but you'll see about 10 times more for "disgusted with." You'll also notice that many of the hits for "disgusted for" will be examples of "disgusted. For" with "disgusted" at the end of one sentence and "For" at the beginning of the next sentence. You can use this method to determine that "disgusted with" is the better choice.

53 Nouns, Articles, and Prepositions

QUICK*TAKE*

- **How do you treat different kinds of nouns?** (see below)
  Incorrect: When we landed at Toronto Island Airport, we asked for **informations** about transportation to Rogers Centre, the Blue Jays baseball team Home field.
  Correct: When we landed at Toronto Island Airport, we asked for **information** about transportation to Rogers Centre, the Blue Jays baseball team **h**ome field.
- **How do you use articles correctly?** (see p. 559)
  Incorrect: **A** mother of **a** soldier held **the** picture of him up to **a** camera.
  Correct: **The** mother of **the** soldier held **a** picture of him up to **the** camera.
- **How do you use prepositions?** (see p. 561)
  Incorrect: Please leave the keys **of** the car **to** the hook.
  Correct: Please leave the keys **for** the car **on** the hook.

53a Kinds of Nouns

There are two basic kinds of nouns. A **proper noun** begins with a capital letter and names a unique person, place, or thing: *Neil Young, Russia, Eiffel Tower*. In the following list, note that each word refers to someone or something so specific that it bears a name.

Proper nouns

Beethoven	Yao Ming	South Korea
Concorde	Toronto Blue Jays	Africa
BC Place	Picasso	Stockholm
Honda	Queen Elizabeth	Lake Huron
Thanksgiving	Virginia Woolf	New Brunswick

The other basic kind of noun is called a **common noun**. Common nouns do not name a unique person, place, or thing: *man, country, tower*. Note that the words in the following list are not names and so are not capitalized.

Common nouns

composer	athlete	country
airplane	baseball team	continent
building	painter	city

company	queen	lake
holiday	writer	province

Common nouns can also refer to abstractions, such as *grace, love*, and *power*. In English, proper nouns are names and are always capitalized, while common nouns are not names and are not capitalized.

53b Count and Non-count Nouns

Common nouns can be classified as either *count* or *non-count*. **Count nouns** can be made plural, usually by adding *s* (*finger, fingers*) or by using their plural forms (*person, people; datum, data*). **Non-count nouns** cannot be counted directly and cannot take the plural form (*information*, but not *informations*; *garbage*, but not *garbages*). Some nouns can be either count or non-count, depending on how they are used. *Hair* can refer to either a strand of hair, when it serves as a count noun, or a mass of hair, when it becomes a non-count noun.

Correct usage of *hair* as count noun

I carefully combed my few **hairs** across my mostly bald scalp.

Correct usage of *hair* as non-count noun

My roommate spent an hour this morning combing his **hair**.

In the same way, *space* can refer to a particular, quantifiable area (as in *two parking spaces*) or to an unspecified open area (as in *there is some space left*).

If you are not sure whether a particular noun is count or non-count, consult a learner's dictionary. Count nouns are usually indicated as [C] (for "countable") and non-count nouns as [U] (for "uncountable").

53c Singular and Plural Forms

Count nouns usually take both singular and plural forms, while non-count nouns usually do not take plural forms and are not counted directly. A count noun can have a number before it (as in *two books, three oranges*) and can be qualified with adjectives such as *many* (*many books*), *some* (*some schools*), *a lot of* (*a lot of people*), *a few* (meaning several, as in *I ate a few apples*), and *few* (meaning almost none, as in *few people volunteered*).

WRITING SMART

Non-count nouns in English

In some languages, all nouns can take singular and plural forms. In English, non-count nouns refer to a collective mass that, taken as a whole, does not have a particular or regular shape. Think of the non-count noun as a mass that can be subdivided into smaller parts without losing its identity. Non-count nouns such as *information, garbage, bread*, and *sand* can be broken down into smaller units and remain unchanged in essence: *bits* of information, *piles* of garbage, *slices* of bread, *grains* of sand. Count nouns such as *train, finger*, and *ocean* cannot be subdivided without becoming something else: a wheel on a train, a knuckle on a finger, but no longer simply a train or a finger.

Non-count nouns can be counted or quantified in only two ways: either by general adjectives that treat the noun as a mass (*much* information, *little* garbage, *some* news) or by placing another noun between the quantifying word and the non-count noun (two *kinds* of information, three *piles* of garbage, a *piece* of news).

COMMON ERRORS

Singular and plural forms of count nouns

Count nouns are simpler to quantify than non-count nouns. But remember that English requires you to state both singular and plural forms of nouns consistently and explicitly. Look at the following sentences.

Incorrect The three **bicyclist** shaved their **leg** before the big race.

Correct The three **bicyclists** shaved their **legs** before the big race.

In the first sentence, readers would understand that the plural form of *bicyclist* is implied by the quantifier *three* and that the plural form of *leg* is implied by the fact that bicyclists have two legs. (If they didn't, you would hope that the writer would have made that clear already!) Nevertheless, correct form in English is to indicate the singular or plural nature of a count noun explicitly, in every instance.

Remember: English requires you to use plural forms of count nouns even when a plural number is clearly stated.

53d Articles

Articles indicate that a noun is about to appear, and they clarify what the noun refers to. There are only two kinds of articles in English, definite and indefinite.

1. **the:** *The* is a definite article, meaning that it refers to (1) a specific object already known to the reader, (2) one about to be made known to the reader, or (3) a unique object.
2. **a, an:** The indefinite articles *a* and *an* refer to an object whose specific identity is not known to the reader. The only difference between *a* and *an* is that *a* is used before a consonant sound (*man, friend, yellow*), while *an* is used before a vowel sound (*animal, enemy, orange*).

Look at these sentences, identical except for their articles, and imagine that each is taken from a different newspaper story:

Rescue workers lifted **the** man to safety.

Rescue workers lifted **a** man to safety.

By use of the definite article *the*, the first sentence indicates that the reader already knows something about the identity of this man and his needing to be rescued. The news story has already referred to him. The sentence also suggests that this was the only man rescued, at least in this particular part of the story.

The indefinite article *a* in the second sentence indicates that the reader does not know anything about this man. Either this is the first time the news story has referred to him or there are other men in need of rescue. When deciding whether to use the definite or indefinite article, ask yourself whether the noun refers to something specific or unique, or whether it refers to something general. *The* is used for specific or unique nouns; *a* and *an* are used for non-specific or general nouns.

A small number of conditions determine when and how count and non-count nouns are preceded by articles.

1. *A* or *an* is not used with non-count nouns.

Incorrect The crowd hummed with **an** excitement.

Correct The crowd hummed with excitement.

2. *A* or *an* is used with singular count nouns whose particular identity is unknown to the reader or the writer.

Detective Johnson was reading **a** book.

3. *The* is used with most count and non-count nouns whose particular identity is known to the reader.

The noun may be known for one of several reasons:

- The noun has already been mentioned.

  I bought a book yesterday. **The** book is about Iraq.

- The noun is accompanied by a superlative such as *highest, lowest, best, worst, least interesting*, or *most beautiful* that makes its specific identity clear.

  This is **the most interesting book** about Iraq.

- The noun's identity is made clear by its context in the sentence.

  The book I bought yesterday is about Iraq.

- The noun has a unique identity, such as *the moon*.

  This book has as many pages as **the Bible**.

4. *The* is not used with non-count nouns meaning "in general."

Incorrect The war is hell.

Correct War is hell.

COMMON ERRORS

Articles with count and non-count nouns

Knowing how to distinguish between count and non-count nouns can help you decide which article to use. Non-count nouns are never used with the indefinite articles *a* and *an*.

Incorrect Maria jumped into a water.

Correct Maria jumped into **the** water.

No articles are used with non-count and plural count nouns when you wish to state something that has a general application.

Incorrect **The** water is a precious natural resource.

Correct Water is a precious natural resource.

Incorrect **The** soccer players tend to be quick and agile.

Correct Soccer players tend to be quick and agile.

Remember:

1. **Non-count nouns are never used with *a* and *an*.**
2. **Non-count and plural nouns used to make general statements do not take articles.**

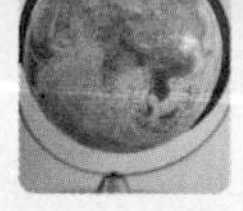

53e Prepositions

Prepositions are positional or directional words such as *to, for, from, at, in, on,* and *with*. They are used before nouns and pronouns, and they also combine with adjectives and adverbs. Each preposition has a wide range of possible meanings depending on how it is used, and each must be learned over time in its many contexts.

Some of the most common prepositional phrases describe time and place, and many are idiomatic.

Incorrect On midnight
Correct At midnight

Incorrect In the counter
Correct On the counter

Incorrect In Saturday
Correct On Saturday

Incorrect On February
Correct In February

Over time, you may notice patterns that help you determine the appropriate preposition. For example, *at* precedes a particular time, *on* precedes a day of the week, and *in* precedes a month, year, or other period of time.

COMMON ERRORS

Misused prepositions

The correct use of prepositions often seems unpredictable to non-native speakers of English. When you are not sure which preposition to use, consult a dictionary.

Of* for *about The report on flight delays raised criticism ~~of~~ about the scheduling of flights.

On* for *into The tennis player went ~~on~~ into a slump after failing to qualify for the French Open.

To* for *in Angry over her low seeding in the tournament, Amy resigned her membership ~~to~~ in the chess club.

To* for *of The family was ignorant ~~to~~ of the controversial history of the house they purchased.

Remember: When you are uncertain about a preposition, consult a learner's dictionary intended for non-native speakers of English. See Chapter 52 on the use of learner's dictionaries.

54 Verbs

QUICK*TAKE*

- **How do you use different kinds of verbs correctly?** (see below)
  Incorrect: She **intending to learn** several skills that **would help** her **becoming** a superhero.
  Correct: She **intends to learn** several skills that **will help** her **to become** a superhero.
- **What are conditional sentences?** (see p. 566)
  Incorrect: If she **had talked** with me in private, **I would not become** so angry.
  Correct: If she **had talked** with me in private, **I would not have become** so angry.
- **What are phrasal verbs?** (see p. 567)
  Incorrect: She **made out** the story.
  Correct: She **made up** the story.

54a Types of Verbs

The verb system in English can be divided between simple verbs such as *run, speak,* and *look* and verb phrases such as *may have run, have spoken,* and *will be looking*. In verb phrases, the words that appear before the main verbs—*may, have, will,* and *be*—are called **auxiliary verbs** (also called **helping verbs**). Helping verbs, as their name suggests, exist to help express something about the action of main verbs: for example, when the action occurs (tense), whether the subject acted or was acted upon (voice), or whether or not an action occurred.

Be Verbs

Indicating tense and voice with *be* verbs

Like the other auxiliary verbs *have* and *do, be* changes form to signal tense. In addition to *be* itself, the *be* verbs are *is, am, are, was, were,* and *been*. To show ongoing action, *be* verbs are followed by the present participle, which is a verb with an *-ing* ending:

Incorrect I **am think** of all the things I'd rather **be do.**

Correct I **am thinking** of all the things I'd rather **be doing.**

Incorrect He **was run** as fast as he could.

Correct He **was running** as fast as he could.

To show that an action is being done to, rather than by, the subject, follow *be* verbs with the past participle (a verb usually ending in *-ed, -en*, or *-t*):

Incorrect The movie **was direct** by John Woo.

Correct The movie **was directed** by John Woo.

Incorrect The complaint **will be file** by the victim.

Correct The complaint **will be filed** by the victim.

WRITING SMART

Verbs that express cognitive activity

English, unlike Chinese, Arabic, and several other languages, requires a form of *be* before the present or past participle. As you have probably discovered, however, English has many exceptions to its rules. Verbs that express some form of cognitive activity rather than a direct action are not used as present participles with *be* verbs. Examples of such words include *know, like, see*, and *believe*.

Incorrect You **were knowing** that I would be late.

Correct You **knew** that I would be late.

But here's an exception to an exception: A small number of these verbs, such as *considering, thinking*, and *pondering*, can be used as present participles with *be* verbs.

I **am considering** whether to finish my homework first.

54c Modal Auxiliary Verbs

Modal auxiliary verbs—*will, would, can, could, may, might, shall, must*, and *should*—are helping verbs that express conditions such as possibility, permission, speculation, expectation, obligation, and necessity. Unlike the helping verbs *be, have*, and *do*, modal verbs do not change form based on the grammatical subject of the sentence (*I, you, she, he, it, we, they*).

Two basic rules apply to all uses of modal verbs. First, modal verbs are always followed by the simple form of the verb. The simple form is the verb by itself, in the present tense, such as *have*, but not *had, having*, or *to have*.

Incorrect	She should **studies** harder to pass the exam.
Correct	She should **study** harder to pass the exam.

The second rule is that you should not use modals consecutively.

Incorrect	If you work harder at writing, you **might could** improve.
Correct	If you work harder at writing, you **might** improve.

Ten conditions that modals express

- **Speculation:** If you had flown, you **would** have arrived yesterday.
- **Ability:** She **can** run faster than Jennifer.
- **Necessity:** You **must** know what you want to do.
- **Intention:** He **will** wash his own clothes.
- **Permission:** You **may** leave now.
- **Advice:** You **should** wash behind your ears.
- **Possibility:** It **might** be possible to go home early.
- **Assumption:** You **must** have stayed up late last night.
- **Expectation:** You **should** enjoy the movie.
- **Order:** You **must** leave the building.

54d Verbs and Infinitives

Several verbs are followed by particular verb forms. An **infinitive** is *to* plus the simple form of the verb. Here are common verbs that are followed by an infinitive:

afford	expect	promise
agree	fail	refuse
ask	hope	seem
attempt	intend	struggle
claim	learn	tend
consent	need	wait
decide	plan	want
demand	prepare	wish

Incorrect	You **learn playing** the guitar by practising.
Correct	You **learn to play** the guitar by practising.

Some verbs require that a noun or a pronoun come after the verb and before the infinitive:

advise	instruct	require
cause	order	tell
command	persuade	warn

Incorrect I would **advise to watch** where you step.

Correct I would **advise you to watch** where you step.

A few verbs, when followed by a noun or a pronoun, take an *unmarked infinitive*, which is an infinitive without *to*:

have	let	make

Incorrect I will **let** her **to plan** the vacation.

Correct I will **let** her **plan** the vacation.

54e Verbs and *–ing* Verbals

Other verbs are followed by **gerunds**, which are verbs ending in *-ing* that are used as nouns. Here are common verbs that are followed by a gerund:

admit	discuss	quit
advise	enjoy	recommend
appreciate	finish	regret
avoid	imagine	risk
consider	practise	suggest

Incorrect She will **finish to grade** papers by noon.

Correct She will **finish grading** papers by noon.

A smaller number of verbs can be followed by either gerunds or infinitives (see Section 54d):

begin	hate	love
continue	like	start

With gerund She **likes working** in the music store.

With infinitive She **likes to work** in the music store.

54f Conditional Sentences

Conditional sentences express *if-then* relationships: They consist of a **subordinate clause** beginning with *if, unless*, or *when* that expresses a condition, and a **main clause** that expresses a result. The tense and mood of the verb in the main clause and the type of conditional sentence determine the tense and mood of the verb in the subordinate clause.

SUBORDINATE CLAUSE — MAIN CLAUSE
When the wind stops, the sea becomes calm.

Conditional sentences fall into three categories: *factual, predictive*, and *hypothetical.*

Factual conditionals

Factual conditional sentences express factual relationships: If this happens, that follows. The tense of the verb in the conditional clause is the same as the tense of the verb in the result clause:

Incorrect When it rains, the ground **would become** wet.

Correct When it rains, the ground **becomes** wet.

Predictive conditionals

Predictive conditional sentences express predicted consequences from possible conditions. The verb in the conditional clause is present tense, and the verb in the result clause is formed with a modal (*will, would, can, could, may, might, shall, must*, and *should*) plus the base form of the verb.

Incorrect If you **take** the long way home, you **enjoy** the ride more.

Correct If you **take** the long way home, you **will enjoy** the ride more.

Hypothetical conditionals

Hypothetical conditional sentences express events that are either not factual or unlikely to happen. For hypothetical events in the past, the conditional clause verb takes the past perfect tense. The main clause verb is formed from *could have, would have*, or *might have* plus the past participle.

Incorrect If we **had fed** the dog last night, he **would not run** away.

Correct If we **had fed** the dog last night, he **would not have run** away.

For hypothetical events in the present or future, the conditional clause verb takes the past tense and the main clause verb is formed from *could*, *would*, or *might* and the base form.

Incorrect If we **paid** off our credit cards, we **can** buy a house.

Correct If we **paid** off our credit cards, we **could** buy a house.

54g Participial Adjectives

The present participle always ends in *-ing* (*boring, exciting*), while most past participles end in *-ed* (*bored, excited*). Both participle forms can be used as adjectives.

When participles are used as adjectives, they can either precede the nouns they modify or come after a connecting verb.

It was a **thrilling** book. [*Thrilling* modifies *book.*]

Stephanie was **thrilled**. [*Thrilled* modifies *Stephanie.*]

Present participles such as *thrilling* describe a thing or a person causing an experience, while past participles such as *thrilled* describe a thing or a person receiving the experience.

Incorrect Students were **exciting** by the lecture.

Correct Students were **excited** by the lecture.

54h Phrasal Verbs

The liveliest and most colourful feature of the English language, its numerous idiomatic verbal phrases, gives many non-native speakers the greatest difficulty.

Phrasal verbs consist of a verb and one or two particles: either a preposition, an adverb, or both. The verb and particles combine to form a phrase with a particular meaning that is often quite distinct from the meaning of the verb itself. Consider the following sentence:

I need to **go over** the chapter once more before the test.

Here, the meaning of *go over*—a verb and a preposition that, taken together, suggest casual study—is only weakly related to the meaning of either *go* or *over* by itself. English has hundreds of such idiomatic constructions, and the best way to familiarize yourself with them is to listen to and read as much informal English as you can.

Like regular verbs, phrasal verbs can be either transitive (they take a direct object) or intransitive. In the preceding example, *go over* is transitive. *Quiet down*—as in *Please quiet down*—is intransitive. Some phrases, such as *wake up*, can be both: *Wake up!* is intransitive, while *Jenny, wake up the children* is transitive.

In some transitive phrasal verbs, the particles can be separated from the verb without affecting the meaning: *I made up a song* is equivalent to *I made a song up*. In others, the particles cannot be separated from the verb.

Incorrect You shouldn't **play** with love **around.**

Correct You shouldn't **play around** with love.

Unfortunately, there are no shortcuts for learning which verbal phrases are separable and which are not. As you become increasingly familiar with English, you will grow more confident in your ability to use phrasal verbs.

55 English Sentence Structure

QUICK*TAKE*

- **What is the subject of a sentence?** (see below)
  Incorrect: Is my favourite flavour of ice cream.
  Correct: **Pistachio** is my favourite flavour of ice cream.
- **What are the correct patterns for English sentences?** (see p. 569)
  Incorrect: The server brought her.
  Correct: The server brought her **a whole salmon.**
- **Where do you place modifiers?** (see p. 571)
  Unclear: After eating a few bites, **the salmon** was not fully cooked.
  Clear: After eating a few bites, **she** realized that the salmon was not fully cooked.

55a Subjects

With the exception of **imperatives** (commands such as *Be careful!* and *Jump!*) and informal expressions (such as *Got it?*), sentences in English usually contain a subject and a predicate. A **subject** names who or what the sentence is about; the **predicate** contains information about the subject.

SUBJECT | PREDICATE
The lion is asleep.

Many languages allow the writer to omit the subject if it's implied, but formal written English requires that each sentence include a subject, even when the meaning of the sentence would be clear without it. In some cases, you must supply an **expletive** (also known as a *dummy subject*), such as *it* or *there*, to stand in for the subject.

Incorrect Is snowing in Alaska.

Correct It is snowing in Alaska.

Incorrect Won't be enough time to climb that mountain.

Correct There won't be enough time to climb that mountain.

Both main and subordinate clauses within sentences require a subject and a predicate. A main clause can stand alone as a sentence, while subordinate clauses can be understood only in the context of the sentence of which they're a part. Still, even subordinate clauses must contain a subject. Look at the underlined subordinate clauses in the following two correct sentences:

We avoided the main highway because it had two lanes blocked off.

We avoided the main highway, which had two lanes blocked off.

In the first example, the subject of the subordinate clause is *it*, a pronoun representing the highway. In the second sentence, the relative pronoun *which*—also representing the highway—becomes the subject. When you use a relative pronoun, do not repeat the subject within the same clause.

Incorrect We avoided the highway, which it had two lanes blocked off.

In this sentence, *it* repeats the subject *which* unnecessarily.

55b English Word Order

All languages have their own rules for sentence structure. In English, correct word order often determines whether or not you succeed in saying what you mean. The basic sentence pattern in English is subject + predicate. A **predicate** consists of at least one main verb (see Section 36a). Although it is possible to write single-verb sentences such as *Stop!*, most English sentences consist of a combination of several words. A simple English sentence can be formed with a noun and a verb.

Birds fly.

In the above sentence, the subject (birds) is taking the action *and* receiving the action. There is no other object after the verb. The type of verb that can form a sentence without being followed by an object is called an **intransitive verb**. If the verb is intransitive, such as *exist*, it does not take a direct object.

Some verbs are **transitive**, which means they require a **direct object** to complete their meaning. The direct object receives the action described by the verb.

Incorrect The bird saw.

Correct The bird saw a cat.

In this sentence, the subject (the bird) is doing the action (saw) while the direct object (a cat) is receiving the action. A sentence with a transitive verb can be transformed into a passive sentence (*A cat was seen by the bird*). See Chapter 31 for active and passive sentences.

Some verbs (*write, learn, read*, and others) can be both transitive and intransitive, depending on how they are used.

Intransitive Pilots fly.

Transitive Pilots fly airplanes.

Most learner's dictionaries and bilingual dictionaries indicate whether a particular verb is transitive or intransitive. See Section 52c on the use of dictionaries.

In another simple pattern, the transitive verb is replaced by a linking verb that joins its subject to a following description:

The tallest player was the goalie.

Linking verbs such as *was, become, sound, look*, and *seem* precede a *subject complement* (in this example, *the goalie*) that refers back to the subject.

At the next level of complexity, a sentence combines a subject with a verb, direct object, and indirect object.

INDIRECT OBJ (her) DIRECT OBJ (the ball)

The goalie passed her the ball.

Passed is a transitive verb, *ball* is the direct object of the verb, and *her* is the indirect object, the person for whom the action was taken. The same idea can be expressed with a prepositional phrase instead of an indirect object:

DIRECT OBJ (the ball) PREP PHRASE (to her)

The goalie passed the ball to her.

Other sentence patterns are possible in English. (See Chapter 36.) However, it is important to remember that altering the basic subject + verb + object word order often changes the meaning of a sentence. If the meaning survives, the result may still be awkward. As a general rule, try to keep the verb close to its subject, and the direct or indirect object close to its verb.

55c Placement of Modifiers

The proximity of a modifier—an adjective or adverb—to the noun or verb it modifies provides an important clue to their relationship. Modifiers, even more than verbs, will be unclear if your reader can't connect them to their associated words. Both native and non-native speakers of English often have difficulty with misplaced modifiers.

Clarity should be your first goal when using a modifier. Readers usually link modifiers with the nearest word. In the following examples, the highlighted words are adjective clauses that modify nouns.

Unclear Many pedestrians are killed each year by motorists **not using sidewalks.**

Clear Many pedestrians **not using sidewalks** are killed each year by motorists.

Unclear He gave an apple to his girlfriend **on a silver platter.**

Clear He gave an apple **on a silver platter** to his girlfriend.

An **adverb**—a word or group of words that modifies a verb, an adjective, or another adverb—should not come between a verb and its direct object.

Awkward The hurricane destroyed **completely** the city's tallest building.

Better The hurricane **completely** destroyed the city's tallest building.

While single-word adverbs can come between a subject and its verb, you should avoid placing adverbial phrases in this position.

Awkward Toronto, **following the SARS scare of 2003**, created an emergency response network to prepare for future health epidemics.

Better **Following the SARS scare of 2003**, Toronto created an emergency response network to prepare for future health epidemics.

As a general rule, try to avoid placing an adverb between *to* and its verb. This is called a **split infinitive**.

Awkward The water level was predicted **to not rise.**

Better The water level was predicted **not to rise.**

Sometimes, though, a split infinitive will read more naturally than the alternative. Note also how the sentence with the split infinitive is more concise:

Without split infinitive	Automobile emissions in the city are expected **to increase by more than two times** over the next five years.
With split infinitive	Automobile emissions in the city are expected **to more than double** over the next five years.

Certain kinds of adverbs have special rules for placement. Adverbs that describe how something is done—called *adverbs of manner*—usually follow the verb.

The student listened **closely** to the lecture.

These adverbs may also be separated from the verb by a direct object:

She threw the ball **well**.

Adverbs of frequency are usually placed at the head of a sentence, before a single verb, or after an auxiliary verb in a verb phrase.

Often, politicians have underestimated the intelligence of voters.

Politicians have **often** underestimated the intelligence of voters.

It's common practice in English to combine two or more nouns to form a compound noun. Where two or more adjectives or nouns are strung together, the main noun is always positioned at the end of the string:

12-speed road **bike**, tall oak **tree**, computer **table**

COMMON ERRORS

Dangling modifiers

A dangling modifier does not seem to modify anything in a sentence; it dangles, unconnected to the word or words it is presumably intended to modify. Frequently, it produces funny results:

When still a girl, my father joined the army.

It sounds like *father* was once a girl. The problem is that the subject, I, is missing:

When I was still a girl, my father joined the army.

COMMON ERRORS *(Continued)*

Dangling modifiers usually occur at the head of a sentence in the form of clauses, with a subject that is implied but never stated.

Incorrect After lifting the heavy piano up the stairs, the apartment door was too small to get it through.

Correct After lifting the heavy piano up the stairs, **we discovered that** the apartment door was too small to get it through.

Whenever you use a modifier, ask yourself whether its relationship to the word it modifies will be clear to your reader. What is clear to you may not be clear to your audience. Writing, like speaking, is an exercise in making your own thoughts explicit. The solution for the dangling modifier is to recast it as a complete clause with its own explicit subject and verb, or to put the implied subject into the main clause with its own verb, as in the example above.

Remember: Modifiers should be clearly connected to the words they modify, especially at the beginning of sentences.

Glossary of Grammatical Terms and Usage

This glossary gives the definitions of grammatical terms and items of usage. The grammatical terms are shown in **blue**. Some of the explanations of usage that follow are not rules but guidelines to keep in mind for academic and professional writing. In these formal contexts, the safest course is to avoid words that are described as *non-standard*, *informal*, or *colloquial*.

a/an Use *a* before words that begin with a consonant sound (*a train*, *a house*). Use *an* before words that begin with a vowel sound (*an airplane*, *an hour*).

a lot/alot *A lot* is generally regarded as informal; *alot* is non-standard.

absolute A phrase that has a subject and modifies an entire sentence (see Sections 36d and 42c).

The soldiers marched in single file, their rifles slung over their shoulders.

accept/except *Accept* is a verb meaning "receive" or "approve." *Except* is sometimes a verb meaning "leave out," but much more often it's used as a conjunction or preposition meaning "other than."

She accepted her schedule except for Biology at 8 a.m.

active A clause with a transitive verb in which the subject is the doer of the action (see Section 31b). See also **passive**.

adjective A modifier that qualifies or describes the qualities of a noun or pronoun (see Sections 36b and 41a).

adjective clause A subordinate clause that modifies a noun or pronoun and is usually introduced by a relative pronoun (see Sections 36c and 41b). Sometimes called a *relative clause*.

adverb A word that modifies a verb, another modifier, or a clause (see Sections 36b, 41a, and 41c).

adverb clause A subordinate clause that functions as an adverb by modifying a verb, another modifier, or a clause (see Sections 36c and 41c).

advice/advise The noun *advice* means a "suggestion"; the verb *advise* means to "recommend" or "give advice."

affect/effect Usually, *affect* is a verb (to "influence") and *effect* is a noun (a "result"):

Too many pork chops affect one's health.

Too many pork chops have an effect on one's health.

Less commonly, *affect* is used as a noun and *effect* as a verb. In the following examples, *affect* means an "emotional state or expression," and *effect* means "to bring about."

The boy's affect changed when he saw his father.

The legislators will attempt to effect new insurance laws next year.

agreement The number and person of a subject and verb must match—singular subjects with singular verbs, plural subjects with plural verbs (see Chapter 38). Likewise, the number and gender of a pronoun and its antecedent must match (see Section 40b).

all ready/already The adjective phrase *all ready* means "completely prepared"; the adverb *already* means "previously."

The tour group was all ready to leave, but the train had already departed.

all right/alright *All right*, meaning "acceptable," is the correct spelling. *Alright* is non-standard.

allude/elude *Allude* means "refer to indirectly." *Elude* means "evade."

He alluded to the fact that he'd eluded capture.

allusion/illusion An *allusion* is an indirect reference; an *illusion* is a false impression.

The painting contains an allusion to the Mona Lisa.

The painting creates the illusion of depth.

among/between *Between* refers to precisely two people or things; *among* refers to three or more.

The choice is between two good alternatives.

The costs were shared among the three participating companies.

amount/number Use *amount* with things that cannot be counted; use *number* with things that can be counted.

A large amount of money changed hands.

They gave him a number of quarters.

an See **a/an**.

antecedent The noun (or pronoun) that a pronoun refers to (see Sections 38c and 40b). *Jeff* is the antecedent of *his* in the following sentence.

Jeff stopped running when his knee began hurting.

anybody/any body; anyone/any one *Anybody* and *anyone* are indefinite pronouns and have the same meaning; *any body* and *any one* are usually followed by a noun that they modify.

Anybody can learn English, just as anyone can learn to bicycle.

Any body of government should be held accountable for its actions.

anymore/any more *Anymore* means "now," while *any more* means "no more." Both are used in negative constructions.

No one goes downtown anymore.

The area doesn't have any more stores than it did in 1960.

anyway/anyways *Anyway* is correct. *Anyways* is non-standard.

appositive A word or phrase placed close to a noun that restates or modifies the noun (see Sections 36d and 42c).

Dr. Lim, my physics professor, is the best.

articles The words *a*, *an*, and *the* (see Sections 36b and 53d).

as/as if/as though/like Use *as* instead of *like* before dependent clauses (which include a subject and verb). Use *like* before a noun or a pronoun.

Her voice sounds as if she had her head in a barrel.

She sings like her father.

assure/ensure/insure *Assure* means "promise," *ensure* means "make certain," and *insure* means to "make certain in either a legal or a financial sense."

Ralph assured the new client that his company would insure the building at full value, but the client wanted higher approval to ensure Ralph was correct.

auxiliary verb Forms of *be*, *do*, and *have* combine with verbs to indicate tense and mood (see Section 54a). The modal verbs *can, could, may, might, must, shall, should, will,* and *would* are a subset of auxiliaries.

bad/badly Use *bad* only as an adjective. *Badly* is the adverb.

He was a bad dancer.

Everyone agreed that he danced badly.

being as/being that Both constructions are colloquial and awkward substitutes for *because*. Don't use them in formal writing.

beside/besides *Beside* means "next to." *Besides* means "in addition to" or "except."

Does anyone, besides your mother, want to sit beside you when you're coughing like that?

between See **among/between**.

bring/take *Bring* describes movement from a more distant location to a nearer one. *Take* describes movement away.

Bring me the most recent issue. You can take this one.

can/may In formal writing, *can* indicates ability or capacity, while *may* indicates permission.

If I may speak with you, we can probably solve this problem.

case The form of a noun or a pronoun that indicates its function. Nouns change case only to show possession: the **dog**, the **dog's** bowl (see discussion of "function" in Section 36b). See **pronoun case** (Section 40a).

censor/censure To *censor* is to edit or ban on moral or political grounds. To *censure* is to reprimand publicly.

The Senate censored the details of the budget.

The Senate censured one of its members for misconduct.

cite/sight/site To *cite* is to "mention specifically"; *sight* as a verb means to "observe" and as a noun refers to "vision"; *site* is most commonly used as a noun that means "location," but is also used as a verb to mean "situate."

He cited as evidence the magazine article he'd read yesterday.

Finally, he sighted the bald eagle. It was a remarkable sight.

The developers sited the houses on a heavily forested site.

clause A group of words with a subject and a predicate. A main or independent clause can stand as a sentence. A subordinate or dependent clause must be attached to a main clause to form a sentence (see Section 36c).

collective noun A noun that refers to a group or a plurality, such as *team*, *army*, or *committee* (see Section 38d).

comma splice Two independent clauses joined incorrectly by a comma (see Section 37c).

common noun A noun that names a general group, person, place, or thing (see Sections 36b and 53a). Common nouns are not capitalized unless they begin a sentence.

complement A word or group of words that completes the predicate (see Section 36c). See also **linking verb**.

Juanita is my aunt.

complement/compliment To *complement* something is to complete it or make it perfect; to *compliment* is to flatter.

The chef complemented their salad with a small bowl of soup.

The grateful diners complimented the chef.

complex sentence A sentence that contains at least one subordinate clause attached to a main clause (see Section 36a).

compound sentence A sentence that contains at least two main clauses (see Section 36e).

compound-complex sentence A sentence that contains at least two main clauses and one subordinate clause (see Section 36a).

conjunction See **coordinating conjunction**; **subordinating conjunction**.

conjunctive adverb An adverb that often modifies entire clauses and sentences, such as *also, consequently, however, indeed, instead, moreover, nevertheless, otherwise, similarly,* and *therefore* (see Sections 36b and 41c).

continual/continuous *Continual* refers to a repeated activity; *continuous* refers to an ongoing, unceasing activity.

Tennis elbow is usually caused by continual stress on the joint.

Archaeologists have debated whether Chaco Canyon was inhabited intermittently or continuously.

coordinate A relationship of equal importance, in terms of either grammar or meaning (see Section 36c).

coordinating conjunction A word that links two equivalent grammatical elements, such as *and, but, or, yet, nor, for,* and *so* (see Section 36b).

could of Non-standard. See **have/of**.

count noun A noun that names things that can be counted, such as *block, cat,* and *toy* (see Section 53b).

dangling modifier A modifier that is not clearly attached to what it modifies (see Section 41e).

data The plural form of *datum*; it takes plural verb forms.

The data are overwhelming.

declarative A sentence that makes a statement (see Section 36a).

Halifax is the capital of Nova Scotia.

dependent clause See **subordinate clause.**

determiners Words that initiate noun phrases, including possessive nouns (*Pierre's violin*); possessive pronouns (*my, your*); demonstrative pronouns (*this, that*); and indefinite pronouns (*all, both, many*) (see Section 41b).

differ from/differ with To *differ from* means to "be unlike"; to *differ with* means to "disagree."

Rock music differs from jazz primarily in rhythm.

Miles Davis differed with critics who disliked his rock rhythms.

different from/different than Use *different from* where possible.

Dark French roast is different from ordinary coffee.

direct object A noun, pronoun, or noun clause that names who or what receives the action of a transitive verb (see Section 55b).

Antonio kicked the ball.

discreet/discrete Both are adjectives. *Discreet* means "prudent" or "tactful"; *discrete* means "separate."

What's a discreet way of saying "Shut up"?

Over the noise, he could pick up several discrete conversations.

disinterested/uninterested *Disinterested* is often misused to mean *uninterested.* Disinterested means "impartial." A judge can be interested in a case but disinterested in the outcome.

double negative The incorrect use of two negatives to signal the same negative meaning (see Section 41a).

We don't have no money.

due to the fact that Avoid this wordy substitute for *because.*

each other/one another Use *each other* for two; use *one another* for more than two.

effect See **affect/effect.**

elicit/illicit The verb *elicit* means to "draw out." The adjective *illicit* means "unlawful."

The teacher tried to elicit a discussion about illicit drugs.

emigrate from/immigrate to *Emigrate* means to "leave one's country"; *immigrate* means to "settle in another country."

ensure See **assure/ensure/insure.**

enthused Non-standard in academic and professional writing. Use *enthusiastic* instead.

etc. Avoid this abbreviation for the Latin *et cetera* in formal writing. Either list all the items or use an English phrase such as *and so forth.*

every body/everybody; every one/everyone *Everybody* and *everyone* are indefinite pronouns referring to all people under discussion. *Every one* and *every body* are adjective-noun combinations referring to all members of a group.

Everyone loves a genuine smile.

Every one of the files contained a virus.

except See **accept/except**.

except for the fact that Avoid this wordy substitute for *except that*.

expletive The dummy subjects *it* and *there* used to fill a grammatical slot in a sentence (see Sections 32c and 55a).

It is raining outside.

There should be a law against it.

explicit/implicit Both are adjectives; *explicit* means "stated outright," while *implicit* means just the opposite, "unstated."

Even though we lacked an explicit contract, I thought we had an implicit understanding.

farther/further *Farther* refers to physical distance; *further* refers to time or other abstract concepts.

How much farther is your home?

I don't want to talk about this any further.

fewer/less Use *fewer* with what can be counted and *less* with what cannot be counted.

There are fewer canoeists in the summer because there is less water in the river.

flunk In formal writing, avoid this colloquial substitute for *fail*.

fragment A group of words beginning with a capital letter and ending with a period that looks like a sentence but lacks a subject or a predicate or both (see Section 37a).

further See **farther/further**.

gerund An *-ing* form of a verb used as a noun, such as *running*, *skiing*, or *laughing* (see Sections 36b, 39b, and 54e).

good/well *Good* is an adjective and is not interchangeable with the adverb *well*. The one exception is health. Both she feels *good* and she feels *well* are correct.

The Yankees are a good baseball team. They play the game well.

hanged/hung Use *hanged* to refer only to executions; *hung* is used for all other instances.

have/of *Have*, not *of*, follows *should*, *could*, *would*, *may*, *must*, and *might*.

I should have [not *of*] picked you up earlier.

he/she; s/he Try to avoid language that appears to exclude either gender (unless this is intended, of course) and awkward compromises such as *he/she* or *s/he*. The best solution is to make pronouns plural (the gender-neutral *they*) wherever possible.

helping verb See **auxiliary verb**.

hopefully This adverb is commonly used as a sentence modifier, but many readers object to it.

I am hopeful [not *Hopefully*] we'll have a winning season.

illusion See **allusion/illusion**.

immigrate See **emigrate from/immigrate to**.

imperative A sentence that expresses a command (see Sections 36a and 55a). Usually the subject is implied rather than stated.

Go away now.

implicit See **explicit/implicit.**

imply/infer *Imply* means to "suggest"; *infer* means to "draw a conclusion."

The ad implied that the candidate was dishonest; I inferred that the campaign would be one of name calling.

in regards to Avoid this wordy substitute for *regarding.*

incredible/incredulous *Incredible* means "unbelievable"; *incredulous* means "not believing."

Their story about finding a stack of money in a discarded suitcase seemed incredible; I was incredulous.

independent clause See **main clause.**

indirect object A noun, pronoun, or noun clause that names who or what is affected by the action of a transitive verb (see Section 36c).

Amir kicked the ball to Mario.

infinitive The word *to* plus the base verb form: *to believe, to feel, to act* (see Sections 36b and 54d). See also **split infinitive.**

infinitive phrase A phrase that uses the infinitive form of a verb (see Section 36d).

To get some sleep is my goal for the weekend.

interjection A word expressing feeling that is grammatically unconnected to a sentence, such as *cool, wow, ouch,* or *yikes* (see Section 36b).

interrogative A sentence that asks a question (see Section 36a).

Where do you want to go?

intransitive verb A verb that does not take an object, such as *sleep, appear,* or *laugh* (see Sections 36c, 39c and 55b).

irregardless Non-standard for *regardless.*

irregular verb A verb that does not use either *-d* or *-ed* to form the past tense and past participle (see Section 39b).

it is my opinion that Avoid this wordy substitute for *I believe that.*

its/it's *Its* is the possessive of *it* and does not take an apostrophe; *it's* is the contraction for *it is.*

Its tail is missing. It's an unusual animal.

-ize/-wise The suffix *-ize* changes a noun or adjective into a verb (*harmony, harmonize*). The suffix *-wise* changes a noun or adjective into an adverb (*clock, clockwise*). Some writers are tempted to use these suffixes to convert almost any word into an adverb or a verb form. Unless the word appears in a dictionary, don't use it.

kind of/sort of/type of Avoid using these colloquial expressions if you mean *somewhat* or *rather. It's kind of hot* is non-standard. Each is permissible, however, when it refers to a classification of an object. Be sure that it agrees in number with the object it is modifying.

This type of engine is very fuel-efficient.

These kinds of recordings are rare.

lay/lie *Lay* means "place" or "put" and generally takes a direct object. Its main forms are *lay, laid, laid. Lie* means "recline" or "be positioned" and does not take an object. Its main forms are *lie, lay, lain.*

He lays the papers down. He laid the papers down.

He lies down on the sofa. He lay down on the sofa.

less See **fewer/less.**

lie See **lay/lie.**

linking verb A verb that connects the subject to the complement, such as *appear, be, feel, look, seem,* or *taste* (see Sections 36b and 36c).

lots/lots of Non-standard in formal writing; use *many* or *much* instead.

main clause A group of words with a subject and a predicate that can stand alone as a sentence (see Sections 36c and 54f). Also called an *independent clause.*

mankind This term offends some readers and is outdated. Use *humans, humanity,* or *people* instead.

may/can See **can/may**.

may be/maybe *May be* is a verb phrase; *maybe* is an adverb.

It may be time to go.

Maybe it's time to go.

media This is the plural form of the noun *medium* and requires a plural verb.

The media in this city are biased.

might of See **have/of**.

modal A kind of auxiliary verb that indicates ability, permission, intention, obligation, or probability, such as *can, could, may, might, must, shall, should, will,* or *would* (see Section 36b).

modifier A general term for adjectives, adverbs, phrases, and clauses that describe other words (see Chapter 41).

must of See **have/of**.

non-count noun A noun that names things that cannot be counted, such as *air, energy,* or *water* (see Section 53b).

non-restrictive modifier A modifier that is not essential to the meaning of the word, phrase, or clause it modifies. It should be set off by commas or other punctuation (see Section 42c).

noun The name of a person, place, thing, concept, or action (see Section 36b). See also **common noun** and **proper noun** (see Section 53a).

number See **amount/number**.

object Receiver of the action within the clause or phrase (see Section 36c).

OK, O.K., okay Informal; avoid using in academic and professional writing. Each spelling is accepted in informal usage.

owing to the fact that Avoid this wordy, colloquial substitute for *because.*

parallelism The principle of putting similar elements or ideas in similar grammatical form (see Section 33c).

participial phrase A phrase formed either by a present participle (for example, *racing*) or by a past participle (for example, *taken*). (See Section 36d.)

participle A form of a verb that uses *-ing* in the present (*laughing, playing*) and usually *-ed* or *-en* in the past (*laughed, played*). (See Sections 36b and 39a.) Participles are either part of the verb phrase (*She had played the game before*) or used as adverbs and adjectives (*the laughing girl*).

parts of speech The eight classes of words according to their grammatical function: nouns, pronouns, verbs, adjectives, adverbs, prepositions, conjunctions, and interjections (see Section 36b).

passive A clause with a transitive verb in which the subject is being acted upon (see Section 31b). See also **active**.

people/persons *People* refers to a general group; *persons* refers to a collection of individuals. Use *people* over *persons* except when you're emphasizing the idea of separate persons within the group.

"People have the power" was the theme of the rally.

Occupancy by more than 135 persons is illegal.

per Try to use the English equivalent of this Latin word except in technical writing or familiar usages such as *kilometres per litre*.

The job paid $20 an hour.

As you requested [not *per your request*], I'll drive up immediately.

phenomena This is the plural form of *phenomenon* ("observable fact" or "unusual event") and takes plural verbs.

The astronomical phenomena were breathtaking.

phrase A group of words that does not contain both a subject and a predicate (see Section 36d).

plenty In academic and professional writing, avoid this colloquial substitute for *very*.

plus Do not use *plus* to join clauses or sentences. Use *and, also, moreover, furthermore,* or another conjunctive adverb instead.

It rained heavily, and it was also [not *plus it was*] bitterly cold.

precede/proceed Both are verbs but they have different meanings: *precede* means "come before," and *proceed* means "go ahead" or "continue."

In Canada, the national anthem precedes every major league baseball game.

We proceeded to the train station.

predicate The part of the clause that expresses the action or tells something about the subject. The predicate includes the verb and all its complements, objects, and modifiers (see Sections 36a, 55a, and 55b).

prejudice/prejudiced *Prejudice* is a noun; *prejudiced* is an adjective.

The jury was prejudiced against the defendant.

She knew about the town's history of racial prejudice.

preposition A class of words that indicate relationships and qualities (see Sections 36b and 53e).

prepositional phrase A phrase formed by a preposition and its object, including the modifiers of its object (see Section 36d).

pronoun A word that stands for other nouns or pronouns. Pronouns have several subclasses, including personal pronouns, possessive pronouns, demonstrative pronouns, indefinite pronouns, relative pronouns, interrogative pronouns, reflexive pronouns, and reciprocal pronouns (see Section 36b and Chapter 40).

pronoun case Pronouns that function as the subjects of sentences are in the **subjective** case (*I, you, he, she, it, we, they*). Pronouns that function as direct or indirect objects are in the **objective** case (*me, you, him, her, it, us, them*). Pronouns that indicate ownership are in the **possessive** case (*my, your, his, her, its, our, their*) (see Section 40a).

proper noun A noun that names a particular person, place, thing, or group (see Sections 36b and 53a). Proper nouns are capitalized.

question as to whether/question of whether Avoid these wordy substitutes for *whether.*

raise/rise The verb *raise* means "lift up" and takes a direct object. Its main forms are *raise, raised, raised.* The verb *rise* means "get up" and does not take a direct object. Its main forms are *rise, rose, risen.*

The workers carefully raised the piano onto the truck.

The piano slowly rose off the ground.

real/really Avoid using *real* as if it were an adverb. *Really* is an adverb; *real* is an adjective.

The singer was really good.

What we thought was an illusion turned out to be real.

reason is because Omit either *reason is* or *because* when explaining causality.

The reason he ran is that he thought he was late.

He ran because he thought he was late.

reason why Avoid using this redundant combination.

The reason he's so often late is that he never wears a watch.

relative pronoun A pronoun that initiates clauses, such as *that, which, what, who, whom,* or *whose* (see Section 36b).

restrictive modifier A modifier that is essential to the meaning of the word, phrase, or clause it modifies (see Section 42c). Restrictive modifiers are usually not set off by punctuation.

rise/raise See **raise/rise**.

run-on sentence Two main clauses fused together without punctuation or a conjunction, appearing as one sentence (see Section 37b).

sentence A grammatically independent group of words that contains at least one main clause (see Section 36a).

sentence fragment See **fragment**.

shall/will *Shall* is used most often in first person questions, while *will* is a future tense helping verb for all persons. British English consistently uses *shall* with first person: *I shall, we shall.*

Shall I bring you some water?

Will they want drinks, too?

should of See **have/of**.

some time/sometime/sometimes *Some time* means "a span of time," *sometime* means "at some unspecified time," and *sometimes* means "occasionally."

Give me some time to get ready.

Let's meet again sometime soon.

Sometimes, the best-laid plans go wrong.

somebody/some body; someone/some one *Somebody* and *someone* are indefinite pronouns and have the same meaning. In *some body*, *body* is a noun modified by *some*, and in *some one*, *one* is a pronoun or an adjective modified by *some*.

Somebody should close that window.

"Some body was found on the beach today," the homicide detective said.

Someone should answer the phone.

It would be best if some one person could represent the group.

sort of See **kind of/sort of/type of**.

split infinitive An infinitive with a word or words between *to* and the base verb form, such as *to boldly go, to better appreciate* (see Sections 41d and 55c).

stationary/stationery *Stationary* means "motionless"; *stationery* means "writing paper."

subject A noun, pronoun, or noun phrase that identifies what the clause is about and connects with the predicate (see Sections 36a, 36c, and 55c).

subject-verb agreement See **agreement**.

subordinate A relationship of unequal importance, in terms of either grammar or meaning (see Section 36c).

subordinate clause A clause that cannot stand alone but must be attached to a main clause (see Sections 33a, 36c, and 54f). Also called a *dependent clause*.

subordinating conjunction A word that introduces a subordinate clause. Common subordinating conjunctions are *after, although, as, because, before, if, since, that, unless, until, when, where,* and *while* (see Section 36b).

such Avoid using *such* as a synonym for *very*.

It was a very [not *such a*] hot August.

sure A colloquial term used as an adverb to mean "certainly." Avoid using it this way in formal writing.

You were certainly [not *sure were*] correct when you said August would be hot.

sure and/sure to; try and/try to *Sure to* and *try to* are correct; do not use *and* after *sure* or *try*.

Be sure to [not *sure and*] take out the trash this morning.

Try to [not *try and*] finish first.

take See **bring/take**.

that/which *That* introduces a restrictive or essential clause. Restrictive clauses describe an object that must be that particular object and no other. Though some writers occasionally use *which* with restrictive clauses, it is most often used to introduce non-restrictive clauses. These are clauses that contain additional non-essential information about the object.

Let's listen to the CD that Clarence bought.

Clarence's favourite music, which usually puts me to sleep, is too mellow for me.

transition A word or phrase that notes movement from one unit of writing to another.

transitive verb A verb that takes a direct object (see Sections 36c, 39c, and 55b).

verb A word that expresses action or characterizes the subject in some way. Verbs can show tense and mood (see Section 36c and Chapter 39).

verbal A form of a verb used as an adjective, adverb, or noun (see Section 36b). See also **gerund**, **infinitive**, **participle**.

well/good See **good/well**.

which/that See **that/which**.

who/whom *Who* and *whom* follow the same rules as other pronouns: *Who* is the subjective pronoun; *whom* is the objective pronoun.

Sharon's father, who served in the Korean War, died last year.

Sharon's father, whom several of my father's friends knew, died last year.

will/shall See **shall/will**.

-wise/-ize See **-ize/-wise**.

would of See **have/of**.

you Avoid indefinite uses of *you*. It should be used only to mean "you, the reader."

The [not *your*] average lifespan in Canada has increased consistently over the past 100 years.

your/you're The two are not interchangeable. *Your* is the possessive form of "you"; *you're* is the contraction of "you are."

Your car can be picked up after 5 p.m.

You're going to need money to live in Manhattan.